Teacher and Language Education

BLOOMSBURY CLASSICS IN LINGUISTICS

Multimodal Teaching and Learning, *Gunther Kress, Carey Jewitt, Jon Ogborn and Charalampos Tsatsarelis*
Opposition in Discourse, *Lesley Jeffries*
Second Language Identities, *David Block*
Worlds of Written Discourse, *Vijay Bhatia*

Teacher Cognition and Language Education

Research and Practice

SIMON BORG

Bloomsbury Academic
An imprint of Bloomsbury Publishing Plc

B L O O M S B U R Y
LONDON • NEW DELHI • NEW YORK • SYDNEY

Bloomsbury Academic
An imprint of Bloomsbury Publishing Plc

50 Bedford Square 1385 Broadway
London New York
WC1B 3DP NY 10018
UK USA

www.bloomsbury.com

BLOOMSBURY and the Diana logo are trademarks of Bloomsbury Publishing Plc

First published 2006

Bloomsbury Classics in Linguistics edition first published in 2015 by Bloomsbury Academic

© David Block 2006, 2015

Simon Borg has asserted her right under the Copyright, Designs and Patents Act, 1988, to be identified as Author of this work.

All rights reserved. No part of this publication may be reproduced or transmitted in any form or by any means, electronic or mechanical, including photocopying, recording, or any information storage or retrieval system, without prior permission in writing from the publishers.

No responsibility for loss caused to any individual or organization acting on or refraining from action as a result of the material in this publication can be accepted by Bloomsbury or the author.

British Library Cataloguing-in-Publication Data
A catalogue record for this book is available from the British Library.

ISBN: PB: 978-1-4725-3206-0
ePDF: 978-1-4725-2504-8
ePub: 978-1-4725-2695-3

Library of Congress Cataloging-in-Publication Data
A catalog record for this book is available from the Library of Congress.

Series: Bloomsbury Classics in Linguistics

Typeset by Deanta Global Publishing Services, Chennai, India
Printed and bound in Great Britain

Contents

Introduction 1
1 The origins of teacher cognition research 5
2 The cognitions of pre-service language teachers 51
3 The cognitions of in-service language teachers 87
4 Teacher cognition in grammar teaching 129
5 Teacher cognition in literacy instruction 159
6 Self-report instruments 197
7 Verbal commentaries 221
8 Observation 265
9 Reflective writing 293
10 A framework for studying language teacher cognition 319

References 341
Index 367

Introduction

In the past 15 years there has been a surge of interest in the study of language teacher cognition – what language teachers think, know and believe – and of its relationship to teachers' classroom practices. It is timely, therefore, to provide an account of the body of work which now exists in this domain of inquiry and to examine the research methods used in this field. These are the two primary aims of this book. In addressing them, it is also my goal to provide an introduction to the study of language teacher cognition which is both comprehensive and accessible. The material covered here will be particularly relevant to researchers, teacher educators, policy makers and programme and curriculum managers working in first (L1), second (L2) and foreign language (FL) education contexts. I use the term 'language teacher' throughout here to refer to classroom practitioners in each of these contexts.

A key factor driving the increase in research in teacher cognition, not just in language education, but in education more generally, has been the recognition of the fact that teachers are active, thinking decision-makers who play a central role in shaping classroom events. Coupled with insights from the field of psychology which have shown how knowledge and beliefs exert a strong influence on human action, this recognition has suggested that understanding teacher cognition is central to the process of understanding teaching. This is one broad but fundamental assumption which unites the body of work discussed in this book. This perspective on teachers and teaching has provided insights into the processes of teacher education and the nature of teachers' instructional practices. It has also helped policy makers become more sensitive to the key role teachers – and their cognitions – play in the implementation of educational innovations. The study of language teacher cognition, then, though relatively speaking still a young domain of inquiry (especially in L2 and FL contexts), has demonstrated its potential for deepening our understandings of what it means to become and to be a teacher. I hope that this book will contribute to a greater understanding of language teacher cognition research and stimulate continued research in this field.

Structure of the book

The book has two parts; the first deals with what we know about language teacher cognition while the second examines the research methods through which it has been studied.

In Chapter 1, I place the study of language teacher cognition in its historical context by outlining the origins of teacher cognition research in education more generally. Chapters 2–5 then examine what we know about language teacher cognition by organizing the research available into four themes. The first of these is examined in Chapter 2, which focuses on research conducted in the context of pre-service teacher education. Salient issues which will be examined relate to the nature of the learning processes prospective and new teachers experience and to the impact which pre-service teacher education programmes have on what teachers know, believe and do. Chapter 3 examines teacher cognition research with reference to the work of in-service teachers. Here the focus is less on how teachers learn and more firmly on the cognitions practising teachers hold and on how these influence what the teachers do in the classroom. In Chapters 4 and 5 I consider the two specific curricular domains which have provided a major focus for language teacher cognition research: the teaching of grammar and literacy instruction. While most of the research on teacher cognition in grammar teaching has been conducted in L2 and FL contexts and appeared in the last ten years, literacy instruction, particularly in relation to the teaching of L1 reading, has been the focus of teacher cognition research for many years. In considering the work in literacy, I will also examine what we know about teachers' knowledge, beliefs and practices in relation to the teaching of writing.

In Chapters 6–9, the focus of the discussion switches to methodological issues in the study of language teacher cognition.

A range of research methods have been applied in investigating what language teachers think, know, believe and do, and the aim of these chapters is to illustrate and examine these. Chapter 6 focuses on self-report instruments. Questionnaires, scenario-rating tasks and tests are three such measures which are commonly used in the study of language teacher cognition. Examples of studies using these methods will be discussed and the rationale for the method used in each case will be outlined. The effectiveness of the different methods in uncovering language teacher cognition will also be considered. Chapters 7–9 follow a similar pattern, with a different approach to studying language teacher cognition being analysed in each case. Chapter 7 focuses on the use of verbal commentaries and various strategies for eliciting these commentaries will be considered, including semi-structured interviews, stimulated recall interviews and repertory grids. In Chapter 8 the research method examined is observation. The use of structured and unstructured observation will be illustrated and recommendations made for the effective use of this strategy in the study of language teacher cognition. Chapter 9 considers the use of reflective writing as a means of collecting data on the cognitions of language teachers. The specific strategies which I consider here are journal writing, autobiography, retrospective accounts and concept mapping.

In Chapter 10, I review the key thematic and methodological issues to emerge from the analyses throughout the book and outline a framework for continued research into language teacher cognition.

1

The origins of teacher cognition research

Language teacher cognition research draws on a tradition of educational research which stretches back over 30 years. My aim in this chapter is to outline the origins and growth of this tradition. The rapid growth of teacher cognition research since the 1970s has been characterized by a number of perspectives from which teachers' mental lives can be studied. I will highlight these here as they provide the conceptual basis for the research I discuss in Chapters 2–5. I will not attempt to provide a comprehensive review of research on teacher cognition in education generally (there are hundreds of individual studies in this domain, across a wide range of curricular areas), but to outline, chronologically, the emergence of this tradition of inquiry and the key perspectives, concepts and findings it has contributed to the study of teaching. In doing so I will draw on a number of reviews of teacher cognition research which have appeared over the years and which readers may want to turn to for more specific detail on particular research perspectives (a list of these reviews appears at the end of this chapter). I will also postpone a discussion of methodological developments in the study of teacher cognition until later in the book.

The 1970s: Changing perspectives in the study of teaching

Dunkin and Biddle (1974: 38) presented a model for the study of teaching which reflected the approach to research on classroom teaching predominant in the 1970s. This model posited relationships between what were called *presage* variables (e.g. teachers' personal characteristics and teacher-training experiences), *context* variables (e.g. learners' personal characteristics), *process* variables (defined through interactions between teachers and learners in the classroom) and *product* variables (e.g. learning outcomes). The approach to the study of teaching implied in this model is what is referred to (often disparagingly in contemporary educational debate) as a process-product approach. The aim was to study what happens in classrooms (i.e. processes, defined primarily in terms of observable teacher and learner behaviours) and to link these causatively with what learners achieve or can do. Although the model does acknowledge presage variables which influence teachers' classroom behaviours, it made no reference to the role teachers' cognitive processes might play in the act of teaching itself. This was the dominant conceptual model of teaching in the 1970s. Learning was seen to be a product of teaching, and teaching was conceived of as behaviours performed by teachers in class. The goal of research on teaching was to describe these behaviours, to identify those which were effective and to study links between these behaviours and learning outcomes.

Alternatives to this conception of teaching had already begun appearing in the late 1960s. Three factors are commonly cited to explain the emergence of these alternatives (see Calderhead, 1987, 1996; Carter, 1990). Firstly, developments in cognitive psychology had highlighted the influence of thinking on behaviour. This, therefore, suggested that understanding teachers required an understanding of teachers' mental lives rather than an exclusive focus on observable behaviours. Secondly, there was an increasing recognition of the fact that teachers played a much more active and central role in shaping educational processes than previously acknowledged. Examining the kinds of decisions teachers made and the cognitive basis of these thus also started to emerge as a central area of research interest. Thirdly, there was growing recognition of the limitations of a concern for quantifying discrete teacher behaviours and the search for generalizable models of teacher effectiveness which had long characterized research on teaching. As an alternative, studies of teaching which examined individual teachers' work and cognitions in a more holistic and qualitative manner began to appear.

Early work reflecting this emerging tradition consisted of rich descriptive and interpretive accounts of classrooms, which illustrated the complexities and the demands of teaching and the manner in which teachers coped with these challenges. Smith and Geoffrey (1968) and Kounin (1970) are representative of such work, though Jackson (1968) is perhaps most often cited as marking a change in the way teaching and teachers could be studied; it was, according to Clark and Peterson (1986: 255), 'one of the first studies that attempted to describe and understand the mental constructs and processes that underlie teaching behaviour'.

In 1975 the National Institute of Education in the United States organized a conference, which had the aim of defining an agenda for research on teaching. Groups of experts in various areas of teaching worked to prepare a plan for research in those areas and one of these groups had as its focus 'Teaching as Clinical Information Processing'. The report of this group argued that:

> it is obvious that what teachers do is directed in no small measure by what they think . . . To the extent that observed or intended teaching behaviour is 'thoughtless', it makes no use of the human teacher's most unique attributes. In so doing, it becomes mechanical and might well be done by a machine. If, however, teaching is done and, in all likelihood, will continue to be done by human teachers, the question of relationships between thought and action becomes crucial.
>
> (National Institute of Education, 1975: 1)

This report marked the start of a tradition of research into teacher cognition. It argued that, in order to understand teachers, researchers needed to study the psychological processes through which teachers make sense of their work. This emphasis on cognitive processes marked a major departure from the views of teaching and teachers dominant at the time; teaching was no longer being viewed solely in terms of behaviours but rather as *thoughtful* behaviour; and teachers were not being viewed as mechanical implementers of external prescriptions, but as active, thinking decision-makers, who processed and made sense of a diverse array of information in the course of their work. As a result of this report, significant research funding for the study of teacher cognition became available to researchers in the USA. Consequently, early thinking in this domain of activity was powerfully shaped by work in North America.

Two key individuals involved in the report just referred to, and whose views at the time on the nature of teaching were influential in promoting a focus on the cognitive dimension of teaching, were Shulman and Elstein. In an early paper (Shulman and Elstein, 1975) they examined psychological studies of problem-solving, judgement and decision-making and considered their relevance to the study of teaching. Both authors had a background in psychology and early work in teacher cognition was in fact primarily psychological in nature, rather than educational (we can contrast this with developments in late 1980s and 1990s, for example, where the study of teacher cognition was aligned more with the field of teacher education rather than with psychology). Reflecting the shift in perspective from teaching behaviours to teacher thinking I have already noted, they commented at the start of their paper that 'research typically slights the problem of how teachers *think about* their pupils and instructional problems; it concentrates instead on how teachers act or perform in the classroom'(p. 3). The aim of their paper was to consider ways in which greater research attention might be focused on teacher thinking; of particular interest was their discussion of teaching as clinical information processing, a metaphor for teaching which dominated early research into teacher thinking (see Kagan, 1988 for an analysis of this analogy). In their words:

> The teacher role can be conceptualized like a physician's role – as an active clinical information processor involved in planning, anticipating, judging, diagnosing, prescribing, problem solving. The teacher is expected to function in a task environment containing quantities of different kinds of information that far exceed the capabilities or capacities of any human information processor.

> Many of the research strategies [we have] discussed above can be used to understand how teachers cope with that overload while somehow responding, diagnosing, judging, making decisions, and taking actions.
> (Shulman and Elstein, 1975: 35)

Research on teaching adopting this perspective was rare at the time, but the position outlined here set the tone for much subsequent work. Teachers' planning, judgements and decision-making were in fact key foci in the emergence of what came to be known as research on *teacher thinking*. An early review of such work is Clark and Yinger (1977).

The introduction to this review reflected the scope of teacher thinking research and the promise it was felt to hold for extending our understandings of teaching:

> A relatively new approach to the study of teaching assumes that what teachers do is affected by what they think. This cognitive information processing approach is concerned with teacher judgment, decision making, and planning. The study of the thinking processes of teachers – how teachers gather, organize, interpret, and evaluate information – is expected to lead to understandings of the uniquely human processes that guide and determine teacher behaviour.
> (Clark and Yinger, 1977: 1)

Four topics were identified here which had been studied from the perspective of teacher thinking: teacher planning, teacher judgement, teacher interactive decision-making (i.e. decisions made during teaching), and teachers' implicit theories or perspectives. The study of planning in teaching was at the time dominated by a prescriptive model in which objectives were the basic initial unit in the planning process followed by the selection of learning activities, decisions about their organization and about their evaluation. Early studies of planning from a teacher thinking point of view, however, suggested that teachers did not follow this rational model and that learning activities and a concern for the content to be taught were the starting points in planning. This kind of finding immediately highlighted the capacity of teacher cognition research to develop theories of teaching grounded in an understanding of teachers' actual thinking and practices. This kind of work also began to reveal the complexity of teaching, indicating that linear, rational models of teachers' work were inadequate. Early teacher thinking research on planning also highlighted teachers' use of instructional routines, developed as a result of experience, and defined as 'methods used to reduce the complexity and increase the predictability of classroom activities, thus increasing flexibility and effectiveness' (Clark and Yinger, 1977: 284). In contrast to this work on planning, the research on teachers' judgements, interactive decision-making and implicit theories available at the time did not suggest many clear conclusions. In each case, the number of studies was small, diverse and conducted in very specific contexts. One interesting point which did emerge from the study of teachers' implicit theories, though, was that teachers' thinking and behaviours are guided by a set of organized beliefs and that these often operate unconsciously. This is a point we take for granted in contemporary research on teaching, but 30 years ago the study of teachers' beliefs and their impact on what teachers do was just emerging. In fact, in all four areas of teaching reviewed by Clark and Yinger, more questions than answers were generated, another reflection of the emergent status of this perspective on the study of teaching in the late 1970s.

The 1980s: Decision-making and teacher knowledge

Building on the bases established late in the previous decade, the 1980s witnessed a rapid expansion in the volume of research conducted into the study of the cognitive basis of teaching.

Shavelson and Stern (1981) provided a review of research on teachers' pedagogical thoughts, judgements and decisions published since 1976. They highlighted two justifications for examining teachers' mental activities. The first was that a behavioural model of teaching, by not accounting for teachers' cognitions, is conceptually incomplete. The second justification posited was that research linking intentions and behaviour can inform teacher education and the implementation of educational innovation. The connections between teacher cognition research and teacher education signalled here were to emerge strongly later in the decade. However, also implied here was the prevailing view at the time that the goal of research on teaching was to provide the basis, somewhat normatively, of more effective teacher preparation and development. For example, in studying teacher planning, there was an interest in identifying effective planning practices and promoting these among teachers generally.

Their diagrammatic overview of teacher thinking research (see Figure 1.1) is indicative of developments in the way the relationship between teacher cognitions and classroom practices were being conceptualized. The various elements in the diagram were organized not linearly (as in the model of teaching by Dunkin and Biddle, 1974, referred to earlier), but as a cycle. The authors explained that 'the figure is circular in order to show that the conditions that inform a decision will, in all likelihood, be changed somewhat by the consequent behavior of the teacher'(p. 460). A recognition of this two-way interaction between

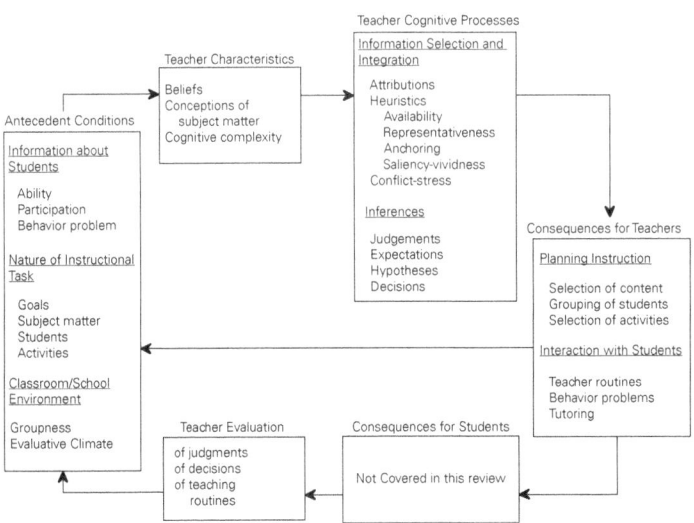

FIGURE 1.1 *Overview of research on teachers' judgements, decisions and behaviour*
(Shavelson and Stern, 1981: 461)

thinking and classroom practice was an important step forward in conceptualizing the field of teacher cognition. Not only was cognition now being affirmed as a key factor in shaping classroom events, it was also becoming recognized that classroom events in turn shaped subsequent cognitions. This was a much more sophisticated view of teaching than that presented by unidirectional linear models starting from antecedent variables and ending with product variables.

Shavelson and Stern's review highlighted a wide range of factors which had been found to impact on teachers' judgements and decisions. Information about students, such as ability, sex and classroom behaviour, were commonly found to influence what teachers did. The immediate classroom and wider school environment were also found to be influential. The latter includes 'extra-classroom pressures in the school such as administrators and policies . . . and in the community (such as parents) [which] set boundaries on teachers' pedagogical decisions' (p. 466). This review also highlighted how existing research had not shown any clear relationship between teachers' beliefs and their pedagogical decisions (i.e. in some studies the two were related while in others they were not). This interest in the congruence between teachers' beliefs and actions remains current today.

Observations highlighted in the earlier review by Clark and Yinger (1977) recur here, particularly teachers' use of instructional routines. Interactive decision-making teaching had previously been thought of as a process in which teachers consider a range of alternative instructional options and then choose, interactively, those which seem most appropriate; teacher thinking research, though, suggested that teachers' employ routinized mental scripts in the classroom and they are generally reluctant to abandon these routines once started – even in the face of evidence that they are not working well. A key reason posited for this behaviour was that a primary concern for teachers was to maintain the smooth flow of activity in the classroom; and abandoning a routine and considering an alternative would interrupt this flow. Drawing on these findings, Shavelson and Stern (1981) proposed a model of interactive decision-making (Figure 1.2) which characterized teaching as the application of well-established routines; during these routines teachers seek cues, by observing learner behaviour, in order to decide whether the routines are working as

THE ORIGINS OF TEACHER COGNITION RESEARCH

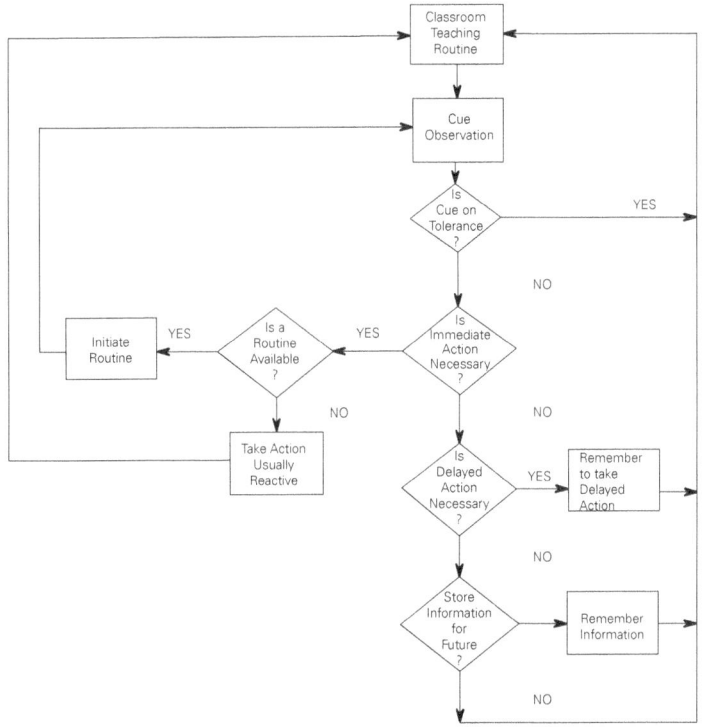

FIGURE 1.2 *A model of interactive decision-making*
(Shavelson and Stern, 1981: 483)

planned or whether an alternative is necessary (where the observed behaviours are not in line with those expected). While this model was valuable in highlighting the role of routines in teachers' interactive decision-making, the observation of learner behaviour was considered the only antecedent to interactive decision-making. This was thus a limited account of decision-making in the classroom (as many other factors may influence the interactive choices teachers make) and later analyses suggested that, with its overemphasis on cues from learners, this model may have pushed subsequent research on teacher thinking in the wrong direction (Clark and Peterson, 1986).

In concluding their review, Shavelson and Stern made several recommendations for continuing research on teacher thinking. One important issue they highlighted related to the role of subject-matter knowledge in teaching. At the time, subject-matter knowledge had received little empirical attention and the authors argued that understanding how such knowledge is integrated into the process of planning and implementing teaching was an important issue deserving greater study. The study of subject-matter knowledge did actually emerge as a major research focus later in the 1980s, as I discuss below.

Practical knowledge

At the same time as the review above appeared, Elbaz (1981), responding to what she perceived as 'the inadequacy of the existing role of the teacher within the field of curriculum' (p. 43) reported on a case study of one teacher through which the notion of *practical knowledge* was explicated and illustrated. This became a widely used concept in subsequent research in the field of teacher cognition and continues to be used today. Elbaz's basic argument is that teachers play a central, autonomous role in shaping curricula, rather than being merely 'a cog in the educational machine' (p. 45) and that 'the single factor which seems to have the greatest power to carry forward our understanding of the teacher's role is the phenomenon of teachers' knowledge' (p. 45). According to Elbaz, teachers' knowledge is practical because much of what teachers know originates in practice and is used to make sense of and deal with practical problems. Elbaz's work was seminal; at a time when the dominant conceptualization of teachers remained firmly behaviourist, her work connected with the emergent interest in teacher thinking, but presented a different, more holistic perspective on the study of teachers' work to that adopted in the earlier, largely psychological studies of teacher decision-making. For example, rather than focusing on the decisions the teacher in her study made and seeking antecedents for them, Elbaz's research on practical knowledge aimed to understand the teacher's conceptions of her work through extensive interviews and some classroom observation. The study of practical knowledge came to be recognized as a distinct orientation to teacher cognition research and generated a tradition which is today associated most strongly perhaps with the work of Clandinin and Connelly (e.g. Clandinin, 1986; Connelly *et al.*,

1997). This tradition contrasts with that encapsulated in research based on decision-making and information-processing models of teaching.

Although these latter models remained dominant in the early 1980s, they were becoming the focus of increasing critiques. The work on practical knowledge, for example, had highlighted that decision-making studies did not capture the process of teaching and teacher cognition in a suitably holistic manner (Mitchell and Marland, 1989 claimed that decision-making accounted for only about 25 per cent of teacher thinking.) Another criticism of the decision-making model was that it 'paid insufficient heed to what one might call teachers' beliefs and repertoires of understandings' (Munby, 1982: 201). The call for teacher cognition research to embrace the study of beliefs marked another important step forward in the development of the field. In making his case, Munby drew on the work of Nisbett and Ross (1980) to argue that 'all human perception is influenced by the perceivers' schema, constructs, existing beliefs and understandings' (p. 206). Munby also highlighted the manner in which, once established, beliefs may be resistant to change even in the face of strong evidence. Given the role of beliefs in human perception and hence in action, Munby argued that the scant attention paid to them in the study of teacher thinking at the time was surprising.

ISATT

Continued expansion in the study of teacher cognition led to the foundation in 1983 of ISATT – the International Study Association on Teacher Thinking. In their introduction to the proceedings of the first ISATT conference, Halkes and Olson (1984a) outlined the perspective on the study of thinking which underpinned the association's work:

> Looking from a teacher thinking perspective at teaching and learning one is not so much striving for the disclosure of 'the' effective teacher, but for the explanation and understanding of teaching processes as they are. Afterall (*sic*) it's the teacher's subjective school related knowledge which determines for the most part what happens in the classroom; whether the teacher

can articulate his/her knowledge or not. Instead of reducing the complexities of teacher-learning situations into a few manageable research variables, one tries to find out how teachers cope with these complexities. The way the complexities and ambiguities of teaching are processed into subjective theories for knowing how to teach in a personal satisfying way might account for actual teaching activities. In short, what's in the 'mind' of teachers could explain classroom processes in one way or another.

(Halkes and Olson, 1984a: 1)

Themes highlighted earlier are evident here, such as an acknowledgement of the complex nature of teaching and the need to understand the subjective cognitive dimensions of teachers' work. Important here, too, was the distinction between the search for the effective teacher and the understanding of teaching processes. As I noted above, early studies of teacher planning and decision-making, despite their focus on teacher thinking, remained aligned to the view that descriptions of what effective teachers do would provide normative guidance for other teachers; what we see here is a move away from this position towards the view that descriptions of teachers' work and of the thinking behind it can deepen our understandings of teaching, but not with the intention of prescribing models of thinking and action for other teachers to follow.

Collections of papers drawn from ISATT events have continued to appear over the years (e.g. Ben-Peretz *et al.*, 1986; Carlgren *et al.*, 1994; Day *et al.*, 1993; Day *et al.*, 1990). These have contributed to advancing teacher cognition research both substantively and methodologically, and also, importantly, provided a largely European perspective in a domain of research which has been dominated by thinking and research in North America. ISATT remains active today, albeit under the broader title of the International Study Association for Teachers and Teaching (see www.ipn.uni-kiel.de/projekte/isatt/).

Teachers' thought processes

By 1986, the field of teacher cognition had changed considerably compared to 1975, and the developments which had taken place during this time were examined by Clark (1986) and in a major review by Clark and Peterson (1986). The first of these argued that a decade earlier teachers were seen as rational decision-makers, akin to physicians in diagnosing and solving problems, whereas in 1986 the view of the teacher was more that of the constructivist, reflective 'sense-maker'. Clark also noted that 'perhaps the most dramatic set of conceptual developments in research on teacher thinking relate to changes in how we have come to think of the context of teaching' (p. 11). He contrasts the earlier view of the classroom as a 'clearly bounded yet complex task environment' (p. 11) with that in 1986 which recognized that 'schools and classrooms are the locus of social, psychological, physical, political, and metaphysical action, embedded in the word and affected by it' (p. 12). This concern for the broader context of teaching contrasts with earlier work on decision-making, where teachers' actions were described and interpreted without reference to the socio-psychological contexts in which they occurred; in fact, many early studies of teacher thinking were conducted in laboratory settings and thus in isolation of the contextual factors which influence teachers in real classroom settings.

There was also an ethical angle to Clark's discussion, particularly with reference to the relationship between research on teacher thinking and teachers' work; he was critical of the prescriptive goal, as noted above, of studies which aimed to discover effective teaching and planning strategies and argued that research be seen as a service to the practice of teaching. Clark summarized this change in perspective as 'a turning away from the goal of making good teaching easier to that of portraying and understanding good teaching in all of its irreducible complexity and difficulty' (p. 14).

A number of criticisms of existing teacher thinking research were also made. In terms of its focus, Clark observed that 'the work on teacher planning and decision-making has been done almost exclusively in nice, well-organized, upper middle class suburban elementary school classrooms' (p. 16). Another gap in research at the time was the lack of attention to issues of quality in the teaching that had been studied; this is a concern which recurs in most subsequent reviews of teacher cognition research.

The review of literature on teachers' thought processes by Clark and Peterson (1986) was a landmark publication. It appeared in the third edition of the authoritative *Handbook of Research on Teaching*;

previous editions of the Handbook had not included a chapter on the study of teacher thinking. Here is the opening to this review:

> The thinking, planning, and decision making of teachers constitute a large part of the psychological context of teaching. It is within this context that curriculum is interpreted and acted upon; where teachers teach and students learn. Teacher behavior is substantially influenced and even determined by teachers' thought processes. These are the fundamental assumptions behind the literature that has come to be called research on teacher thinking. Practitioners of this branch of educational research seek first to describe fully the mental lives of teachers. Second, they hope to understand and explain how and why the observable activities of teachers' professional lives take on the forms and functions that they do. They ask when and why teaching is difficult, and how human beings manage the complexity of classroom teaching. The ultimate goal of research on teachers' thought processes is to construct a portrayal of the cognitive psychology of teaching for use by educational theorists, researchers, policymakers, curriculum designers, teacher educators, school administrators, and by teachers themselves.
>
> (*op. cit.*, p. 255)

Figure 1.3 is the model of teacher thought and action which Clark and Peterson presented to make sense of the literature they cover in their review. The 'action' component covered the observable components of the classroom while the 'thought' component accounted for the unobservable psychological context of teaching. The arrows between the two components of the diagram highlighted the interaction between them – with thoughts both influencing and being influenced by behaviours. Warning against research which neglected either thought or action, Clark and Peterson argued that 'the process of teaching will be fully understood only when these two domains are brought together and examined in relation to one another' (p. 258). The figure also acknowledged the impact on teaching of the constraints and opportunities which teachers face in their work, and recognized that attention to these factors was central to a fuller understanding of teachers' thoughts and actions.

THE ORIGINS OF TEACHER COGNITION RESEARCH

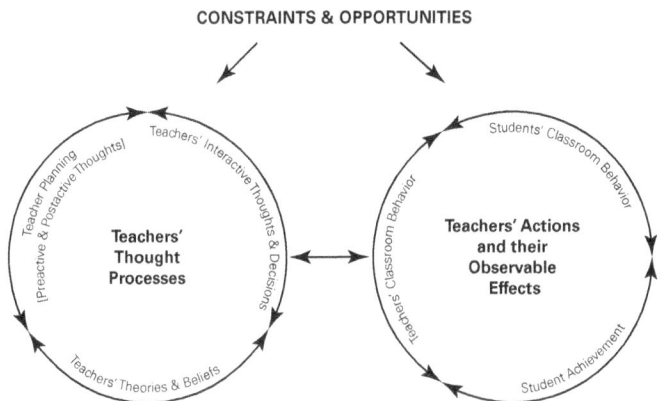

FIGURE 1.3 *A model of teacher thought and action*
(Clark and Peterson, 1986: 257)

Clark and Peterson (1986) organized their review of work on teacher thinking into three mutually informing categories: teacher planning (preactive and postactive thoughts); teachers' interactive thoughts and decisions; and teachers' theories and beliefs. The inclusion of the latter category was significant; as we saw above, Munby (1982) had noted the lack of research on teachers' beliefs; a few years later, although the volume of research on teachers' theories and beliefs was still not large, there was nonetheless sufficient work for it to constitute a distinct category of inquiry in the field of teacher cognition.

For each of these categories, the findings and methods used in teacher cognition research available at the time were analysed. Many of the issues highlighted in previous reviews in relation to teacher planning and decision-making were confirmed here; additional insights were also provided. For example, in relation to the frequency of interactive decision-making, the conclusion was that findings across studies were consistent in suggesting that decision-making is an intense activity (on average, teachers were found to make an interactive decision once every two minutes); in terms of the content of teachers' interactive thoughts, the most commonly reported focus was consistently the learner. Critiques of existing teacher cognition research were also provided; for example, it was again noted that studies of planning had focused largely on the work of experienced elementary teachers (working, I would add, in the USA). One recommendation for continuing research, then, was that planning be studied longitudinally, focusing also on novices, 'instead of continuing to accumulate descriptions of the planning of experienced teachers' (p. 268). And the review of research on interactive decision-making concluded, as suggested earlier, that existing models (e.g. Shavelson and Stern, 1981 – see Figure 1.2) of this process were inadequate, for whereas these models suggested that teachers' interactive decisions were triggered by teachers' judgements about learners, the research available in the mid-1980s suggested that other factors also needed to be included in models of this kind. Clark and Peterson concluded that

> while a large proportion of a teacher's interactive decisions do seem to occur as a result of a teacher's judgment about student behavior, a model that focuses only on student behavior as the antecedent of teacher interactive decisions . . . does not accurately portray the processes involved in teacher interactive decision making.
>
> (Clark and Peterson, 1986: 277)

The review of literature on teachers' theories and beliefs was divided into two sections. The first focused on teachers' beliefs about students; the second focused on teachers' implicit theories about teaching and learning. The latter was at the time described as 'the smallest and youngest part of the literature on teacher thinking' (p. 285) and its purpose was 'to make explicit and visible the frames of reference through which individual teachers perceive and process information' (p. 286). Even at that early stage in the study of teachers' beliefs, Clark and Peterson noted that this field was characterized by a proliferation of concepts and terminology. This remains a characteristic of the field of teacher cognition research today.

Teacher knowledge

From the mid-1980s onwards, the work of Lee Shulman and his associates at Stanford University working on the Knowledge Growth in Teaching research programme made an influential contribution to the field of teacher cognition (e.g. Grossman *et al.*, 1989; Shulman, 1986a, 1986b, 1987; Wilson *et al.*, 1987). The focus of this research was the role of subject matter knowledge in teaching, an issue which Shulman (1986b) argued had been awarded scant attention in research on teaching. In referring to this gap as the 'missing paradigm problem' (p. 6) he was not only criticizing process-product approaches to research on teaching; even teacher cognition researchers, he argued, had shown little concern for subject-matter knowledge. And with reference to work at the time on practical knowledge (e.g. Elbaz, 1983), Wilson, Shulman and Richert (1987: 108) wrote that

> by emphasizing the practical, and to some extent, idiosyncratic knowledge that teachers use, these researchers present a truncated conceptualization of teacher knowledge. Teachers have theoretical, as well as practical, knowledge of the subject matter that informs and is informed by their teaching: any portrait of teacher knowledge should include both aspects.

The work of Shulman and colleagues examined the sources of teacher knowledge, how it is acquired, transformed and used in the classroom. In particular, this programme of research focused on the ways in which college graduates who become teachers transform the subject-matter knowledge obtained from college into knowledge which can be communicated to and understood by learners. An influential product of this work were various classifications of teachers' content knowledge (Shulman, 1986b; 1987). Seven headings under which teacher knowledge could be organized were proposed; subject-matter content knowledge, pedagogical content knowledge, curricular knowledge, general pedagogical knowledge, knowledge of learners and their characteristics, knowledge of educational contexts and knowledge of educational ends. Of these, pedagogical content knowledge (PCK) is perhaps that which had the largest impact on continuing thinking and research on teacher cognition (though there has been much debate about the precise value of the concept, e.g. Segall, 2004; Sockett, 1987). PCK implies that teachers transform their knowledge of the subject matter into a form which makes it amenable to teaching and learning – 'it represents the blending of content and pedagogy into an understanding of how particular topics, problems, or issues are organized, represented, and adapted to the diverse interests and abilities of learners, and presented for instruction' (Shulman, 1987: 8). PCK is subject-specific, as distinct from general pedagogical knowledge, and has generated much research into the kinds of knowledge that teachers of specific subjects have, particularly in science and mathematics (see, respectively, Cochran and Jones, 1998; Fennema and Franke, 1992).

The year 1987 also saw the publication of *Exploring Teachers' Thinking*, a collection of papers edited by James Calderhead, who is perhaps the British academic most strongly associated with research on teacher cognition. (Despite the British editor, though, this collection contained papers largely from North America.) The work reported here was grounded in the notion of teaching as a professional thinking activity and dealt with three broad themes: the nature of teachers' professional knowledge, the ways in which knowledge is used in the task of teaching (including work by Clark and Yinger on planning and Shulman and his associates on teacher knowledge), and the role of teachers' thinking and knowledge in the processes of educational change. Despite the use of teacher *thinking* in the title, it was teacher *knowledge* that was the unifying conceptual concern of this volume. In fact, the study of teachers' subject-matter knowledge generated sufficient research interest for it to become recognized as an orientation to the study of teacher cognition distinct from three already discussed in this chapter and which focused respectively on decision-making, practical knowledge and teachers' theories and beliefs. From the late-1980s, *teacher knowledge* began to challenge and in time to displace *teacher thinking* as the term most strongly associated with the study of teacher cognition. It remains the dominant concept today.

Another review of research on teacher thinking appeared in 1987 (Clandinin and Connelly, 1987). This paper examined studies focusing specifically on teachers' theories and beliefs; the fact that only 12 such studies were identified reflects the manner in which the study of beliefs remained the least developed of the different orientations to teacher cognition research I have identified here. One point highlighted by this review was the confusion being caused in the field by the proliferation of terminology and concepts (a point also noted by Eisenhart *et al.*, 1988), such that the commonality among studies of teachers' beliefs was often masked through the use of diverse terms for describing their focus. (Some 20 years on, the wide range of concepts and terms in the field of teacher cognition still presents researchers with significant challenges in attempting to relate different studies and, seemingly different perspectives, to one another.) This analysis made two general critiques of the available studies of teachers' theories and beliefs. One was that teacher thought had been studied largely without reference to teachers' actions in the classroom and to their biographical histories. This, for the authors, was a shortcoming. A second, related observation was that the research reviewed was grounded in a predominantly cognitive perspective on teacher thinking. The view of Clandinin and Connelly was, in contrast, 'that a cognitive and affective understanding of the personal practical knowledge of teachers will help produce more living, viable understandings of what it means to educate and to be educated' (p. 499). These authors have in fact made a major contribution in the study of teaching by advancing a holistic view of teacher knowledge; their work has been based on analyses of teachers' personal experiences and biographies which transcend a concern with the cognitive (e.g. Clandinin, 1986; Connelly and Clandinin, 1990; Connelly et al., 1997). Their work on personal practical knowledge – which they defined as 'knowledge which is experiential, embodied, and reconstructed out of the narratives of a teacher's life' (p. 490) – has been instrumental in furthering the tradition of teacher cognition research stimulated by Elbaz (1981, 1983).

Teachers' Professional Learning (Calderhead, 1988b) provided further evidence of developments in the field of teacher cognition research. The focus of this volume was on understanding the process of *learning to teach,* a term which was to become widespread in the teacher education literature in the 1990s (see also, for example, Kennedy, 1991). As Calderhead writes in the introduction to the volume, 'Learning to teach involves complex cognitive, affective and behavioural changes, and research into this complexity has only recently acquired momentum. This research clearly promises to be of value in informing current policy and the practices of teacher educators' (p. 2). The connections, then, between the study of teacher cognition and the process of teacher education were continuing to become stronger, and many of the papers in this collection were by academics well known for their commitment not just to research, but to the practice of teacher education (e.g. Tom Russell and Fred Korthagen). Orientations to teacher cognition which had emerged earlier in the 1980s, such as the focus on teachers' theories and on planning, were also in evidence here in relation to teacher learning (Anning, 1988; Borko et al., 1988 respectively). The processes of learning to teach highlighted in this volume became central in the study of teacher cognition in the subsequent decade and remain so today. We can contrast this with the situation in the 1970s where the impetus for teacher cognition research came from educational psychologists.

In relation to this volume, it is also important to note the influence which the notion of reflective practice and in particular the work of Schön (1983, 1987) was starting to have on thinking in teacher education. As reflection by teachers emerged as a central component in professional development, understanding the process of reflection, what it involved and how it affected teacher learning became central to research in teacher education (e.g. Calderhead, 1989; Calderhead and Gates, 1993; Grimmett and Erickson, 1988; Russell and Munby, 1992). In his review of research on teacher knowledge, Fenstermacher (1994) later conceived research with a reflective orientation as part of an approach to teacher cognition research which, along with the work on practical knowledge, was concerned with examining and understanding what teachers do; he contrasted this orientation with earlier work on decision-making and planning, where the focus was on producing knowledge that teachers could use.

The 1980s was, then, an intensive period of growth in teacher cognition research. Teacher knowledge emerged as a key concept, though at the same time the field continued to be strongly associated with earlier work on teacher decision-making. In 1988 Clark wrote that 'research on teacher thinking has established a place for itself within the international education research enterprise (1988: 5), while a further review of the field noted that 'interest in the study of teacher thinking has intensified to the point where it has become a dominant field of inquiry within research on teaching' (Mitchell and Marland, 1989: 115). In this review, Mitchell and Marland again drew attention to limitations of the view of teaching as decision-making; as noted earlier, it accounted for only a part of teachers' mental activity in the classroom; it also often focused on a limited and trivial set of classroom issues (Shulman, 1986a: 24, called this 'a severely attenuated menu of teacher cognitions') and some of the issues which this research had focused on (e.g. how many interactive decisions teachers make) were criticized for being of little practical or theoretical interest. Mitchell and Marland concluded that

> we consider the value of representing teachers' thinking as decision-making is at best problematical. We agree that the decision-making model can be best used to describe some of the conscious processing of teachers but we remain sceptical as to its validity. We submit that such an account may not capture the real essence of teachers' interactive thinking. Our position is that describing teacher thinking in terms of decision making is somewhat analogous to representing the real significance of Christmas to Christian communities in terms of holidaying or exchanging gifts. Our research has indicated that teachers, at both primary and secondary levels, process information in classrooms in accordance with other models.
> (Mitchell and Marland 1989: 117)

The key point of this review, then, was that notions of teacher thinking as decision-making did not adequately capture the manner in which teachers processed information in the classroom and that more complex models accounting for the greater range of the thinking that teachers engage in needed to be developed. A focus on teacher decision-making as conceived of in the early 1980s did in fact become less common in the subsequent decade.

The 1990s: Knowledge, beliefs and learning to teach

In response to the proliferation of research on teacher cognition in the late 1980s and early 1990s, this decade was characterized by a series of important reviews of different aspects of the literature on teacher cognition. (By this point the volume of material for reviewers to deal with had grown to the extent that a single comprehensive analysis of all existing material, as that produced by Clark and Peterson in 1986 was no longer feasible.) Both Thompson (1992) and Fennema and Franke (1992) examined relevant work in the field of mathematics, while Pajares (1992) focused on explicating the meaning of 'belief' in research on teaching. Several reviews were driven by the concerns of teacher education: Carter (1990), Borko and Putnam (1996) and Carter and Doyle (1996) all focused on learning to teach; Ball and McDiarmid (1990) and Shulman and Quinlan (1996) examined research on subject-matter knowledge, while Grimmett & Mackinnon (1992) reviewed research on teachers' craft knowledge (a concept that shares much in common with practical knowledge). Richardson (1996) focused on attitudes and beliefs, while Calderhead (1996) examined beliefs and knowledge. Fenstermacher (1994) also focused on teacher knowledge. To give a sense of how the field of teacher cognition continued to develop in the 1990s, I will highlight below key issues emerging from a selection of these publications.

Teacher knowledge and learning to teach

Carter (1990) organized her review of what teachers know and how that knowledge is acquired around three categories of teacher knowledge: (a) teachers' information-processing, including decision-making and expert-novice studies; (b) teachers' practical knowledge including personal knowledge and classroom knowledge and (c) pedagogical content knowledge. These distinctions reflect perspectives on the study of teacher cognition which I have already highlighted and represent an attempt to organize these under the general heading of teacher knowledge. The distinctions between the information-processing and decision-making perspectives which were made more starkly in the 1980s (see, for example, Clark, 1980) here appear to be less marked. Discussions of 'personal knowledge', including beliefs and implicit theories, are also subsumed under the heading of 'practical knowledge'.

I have already discussed early teacher cognition studies of decision-making and Carter's review reiterates findings highlighted in earlier analyses of this material. Within an information-processing tradition, though, the expert-novice strand of research is not one I have commented on. This emerged in the late 1980s (e.g. Berliner, 1987;

Borko and Livingston, 1989), drawing on work in cognitive psychology which examined differences in the thinking of experts and novices. Carter's summary of this work was that

> these studies suggest that expert teachers, in contrast with novices, draw on richly elaborated knowledge structures derived from classroom experience to understand teaching tasks and interpret classroom events. Expert teachers know the common forms of activities (recitations, seatwork, discussions) and academic assignments as classroom occurrences. They are familiar with typical behaviors, interactions, and situations associated with such events. This event-structured knowledge appears to help experts make highly accurate predictions about what might happen in a classroom.
>
> (Carter, 1990: 299)

As Carter pointed out, though, such insights into differences in the knowledge of experts and novices were not especially helpful in understanding how such knowledge is acquired. The longitudinal dimension required to inform our understandings of how teachers learn was lacking in expert-novice studies at the time. There was also the danger in some of this work that expert knowledge was being used normatively, to define what teachers generally should be doing; in this sense, the teacher effectiveness orientation to the study of teacher cognition which characterized early work in the field was still exerting some influence.

Throughout her review, Carter's focus was conceptual more than substantive; that is, she was attempting to clarify some of the theoretical confusion she felt characterized research on teacher knowledge at the time. Her attempt to clarify the distinction between pedagogical content knowledge and practical knowledge is a good example of the contribution this review made to the field:

> From a learning-to-teach perspective, pedagogical content knowledge is a domain distinct from, but not unrelated to, practical knowledge. The major difference is that pedagogical content knowledge is to a greater extent grounded in disciplines and in formulations related to school curriculum and the

collective wisdom of the profession than practical knowledge. It is, in other words, more formal than personal and situational knowledge.

(ibid., p. 306)

In concluding her review, Carter indicated that the research on teacher knowledge available at the time had focused more on the characteristics of such knowledge (e.g. it is complex, holistic, personal) and on the topics teachers think about (e.g. routines, students, classroom management) than on the substance of that knowledge – what it is teachers know or need to know about classrooms, content and pedagogy, and how that knowledge is organized.

Teachers' beliefs

Although the study of teachers' implicit theories and beliefs was highlighted as a key category of research on teacher thinking by Clark and Peterson (1986), there had been little explicit discussion in the literature of ways in which the study of beliefs might be different to the study of related psychological constructs such as knowledge, conceptions and attitudes. Pajares (1992) made a significant contribution to this issue with what remains the most comprehensive review of literature on teachers' beliefs available. As he outlines at the start of his paper, although the influence of beliefs on the perceptions, judgements and classroom behaviours of teachers was widely acknowledged, research on teachers' beliefs had been hampered by the lack of a clear definition for the concept. In working towards such a definition, Pajares argued that talking about teachers' beliefs generally is inadequate as this term is far too broad:

> The construct of educational beliefs is itself broad and encompassing. For purposes of research, it is diffuse and ungainly, too difficult to operationalize, too context free. Therefore, as with more general beliefs, *educational beliefs about* are required – beliefs about confidence to affect students' performance (teacher efficacy), about the nature of knowledge (epistemological beliefs), about causes of teachers' or students' performance (attributions, locus of control,

motivation, writing apprehension, math anxiety), about perceptions of self and feelings of self-worth (self-concept, self-esteem), about confidence to perform specific tasks (self-efficacy). There are also educational beliefs about specific subjects or disciplines (reading instruction, the nature of reading, whole language).

(Pajares, 1992: 316)

This deconstructing of the notion of teachers' beliefs into the many different foci it could represent opened up a wide range of specific issues for subsequent research to examine. Pajares proposed that beliefs can be defined as 'an individual's judgment of the truth or falsity of a proposition, a judgment that can only be inferred from a collective understanding of what human beings say, intend, and do' (p. 316). He then drew on the work of cognitive psychologists Rokeach (1968), Nisbett and Ross (1980) and Abelson (1979), as well as on existing educational research on teacher beliefs to identify a list of 16 'fundamental assumptions that can be made when initiating a study of teachers' educational beliefs' (p. 324). These are summarized in Figure 1.4 and provide a framework which remains helpful today.

In concluding his review, Pajares noted that 'little will have been accomplished if research into educational beliefs fails to provide insights into the relationship between beliefs, on the one hand, and teacher practices, teacher knowledge, and student outcomes on the other' (p. 327). While the connections between beliefs, practices and knowledge have attracted much attention in the last 15 years, the relationship of teacher cognition to student outcomes remains an issue which researchers have failed to address in any substantial manner.

Subject-specific teacher cognition

Sufficient teacher cognition research had accumulated by the early 1990s to justify literature reviews grounded in specific curricular areas. Mathematics and science were (and remain) the two areas where most subject-specific teacher cognition research had taken place, and here I will discuss briefly one review in the field of mathematics (see Cochran and Jones, 1998 for a review in science).

1. Beliefs are formed early and tend to self-perpetuate even against contradictions caused by reason, time, schooling or experience.
2. Individuals develop a belief system that houses all the beliefs acquired through the process of cultural transmission.
3. The belief system has an adaptive function in helping individuals define and understand the world themselves.
4. Knowledge and beliefs are inextricably intertwined, but the potent affective, evaluative and episodic nature of beliefs makes them a filter through which new phenomena are interpreted.
5. Thought processes may be precursors to and creators of belief, but the filtering effect of belief structures ultimately screens, redefines, distorts or reshapes subsequent thinking and information-processing.
6. Epistemological beliefs play a key role in knowledge interpretation and cognitive monitoring.
7. Beliefs are prioritized according to their connections or relationship to other beliefs or other cognitive and affective structures.
8. Belief substructures, such as educational beliefs, must be understood in terms of their connections not only to each other but also to other, perhaps more central, beliefs in the system.
9. By their very nature and origin, some beliefs are more incontrovertible than others.
10. The earlier a belief is incorporated into the belief structure, the more difficult it is to alter. Newly acquired beliefs are most vulnerable to change.
11. Belief change during adulthood is a very rare phenomenon, the most common cause being a conversion from one authority to another or a gestalt shift.
12. Beliefs are instrumental in defining tasks and selecting the cognitive tools with which to interpret, plan and make decisions regarding such tasks.
13. Beliefs strongly influence perception, but they can be an unreliable guide to the nature of reality.
14. Individuals' beliefs strongly affect their behaviour.
15. Beliefs must be inferred, and this inference must take into account the congruence among individuals' belief statements, the intentionality to behave in a predisposed manner, and the behaviour related to the belief in question.
16. Beliefs about teaching are well established by the time a student gets to college.

FIGURE 1.4 *Findings on teacher beliefs*
(Pajares, 1992: 324 6)

Thompson (1992) appeared in a handbook of research on mathematics teaching. The focus of this review was teachers' beliefs (Fennema and Franke, 1992, in the same volume, examined research on teacher knowledge in mathematics education.) In addressing the knotty issue of the distinction between beliefs and knowledge, Thompson cited authors who had argued that in educational research there is no need to distinguish beliefs and knowledge in any definitive way, and that what matters more is understanding how these concepts affect what teachers do. Nonetheless, her position was that it is important to clarify the nature of beliefs and she aimed to do this with reference to literature from psychology and philosophy (e.g. Abelson, 1979; Green, 1971; Scheffler, 1965).

Thompson highlighted two key features of beliefs: that they can be held with various degrees of conviction and that they are non-consensual (i.e. they can be disputed). (Nespor, 1987 had noted similar points.) She also discussed belief systems, with particular reference to the work of Green (1971). Beliefs are seen to exist in relation to other beliefs in such a way that some beliefs may be *primary* (e.g. learning is facilitated when there is a positive climate in the classroom) and others *derivative* (e.g. the teacher should have a sense of humour – this is derivative in that it is based on the primary belief just cited). Green also distinguished between beliefs which are central and those which are peripheral, with the former being more firmly held and less susceptible to change.

At the end of her discussion of the conceptual background to the review, Thompson stated that she will also refer to teacher's conceptions, 'viewed as a more general mental structure, encompassing beliefs, meanings, concepts, propositions, rules, mental images, preferences, and the like' (p. 130). Knowledge was not included here though its omission seemed arbitrary. In fact, in her summary Thompson concluded that 'it seems more helpful for researchers to focus their studies on teachers' conceptions – mental structures encompassing both beliefs and any aspect of the teachers' knowledge that bears on their experience, such as meanings, concepts, propositions, rules, mental images, and the like – instead of just beliefs' (p. 141). This is further evidence of the difficulties teacher cognition researchers have constantly faced in separating the study of teacher beliefs and knowledge (other than knowledge which is obviously propositional).

Two conclusions of general importance to research on teacher cognition emerged from this review of research on teachers' beliefs and conceptions in mathematics:

> Studies of the relationship between teachers' beliefs and practice lead us to question the adequacy of two related assumptions underlying a number of studies. One of them is that belief systems are static entities to be uncovered. The second assumption is that the relationship between beliefs and practice is a simple linear-causal one. Thoughtful analyses of the nature of the relationship between beliefs and practice suggest that belief systems are dynamic, permeable mental structures, susceptible to change in light of experience. The research also strongly suggests that the relationship between beliefs and practice is a dialectic, not a simple cause-and-effect relationship. Thus, future studies, particularly those having to do with effecting change should seek to elucidate the dialectic between teachers' beliefs and practice, rather than try to determine whether and how changes in beliefs result in changes in practice.
> (Thompson, 1992: 140)

The dialectic highlighted here between cognitions and practices had been suggested as far back as 1986 by Clark and Peterson (see Figure 1.3); Thompson's review found empirical support for it. She also, once again, pointed out the lack of connections in existing research between teachers' cognitions and student learning. This is a separation which has remained problematic until today.

Conceptions of knowledge

A great deal of work in teacher cognition in the 1990s was conceptual; the need was felt not only to generate more substantive findings, but also to make sense of the wide range of often confusing and conflicting conceptions of teacher cognition which had emerged. Fenstermacher (1994) is a key paper in this vein. His focus was on teacher knowledge, but his perspective was philosophical as he examined 'how notions of knowledge are used and analyzed in a number of programs that study teachers and teaching' (p. 3).

He addressed this question by discussing three types of research; the first was typified by process-product studies often grounded in psychology and where the goal was to discover effective teaching and to use this as the basis of prescriptions for practice; the second included studies of practical knowledge and reflective practice; and the third tradition was that focusing on subject-matter knowledge. Fenstermacher distinguished between formal teacher knowledge – 'the concept of knowledge as it appears in standard or conventional behavioral science research' (p. 5) and practical teacher knowledge – what teachers know as a result of experience – and argued that the first of the three traditions above focused on formal knowledge, the second on practical knowledge, while the orientation of the third was ambiguous, though with a possible leaning towards formal knowledge. It is clear here that Fenstermacher was seeking to make sense of teacher cognition research from an epistemological perspective, examining not just the focus of different traditions of research but also the assumptions about knowledge underlying them.

In the course of this analysis, Fenstermacher highlighted two senses in which the term *knowledge* can be used in teacher cognition research. One is to use *knowledge* as a grouping or classifying term (in which case it is acceptable to group other constructs, such as beliefs or conceptions, under it). A different use of the term, though, is to use it to make claims about the epistemological status of an entity. (As a philosopher, Fenstermacher saw clear distinctions between belief and knowledge.) This distinction is expanded on below:

> The main point of this discussion of knowledge and belief is that there are important differences between the two if one intends to make claims about epistemic import. When, for example, a researcher argues that teachers produce knowledge in the course of acting on experience, he or she could be saying merely that teachers generate ideas, conceptions, images, or perspectives when performing as teachers (the grouping sense of knowledge) or that teachers are justified in performing as they do for reasons or evidence they are able to provide (the epistemic status sense of knowledge).
>
> (Fenstermacher, 1994: 31)

The question Fenstermacher left readers with, on the basis of his analysis, relates to the status of practical knowledge: does it have an epistemic merit (i.e. can evidence be cited to support the claim that it is knowledge?), or is it rather an umbrella label used to group together a range of related psychological constructs without making any claims about their epistemological status?

Perspectives from teacher education and educational psychology

I conclude this overview of developments in the 1990s with reference to two further literature reviews. Richardson's (1996) review of the role of attitudes and beliefs in learning to teach appeared in the second edition of the *Handbook of Research on Teacher Education* (Sikula *et al.*, 1996), while Calderhead (1996) analysed research on teachers' beliefs and knowledge in the *Handbook of Educational Psychology* (Berliner and Calfee, 1996). These two handbooks reflect the two areas of activity which teacher cognition research has been most strongly associated with – psychology and teacher education – though by the mid-1990s it was the latter that seemed most strongly aligned with continuing developments in the study of teacher cognition.

Richardson examined literature both on the ways that pre-service students' and teachers' beliefs influence learning to teach, as well as on teacher education programmes that are designed to change beliefs and attitudes. In common with most reviews in the field, Richardson dedicated space early in the work to addressing issues of definition; in this case, belief was defined as 'a proposition that is accepted as true by the individual holding the belief' (p. 104) and a distinction between beliefs and knowledge similar to that made by Fenstermacher (i.e. knowledge implies epistemic warrant) was drawn.

The role of beliefs in learning to teach is discussed from two perspectives: the first relates to constructivist theories of learning that state that students bring beliefs to teacher education which influence what and how they learn. The second relates to belief change as a focus for teacher education. In relation to the former, three categories of experience were identified as influencing the development of beliefs and knowledge about teaching. (Richardson does in fact dedicate space to the discussion of knowledge, despite the avowed focus on attitudes and beliefs; attitudes actually play a minor role in the review.) These are personal experience, experience of schooling and instruction and experience with formal knowledge ('understandings that have been agreed on within a community of scholars as worthwhile and valid', p. 106). In discussing the second of these, reference is made to Lortie's (1975) widely cited notion of the 'apprenticeship of observation' – the impact of schooling experiences on the development of beliefs about teaching – and the manner in which beliefs formed during this apprenticeship may be resistant to change during teacher education. The extent to which beliefs could be changed through teacher education was an issue of much controversy at the time. On the basis of the available research, Richardson's conclusion was that 'the results are complex. Some programs effect change and others do not; some programs affect certain types of students and not others; and some beliefs are more difficult to change than others' (p. 111). Overall, she concluded that teacher education seemed to be a weak intervention, 'sandwiched between two powerful forces – previous life history, particularly that related to being a student, and classroom experience as a student teacher and a teacher' (p. 113).

Calderhead's (1996) review examined research on teachers' beliefs and knowledge published between 1985 and 1995. Here, the domain of teacher cognition research was classified into three distinct phases of research: (a) decision-making, (b) perceptions, evaluations and related issues (this phase covered a broader range of constructs than decision-making) and (c) knowledge and beliefs. This classification varies from those mentioned earlier in Carter (1990) and Fenstermacher (1994), a point which reinforces the variety of ways in which distinct orientations to teacher cognition research have been conceptualized over the years.

Unsurprisingly perhaps, although this review provides a helpful discussion of the field, it adds little to previous reviews; for example, in the discussion of research on interactive decision-making, we are reminded of the conclusion that 'teachers make few decisions in the classroom' (p. 714) – in other words, they rely largely on well-established routines, as discussed earlier.

Calderhead's discussion of both knowledge and beliefs highlights several sub-types in each category which had been noted in the literature. Under knowledge, there is subject knowledge, craft knowledge ('the knowledge that teachers acquire within their own classroom practice, the knowledge that enables them to employ the strategies, tactics, and routines that they do', p. 717), personal practical knowledge, case knowledge ('a knowledge based of significant incidents, events, and people that enables new situations to be identified and helps guide teachers' practice', p. 718), theoretical knowledge and metaphors and images.

Teachers' beliefs are also discussed under a number of headings: beliefs about learners and learning, beliefs about teaching, beliefs about subject, beliefs about learning to teach and beliefs about self and the teaching role. This specific treatment of different types of beliefs suggests that teacher cognition research had moved away from the study of beliefs generically to more focused analysis of beliefs about particular issues, as recommended by Pajares (1992).

In concluding his review, Calderhead highlighted the valuable contribution to the study of teaching made by teacher cognition research:

> Research on teachers' cognitions has highlighted the complex array of factors that interact in the processes of teaching and learning. In particular, research has pointed to the elaborate knowledge and belief structures that teachers hold, to the influence of their past experiences, even experiences outside of teaching, in shaping how teachers think about their work, and to the diverse processes of knowledge growth involved in learning to teach. Research also has begun to unravel some of the pedagogical processes involved in classroom teaching and the different types of knowledge that teachers draw on in their efforts to help children to learn and understand.
>
> (Calderhead, 1996: 721)

The issues highlighted here constituted the basis of research on teacher cognition throughout the rest of the 1990s, and continue to influence the direction of such research today.

Developments since 2000

As we moved into a new millennium, interest in the study of teacher cognition showed no sign of abating. The year 2001 saw the publication of two further reviews of literature – both focused on teacher knowledge (which had become the most widely used term in the study of teacher cognition). That by Munby, Russell and Martin (2001) did not attempt a comprehensive review of research on teachers' knowledge – given the volume of work available on this topic and the many reviews of it already available, the authors opted rather to present a guide to research which had appeared since the previous edition of the *Handbook of Research Teaching* in 1986. An issue which is stressed in this review is that making sense of the literature on teacher cognition presents a major challenge stemming from

> the legion of interpretations not just of teachers' knowledge but also, importantly, of knowledge itself . . . the literature seems characterized by a root tension: Different views have developed about what counts as professional knowledge and even how to conceptualize knowledge.
> (Munby, Russell and Martin, 2001: 878)

Many of the key publications in the field which appeared in the 1990s (several of which I discussed above) are reviewed in this analysis and a key tension is highlighted between accounts of teacher knowledge which view it as largely propositional – information generated through (psychological) research and which teachers learn and apply – (e.g. Reynolds, 1989) and those based on more practice-oriented conceptions – where knowledge derives from and makes sense in relation to teachers' work in the classroom (e.g. Russell and Munby, 1992). This relates to the tension (between formal and practical teacher knowledge) highlighted earlier in Fenstermacher (1994). Proposals for addressing this tension and establishing connections between propositional and practical knowledge are discussed by Munby et al. (2001), focusing in particular on the notions of practical reasoning and practical argument (see Fenstermacher, 1986) and on Schön's (1983) concepts of knowing-in-action and reflection-in-action.

Verloop, Van Driel and Meijer (2001) also focused on teacher knowledge. They offer a broad definition of teacher knowledge (or teacher practical knowledge as they also call it) as 'the whole of the knowledge and insights that underlie teachers' actions in practice' (p. 446). Knowledge is being used here as the superordinate term for all kinds of cognitive constructs:

> It is important to realize that in the label 'teacher knowledge', the concept 'knowledge' is used as an overarching, inclusive concept, summarizing a large variety of cognitions, from conscious and well-balanced opinions to unconscious and unreflected intuitions. This is related to the fact that, in the mind of the teacher, components of knowledge, beliefs, conceptions, and intuitions are inextricably intertwined. As Alexander, Schallert, and Hare (1991) noted, the term 'knowledge' is mostly used to encompass 'all that a person knows or believes to be true, whether or not it is verified as true in some sort of objective or external way' (p. 317). This is particularly relevant with respect to research on teacher knowledge. In investigating teacher knowledge, the main focus of attention is on the complex totality of cognitions, the ways this develops, and the way this interacts with teacher behaviour in the classroom. Following Pajares (1992), knowledge and beliefs are seen as inseparable, although beliefs are seen roughly as referring to personal values, attitudes, and ideologies, and knowledge to a teacher's more factual propositions
>
> (Meijer, Verloop and Beijaard, 2001: 446)

The argument here, then, is that aiming to separate knowledge, belief and related concepts is not a particularly fruitful exercise given that in the mind of the teachers these constructs are not held or perceived distinctively. Scholars in the field with a more philosophical orientation would perhaps find this position untenable, but this is a position which is reflected, often tacitly, even in some of the major reviews of teachers' beliefs and knowledge discussed earlier.

Two final points raised in this review merit a comment here. Firstly, a distinction was made between individual teacher cognitions and more generalized, shared components of teacher knowledge. The idea of shared teacher cognitions is not one that had (or has) received much empirical attention in the field, in contrast to the intense study of individuals. Secondly, the authors examine the manner in which teacher education can make teacher knowledge available or accessible to prospective teachers. The programme of research conducted by Verloop and colleagues at Leiden University has made an important contribution to the field in both these respects (e.g. Meijer *et al.*, 2002; Zanting *et al.*, 2003).

As we move past the midpoint of the current decade, the contents pages of key research journals in education, and particularly in teacher education, highlight the continuing interest in the study of teacher cognition (e.g. Angeli and Valanides, 2005; Graham, 2005; Huang *et al.*, 2005; Olson and Craig, 2005; Verjovsky and Waldegg, 2005). Concepts which have been in circulation for almost 20 years continue to exercise the minds of scholars in this field (see, for example, Hashweh, 2005, who reviews the notion of pedagogical content knowledge and proposes an alternative 'called teacher pedagogical constructions'), while there is evidence of continued development in the work of key figures in the field; Shulman and Shulman (2004), for example, outline how their thinking about teacher learning 'has moved from a concern with individual teachers and their learning to a conception of teachers learning and developing within a broader context of community, institution, polity, and profession' (pp. 267–9). This new perspective contrasts with the largely individual focus on teacher learning which characterized Shulman's earlier work on subject-matter knowledge. Debates I have highlighted in this historical overview related to matters of definition also remain current, as evidenced, for example, by exchanges on the differences between knowledge and belief between Smith and Siegel (2004) and Davson-Galle (2004), in the context of science education. And for some problematic areas, such as the relationship between teacher cognition and learning outcomes, little progress has been achieved. Despite the dilemmas which continue to surround key issues in the study of teacher cognition, it has as a field of inquiry experienced enormous growth in the past 30 years.

Summary

Here are some conclusions that we can extract from the overview I have presented here.

1 The development of teacher cognition research has been characterized by changing orientations to both how teaching has been conceptualized and why teachers' mental lives are a valuable research focus. From an initial concern with information-processing, decision-making and teacher effectiveness, the predominant focus today is on understanding teacher knowledge (used as an umbrella term for a range of psychological constructs), its growth and use. Teacher cognition research today is aligned particularly closely with work in teacher education: a key role for such research is to support teacher learning at both pre-service and in-service level.

2 The field is characterized by an overwhelming array of concepts. Table 1.1 presents a list of terms from the literature which have been used in describing teachers' cognitions with the definitions assigned to these terms. The need for such diversity may be justified by the inherently complex nature of the phenomena under study; however, the confusion is also due to the fact identical terms have been defined in different ways and different terms have been used to describe similar concepts.

3 An analysis of the concepts used in teacher cognition research suggests a number of recurrent ideas which, collectively, characterize the essence of this phenomenon. These are (a) personal, (b) practical (though informed by formal knowledge), (c) tacit, (d) systematic and (e) dynamic. Teacher cognition can thus be characterized as an often tacit, personally-held, practical system of mental constructs held by teachers and which are dynamic – that is defined and refined on the basis of educational and professional experiences throughout teachers' lives. These constructs have been characterized using a range of psychological labels (particularly belief and knowledge) which may often

Table 1.1 Concepts in teacher cognition research

Term	Definition	Source
belief	a form of personal knowledge consisting of implicit assumptions about students, learning, classrooms and the subject matter to be taught	Kagan (1992b)
belief	knowledge that is viable in that it enables an individual to meet goals in specific circumstances	Tobin & LaMaster (1995)
beliefs	preconceptions and implicit theories; an eclectic aggregation of cause-effect propositions from many sources, rules of thumb and generalizations drawn from personal experience	Crawley & Salyer (1995)
beliefs	convictions or opinions that are formed either by experience or by the intervention of ideas through the learning process	Ford (1994)
beliefs	attitudes and values about teaching, students, and the educational process	Pajares (1993)
case knowledge	knowledge of specific, well-documented and richly defined events, which enable new situations to be identified and help guide teachers' practice	Shulman (1986)
cognition	teachers' self-reflections; beliefs and knowledge about teaching, students and content; and awareness of problem-solving strategies endemic to classroom teaching	Kagan (1990)
conceptions of subject matter	conscious or subconscious beliefs, concepts, meanings, rules, mental images and preferences concerning the discipline to be taught	Thompson (1992)

(*Continued*)

Table 1.1 (Continued)

Term	Definition	Source
conceptions of teaching	what a teacher considers to be desirable goals, his or her own role in teaching, the students' role, appropriate classroom activities, desirable instructional approaches and emphases, legitimate procedures and acceptable outcomes of instruction	
conceptions of teaching	the set of ideas, understandings and interpretations of experience concerning the teacher and teaching, the nature and content of the subject matter and the learners and learning that the teacher uses in making decisions about teaching, both in planning and execution	Hewson, Kerby & Cook (1995)
conditional/ situational knowledge	knowledge about how to act and react during specific events and situations	Roehler et al. (1988)
content knowledge	factual information, organizing principles, central concepts of a discipline	Grossman, Wilson & Shulman (1989)
substantive knowledge	the explanatory frameworks or paradigms that are used both to guide inquiry in the field and to make sense of data	
syntactic knowledge	knowledge of the ways in which new knowledge is brought into the field	
craft knowledge	a rubric for describing a number of different approaches to studying the psychological context of teaching	Zeichner, Tabachnick & Densmore (1987)
general pedagogical knowledge	knowledge of pedagogical principles and techniques that is not bound by topic or subject matter	Wilson, Shulman & Richert (1987)

Table 1.1 (Continued)

Term	Definition	Source
knowledge of learners	knowledge of student characteristics and cognitions as well as knowledge of motivational and developmental aspects of how students learn	
images	general metaphors for thinking about teaching; overall concepts of a lesson; memorized snapshots of particular experiences; conceptions of a subject; ideas about how students learn	Calderhead & Robson (1991)
implicit theories	the complex aggregate of cause-effect propositions, rules of thumb, generalizations based in personal experiences, beliefs, values and assumptions that teachers use to guide their behaviours	Dirkx & Spurgin (1992)
knowing-in-action	actions, recognitions and judgements which professionals carry out spontaneously and based on their tacit knowledge of the situation	Schön (1983)
lay theories	beliefs developed naturally over time without the influence of instruction	Holt Reynolds (1992)
orientations to teaching	beliefs and opinions about teaching	Brousseau, Book & Byers (1988)
personal practical knowledge	an individual's particular way of reconstructing the past and intentions for the future to deal with the exigencies of a present situation	Connelly & Clandinin (1988)
personalized pedagogy	a belief system that constrains the teachers' perception, judgement and behaviour	Kagan (1992b)

(Continued)

Table 1.1 (Continued)

Term	Definition	Source
perspective	a coordinated set of ideas and actions which a person uses in dealing with some problematic situation; perspectives differ from attitudes since they include actions and not merely dispositions to act; similar to beliefs and implicit theories	Tabachnick & Zeichner (1986)
practical knowledge	first-hand experience of students' learning styles, interests, needs, strengths and difficulties and a repertoire of instructional techniques and management skills. This knowledge ranges over five areas (self, milieu, subject matter, curriculum and instruction)	Elbaz (1981)
practical knowledge	the knowledge that is directly related to action, that is readily accessible and applicable to coping with real-life situations, and is largely derived from teachers' own classroom experience	Calderhead (1988a)
practical theories	the conceptual structures and visions that provide teachers with reasons for acting as they do, and for choosing the teaching activities and curriculum materials they choose in order to be effective; they are the principles or propositions that undergird and guide teachers' appreciations, decisions and actions	Sanders & McCutcheon (1986)
practical theory	a person's private, integrated, but ever-changing system of knowledge, experience, and values which is relevant to teaching practice at any particular time	Handal & Lauvas (1987)
professional craft knowledge	knowledge which is embedded in, and tacitly guiding, teachers' everyday actions in the classroom; related to the intuitive, spontaneous and routine aspects of teaching rather than to the more reflective and thoughtful activities in which teachers may engage at other times.	Brown & McIntyre (1986)

Table 1.1 (Continued)

Term	Definition	Source
prototypical/case knowledge	knowledge of significant events, people, places and procedures which act as typifications, enabling teachers to readily identify the situations they confront	Calderhead (1991)
schema	an ordered representation of objects, episodes, actions or situations that contain slots or variables into which specific instances of experience in a particular context can be fitted	Carter & Doyle (1987)
situated knowledge	contextually developed automatic knowledge consisting of a highly efficient collection of heuristics for the solution of very specific problems in teaching	Leinhardt (1988)
subject-matter knowledge	knowledge of the facts of a discipline	(Shulman (1986)
pedagogical content knowledge	knowledge of the ways of representing and formulating the subject that makes it comprehensible to others	
curricular knowledge	knowledge of programmes designed for the teaching of particular subjects and topics at a given level and of the variety of instructional materials available in relation to those programmes	
pedagogical knowledge of teaching	knowledge of generic principles of classroom organization and management	
teaching criteria	personal values a teacher tries to pursue or keep constant while teaching	Halkes & Deijkers (1984b)
theoretical orientations	belief systems and philosophical principles employed by teachers to develop expectations about students and make decisions about classroom life	Harste & Burke (1977)

be distinguished at the level of theoretical or philosophical debate but which seem to defy compartmentalization when teachers' practices and cognitions are examined empirically. This inclusive description of teacher cognition reminds us of the characteristics of the central concept which unifies the field. The proliferation of specialized terminologies has tended to obscure the existence of these recurrent characteristics.

4 Empirically, teacher cognition research has affirmed the active role which teachers play in shaping classroom events and highlighted the complex nature of classroom decision-making. It has provided evidence of the way in which teachers' beliefs and knowledge influence what teachers do in the classroom, though evidence also exists that teachers' beliefs about instruction are not always fully realized in their work. This lack of congruence between teachers' observed practices and their explicitly stated beliefs has been attributed to the influence on teaching of the social, psychological and environmental factors which exist in schools and classrooms and which teachers may perceive as external forces beyond their control. It is now accepted that the study of teachers' practices and cognitions must also take into account such factors.

5 The development of teachers' cognitions and their growth through teacher education and experience have also been key empirical areas of study. This had led to a recognition of the influence which teachers' educational biographies, generated by their vast experience as learners, have on their initial thinking. The impacts of teacher education on teachers' prior cognitions remains a matter of debate; there has been much research suggesting that teacher education is a weak intervention, though contemporary views are less pessimistic about the impact of teacher education than was the case in the early 1990s. There is now growing evidence of the ways in which teacher education can make explicit and promote change in the teachers' prior knowledge and beliefs. A concern for the role of teachers' subject-matter knowledge and how this is transformed in the act of teaching has been, and remains, a key feature of teacher cognition research.

THE ORIGINS OF TEACHER COGNITION RESEARCH

6 The role of teachers' experience has also been highlighted in studies of teacher cognition. Classroom experience has been shown to have a powerful influence on teachers' practical knowledge and hence to shape teachers' actions. Comparisons of expert and novice teachers (though generally lacking a longitudinal dimension) have also highlighted differences in their cognitions; experienced teachers have more fully developed schemata of teaching on which to base their instructional decisions; they also possess vast amounts of knowledge about typical classrooms and students to the extent that they often know a lot about their students even before they meet them. Such expert knowledge is not available to inexperienced teachers.

To conclude this chapter, then, Figure 1.5 (Borg, 2003c: 82) represents a schematic conceptualization of teaching within which teacher

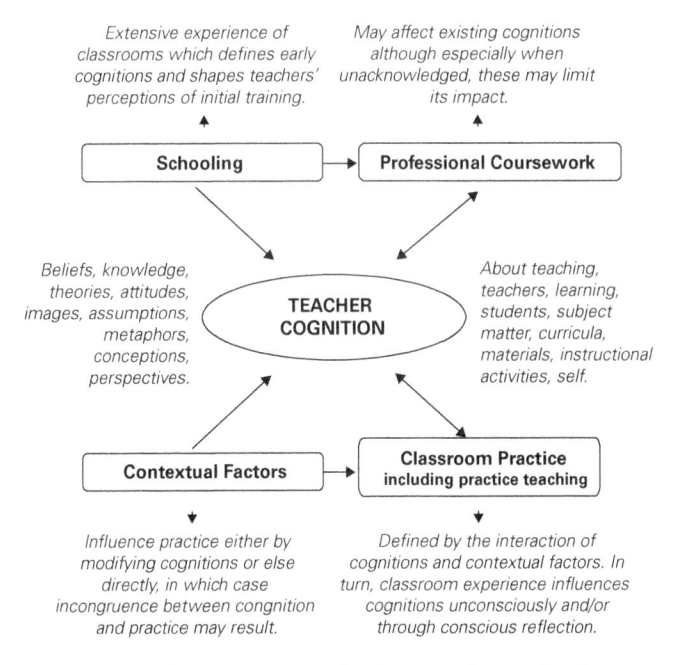

```
Extensive experience of          May affect existing cognitions
classrooms which defines early     although especially when
cognitions and shapes teachers'  unacknowledged, these may limit
perceptions of initial training.           its impact.
               ▲                              ▲
        ┌───────────┐            ┌───────────────────────┐
        │ Schooling │ ─────────▶ │ Professional Coursework│
        └───────────┘            └───────────────────────┘

 Beliefs, knowledge,                          About teaching,
  theories, attitudes,        ╭──────────╮    teachers, learning,
 images, assumptions,   ◀──── │ TEACHER  │    students, subject
     metaphors,               │ COGNITION│    matter, curricula,
    conceptions,              ╰──────────╯    materials, instructional
    perspectives.                              activities, self.

        ┌──────────────────┐    ┌──────────────────────────┐
        │ Contextual Factors│──▶│ Classroom Practice        │
        │                   │   │ including practice teaching│
        └──────────────────┘    └──────────────────────────┘
               ▼                              ▼
  Influence practice either by      Defined by the interaction of
    modifying cognitions or else    cognitions and contextual factors. In
       directly, in which case      turn, classroom experience influences
  incongruence between congnition   cognitions unconsciously and/or
       and practice may result.        through conscious reflection.
```

FIGURE 1.5 *Teacher cognition, schooling, professional education and classroom practice*
(Borg, 2003c: 82)

cognition plays a pivotal role in teachers' lives. It indicates that teachers have cognitions about all aspects of their work, and lists recurrent labels used to describe the various psychological constructs which I collectively refer to here as teacher cognition. The diagram also outlines relationships discussed above among teacher cognition, teacher learning (both through schooling and professional education), classroom practice and contextual factors. It is within this framework, grounded in an analysis of mainstream educational research, that language teacher cognition research has emerged and become an established domain of inquiry, particularly in the past ten years. In the next chapter I begin to discuss this domain of inquiry. I will return to Figure 1.5 at the end of the book and revise it with reference to the literature on language teacher cognition I consider between now and then.

Further reading: Reviews of research on teacher cognition

Readers wanting to explore in more detail the reviews of teacher cognition discussed in Chapter 1 will find the following sources relevant.

Ball, D. L. and McDiarmid, G. W. (1990). The subject-matter preparation of teachers. In W. R. Houston (ed.), *Handbook of Research on Teacher Education* (pp. 437–9). New York: Macmillan.

Block, J. H. and Hazelip, K. (1995). Teachers' beliefs and belief systems. In L. W. Anderson (ed.), *International Encyclopedia of Teaching and Teacher Education* (pp. 25–8). Oxford: Elsevier.

Borko, H. and Putnam, R. (1996). Learning to teach. In D. C. Berliner and R. C. Calfee (eds), *Handbook of Educational Psychology* (pp. 673–708). New York: Macmillan.

Calderhead, J. (1996). Teachers: Beliefs and knowledge. In D. C. Berliner and R. C. Calfee (eds), *Handbook of Educational Psychology* (pp. 709–25). New York: Macmillan.

Carter, C. and Doyle, W. (1996). Personal narrative and life history in learning to teach. In J. Sikula (ed.), *Handbook of Research on Teacher Education* (2nd ed., pp. 120–42). New York: Macmillan.

Carter, K. (1990). Teachers' knowledge and learning to teach. In W. R. Houston (ed.), *Handbook of Research on Teacher Education* (pp. 291–310). New York: Macmillan.

Clandinin, D. J. and Connelly, F. M. (1987). Teachers' personal knowledge: What counts as personal in studies of the personal. *Journal of Curriculum Studies*, 19, 487–500.

Clark, C. and Yinger, R. (1977). Research on teacher thinking. *Curriculum Inquiry*, 7, 279–304.

— (1979). Teachers' Thinking. In P. Peterson and H. Walberg (eds), *Research on Teaching and Learning: Concepts, Findings and Implications* (pp. 231–63). Berkeley: McCutchen.

Clark, C. M. (1980). Choice of a model for research on teacher thinking. *Journal of Curriculum Studies*, 12, 41–47.

— (1986). Ten years of conceptual development in research on teacher thinking. In M.Ben-Peretz, R. Bromme and R. Halkes (eds), *Advances of Research on Teacher Thinking.* (pp. 7–20). Lisse: Swets and Zeitlinger.

Clark, C. M. and Peterson, P. L. (1986). Teachers' thought processes. In M. C. Wittrock (ed.), *Handbook of Research on Teaching* (3rd ed., pp. 255–96). New York: Macmillan.

Cochran, K. F. and Jones, L. L. (1998). The subject matter knowledge of preservice science teachers. In B. Fraser and K. Tobin (eds), *International Handbook of Science Education* (pp. 707–18). Dordrecht, The Netherlands: Kluwer.

Eisenhart, M. A., Shrum, J. L., Harding, J. R. and Cuthbert, A. M. (1988). Teacher beliefs: definitions, findings and directions. *Educational Policy*, 2), 51–70.

Fennema, E. and Franke, M. L. (1992). Teachers' knowledge and its impact. In D. A. Grouws (ed.), *Handbook of Research on Mathematics Teaching and Learning* (pp. 147–64). New York, NY: Macmillan Publishing Co, Inc.

Fenstermacher, G. D. (1979). A philosophical consideration of recent research on teacher effectiveness. *Review of Research in Education*, 6, 157–85.

— (1986). Philosophy of research on teaching: three aspects. In M. C. Wittrock (ed.), *Handbook of Research on Teaching* (3rd ed., pp. 37–49). New York: Macmillan.

— (1994). The knower and the known: The nature of knowledge in research on teaching. *Review of Research in Education*, 20, 1–54.

Fenstermacher, G. D. and Richardson, V. (1993). The elicitation and reconstruction of practical arguments in teaching. *Journal of Curriculum Studies*, 25, 101–14.

Grimmett, P. P. and Mackinnon, A. M. (1992). Craft knowledge and the education of teachers. *Review of Research in Education*, 18, 385–456.

Grossman, P. L. (1995). Teachers' knowledge. In L. W. Anderson (ed.), *International Encyclopedia of Teaching and Teacher Education* (pp. 20–4). Oxford: Elsevier.

Mitchell, J. and Marland, P. (1989). Research on teacher thinking: The next phase. *Teaching and Teacher Education*, 5, 115–28.

Morine-Dershimer, G. (1991). Learning to think like a teacher. *Teaching and Teacher Education*, 7, 159–68.

Munby, H. (1982). The place of teachers' beliefs in research on teacher thinking and decision making, and an alternative methodology. *Instructional Science*, 11, 201–25.

Pajares, M. F. (1992). Teachers' beliefs and educational research: Cleaning up a messy construct. *Review of Educational Research*, 62, 307–32.

Richardson, V. (1996). The role of attitudes and beliefs in learning to teach. In J. Sikula (ed.), *Handbook of Research on Teacher Education* (2nd ed., pp. 102–19). New York: Macmillan.

Shavelson, R. J., Atwood, N. K. and Borko, H. (1977). Experiments on some factors contributing to teachers' pedagogical decisions. *Cambridge Journal of Education*, 7, 51–70.

Shavelson, R. J. and Stern, P. (1981). Research on teachers' pedagogical thoughts, judgements and behaviours. *Review of Educational Research*, 51, 455–98.

Shulman, L. S. (1986). Paradigms and research programmes in the study of teaching: A contemporary perspective. In M. C. Wittrock (ed.), *Handbook of Research in Education* (pp. 3–36). New York: Macmillan.

Shulman, L. S. and Quinlan, K. M. (1996). The comparative psychology of school subjects. In D. C. Berliner and R. C. Calfee (eds), *Handbook of Educational Psychology* (pp. 399–422). New York: Macmillan.

Thompson, A. G. (1992). Teachers' beliefs and conceptions: A synthesis of the research. In D. A. Grouws (ed.), *Handbook of Research on Mathematics Teaching and Learning* (pp. 127–46). New York: Macmillan.

Verloop, N., Van Driel, J. and Meijer, P. C. (2001). Teacher knowledge and the knowledge base of teaching. *International Journal of Educational Research*, 35, 441–61.

2

The cognitions of pre-service language teachers

In this chapter I will consider research which has been conducted into the cognitions of pre-service language teachers. Before proceeding, though, it is necessary to provide a brief introduction to the work I will be discussing in this and the subsequent three chapters.

The scope of language teacher cognition research

In an earlier review of research (Borg, 2003c) I identified 64 studies of teacher cognition conducted in second or foreign language contexts and published between 1976 and 2002. The analysis I present in Chapters 2–4 of this book extends this significantly by examining over 180 studies published up to 2006 in a wide range of first language (L1), second language (L2) and foreign language (FL) contexts. The majority of work in this field has appeared since the mid-1990s and has been conducted largely – but not exclusively – in contexts where English is taught as a first, second or foreign language; other languages represented in work I cover here (in either L1 or FL instructional contexts) are Japanese, German, Dutch, Spanish,

French, Latin, Malay, Tamil, Greek and Chinese. It is clear from the substantial body of work that is now available that the study of language teacher cognition is a well-established domain of research activity. It is also, however, diverse, with little evidence of replication or of programmatic approaches to research whereby a particular theme or methodological approach is engaged within a sustained manner by different researchers. Rather, the field is a largely fragmented one, with an array of diverse issues being studied from different perspectives. This diversity extends, though to a much lesser extent, to the geographical contexts in which language teacher cognition has been studied; for while much work has been conducted in the USA, the research I discuss also comes from the United Kingdom, Hong Kong, Canada, Singapore, Germany, Turkey, Malta, Hungary, Australia, New Zealand, Colombia, Oman, Brazil, Greece, the Netherlands, Puerto Rico, Indonesia and Sri Lanka. The study of language teacher cognition, then, is increasingly an international phenomenon.

Given the diversity of this field, a coherent system for classifying the studies which constitute it is required before these can be systematically analysed. A number of criteria – for example chronological, methodological or geographical – might provide the basis of such a system. For the purposes of making substantive sense of language teacher cognition research, though, I have opted for a thematic classification. This is presented in Table 2.1.

This classification broadly divides language teacher cognition research into studies which have examined pre-service teachers' cognitions, those which have examined the cognitions of in-service (i.e. practising) teachers and those which have examined specific curricular domains in language teaching. Whereas in the first two groups the focus is on the teachers' experiences, beliefs, decisions and knowledge without reference to any particular curricular area, studies in the third group examine cognitions in relation to particular domains: those which have been the focus of substantial work are grammar and literacy (i.e. reading and writing). This classification provides the organizational framework for this chapter and the three that follow; the discussion here of pre-service teachers' cognitions will be followed in Chapter 3 by a focus on those of in-service teachers; Chapters 4 and 5 examine studies of teacher cognition in relation to grammar and literacy respectively.

Table 2.1 A classification of research on language teacher cognition

Broad focus	Specific concerns
Pre-service Teachers	• trainees' prior learning experiences and cognitions
	• trainees' beliefs about language teaching
	• trainees' decision-making, beliefs and knowledge during the practicum
	• change in trainees' cognitions during teacher education
In-service Teachers	• the cognitions of novice language teachers
	• cognitions and reported practices of in-service teachers
	• cognitions and actual practices of in-service teachers
	• cognitive change in in-service teachers
	• comparisons of expert-novice cognitions and practices
Specific Curricular Domains	Teachers' cognitions and/or practices in relation to the teaching of
	• grammar
	• reading
	• writing

Terminology in language teacher cognition research

In introducing language teacher cognition research, it is important to note that it is characterized by the same multiplicity of concepts and labels which was highlighted in relation to teacher cognition research more generally in Chapter 1. Table 2.2 illustrates this point by listing a number of labels which appear in the literature on language teacher cognition, together with the definitions provided by the respective researchers.

The superficial diversity created by the terms in this table should not mask the considerable overlap which exists among them. Collectively, they highlight the personal nature of teacher cognition, the role of experience in the development of these cognitions and the way in which instructional practice and cognition are mutually informing. Teacher cognition also emerges here as a multidimensional concept within which, philosophical arguments apart (see, for example, Fenstermacher, 1994; Orton, 1996), untangling closely related notions such as belief and knowledge remains problematic. As we saw in Chapter 1, literature reviews aiming to focus on one psychological construct in particular have found it difficult not to include others in their discussion; additionally, empirical studies which have attempted to focus on a specific construct have also found this to be difficult. For example, Grossman, Wilson and Shulman (1989: 31) set out to study teacher knowledge. Yet they concluded that 'while we are trying to separate teachers' knowledge and belief about subject matter for the purposes of clarity, we recognize that the distinction is blurry at best'. In their review of how researchers in literacy talk about knowledge, Alexander, Schallert and Hare (1991) also concluded that the distinction between knowledge and belief was not tenable. And as we see later, Woods (1996) came to a similar conclusion in his study of language teachers. This is because, as Verloop *et al.* (2001: 446) explain, 'in the mind of the teacher, components of knowledge, beliefs, conceptions, and intuitions are inextricably intertwined'.

Throughout this book, therefore, I use the term teacher cognition as an inclusive term to embrace the complexity of teachers' mental lives. Studies of teacher cognition are taken here as published works in English which examine, in language education contexts, what teachers at any stage of their careers think, know or believe in relation to any aspect of their work, and which, additionally but not necessarily, also entail the study of actual classroom practices and of the relationships between cognitions and these practices.

Table 2.2 Terminology in language teacher cognition research

Term	Description	Source
BAK	a construct analogous to schema, but emphasizing the notion that beliefs, assumptions and knowledge are included	Woods (1996)
beliefs	statements teachers make about their ideas, thoughts and knowledge that are expressed as evaluations of what 'should be done', 'should be the case' and 'is preferable'	Basturkmen, Loewen & Ellis (2004)
conceptions of practice	a set of ideas and actions teachers use to organize what they know and to map out what is possible; they guide individual action but are also affected by new situations	Freeman (1993)
culture of teaching	the nature of teachers' knowledge and beliefs systems, their views of good teaching and their views of the systems in which they work and their role within them	Richards et al. (1992)
epistemological beliefs	implicit or intuitive beliefs or theories about the nature of knowledge, knowing and learning	Flores (2001)
folklinguistic theories	teacher adaptations of expert theories/systems	Warford & Reeves (2003)
idealized cognitive models (ICMs)	propositions or constructs that combine two or more concepts to form a subjective mini-theory	Murray (2003)
image	a personal meta-level, organizing concept in personal practical knowledge in that it embodies a person's experience; finds expression in practice; and is the perspective from which new experience is taken	Golombek (1998)

(Continued)

Table 2.2 (Continued)

Term	Description	Source
images	general metaphors for thinking about teaching that not only represent beliefs about teaching but also act as models of action	Johnson (1994)
knowledge about language	the collection of attitudes towards language and knowledge about English grammar which teachers possess	Borg (2005b)
maxims	personal working principles which reflect teachers' individual philosophies of teaching	Richards (1996)
pedagogic principles	shaped and generated by underlying and more abstract beliefs, these serve to mediate between beliefs and ongoing decision-making in particular instructional contexts	Breen et al. (2001)
pedagogical knowledge	the teacher's accumulated knowledge about the teaching act (e.g. its goals, procedures, strategies) that serves as the basis for his or her classroom behaviour and activities	Gatbonton (1999)
pedagogical reasoning	the process of transforming the subject matter into learnable material	Richards et al. (1998)
perception	a physical and intellectual ability used in mental processes to recognize, interpret and understand events	da Silva (2005)
personal pedagogical systems	stores of beliefs, knowledge, theories, assumptions and attitudes which play a significant role in shaping teachers' instructional decisions	Borg (1998b)

Table 2.2 (Continued)

Term	Description	Source
personal practical knowledge	a moral, affective and aesthetic way of knowing life's educational situations	Golombek (1998)
personal theories	an underlying system of constructs that student teachers draw upon in thinking about, evaluating, classifying and guiding pedagogic practice	Sendan & Roberts (1998)
practical knowledge	the knowledge teachers themselves generate as a result of their experiences as teachers and their reflections on these experiences	Meijer *et al.* (1999)
routines	habitualized patterns of thought and action which remove doubts about what to do next, reduce complexity and increase predictability	Crookes & Arakaki (1999)
specific pedagogical knowledge	knowledge related specifically to the teaching of a particular subject	Spada & Massey (1992)
teacher cognition	the beliefs, knowledge, theories, assumptions and attitudes that teachers hold about all aspects of their work	Borg (1999c)
theoretical beliefs	the philosophical principles, or belief systems, that guide teachers' expectations about student behaviour and the decisions they make	Johnson (1992b)
theories for practice	the thinking and beliefs which are brought to bear on classroom processes	Burns (1996)

The cognitions of pre-service language teachers

In Chapter 1 I highlighted the strong links which have developed in education generally between the concerns of teacher educators and the focus of teacher cognition research; a similar trend is evident in the field of language teaching and this will be the focus of the rest of this chapter. In discussing studies of pre-service language teacher cognition I will distinguish between studies which describe teachers' cognitions during teacher education and those which examine the impact of teacher education on pre-service teachers' cognitions. This distinction reflects differences in emphasis rather than in overall purpose; all the work discussed in this chapter shares a concern for understanding the cognitions of pre-service language teachers; some studies, however, focus on capturing, describing and classifying these cognitions, while others do so with attention to development or change in them during teacher education. For the purpose of this discussion, pre-service teachers are those engaged in initial teacher education programmes (at undergraduate or postgraduate level) and who typically have no formal language teaching experience. I will avoid the term novice here, using it rather in the next chapter to refer to qualified teachers at the start of their careers.

Describing pre-service language teachers' cognitions

A number of studies have aimed to describe and analyse pre-service language teachers' beliefs, thinking, knowledge and decision-making. These are listed in Table 2.3.

These studies shed light on a number of themes in the study of pre-service language teacher cognition: (a) the influence of prior language learning experience on pre-service teachers' cognitions; (b) pre-service teachers' beliefs about language teaching; (c) cognitions in relation to practicum experiences and (d) pre-service teachers' instructional decision-making and practical knowledge. I will now discuss each of these in turn.

Table 2.3 Studies of pre-service language teachers' beliefs, thinking, knowledge and decisions

Source	Focus	Context
Bailey et al. (1996)	the influence of prior language learning experience on teaching philosophies and practices	7 teachers in the USA
Brown & McGannon (1998)	beliefs about language learning and the roles of teachers	35 trainee teachers of LOTE and ESL in Australia
Cumming (1989)	conceptions of curriculum decision-making	37 pre-service ESL teachers in Canada
Farrell (2001)	socialization processes during the practicum	1 EFL student teacher in Singapore
Golombek (1998)	personal practical knowledge and its role in practice	2 ESL teachers in the USA
Johnson (1992a)	instructional actions and decisions	6 pre-service ESL teachers in the USA
Johnson (1994)	beliefs about L2 learning and teaching and perceptions of instructional practice	4 pre-service ESL teachers in the USA
Johnson (1996)	perceptions of initial teaching experiences	1 TESOL pre-service teacher in the USA
Numrich (1996)	perceptions of needs during a practicum	26 pre-service ESL teachers in the USA
Tsang (2004)	the practical knowledge underlying interactive decision-making	3 pre-service ESL teachers in Hong Kong
Warford & Reeves (2003)	conceptions of TESOL	9 pre-service teachers on a TESOL programme in the USA

Pre-service teachers' prior language learning experience

The work reviewed in Chapter 1 highlighted how, in studies of learning to teach, a key influence on prospective teachers' cognitions was their experiences as learners – what Lortie (1975) called the apprenticeship of observation (see Borg, 2004; also John, 1996 for a discussion of this issue in relation to initial teacher education). There have been few studies dedicated specifically to the study of pre-service language teachers' prior experiences and of how these impact on their understandings and practices during teacher education, though a number of studies where it was not the main focus of study do also shed light on this issue. I will now discuss this work.

Bailey *et al.* (1996) describe a project in which seven MA candidates (all teachers in training) and a teacher educator investigated, through autobiographical writing and reflection on it, the role of their language learning histories in shaping their current teaching philosophies and practices. As a result, the writers identified several factors related to teaching and learning situations which had made their own language learning experiences positive: (1) teacher personality and style mattered more than methodology; (2) teachers were caring and committed, and had clear expectations of their students; (3) teachers respected, and were respected by, the students; (4) as students, their motivation to learn enabled them to overcome inadequacies in the teaching and (5) learning was facilitated by a positive classroom environment. By exploring their experiences in this manner, the authors of this study felt they were able to begin to articulate their own theories of teaching and to become aware of their origins. They felt, quoting Freeman (1992), that 'the memories of instruction gained through their apprenticeship of observation function as de facto guides for teachers as they approach what they do in the classroom' (p. 11). Analyses of actual practices, however, were not reported here to demonstrate how they might have been influenced by the teachers' apprenticeship of observation.

Johnson (1994) and Numrich (1996) do, however, shed light on how prior experience relates to classroom practice. Johnson found that pre-service teachers' instructional decisions during a practicum were based on images of teachers, materials, activities and classroom organization generated by their own experiences as L2 learners. She concluded that

> these preservice teachers judged the appropriateness of certain theories, methods, and materials in terms of their own first hand experiences as second language learners. Furthermore, the extent to which they accepted or rejected the content of their teacher preparation courses appeared to rest on their prior formal and informal language learning experiences.
>
> (Johnson, 1994: 445–6)

and that

> the most striking pattern that emerged from these data is the apparent power that images from prior experiences within formal language classrooms had on these teachers' images of themselves as teachers, and their perceptions of their own instructional decisions.
>
> (*ibid.*, p. 449)

Numrich, also working with teachers in training, found that they decided to promote or to avoid specific instructional strategies on the basis of their positive or negative experiences of these respective strategies as learners. For example, 27 per cent of the teachers reported in their diaries that they attempted to integrate a cultural component into their teaching because they had found learning about the L2 culture to be an enjoyable part of their own L2 learning experience. In contrast, the teachers noted that they avoided teaching grammar or correcting errors because their own experiences of these aspects of L2 instruction had been negative. With respect to the latter, Numrich reports that

> Error correction was most often cited as a technique that had been used by their language teachers and that had inhibited them from speaking. In some cases it had even turned them off to [*sic*] language learning because they had felt so humiliated and uncomfortable being corrected. Because of negative

experiences of being corrected, several teachers chose not to interrupt their students' flow of speech in the classroom to correct errors.

(Numrich, 1996: 139)

Further evidence of how pre-service teachers' beliefs about language teaching can be shaped by their prior experience is provided in Farrell (1999), Gutierrez Almarza (1996), Richards and Pennington (1998), Urmston (2003), Pennington and Urmston (1998) and Warford and Reeves (2003), all of which I discuss in more detail later. The latter suggest that the impact of the apprenticeship of observation may be more powerful on non-native teachers (NNS) of a language than on native speakers; they explain that 'this may be a function of the fact that the NNS, being in an L2 context, are still in the language learning experience' (p. 57).

The general picture to emerge here, then, is that prospective teachers' prior language learning experiences establish cognitions about learning and language learning which form the basis of their initial conceptualizations of L2 teaching during teacher education. It is perhaps surprising that more specific research into the prior cognitions of pre-service language teachers has not been conducted given the recognized influence such cognitions have on what and how teachers in training learn and on the practices which they adopt during their early teaching experiences in the classroom (see, for example, Holt Reynolds, 1992: 95; Joram and Gabriele, 1998: 314; Tillema, 1994: 130). Within contemporary constructivist views of teacher education (see Richardson, 1997), teacher learning takes place through the interaction between what trainees bring to a teacher education programme and the experiences and content they encounter on it; ignoring the former is likely to hinder the internalization by teachers of the new ideas they are exposed to and practices they are encouraged to adopt. Loughran and Russell (1997: 165–6) in fact list the following as one of their principles for pre-service constructivist teacher education: 'The student-teacher is a learner who is actively constructing views of teaching and learning based on personal experiences strongly shaped by perceptions held before entering the program'. This is, therefore, clearly an issue of continuing interest in the study of pre-service language teacher cognition.

Pre-service language teachers' beliefs about language teaching

A few studies of pre-service language teachers have also focused on eliciting and describing the beliefs which these teachers hold about all aspects of their work. Mainstream educational research has shown that at the start of teacher education programmes, students may have inappropriate, unrealistic or naive understandings of teaching and learning (e.g. Brookhart and Freeman, 1992). Studies by Cumming (1989) and Brown and McGannon (1998) illustrate this point in the field of language teaching. Cumming explored student teachers' conceptions of curriculum and concluded that these were inadequate as the basis of principled and effective programme design in ESL. Students were asked to produce 'a schematic chart outlining the curriculum decisions they would consider to be most important in teaching an ESL course' (p. 35). The author reported that the charts produced by the student teachers were generally inadequate in terms of the relationships they posited between theoretical and practical issues, the way different components of the curriculum were related and sequenced and the relative emphasis they placed on particular components. Brown and McGannon (1998) administered a questionnaire about L2 acquisition (taken from Lightbown and Spada, 1993) to a total of 35 TESL and LOTE (languages other than English) method students in the initial stages of their programme. Two beliefs held by both groups were that languages were learned mainly by imitation and that errors were mainly due to L1 interference. These beliefs were clearly inadequate as the basis for effective L2 pedagogy. Urmston (2003), which I discuss later in this chapter, also found evidence that pre-service teachers held beliefs about language teaching which were unlikely to provide the basis of successful classroom experience; for example, there was a prevalent belief that teachers should be learners' friends.

Warford and Reeves (2003) studied pre-service teachers' cognitions by analysing the metaphors nine trainees used to talk about their conceptions of TESOL. Three categories of metaphors were identified: those for describing how the respondents had moved into the field of language teaching (most teachers indicated that they had 'fallen into it'); those for describing the English language, mainly as a source of power (e.g. 'ammunition', in the words of one teacher) and metaphors for English language teaching (e.g. teachers' 'blindness' to students). The teachers also expressed their conceptions through folklinguistic theories – adaptations of expert theories or systems. For example, the teachers frequently used the language of constructivism and learner-centredness (thus drawing on these theories) to express their conceptions of TESOL. One further characteristic of these teachers' cognitions was 'presentism' (a term taken from Lortie, 1975); that is, the teachers adopted a day-to-day outlook on their careers, and 'very few . . . dared to visualize, with confidence and clarity what their in-service experience might be like' (p. 59). The authors argue that these different ways of representing teachers' conceptions of TESOL – metaphors, folklinguistic theories and presentism (together with the apprenticeship of observation, which was mentioned earlier) – can be examined to understand pre-service teachers' cognitions.

Practicum experiences

A further group of studies have focused on understanding the concerns of pre-service teachers during teaching practice. Numrich (1996) analysed diaries kept by 26 teachers during a practicum. The diaries revealed that teachers' early preoccupations while teaching were most frequently related to the following needs (p. 135):

- to make the classroom a safe and comfortable environment;
- for control when learners talk;
- to be creative and varied in teaching;
- to experience teaching individually (rather than being paired up with another pre-service teacher);
- to clarify the value of the textbook.

This study also indicated that new teachers made unexpected discoveries about effective teaching during the practicum (e.g. that positive language learning can occur outside the classroom). Continued frustrations that teachers experienced during their practicum were also highlighted; those most mentioned, in descending order, were:

- managing class time;
- giving clear directions;
- responding to students' various needs;
- teaching grammar effectively;
- assessing students' learning;
- focusing on students rather than on self (p. 142).

In addition to her 1994 study of practicum experiences which was discussed earlier in relation to the impact of pre-service teachers' prior beliefs, Johnson (1996) also examined how the practicum shaped the perceptions a pre-service teacher had of herself as a teacher, of L2 teaching and of the TESOL practicum. A key issue to emerge here was the gap between the teacher's vision of TESOL and the reality she experienced during her teaching practice. The teacher experienced frustrations similar to some of those highlighted in Numrich (1996): interruptions, time constraints, low-status awarded to ESL, uninspiring materials, not knowing enough about the students, needing to develop relationships with students but not having time and having to ensure content was covered even though it meant there was less time to respond to students' questions. The gap between the teacher's vision and the reality she experienced is presented in terms of 'tensions' (contrasts between what teachers aim for and what they experience). The teacher's initial response to these tensions was a loss of motivation and giving up; conflicts between the teachers' beliefs and practices also emerged:

> I don't like it when I see myself teaching this way. I want it to be more student-centred and not teacher-centred, but sometimes it's just easier to stand up there and tell them what they need to know. This is not my vision of good teaching but sometimes I find myself doing it anyway.
>
> (Johnson, 1996: 37)

However, over time she developed strategies to minimize these conflicts:

> As Maja came to terms with the realities of teaching, she began to develop strategies to cope with them. This meant anticipating the ways in which these realities would affect what went on in her classroom, and then arranging her classroom instruction in such a way as to deal with the realities up front; in doing so, her lessons would have the best possible chance of proceeding in the way she envisioned them. While Maja's vision of teaching did not change drastically over the course of the TESOL practicum, her understanding of how to create a classroom environment in which that vision could become realized did. And in the process, she began to develop instructional strategies that enabled her to cope with the social and pedagogical realities she faced in the classroom.
>
> (Johnson, 1996: 47)

The challenges of the practicum are further highlighted by Farrell's (2001) study of the socialization of an EFL teacher on teaching practice in Singapore. In this study, the teacher's largely negative experiences stemmed from the lack of positive working relationships among staff in the school and from the belittling way he felt treated by superiors; this in particular hindered his ability to establish any credibility with the learners. For example, the teacher reported that the learners initially mistook him for a salesman promoting books. A lack of communication between superiors and the teacher also meant he was unable to participate fully in school events (as he was never properly informed about these). At the end of this practicum the teacher was uncertain as to whether he wanted to pursue a teaching career. This study suggests that the socialization processes prospective teachers experience during the practicum can have a powerful influence on their conceptions of language teaching and of what it means to be a language teacher.

Collectively, the studies of the practicum discussed here highlight the potential of teacher cognition research for making explicit and understanding pre-service teachers' early classroom experiences, the difficulties they face and how they respond to these challenges. Insight into such matters is valuable to teacher educators concerned with providing support during the practicum, a time which can be stressful for many new teachers.

Instructional decision-making and practical knowledge

Studies of pre-service teachers have also examined the nature of the decisions they make in the classroom and the practical knowledge underlying these. Such studies are obviously also contextualized within the practicum; however, I discuss them separately here given their explicit focus on understanding the decisions pre-service teachers make while teaching. Johnson's (1992a) study was grounded in the tradition of research on teachers' decision-making discussed in Chapter 1. It examined the instructional decision-making of six pre-service teachers in the USA by attending to the cues which prompted interactive decisions and by exploring teachers' concerns in making these decisions. Eight types of considerations behind instructional decisions (described in more detail in Johnson, 1999) were identified, the most commonly cited by the teachers being a consideration of student understanding:

- student involvement and motivation;
- instructional management;
- curriculum integration;
- student affective needs;
- subject-matter content;
- student understanding;
- student language skills and ability;
- appropriateness of teaching strategy.

Two key findings here reflected those in mainstream educational research. One was that unexpected student behaviour was the most common antecedent of pre-service teachers' instructional behaviour. The second was that pre-service teachers' predominant concern in making decisions was to maintain the flow of activity in the classroom. The similarities between the mainstream and TESOL findings led Johnson to conclude that 'the field of second language teacher education can, and should, look to L1 educational literature as it continues to explore the cognitive dimensions of second language teaching' (pp. 527–8).

This has certainly occurred in the time since Johnson's article appeared and is evident in the work of Golombek (1998), who used the notion of personal practical knowledge (PPK) as the basis of an examination of the practices of two ESL teachers. The account presented here goes beyond an analysis of interactive decisions and of the immediate factors motivating these; rather, the study shows how the teachers' work was shaped by four overlapping and interacting categories of PPK (knowledge of self, of subject matter, of instruction and of context) which the teachers held and used in a holistic manner. Echoing Freeman's (1993) use of the term, Golombek shows the working of these categories by exploring *tensions* in the teachers' work. For example, in one case the tension is discussed in terms of the teacher's desire to achieve a balance in her lessons between attention to both accuracy and fluency; however, her own negative experiences of language learning, where she was hypercorrected, discourage her from attending to accuracy as much as she would like to (and is expected to) for fear of making her students feel bad too. The multifaceted nature of this teacher's PPK surfaces as she articulates and attempts to make sense of this tension. Influenced by the work of Clandinin and Connelly discussed in Chapter 1, the study illustrates how L2 teachers' PPK is 'personally relevant, situational, oriented towards practice, dialectical, and dynamic as well as moralistic, emotional, and consequential' (p. 452) and concludes that classroom practice and PPK exert a powerful and continual influence on one another:

> The teachers' personal practical knowledge informed their practice by serving as a kind of interpretive framework through which they made sense of their classrooms as they recounted their experiences and made this knowledge explicit. The teachers' sense-making processes were dynamic; the teachers' practice at any point represented a nonlinear configuration of their lived experience as teachers, students, and people, in which competing goals, emotions, and values influenced the process of and the

classroom strategies that resulted from the teachers' knowing. Thus, personal practical knowledge informs practice, first, in that it guides teachers' sense-making processes; that is, as part of a teacher's interpretive framework, it filters experience so that teachers reconstruct it and respond to the exigencies of a teaching situation. Second, it informs practice by giving physical form to practice; it is teachers' knowledge in action.

(Golombek, 1998: 459)

A more recent study of pre-service teachers' decision-making is Tsang (2004), who studied the role of teachers' personal practical knowledge in the interactive decision making of three pre-service non-native ESL teachers in Hong Kong. The explicit linkage here of decision-making and practical knowledge – traditionally distinct perspectives in teacher cognition research – is interesting; the framework for the study (unlike in Golombek, 1998 above) emphasizes the metaphor of teacher as decision-maker – a conceptualization of teaching which, as noted earlier, has been critiqued for being insufficiently narrow in its portrayal of what teaching involves; work on personal practical knowledge, in contrast, adopts a more holistic view of the dimensions of teaching. The definition of terms in this study also seems to highlight further the problems besetting the field; here, personal practical knowledge is defined simply as 'teaching maxims' (see Table 2.2 for a definition of 'maxims' as used by Richards, 1996); the seemingly interchangeable use of maxims and personal practical knowledge in this study does provide readers with a conceptual challenge.

The study itself presents an analysis of the interactive decisions of three teachers and elicits from them the maxims underlying these decisions (see Table 2.4 for examples). The influences on these maxims are also examined. The sources of influence identified were practice teaching, previous learning experience, both L2 learning and schooling more generally, former teachers and variables in the local language teaching context, such as the status of English in Hong Kong. This study, then, provides further evidence of the manner in which experiences throughout teachers' lives impinge on their cognitions and decisions, but also highlights the role which contextual factors, both in and outside the classroom, play in influencing what teachers do. Additionally, the study reports that although in many cases it

Table 2.4 Sample teaching maxims of three pre-service ESL teachers (Tsang, 2004)

Jodie	Anna	Polly
provide the best input for students	establish authority and keep things under control	use vocabulary notebooks to facilitate vocabulary learning
be reflective in identifying strengths and weaknesses after teaching a lesson	adopt and model the right attitude for students to follow suit	play different teacher roles to go beyond that of transmitting knowledge
prepare well and anticipate	be innovative and lively	promote a relaxing learning environment
possess good subject knowledge	be proficient	adopt communicative language teaching
use materials appropriate for students' levels	avoid lecturing or monotony	get students ready for reading – more important than meeting the teaching schedule
be flexible	possess good subject knowledge	give ample examples to make understanding of grammar points easier

was possible to relate interactive decisions to teachers' maxims, 'only about half of the interactive decisions were guided by teaching maxims' (p. 193). It is not clear what factors accounted for the other half, but contextual factors inside the classroom (e.g. lack of time) would seem to be prime candidates here.

Conceptually, this study offers three conclusions about the nature of teachers' personal practical knowledge (PPK). Firstly, 'Some parts of personal practical knowledge are competing among themselves and conditional upon classroom variables' (p. 183). From the examples provided to illustrate this, the point being made here is that different maxims teachers hold may often not be compatible (e.g. teachers may want to value rapport with students but at the same time believe that firm discipline is necessary). The second point made about PPK is that it is 'open and developing rather than stable and exhaustible' (p. 189).

In other words, teachers' maxims are subject to change over time. The third conclusion drawn about PPK from this study is that it informs postactive decisions (those made after a lesson) as well as interactive ones. All three conclusions reinforce, in the context of language teaching, understandings of teacher cognition developed in educational research generally.

As a more recent example of teacher cognition research in preservice language teaching, this paper highlights a number of issues which I believe are central to the continued development of research in this field. As already noted, I do not feel that, conceptually, the research is sufficiently clear in the manner in which terms are defined (equating personal practical knowledge with maxims does require further justification). Secondly, the merging of distinct traditions of teacher cognition research (decision-making and PPK), while certainly possible, needs to be grounded in a more detailed acknowledgement of the different conceptions of teaching each is informed by. Thirdly, the lists of maxims provided for each teacher seem to operate at different levels of generalization; for example, the maxim 'adopt the communicative approach' would seem to encompass several other maxims (e.g. use authentic materials). There are unexplored questions here, then, about the relationships between the maxims each teacher held, the relative strength of each maxim and the ways in which these might operate as a system. Most accounts of teachers' beliefs do highlight the manner in which these operate as a system of sorts – for example a belief system (Pajares, 1992), a pedagogical system (Kagan, 1992b) or a coherence system (Warford and Reeves, 2003). Exploring how, methodologically, we might study the systemic nature of teacher cognition is clearly an issue which merits continued attention.

The impact of pre-service teacher education

The second broad group of studies I want to discuss in this chapter examines the manner in which pre-service language teacher cognitions change during the process of teacher education. The impact of teacher education on what teachers believe, know and do has, as I highlighted in Chapter 1, been a widely debated issue in the last 15 years. Kagan (1992a), for example, concluded that teacher education had a limited impact on the prior cognitions of pre-service teachers (but see critiques of this analysis by Dunkin, 1995; 1996); Richardson (1996) also concluded that teacher education was a weak intervention. On the other hand there is also evidence of ways in which teacher education can exert an influence on teachers' beliefs and knowledge (e.g. Adams and Krockover, 1997; Dunkin *et al.*, 1994; Graber, 1995; Kettle and Sellars, 1996; Sariscany and Pettigrew, 1997). Analyses of the impact of teacher education continues to be a central concern in educational research (for reviews see Wideen *et al.*, 1998; Wilson *et al.*, 2002), and several studies have examined this issue in the context of language teaching. These are listed in Table 2.5 (additional studies which examine the impact of teacher education with specific reference to grammar and literacy instruction are covered in Chapters 4 and 5 respectively).

Overall, but not in all cases, these studies provide some evidence of changes in one or both of cognitions and instructional practices during or subsequent to pre-service language teacher education. In comparing these studies, though, two key issues must be noted. Firstly, the range of teacher education programmes studied is diverse – for example intensive short certificate courses, undergraduate degree programmes and master's programmes. Secondly, there are variations in what is considered to be evidence of change (e.g. responses to questionnaires, interviews, journal entries and classroom practice). These variations complicate the task of attempting to compare the findings from different studies, and need to be kept in mind throughout here.

Change in cognitions during CELTA programmes

In the context of the CELTA (Certificate in English Language Teaching to Adults), an internationally recognized, practically oriented introductory training course, Richards, Ho and Giblin (1996) studied five trainees and found changes in their cognitions in relation to (1) their conception of their role in the classroom, (2) their knowledge of professional

Table 2.5 Studies of the impact of teacher education on pre-service language teachers

Source	Focus	Context
Borg (2005a)	changes in beliefs	1 teacher on a TEFL certificate programme in the UK
Cabaroglu (2000)	changes in beliefs	20 students on a PGCE in Modern Languages in the UK
da Silva (2005)	congruence of input and practice teaching in teacher education	3 Language Arts undergraduate students in Brazil
Gutierrez Almarza (1996)	origins, content and change in knowledge and its impact on classroom practice	4 foreign language teachers on a PGCE in the UK
MacDonald, Badger & White (2001)	influence of a course in SLA on beliefs about English language learning	55 students on BA/MSc programmes in TESOL in the UK
Peacock (2001)	changes in the beliefs about L2 learning	146 trainee ESL teachers in Hong Kong
Pennington & Urmston (1998)	beliefs held by trainees at start and end of a teacher education programme	40–48 trainee teachers on a BA TESL in Hong Kong
Richards, Ho & Giblin (1996)	changes in conceptions and beliefs related to teaching EFL	5 teacher trainees on a TEFL certificate course in Hong Kong
Sendan & Roberts (1998)	the development of personal theories about teaching effectiveness	1 student EFL teacher on a degree programme in Turkey
Urmston (2003)	changes in beliefs	30/40 trainee teachers on a BA TESL in Hong Kong

discourse, (3) their concerns for achieving continuity in lessons, (4) common dimensions of the teaching they found problematic (e.g. timing, presenting new language) and (5) the manner in which they evaluated their own teaching. For example, with respect to the development of a professional discourse, the authors report that

> by the end of the course the trainees had completely internalized the discourse and metalanguage promoted and were able to talk spontaneously and thoughtfully about their own and others' lessons, to compare and contrast performances, and to discuss causes and effects of teaching behavior using the appropriate technical terminology.
> (Richards, Ho and Giblin, 1996: 248)

The trainees, though, did not change in a homogeneous way; there was variability in the extent to which each of the trainees mastered the principles underlying the course, with each interpreting these 'in individual ways on the basis of their teaching experiences and their own beliefs and assumptions about themselves, teachers, teaching, and learning' (p. 258).

Also in the context of the CELTA, Borg (2005a) studied development in the pedagogical thinking (using the concept of belief) of one pre-service teacher. Three categories of *belief* were studied: about teachers and teaching; about language and language learning and about learning to teach. Data were collected over the duration of a four-week course, so that conclusions about development in these beliefs over that time could be made. By the end of the course, the teacher had a greater awareness of the 'backstage' elements of teaching (e.g. planning) compared to the performative aspects (e.g. giving instructions), and the teacher's perspective on grammar had also developed so that she was able to see it from a teacher's point of view, not just as a language learner. Overall, though, little change in the teacher's beliefs was noted; for example, at the start of the course the teacher was clear in her rejection of didactic approaches to teaching, favouring rather an approach which focused on learners and which aimed to make them active and relaxed participants in class; such views remained in place at the end of the course.

An explanation postulated in this study for the similarity between the teacher's pre- and post-course beliefs is that the course did actually allow the teacher to implement an approach to teaching which was in line with her prior beliefs; that is the CELTA is a programme which discourages didacticism and encourages active learner participation, and as such it provided fertile ground for the teacher to develop teaching practices which were consonant with her beliefs. Thus, I would argue, although the lack of change in the teacher's beliefs during the programme may be taken as evidence of limited impact, the fact that the programme affirmed her prior beliefs and allowed them to flourish can actually be construed as a form of impact in itself. Impact, then, does not necessarily imply change, but can also take the form of reinforcement in prior cognitions.

In the case of the CELTA, a number of other features of the programme – for example the promotion of reflection, modelling by trainers of practices they wanted the trainees to adopt and a coherent, unified professional discourse – may have strengthened its impact on the teachers in both this and the previous study. These findings reflect those in Borg (1998b), where I also found that particular features of the CELTA (at that time known as the CTEFLA) – such as its intensity, strong practical orientation and daily teaching practice – enabled it to exert a powerful influence on a teacher's beliefs.

Much mainstream educational research on the impact of teacher education on teacher cognition has taken place within the context of programmes extending over a year or more; the existence (particularly in the field of English as a foreign language) of intensive courses such as the CELTA which last a matter of weeks thus creates a somewhat unique context for the study of how teacher education shapes teachers' beliefs and knowledge. The CELTA in particular has a number of features, as noted above, which may enable it to impact on trainees, at least in the short-term, more than longer programmes might. Studies comparing the impacts of shorter and longer teacher education programmes have not yet been conducted and may provide an interesting focus for continuing research.

Cognitive and behavioural change in teacher education

Further evidence of the variable influence of teacher education on trainees is shown in Gutierrez Almarza (1996), who tracked the learning of four student teachers on a PGCE (Postgraduate Certificate in Education) course in the United Kingdom. In particular, the findings here highlight the distinction between the cognitive and behavioural changes which teacher education programmes may induce. Behaviourally, all four students adopted the specific teaching method they were taught on their programme, and implemented this in their classrooms during practice teaching. This behaviour, though, was at least partly a result of the need felt by the student teachers to conform to certain standards (they were, after all, being assessed). Cognitively, though, the student teachers varied in their acceptance of the suggested approach to teaching. These variations emerged when the students talked about their work, rather than through their practice, and were largely rooted in the different cognitions about language, learning and teaching they held prior to their training. For example, on completion of her teaching practice, one of the student teachers 'saw herself free from the constraints imposed by the context of the classroom, she was back in a position in which she could continue to explore the ideas she had about language prior to the beginning of the course' (p. 69). This study concludes that, although teacher education played a powerful role in shaping the student teachers' behaviour during teaching practice, it did not alter significantly the cognitions the students brought to the course. This study also suggests that caution must be exercised in concluding that trainees' behaviours during assessed teaching practice are evidence that the teacher education programme has had an impact on their cognitions and instruction; in such situations, trainees' behaviours may be influenced by the need to pass the assessment rather than being a reflection of their own beliefs about how to teach.

This same point is relevant to da Silva (2005), which examined the perceptions held by three Brazilian undergraduate students of Language Arts of the teaching of the four skills – speaking, listening, reading and writing – in the EFL classroom. Conceptually, the choice of *perception* as the key concept here is immediately striking; given the terminological challenges the field is already facing, it seems unnecessary for researchers to continue introducing new terms rather than consolidating the use of a smaller group of more established ones.

In this study, participants' perceptions were identified through the analysis of classroom observation reports they wrote, stimulated recall interviews, lesson plans they produced and written self-evaluations of their work. Of key interest here is insight into the way the trainees utilized in their practices the framework for teaching the four skills they were trained to use – 'a version of the communicative approach to language teaching, task-based thematic teaching' (p. 3). The results indicated that in terms of how lessons were planned, the trainees did adopt this framework. (This is not wholly surprising, as it is noted that a framework for planning lessons was provided to trainees by their supervisors and that the trainees were assessed against this framework.) Classroom practices also reflected the communicative framework, though there were variations in the manner in which this occurred. Particularly in relation to speaking, the trainees at times engaged students in activities (e.g. oral practice through dialogues absent of any communicative purpose) which, according to the researcher, were at odds with the communicative principles underlying their plans. The trainees also cited contextual factors which they felt made it difficult for them to adhere to their theoretical principles. For example, in commenting on the challenges involved in developing students' pronunciation, one trainee said that

> it's difficult to create opportunities. There are more than 20 students in class and if we want to observe pronunciation, teach pronunciation, and observe pronunciation again . . . It's difficult to create situations in which the use of the language could be real . . . it takes time.
>
> (da Silva, 2005: 7)

Inconsistencies between trainees' theoretical knowledge and classroom practices in teaching listening, reading and writing were not evident; the communicative tenets promoted during their training were reflected in the way these skills were taught and in the beliefs about them the trainees expressed.

Key conclusions to emerge from this work emphasize themes already highlighted in this chapter; trainees experiencing the same theoretical input will not necessarily interpret and apply this input in an isomorphous manner; and trainees' classroom practices and theoretical beliefs may not concur due to contextual factors. In relation to the impact of teacher education, a high level of consistency was observed here between methodological input, planning, and classroom practices. As already noted, though, the structured and assessed nature of what the trainees were doing must be considered when interpreting these findings.

Structure and process in cognitive change

Even stronger claims about the manner in which trainees' cognitions do change during teacher education are provided by Sendan and Roberts (1998) and Cabaroglu and Roberts (2000). In the first of these studies, a key research question was 'what is the nature of observed changes (if any) in the structure and content of the student teachers' personal theories at different stages of the training programme?' (p. 234). Repertory grid data (see Chapter 7) were used to represent changes in one student teacher's personal theories about teaching effectiveness over a period of 15 months. A distinction between changes in the content (i.e. what the trainee thought about effective teaching) and in the structure – 'the ways in which individual constructs are hierarchically organised into a whole system of construction' (p. 231) – was central to this study. An analysis of the grids generated at three points in the student teacher's progress through the course suggests that although there were no major changes in the content of his personal theories about effective teaching, there were clear developments in the organization of this content. Underpinned by a basis of stable constructs, changes in the student teacher's thinking were characterized by the addition of new constructs, the reorganization of the existing structures to accommodate these, the existence of 'mobile constructs' (p. 238), which were associated with different clusters of constructs at different times, and the formation of a more stable overall structure in which previously disassociated constructs were integrated into internally tight ones. On the basis of their findings, the authors argue that initial training does promote change in trainees' thinking, at least at the structural level. They conclude that

> the process of professional development is one in which new information and new experiences lead student teachers to add to, reflect upon and restructure their ideas in a progressive, complex and

non-linear way, leading towards clearer organisation of their personal theories into thematically distinct clusters of ideas. It is therefore inappropriate to conceptualise student teacher cognitive development in terms of a simple process of aggregation of new ideas.

(Sendan and Roberts, 1998: 241)

Cabaroglu and Roberts (2000) used a sequence of three in-depth interviews to analyse the processes, rather than the content, of belief development in 20 PGCE Modern Languages students. They found that only one participant's beliefs remained unchanged during the programme. In this study, evidence of change emerged from the analysis of interview data, from which the authors established categories of belief development processes (listed with definitions and examples on p. 393). One category, for example, was called 're-ordering', defined as the 'rearrangement of beliefs regarding their importance'; a second was 're-labelling', which involves the renaming of a construct; a third example is 'reversal', the 'adoption of opposite of previous belief'. In reflecting on the widespread changes in beliefs found in this study, the authors conclude that contrary to views about conceptual inflexibility in student teachers' professional growth, the processes they described in their study are a more realistic picture of the changes that can occur during teacher education in student teachers' belief systems.

Pre- and post-course comparisons of beliefs and knowledge

A common strategy for evaluating cognitive change in teacher education is to compare questionnaire data at the start and end of a programme. Four studies of pre-service language teachers illustrate this approach. MacDonald, Badger and White (2001) examined the impact on participants' beliefs of courses in second language acquisition (SLA). Most of the respondents in this study had little or no experience of teaching. A questionnaire about L2 acquisition from Lightbown and Spada (1993) was administered before and after the SLA course to a total of 28 postgraduates and 27 undergraduates. Before the course, the combined results showed that students agreed strongly with two of the 12 statements on the questionnaire; they did not disagree strongly with any of the statements though. After the course, students still agreed strongly with one of the statements they had strongly agreed with before the course: teachers should teach simple language structures before complex ones. Students also now disagreed strongly with three statements: languages are learned mainly through imitation; teachers should use materials that expose students only to those structures which they have already been taught and students learn what they are taught. The authors conclude that 'after the course, the subjects had at least taken on board one of the few certainties afforded by SLA research: a rejection of the behaviourist model of learning' (pp. 956–7). Thus there is some evidence that the participants' cognitions had been affected by the course, though not all students' responses to the questionnaire showed belief change in the direction promoted by this course. Also, it is possible that these results could have simply been the product of participants answering the questionnaire in a way which they felt best matched course content and/or the responses desired by the course tutors; if this were the case, these responses would not be indicative of any real cognitive change.

In contrast to the general conclusions emerging from the above study, three further questionnaire-based studies suggested that teacher education had a limited effect on pre-service teachers' cognitions. All three studies were conducted on the same three-year BA TESL programme in Hong Kong. Two of these (Peacock, 1998; Urmston, 2003) had a longitudinal dimension; the third (Pennington and Urmston, 1998) compared the beliefs of two different groups of trainees in the first and final year of the programme and used the results as indirect evidence of change over the course of the programme.

Peacock (2001) studied changes in the beliefs about L2 learning of 146 trainee ESL teachers. The beliefs of first-year trainees were collected using the Beliefs about Language Learning Inventory (BALLI, Horwitz, 1985), and these were compared with the beliefs of experienced ESL teachers. Three key differences between trainees' beliefs and those of experienced teachers were identified in relation to the following statements:

- Learning a foreign language is mostly a matter of learning a lot of new vocabulary words.

- Learning a foreign language is mostly a matter of learning a lot of grammar rules.
- People who speak more than one language well are very intelligent.

In each case, the percentage of first year trainees agreeing with these statements was much higher than that for experienced teachers (e.g. only 7 per cent of experienced teachers agreed with the second statement, compared to 52 per cent of trainees). Such beliefs were seen by the author as 'detrimental to their [trainees'] own language learning or to their future students' learning' (p. 183) and he hoped that they would be eliminated in the course of the teacher education programme (where explicit attention was given to the nature of L2 learning). To monitor this, he asked the trainees to complete the BALLI at two further points in their course. On the basis of the results, Peacock concluded that 'there was surprisingly little change over the three years on Horwitz's two core beliefs about vocabulary and grammar, or . . . about the role of intelligence in language learning' (p. 184) and that the 'data do not support the belief that trainees' beliefs are shaped by their preservice methodology courses' (p. 187). These results, though, perhaps tell us more about the limitations of questionnaires in studying teachers' beliefs than about the impact of teacher education on teacher cognition.

In two related studies, Urmston (2003) compared the beliefs and knowledge of trainees at the beginning and end of their programme (the same trainees) while Pennington and Urmston (1998) conducted a cross-sectional comparison of the data from the first year students in Urmston's study and of responses from trainees who were at that time in their final year. The same instrument (reported in full in Urmston, 2003) was used in both these studies. The longitudinal study provides a stronger source of evidence of change (or lack of it) in trainees' cognitions over a three year period. Changes were found in trainees' beliefs about the out-of-class activities they would have to do (e.g. marking examinations, extra-curricular activities) and in their views about whether they had a definite philosophy of teaching. There were also some changes in trainees' perceptions of their roles and responsibilities, although the belief prevalent in the first year that teachers should be friends with students was still strongly held at the end of the programme. This was an example of a fundamental belief where evidence of change was limited. In fact, the conclusion this paper reaches is that despite a number of differences in the beliefs expressed by trainees at the start and end of their programme, 'their views on some of the most crucial aspects of teaching showed just a few changes during the period of their course'. These results are attributed to the powerful influence of the trainees' prior beliefs.

Pennington and Urmston (1998) reached similarly pessimistic conclusions, though, as noted above, the findings here are limited by the cross-sectional nature of the comparisons being made. In any case, the conclusion here was that 'the views of these graduating TESL teachers were not greatly affected by their coursework but were rather largely a reflection of the teaching culture of the Hong Kong education context' (p. 34).

The negative conclusions of the questionnaire studies of belief change in Hong Kong are in general contrast to the findings of more qualitative studies of change during pre-service teacher education. Differences in the research instruments, the characteristics of the teacher education programmes studied, trainee attributes and educational context for each study may together go some way to explaining these differences. I discuss how research findings are often a product of the investigative methods used in Chapters 6–9 of this book.

Summary

The focus of this chapter has been on research on language teacher cognition in the context of pre-service teacher education. The following are key themes to emerge from this work:

1 Even allowing for the fact that some additional studies of pre-service language teacher cognition will be discussed in later chapters on specific curricular areas, the volume of research in this area remains small; additionally, given the global nature of language teaching, the geographical spread of this work is limited too (eight countries, with a third of the studies being from the USA).

2 The notions of *variable outcomes* and *individual developmental pathways* seem central to an understanding of the impact of teacher education on language teacher cognition. Individual trainees make sense of and are affected by training programmes in different and unique ways. Further longitudinal studies of individual teachers' development on pre-service language teacher education programmes, then, are to be encouraged.

3 The distinction between *behavioural* change and *cognitive* change during or as a result of teacher education, and of the relationships between the two, is also key to continuing research on this topic. As we have seen here, behavioural change does not imply cognitive change, and the latter (because of contextual influences on what teachers do) does not guarantee changes in behaviour either.

4 Even where evidence of cognitive and/or behavioural change is found, caution must be exercised in interpreting such findings if they were obtained in the context of programmes which are assessed on the basis of trainees' abilities to conform to particular ways of thinking or behaving. In such cases, the changes discovered may reflect trainees' understandings of what is required for them to pass their course rather than any real change.

5 Much existing literature about the ineffectiveness of teacher education in changing trainees' cognitions has focused on the *content* of these cognitions; this is also the case with some of the studies I have discussed here. Work examining the *processes* and the *structure* of cognitive development, however, suggests significant changes in trainees do take place during teacher education. Continued research, then, can benefit from attention to the content, structure, and development processes involved in language teacher trainees' cognitive change.

6 Pre-service teacher education can take a number of forms; an obvious distinction is that between three- or four-year programmes typically run by universities or teacher training

colleges, and intensive four-week courses such as the CELTA. There is evidence that the nature of the programme is a variable which may influence the findings of research into the impact it has on trainees. Greater attention to programme characteristics is therefore required in continuing work of this kind.

7 Terminology continues to be an issue in the work discussed here. Established terms such as *belief, pedagogical knowledge, interactive decisions* and *practical knowledge* appear, but other, less necessary constructs have also been adopted (e.g. *perceptions*). The development of a more programmatic orientation to research into pre-service language teacher education can be further facilitated through the adoption of a limited range of terms with well-defined and commonly used definitions.

8 These studies vary in what is considered to be evidence of cognition and cognitive change. Questionnaire responses, repertory grids and in-depth interview responses, for example, are very different forms of data, and the extent to which they can capture the content, structure and change processes of cognitive phenomena is clearly an issue for continuing methodological discussion. I consider such issues in Chapters 6–9.

9 The body of research discussed here evinces little evidence of replication; in a few cases similar research questions have been addressed, though even in such cases different investigative approaches have been deployed. This variability may to some extent be an inevitable consequence of the idiosyncratic nature of teacher cognition and the uniqueness which characterizes every different context; however, this situation does contribute to the lack of any evident programmatic trends in the body of work I have reviewed. The development of more programmatic approaches to the study of teacher cognition would seem to be a key issue for the field to address in taking this domain of inquiry forward. What this implies, in the context of this chapter, is the development

of a set of questions related to teacher cognition in pre-service language teacher education which merit addressing and the concentration of research effort on these questions; the goal of this programmatic approach which would be to generate findings which allow a greater deal of comparability than is at present possible. For example, given the numbers of teachers who take the CELTA training programme, there is clearly scope for a programme of research focusing on this teacher education context and which addresses questions such as:

- what prior cognitions do trainees bring to the programme?
- which of these prior cognitions seem to be central or core, and which more peripheral?
- what beliefs and knowledge does the programme aim to promote?
- how congruent with trainees' prior cognitions are these?
- do trainees' cognitions about language learning and teaching change during the programme?
- what processes characterize change in pre-service teachers' cognitions?
- what factors stimulate cognitive change?
- what are the characteristics of trainees' classroom practices during the programme?
- what influences underlie these practices?
- to what extent are these practices congruent with the programme's goals?
- how do trainees' exit cognitions compare to those they entered with?

3

The cognitions of in-service language teachers

A number of studies have been conducted in the field of language teaching which focus on what in-service teachers (i.e. those who have completed their initial training and work in classrooms) believe and know. Such work is the focus of this chapter. In some cases, practising teachers' cognitions have been investigated in isolation of their classroom practices, while in others the study of cognitions and classroom practices have been linked. Here I will discuss what studies of both types tell us about the thinking and actions of language teachers, using the five themes identified earlier in Table 2.1 to organize the discussion. I will thus consider in turn

- the cognitions of novice language teachers;
- the cognitions and *reported* practices of in-service language teachers;
- the cognitions and *actual* practices of in-service language teachers;
- cognitive change in in-service teachers;
- comparisons of the cognitions of expert and novice language teachers.

The focus throughout here is on the study of generic cognitions and practices; studies of in-service teachers with an interest in specific curricular areas will be considered in Chapters 4 and 5.

The cognitions of novice language teachers

Table 3.1 lists studies which have examined the cognitions of language teachers in their first year in the classroom.

In an early study, Spada and Massey (1992) examined the extent to which knowledge obtained in pre-service ESL teachers' methodology courses was transferred to the classroom practice of novice teachers. This work was influenced and modelled on the teacher knowledge research conducted by Shulman and his associates (see Chapter 1).

The study was inconclusive; some evidence of transfer was found in two of the teachers investigated, yet such evidence was lacking in the third teacher studied. Also, none of the teachers felt certain that their classroom practices could be directly attributed to their methodology courses during teacher education. The researchers

Table 3.1 The cognitions of novice language teachers

Source	Focus	Context
Farrell (2003)	learning to teach English in the first year	1 novice EFL teacher in Singapore
Grossman (1989)	pedagogical content knowledge of teachers of English	6 novice teachers of English in the USA
Richards & Pennington (1998); Pennington & Richards (1997)	learning to teach English in the first year	5 BA TESL graduates in Hong Kong
Spada & Massey (1992)	transfer from teacher education to classroom practice	3 novice ESL teachers in Canada

suggest that the lack of transfer apparent in one case may have been due to the contextual factors of the school in which this teacher worked. In the quote below, Alice is a teacher where transfer from teacher education was evident, Neil was the one where this was not the case:

> It will be recalled that Alice was teaching in a private school and given considerable flexibility as to what she could do in her classroom. It was a tranquil school setting with exemplary behaviour exhibited on the part of the students. It is possible that this factor was an important one in that it enabled Alice to use the knowledge she obtained in her training and concentrate on the development and application of her lessons in creative ways without any distractions. Neil, on the other hand, was teaching in a public school known to have serious discipline problems . . . this meant that he was rarely able to follow through with his lesson plans and spent most of his time managing student behaviour.
> (Spada and Massey, 1992: 33)

Further evidence of the powerful contextual factors which influence novice language teachers comes from the work of Richards and Pennington, who studied five teachers of English in their first year of teaching in Hong Kong (Pennington and Richards, 1997; Richards and Pennington, 1998). These teachers had been trained in a version of the communicative method and, thus, encouraged to base their teaching on the following principles:

- Emphasize meaningful language use
- Give equal attention to form and function
- Focus on learners' needs and interests
- Be in charge of your class
- Plan lessons carefully
- Be responsive to classroom context
- Use English as the medium of instruction

(Richards and Pennington, 1998: 180)

At the start of their first year, all five teachers expressed a belief in such principles; however, in the course of the year, without exception, their practices diverged from communicative principles. Rather than focusing on these principles, the teachers focused their attention on two main themes: (1) establishing their role and relationship with the students and (2) covering the required material and preparing for examinations. Concentrated attention to such issues led to teaching in which

> none of the teachers departed from their lessons for more than a brief moment to pursue a topic or an example raised by a student, and none allowed spontaneous communicative tangents to develop to any extent as part of their lessons. In fact, more often than not, they followed their textbooks or lesson materials closely and did little teaching that was genuinely communicative. Much of the philosophy of the [teacher education] course was thus stifled by the overriding concern to maintain an orderly class and to cover the prescribed material of the school syllabus.
> (Richards and Pennington, 1998: 183–4)

A number of factors were seen to have influenced the teachers' decision to abandon the principles promoted during their training: the impact of large classes, unmotivated students, examination pressures, a set syllabus, pressure to conform from more experienced teachers, students' limited proficiency in English, students' resistance to new ways of learning and heavy workloads. As the authors conclude:

> Such factors discourage experimentation and innovation, and encourage a 'safe' strategy of sticking close to prescribed materials and familiar teaching approaches. Without any relief from these factors and without any reward for innovating in the face of them, the teachers would naturally be led back toward a conservative teaching approach to align themselves with the characteristics of the existing teaching context.
> (Richards and Pennington, 1998: 187–8)

Another perspective on the study of novice language teachers' cognitions is evident in Farrell (2003), who examined the early socialization experiences of an EFL teacher in Singapore. In particular, the study focused on the role that support from the school and from colleagues played in a teacher's development during his first year.

A key challenge faced by the teacher studied was reality shock, particularly in relation to what he perceived to be a very heavy workload compared to that he experienced during his practicum. His was teaching 35 periods of 35 minutes each week, plus additional extra-curricular activities and setting and marking examination papers for levels he was not teaching (and marking examinations for subjects other than English too). Another theme explored in this paper was the support that the teacher received from the school and from colleagues during this first year. The individualistic culture of the school meant that the teacher had few opportunities for collegial sharing – for example he was not allowed to observe experienced colleagues and was based in a separate office away from other teachers. A lack of communication with colleagues was seen by the teacher as a major challenge during his first year. On a more positive note, the teacher did receive some support from the school principal, though the mentoring which had been expected (and for which purpose a more experienced colleague had been officially appointed) never materialized.

In considering the teacher's reflections on his experience over the year, Farrell identifies a number of stages of development which the teacher went through:

- early idealism and strong identification with the students;
- reality shock during the first semester when faced with classroom reality;
- recognition of his difficulties and their causes, plus a questioning of his ability to succeed as a teacher;
- adjusting to the school culture and establishing routines to enable him to cope better both in and out of the classroom;
- focusing more on the quality of student learning.

The student did not move through these phases in a linear manner and there was evidence of overlap and simultaneity among them, as well of cyclical development (e.g. repeated phases of recognizing difficulties and developing coping strategies).

Overall, this study shows that while the teacher eventually managed to cope with the demands of being a first year teacher of English, he did so largely on his own. His induction into a new profession was not a positive experience as he struggled with unsupportive colleagues, a demanding teaching load and classes which presented instructional and management challenges. Once again, there is ample evidence here of how the institutional and social contexts novice language teachers work in can shape their initial cognitions, particularly in relation to their professional identity (i.e. their understandings of what it means to be a teacher).

One final study I will discuss in this group is Grossman (1989). Although not technically about language teaching (given its focus on teaching English literature), I include it here due to the particular perspective on the study of teacher cognition it illustrates. Grossman was one of Shulman's associates (see Chapter 1) and this study examined the nature of the pedagogical content knowledge (PCK) used by six beginning teachers of English in the USA (see Grossman, 1990 for an expanded account of this work).

All six teachers in this study had strong backgrounds in English as a subject but only three had undergone formal teacher education. A key concern in this study was thus to examine the impact which teacher education had on teachers' work; or, put differently, there was an interest here in examining whether sound subject-matter knowledge was a sufficient basis for skilled teaching. In comparing the case studies of the six teachers, Grossman's conclusion was that

> the results of this study suggest that, in this case, subject specific coursework did make a difference in these beginning teachers' pedagogical content knowledge of English. The two groups of teachers differed in their conceptions of the purposes for teaching English, their ideas about what to teach in secondary English, and their knowledge of student understanding.
>
> (Grossman, 1989: 26)

Grossman sees all three kinds of knowledge referred to here – conceptions of subject matter and of the purposes for teaching it; conceptions of curricular content; and conceptions of students' understanding of the subject – as being components of PCK. In her view, the teachers who had undergone formal teacher education demonstrated PCK which was qualitatively different to that of the teachers who had not. For example, in terms of the conceptions of subject matter (i.e. of English), two of the teachers with no professional preparation did not distinguish between English as a discipline and English as a school subject; thus teaching English for them was about the analysis of literary texts. The teachers with a teacher education background saw English more as an opportunity for self-expression and communication in reading and writing. Differences were also apparent in curricular knowledge – 'knowledge and beliefs about the selection and organization of content for instruction' (p. 27). Here again, the two teachers who viewed English as a discipline concerned with literary analysis made curricular choices which reflected this orientation; a hypothetical course they planned as part of the research was organized around literary texts. Teachers with professional preparation made curricular decisions based on their understandings of the students they would be teaching and of the context that this teaching would take place in.

While conducted with novice teachers, this study has obvious implications for our understandings of the relationship between initial teacher education and teacher cognition. One overall finding of this study was that subject-specific coursework during teacher education can be a powerful influence on how teachers think about and teach their subjects. Interestingly, there has been little work of this kind in the field of language teaching (but see, for example, Richards *et al.*, 1998). Given the impact of the notions of subject-matter knowledge and PCK on teacher cognition research generally, their absence in language teacher cognition research is noteworthy; it may be that a concept such as PCK does not lend itself easily to an area such as language teaching where the content and medium of learning are often seen to be inextricably linked. Freeman (2002: 6), for example, has suggested that 'when applied to language as subject matter, PCK becomes a messy and unworkable concept'. Thus while in education generally it has often been assumed that PCK can be usefully applied to all disciplines, this is an assumption that would merit further critical analysis in the context of language teaching.

Overall, the limited number of studies I have discussed in this section are indicative of how little is currently known about the early experiences of qualified language teachers, particularly in L2 and FL contexts (in Chapter 5 I discuss some additional examples from L1 contexts in the USA). The particular needs of novice teachers have been recognized and acknowledged with empirical attention in mainstream educational research (e.g. Bianchini *et al.*, 2003; Bullough, 1989) but much less so in the field of language teaching. The studies available in language teaching highlight a range of perspectives from which the cognitions of novice teachers can be studied – through analysis of the congruence between their early classroom practices and those promoted during initial teacher education, by studying their early socialization processes, and by focusing specifically on the nature of teachers' subject matter and pedagogical content knowledge. These studies, despite their diversity, highlight two general points about novice teachers' cognitions and practices. Firstly, it is clear that the transfer of knowledge and beliefs from initial teacher education to classroom practice does not happen in a smooth, linear manner; contextual factors in schools and classrooms, including novice teachers' professional relationships with colleagues, together with immediate concerns with managing learners, exert a powerful influence on novice teachers' cognitions and practices which may outweigh principles learned during teacher education. Second, there is evidence that knowing a subject is insufficient as the basis for teaching that subject skilfully. This is particularly pertinent to the field of language teaching, where the belief may still persist in some quarters that one's status as a native speaker of a language (and the knowledge of the language which that status is assumed to imply) in itself qualifies one to teach it.

In-service language teachers' cognitions and reported practices

In this group of studies (see Table 3.2) the focus is on describing the cognitions of experienced language teachers without, however, analysing observed classroom practices. In each of these studies the key data collection method is the questionnaire.

Table 3.2 Questionnaire studies of in-service language teachers' beliefs

Source	Focus	Context
Allen (2002)	teachers' beliefs about foreign language learning	613 FL teachers (mostly of Spanish) in the USA
Flores (2001)	beliefs and reported practices of bilingual educators	176 bilingual teachers in the USA
Kern (1995)	teachers' and students' beliefs about language learning	288 undergraduate students of French and their 12 instructors in the USA
Richards et al. (1992)	the culture of teaching	249 teachers of English in Hong Kong secondary schools

Richards *et al.* (1992), drawing on a research tradition on the culture of teaching (see, for example, Feiman-Nemser and Floden, 1986), analysed the beliefs and reported practices of 249 secondary school teachers of English in Hong Kong (the average length of experience of these teachers was seven years). The results were described under five headings, which reflect a range of issues that language teachers have beliefs about:

- views of the ESL curriculum;
- views of language and language teaching;
- views of classroom practices;
- views of the teacher's role;
- views of the profession.

The analysis of the questionnaire responses focused on the relationships between teachers' experience and training on the one hand and their beliefs and practices on the other. Teachers with more experience and training differed from those with less in three areas: their views of the aims and approach of language teaching in Hong Kong; some aspects of their classroom practice and their views of professional support and professional development. For example, inexperienced and untrained teachers reported being more likely than experienced and trained teachers to think that grammatical theories of language are useful to language teaching and that writing is the most important skill at both elementary and secondary school. Also, experienced teachers felt that training and in-service support are most important for their teaching; inexperienced teachers said their personal philosophy of teaching is most important.

In terms of classroom practices, teachers' reports of what they do or prefer suggested the existence of two distinct orientations to language teaching – functional-based and grammar-based. The former group, for example, reported more frequent use of audio tapes and pair and group work, while the latter reported more frequent use of written grammar exercises.

Overall, the study reported a relationship between teachers' goals, values and beliefs, and their teaching experience, training and reported approach to language teaching. These findings are thus also relevant to the research comparing novice and expert language teachers which I discuss later in this chapter.

In the context of the teaching of French, Kern (1995) administered the Beliefs about Language Learning Inventory questionnaire (BALLI, Horwitz, 1985: 373) to 288 undergraduate students and to their instructors. His goals were to describe and compare students' and instructors' beliefs about language learning and teaching, on the assumption that congruence between these beliefs might impact on the learning experience (similar concerns underpin the work of Berry, 1995, 1997; Cathcart and Olsen, 1976; Peacock, 1998; Schulz, 1996). The study also looked for evidence of change in the students' beliefs over a 15-week period (the BALLI was completed twice).

In terms of what this study tells us about language teacher cognition (the students in this study were not trainee teachers), the views of instructors as expressed through the BALLI were in general quite uniform; for example they all disagreed with the statement that students shouldn't say anything in the foreign language until they can say it correctly, while 79 per cent agreed that it is OK to guess when you do not know a word in the foreign language. Additionally, while there was a strong overall correlation between the initial views of students and those of their instructors, when comparisons were made between individual instructors and the specific students they taught differences were apparent:

> These differences cover a wide range of issues, from the nature of language learning (students gave more credence to the importance of good accent, grammar rules, and translation than did teachers) to pedagogy (error correction, cultural knowledge) to length of time needed to become fluent. The instructors, on the whole, tended to take a more definite stand on the issues than did the students. Presumably, this is due to their considerable experience as both learners and teachers of a foreign language. Like the students, the instructors indicated high optimism that everyone can learn a foreign language, but they also expressed more realistic expectations concerning the time needed to become proficient in the language, as well as greater awareness of the complexity and multifaceted nature of language learning.
>
> (Kern, 1995: 78)

Many of the differences between students' and instructors' beliefs persisted at the end of the semester; in some cases – beliefs about pronunciation, error correction and grammar rules – the differences between students and instructors were actually greater than at the start of the semester. On the basis of these findings, the study concluded that teachers' beliefs have less influence on students' beliefs than do textbooks, classroom practices, peers' beliefs and learners' self-awareness.

A third questionnaire study of practising language teachers' beliefs is Allen (2002), who compared the beliefs of 613 foreign-language teachers in the USA to the principles embodied in a set of national standards for foreign language instruction called the *Standards for Foreign Language Learning in the 21st Century*. The argument in this case was that congruence between teachers' beliefs and the standards had implications for the extent that these standards could be properly implemented.

The results indicated that, overall, teachers' beliefs were generally consistent with those articulated in the *Standards*. In particular, teachers believed that foreign language instruction should be delivered in the target language; in the study of Hong Kong teachers reported earlier (Richards et al., 1992), beliefs about the use of the target language were less definite (42 per cent felt it was better to use Chinese only and 21 per cent felt that using English all the time was sound educational practice.) There were differences, however, in the extent to which teachers were familiar with the standards; teachers in rural schools were more familiar with these than teachers in urban schools (and the difference was statistically significant), while teachers belonging to two or more professional associations were also significantly more familiar with the standards than those who belonged to none. Membership of professional associations did in fact emerge here as a key factor which related to teachers' beliefs; higher levels of involvement in professional associations correlated with beliefs more consistent with those in the standards. Highest educational degree related to teachers' beliefs on only one statement out of the 32 on the instrument.

The final study in this group comes from the field of bilingual education in the USA; in this context students have limited or no proficiency in English and their first language is used for teaching while they are acquiring proficiency in English for academic purposes. Flores (2001) surveyed the beliefs of 176 bilingual educators and also asked them, through interviews, to report on their practices. Thus, as in Richards *et al.* (1992), although relationships between beliefs and practices were studied here, no actual classroom observations were conducted by the researcher. Drawing on work by Schommer (1990) on the dimensions of epistemological beliefs, this study used an instrument called the Survey of Bilingual Teachers Epistemology and Teaching Practices (SBTETP). Three specific questions were investigated here:

1 What is the nature of bilingual teachers' beliefs about bilingual children's cognition?

2 What prior experiences (personal and sociocultural experiences, K-12 schooling, background, educational theory and teacher preparation and professional teaching) influence bilingual teachers' epistemological beliefs about bilingual children's cognition?

3 Do bilingual teachers' epistemological beliefs about bilingual children's cognition influence their teaching behaviour? If so, how?

A number of findings emerged here in relation to the beliefs of bilingual educators. For example, most bilingual education teachers recognized the importance of language and culture in the acquisition of knowledge. In addition,

> the findings support the position that bilingual education teachers' beliefs do appear to be socially constructed. Experiences as bilingual learners are also unique to the bilingual education teacher. When bilingual teachers have a conscious, shared ethnic identity, they are likely to intuitively recognize the needs of their bilingual learners. This finding also speaks to the importance of having bilingual teachers, especially those with a conscious, shared ethnic identity, as role models for language minority children.
>
> (Flores, 2001: 268)

A number of other findings reflected issues highlighted in mainstream educational research on teacher cognition; for example, there was evidence that beliefs are not static, but dynamic. Evidence was also found that while bilingual teachers' beliefs were influenced by personal experience, they were subject to modification as a result of teacher education. This was especially true when teacher education programmes had a strong and coherent theoretical and philosophical base; for example, it emerged here that such programmes 'influenced bilingual teachers' beliefs that learning is incremental and that the language, culture, and thought are interactive processes in the creation of knowledge' (p. 269). In relation to the third research question listed above, the study reported a significant relationship between the stated beliefs and the reported practices of the bilingual teachers (though the correlation of .31 reported was weak to moderate in strength).

The four studies I have discussed in this section share a common focus on describing the beliefs – about knowledge, teaching, learning, students and curricula – of experienced language teachers. They also share a common methodological trend – their use of questionnaire data.

Apart from these general similarities, though, extracting commonalities presents a recurrent challenge given the diversity of the specific issues examined and of the contexts in which the studies took place. Three of the studies involved teachers from the USA (the other study took place in Hong Kong) but even within the USA studies the contexts examined were distinct – university instructors in a French department, foreign language teachers in three states and bilingual educators from a further state. Four general points from this work are worth noting:

1. Both Richards *et al.* (1992) and Flores (2001) suggest a relationship between teachers' stated beliefs and their reported practices. We must not, however, interpret this to mean that teachers reported their practices accurately or that their actual practices are consistent with their beliefs. Particularly in the Hong Kong context, there is evidence from other studies that contextual factors in the system can exert a powerful influence on what teachers do, thus creating tensions between their beliefs and actual practices (e.g. Pennington and Richards, 1997; Tsui, 1996).

2. The study by Kern (1995) was the only one here which considered potential connections between teachers' beliefs and students' beliefs. On the basis of the discrepancies he found between teachers and students both at the start and end of the semester, his conclusion was that teachers' beliefs about language learning did not exert a powerful influence on those of their learners. Other studies I discuss in Chapters 4 and 5 have examined teacher and student beliefs in this way; the focus, though, has been mainly on the degree of congruence between these beliefs rather than on understanding the extent to which teachers' beliefs influence those of students. This is an area for further research.

3. While Kern (1995) was interested in comparing students' and teachers' cognitions, Allen (2002) examined congruence between teachers' cognitions and national standards for language teaching. In both these studies, higher levels of congruence were assumed to be positive, for learning on one hand and for the implementation of the standards on the

other. The notion of congruence among teachers' cognitions, students' cognitions and curricular principles is a useful one in analysing the coherence of educational systems.

4   In terms of potential influences on teachers' beliefs, a number of factors were suggested in the studies discussed here. Prior experience of language learning, years of teaching experience, type of professional training and involvement in professional associations were four that were highlighted (Allen, 2002; Flores, 2001; Richards *et al.*, 1992). No clear trends across the studies were evident (e.g. in relation to the impact of experience and qualifications on teachers' cognitions). The impact of teachers' associations is not a factor that has been highlighted in research on language teacher cognition and may provide an interesting focus for continuing inquiry.

The cognitions and practices of in-service teachers

Numerous studies in mainstream educational research have shown that teacher cognition and classroom practice exist in 'symbiotic relationships' (Foss and Kleinsasser, 1996: 441). Several studies have also studied these relationships in the work of language teachers. In this work, what teachers know and believe has been studied through an analysis of their actual classroom practices and of how they talk about these. This is the key common characteristic of the work I discuss here and the major point of contrast to the studies I discussed in the previous section. In addition, there is little or no reliance on questionnaire data in this group of studies, with interviews and observations being the predominant strategies used to collect evidence about teachers' cognitions and practices. Table 3.3 provides details of the studies I include in this group.

The diversity of these studies is clear even from the summary information provided in the table; a range of foci have been analysed, drawing on different traditions in teacher cognition research (e.g. decision-making and practical knowledge), investigating teachers in different geographical contexts (eight different countries are

Table 3.3 Cognitions and practices of in-service language teachers

Source	Focus	Context
Bailey (1996)	teachers' departures from their lesson plans	6 ESL teachers in the USA
Bartels (1999)	the knowledge and skills teachers use to realize lesson plans	3 EFL teachers in Germany
Breen (1991)	the implicit theories of experienced language teachers	106 language teachers in UK
Breen et al. (2001)	relationships between individual and collective principles and practices	18 ESL teachers in Australia
Burns (1996)	teachers' theories and practices in the beginning adult L2 classroom	6 ESL teachers in Australia
Crookes & Arakaki (1999)	the sources of ESL teachers' ideas for teaching	20 ESL teachers in the USA
Freeman (1992, 1993)	changes in teachers' practices and thinking	4 French and Spanish teachers in the USA
Gatbonton (1999)	the pedagogical knowledge of experienced ESL teachers	7 ESL teachers in the USA
Golombek & Johnson (2004)	the use of narrative to explore teacher development	3 ESL teachers; 2 based in the USA, 1 in Spain
Hayes (2005)	the life history of non-native speaking English educators	3 ELT teacher educators in Sri Lanka
Mangubhai et al. (2004)	the practical theory of a teacher in relation to CLT	1 LOTE (German) teacher in Australia
Richards (1996)	the nature and role of the teachers' maxims	ESL teachers in Hong Kong

Table 3.3 (Continued)

Source	Focus	Context
Sato & Kleinsasser (1999)	teachers' understandings and practices in relation to CLT	10 teachers of Japanese in Australia
Smith (1996)	the relationship between instructional decisions, teachers' beliefs, and contextual factors	9 ESL teachers in Canada
Ulichny (1996)	departures from lesson plans	1 ESL teacher in the USA
Woods (1991; 1996)	planning and decision-making in the ESL classroom	8 ESL teachers in Canada

represented) and involved in different domains of language teaching (ESL, EFL and LOTE). Diverse, too, is the range of concepts which have been invoked in accounting for the cognitions which shape in-service language teachers' classroom practices. As Table 3.4 shows, these cognitions have been described in terms of *instructional concerns* or *considerations* teachers have, *principles* or *maxims* they are trying to implement, their thinking about different *levels of context*, the *pedagogical knowledge* they possess, their *personal practical knowledge* and their *beliefs*. This variety highlights points I have already made about the somewhat fragmented nature of language teacher cognition research and the need to develop a more consistent set of substantive, conceptual and methodological frameworks to guide continuing development in the field. It is my hope, of course, that this book is a contribution in this direction.

An analysis of the studies in Table 3.3 suggests that the following six themes are central in the study of in-service language teachers' cognitions and practices:

- reasons for instructional decisions;
- departures from lesson plans;

Table 3.4 Cognitive influences on language teachers' classroom practices

Source	Cognitive influences
Bailey (1996)	Teachers' in-class decisions to depart from their lesson plan were based on a number of *principles*: (1) serve the common good (2) teach to the moment (3) further the lesson (4) accommodate students' learning styles (5) promote students' involvement and (6) distribute the wealth.
Breen (1991)	*Seven pedagogic concerns,* focused on three main variables: Focus on the *learners*: concern with the learners' (1) affective involvement (2) background knowledge (3) cognitive processes assumed to facilitate learning. Focus on the *subject matter*: concern with language as (4) usage (5) use. Focus on the *teacher*: concern with (6) guidance (7) classroom management.
Breen *et al.* (2001)	Five superordinate categories of *teacher concern*: • a concern with how the learner undertakes the learning process • a concern with particular attributes of the learner • a concern with how to use the classroom and its human and material resources to optimize learning • a concern with the subject matter of learning – with what is being taught and learned • a concern with the specific contributions that they can make in their role as teacher.

Table 3.4 (Continued)

Source	Cognitive influences
Burns (1996)	Three interacting *contextual levels* of teacher thinking: • thinking about the institutional culture • teachers' beliefs about language, learning and learners • thinking about specific instructional activities.
Gatbonton (1999)	Six general domains of *pedagogical knowledge*: • knowledge of how to manage specific language items so that students can learn them • knowledge about the students and what they bring to the classroom • knowledge about the goals and subject matter of teaching • knowledge about techniques and procedures • knowledge about appropriate student-teacher relationships • knowledge about evaluating student task involvement and progress during the lessons.
Richards (1996)	Teachers explained their decisions in terms of *maxims*: • The maxim of involvement: follow the learners' interests to maintain student involvement • The maxim of planning: plan your teaching and try to follow your plan • The maxim of order: maintain order and discipline throughout the lesson • The maxim of encouragement: seek ways to encourage student learning • The maxim of accuracy: work for accurate student output • The maxim of efficiency: make the most efficient use of classroom time • The maxim of conformity: make sure your teaching follows the prescribed method • The maxim of empowerment: give the learners control.

- collective principles and practices;
- change in cognitions and practices during in-service training;
- practical theories about communicative language teaching (CLT);
- narrative accounts of cognitions and practices.

I will now discuss each of these in turn. Before I do, it is appropriate to highlight in advance that, despite a shared general interest in the work and thinking of practising language teachers, the studies I will be discussing here are quite diverse: they are generally grounded in different conceptual frameworks, utilize different labels in talking about teacher cognition and are characterized by individual research concerns, examined in distinct contexts. There are no examples here of replicated studies. This diversity makes it hard to extract any specific commonalities. To support the reader in working through the sub-sections which follow, each section is given a number in addition to a heading.

Theme 1: Reasons for instructional decisions

Some studies have attempted to identify the reasons most commonly cited by practising language teachers in explaining their instructional decisions. In Breen (1991), the most common reason teachers gave for choosing instructional techniques was that they were believed to engage learners in cognitive processes which facilitated L2 learning. In Gatbonton (1999), a concern for language management (e.g. explaining vocabulary, creating contexts for meaningful use) was overall the most common focus of teachers' pedagogical thoughts. (The quantitative analysis in this study yielded the statistic that the two groups of participant teachers averaged 3.48 and 3.77 pedagogical thoughts per minute respectively.) Nunan (1992), in contrast with Gatbonton, found that teachers' comments on their decisions did not reveal a concern for language (especially in the case of the inexperienced teachers in his study); in this case, teachers' concerns related mostly to the pacing and timing of lessons, the quantity of teacher-talk and the quality of their explanations and instructions. Richards (1996) analysed data from a corpus of teacher narratives about their work to suggest that teachers accounted for their pedagogical choices with reference to maxims (i.e. personal working principles – see Table 3.4). Similar principles were reported in the work of Bailey (1996), which I discuss below. The study by Bartels (1999), grounded in the work of Shulman (1987), was also concerned with the manner in which teachers realize their lesson plans and in particular with the kinds of knowledge teachers drew on to do so. His study of 3 EFL teachers in Germany highlighted their use of three types of knowledge in implementing instruction: knowledge of instructed L2 learning (e.g. getting students to figure out things for themselves led to more effective learning); knowledge of students interlanguage; and knowledge of curriculum and materials.

Woods (1991, 1996) conducted a longitudinal study of planning and decision-making in ESL classrooms in Canada which tracked a group of teachers as they went through the process of planning and teaching their courses. This work provides detailed insight into teachers' decision-making processes and the factors shaping these. These factors relate not only to immediate antecedent conditions, but also to influences stemming from teachers' professional lives as a whole (e.g. their prior language-learning experiences). Woods divides these factors into two groups, which he labels *external* and *internal*.

As an example of the complex range of external (i.e. situational) factors which impact on the decision-making process, Woods (p. 129) cites the following list which emerged from the analysis of one teacher's approach to planning a lesson:

- how many students will probably turn up
- availability of photocopying
- knowledge about students' prior course experience
- a recent conversation with another teacher
- estimation of the complexity of a task

- estimation of how well the students as a group are moving
- estimation of what the group can handle
- estimation of how well particular individuals in the class are moving
- estimation of what particular individuals can handle
- class dynamics and individual dynamics in class.

Internal factors relate to temporal and logical relationships among instructional decisions. Temporally, teachers need to organize instruction chronologically and hence to make decisions about what comes first, what follows and so on. Logical relationships refer to the different levels of generality at which planning occurs (e.g. course, lesson, activity, text); teachers' decisions are thus also shaped by their understandings of the relationships among different levels of course units.

Woods' data also highlighted for him the problems inherent in attempting to distinguish between constructs such as belief and knowledge. He proposed the notion of BAK (beliefs, assumptions, knowledge) to reflect his view that, rather than being distinct concepts, beliefs, assumptions and knowledge are points on a spectrum of meaning.

One obvious difficulty in synthesizing the studies of teachers' instructional decisions I have outlined here is that each study utilizes a set of distinct concepts; multiple perspectives have been brought to bear on the conceptualization of the cognitions underpinning instructional decision-making and these tend to obscure any substantive overlap which these studies might have. The distinction between preactive (i.e. planning) and interactive decisions provides a useful way of separating out different phases of decision-making, but with regard to the latter, the existence of multiple conceptual frameworks for accounting for the choices teachers make has hindered the development of research into this issue. What we have, consequently, are several studies which seemingly fail to build on one another in any structured manner (see, though, Tsang, 2004, who in a pre-service context does attempt to build on existing concepts in the study of instructional decision-making).

Theme 2: Departures from lesson plans

The notion of improvisational teaching has been examined in the educational literature (e.g. Borko and Livingston, 1989) and studies of language teaching have also looked specifically at the reasons in-service teachers give for departing from their lesson plans. Ulichny (1996) presents a case study of a teacher who started a lesson with specific plans and principles in mind (e.g. promoting learner-centred reading) but who during the lesson had to modify her plans in the face of the unexpected difficulties the students experienced in completing the planned activities. The outcome was a lesson in which the teacher engaged in practices which did not reflect her principles (e.g. the lesson became very teacher-centred). Bailey (1996) found that teachers' in-class decisions to depart from their lesson plans were based on a number of principles (see Table 3.4). For example, one principle was 'serve the common good'. This means that when an unexpected issue or question arises during a lesson, a teacher may depart from the plan to deal with it if it is perceived to be of general relevance to the whole class. In his study of teachers' use of lesson plans, Richards (1998) also found evidence of 'on-the-spot modification of planned activities in order to maintain students' engagement and interest level' (p. 115). These modifications (more common in the work of experienced teachers) were prompted by pedagogical factors (e.g. the need to simplify a task) and by a perceived need for more focused language work. Smith (1996) too highlights the distinction between planned and unplanned interactive decisions; in her study, unanticipated decisions were prompted by student factors (e.g. students' affective state) or teacher factors (e.g. forgetting to bring a key resource to class). Smith reports that student misbehaviour and student noncomprehension, two factors typically associated with unplanned interactive decisions, were not in evidence in the classes she studied. Rather than seeing teachers' departures from their lesson plans as a shortcoming, then, teacher cognition research shows that such departures are the result of the constant interaction between teachers' pedagogical choices and their perceptions of the instructional context, particularly of the students, at any particular time.

Theme 3: Collective principles and practices

The study by Breen *et al.* (2001) makes a distinctive contribution to our understanding of the relationships between cognition and practice in language teaching. Through observations and elicitation procedures, five researchers examined the relationship, at both an individual and group level, between the practices and principles of 18 teachers working in a similar context in Australia. An analysis of the profiles generated by this study showed that individual teachers realize specific principles through particular sets of favoured practices, and that at an individual level these configurations of practices and principles are unique. At group level, though, there were several pedagogic principles which were common to the majority of the teachers (e.g. a belief in the importance of taking individual differences among students into account). An analysis of the practices which were justified by the teachers with reference to these shared principles showed that any one principle was realized through several distinct practices (see Figure 3.1 for an example). However, the set of practices related to any one principle was largely distinct from the set related to a different principle. The study thus showed that teachers working in a similar context may implement a set of shared principles through diverse practices, but that behind this apparent diversity of practices there is 'a collective pedagogy wherein a widely adopted classroom practice is . . . an expression of a specific and largely distinctive set of principles' (p. 496). This attention to collective cognitions and practices is unique in our field (see, though, Andrews, 2003a in Chapter 4).

Theme 4: Cognitive change during in-service training

In comparison to the study of pre-service language teacher cognition, studies of practising language teachers engaged in in-service teacher education are limited. There are some examples in the context of literacy instruction (e.g. McCarthey, 1992; Mosenthal, 1995; Scott and Rodgers, 1995), which I discuss in Chapter 5, but in terms of

- Shows interest in students' personal lives; e.g. asked about a student's relative who was sick.
- Accepts all students' responses without saying they're wrong: 'You would be understood, but a better way to say that is . . .'
- Integrates within lessons items needed for competencies to be covered in the term.
- Assesses students individually when they say they are ready
- Goes from individual to individual during desk work to check understanding or correctness.
- Makes worksheets on same topic but at different levels.
- Links vocabulary/concepts back to students' culture/experience (e.g. 'gnome': do they have similar creatures in their culture)
- Models orally and on board as visual support
- Uses colours to mark inflections of works on board.
- Uses variety of resources: video, tapes, & workbook exercises.
- Accompanies oral input with written, pictorial, diagrammatic, input using colour coding.
- Uses videos, real experiences, tapes, gesture, mime, groupwork.
- Listens to everyone. Asks their opinions, asks when they want a break.
- Incompleted homework, inability to do a task, or being late to class not admonished by the teacher(s).
- Pairs stronger person with one with less developed English.
- Negotiates breaks and outings.
- Explains detailed rules, exceptions, generalizations.
- Much input to whole class, especially feedback when groups reporting back.
- Chooses topic that is seen as relevant to students' daily lives ('fast foods').
- Corrects sentences in students' writing.
- Uses students' names to illustrate comparative/superlative forms of adjectives.
- Chooses topics that are 'jazzy/groovy' to suit 18–20 age group.
- Video replay of students' own oral presentations.
- Adopts informal, non-authoritarian manner.
- Explains how a person could take a book from the local library.
- Gets feedback from students on their community involvement (e.g. conversations with other parents at their children's school).

FIGURE 3.1 *Practices realizing the principle of accounting for individual differences*

(Breen *et al.*, 2001: 490). By permission of Oxford University Press.

studies looking at generic processes (rather than specific curricular areas), Freeman (1992, 1993) is the only example I am aware of. This longitudinal study examined the changes in practice and thinking of four high school French and Spanish teachers doing an in-service teaching degree in the USA. In analysing the process of change the teachers' underwent over a period of almost two years, four issues were highlighted: (a) teachers' conceptions of practice; (b) tensions in those conceptions; (c) the process of articulation; and (d) local and professional language. At the start of the programme, the teachers held tacit, unanalysed, conceptions about teaching. During the in-service programme, aspects of these tacit understandings of teaching surfaced in the form of tensions in the teachers' work; tensions were defined here as 'divergences among different forces or elements in the teacher's understanding of the school context, the subject matter, or the students. They are expressed as discomforts or confusions which interfere with the teacher's translating intention into action in the classroom' (p. 488). Here is an example of one of the teachers talking about the tension between her experience of Spanish in and out of the classroom:

> Everything I liked and learned [about Spanish] was outside the classroom and [I'm] trying to bring that into the classroom. It's not in the book, and it's tough to heighten students' awareness of the outside world and get them as excited about it as I was living it, but through the classroom.
> (Freeman, 1993: 488)

The study argues that recognizing these tensions was an important factor in enabling the teachers to develop their classroom practice. This study also highlights the role which learning to talk about teaching using the professional discourse of education plays in enabling teachers to become more effective at critiquing their own practices, and hence in changing their cognitions and practices. Teachers initially talked about their practice using a local language, derived from their own experiences as learners and the ways of talking about teaching used in their particular school environments. The programme, however, had as one of its goals the development of teachers' understandings of the professional discourse of education. By combining this new professional language with their local language explanations of their work, the teachers were able to reflect on and critique their practice (this is the process of articulation). The teachers in Richards *et al.* (1996) (in Chapter 2) were also keen to learn to talk like teachers, and one aspect of their development during their pre-service course was the manner in which they learned to use the metalanguage of teaching in discussing their work. The development of a professional discourse may thus have a role to play in enabling cognitive change during teacher education.

In terms of changes in practices, the study found that specific aspects of the teachers' practices did change as a result of this process of articulation, but some patterns endured. However, the important argument is made that considering change in behavioural terms is limited and that by examining teachers' thinking a more complex picture of the impact of the teacher education programme on the teachers emerges:

> By viewing thought and activity as interrelated components, the findings offered a view of classroom teaching which highlighted the development of teachers' thought as a major component of that practice. Within this view, the notion of change becomes more complicated because it is no longer possible to simply use behavior as the criterion by which to assess it.
>
> (Freeman, 1993: 495)

This conclusion echoes points raised in Chapter 2, where the distinction between behavioural and cognitive change was made and the importance stressed of distinguishing between the two in studies of the relationship between teacher education, teacher cognition and classroom practice.

Theme 5: Practical theories of CLT

Another perspective on the study of in-service language teachers' cognitions and practices is reflected in two studies, both conducted in Australia, which examined teachers' practical theories with reference to communicative language teaching (CLT). In Sato and Kleinsasser (1999), the practical understandings of CLT of ten teachers of

Japanese were analysed through interviews, observations and a survey. The data revealed that the teachers held four particular theoretical understandings of CLT:

- CLT is about learning to communicate in the second language;
- CLT uses mainly speaking and listening;
- CLT involves little grammar instruction (this view was reflected clearly in the words of the teacher who explained that 'I'm not particularly a communicative language teacher, because I love teaching grammar' (p. 504);
- CLT uses activities that are time-consuming.

Despite teachers' positive beliefs about CLT, though, the analysis of actual teaching showed little evidence of CLT in practice:

> The observation data showed reluctance on the part of teachers to promote CLT and indicated that many teachers avoided (or at least challenged or mutated) the few conceptions of CLT that they held. . . . Although most teachers reported using communicative activities such as role-play, games, survey, group work, and simulations, unfortunately, these things were rarely observed. There were few observed student-student interactions in most of the classrooms. Only two teachers actually used role-play of any type, while most relied on traditional practices: teacher-fronted, repetition, translation, explicit grammar presentation practice from textbook, and little or no L2 use or culture integration.
> (Sato and Kleinsasser, 1999: 509–10)

This finding reflects that from Karavas-Doukas (1996), who also found a lack of congruence between the attitudes towards CLT as indicated on a survey by EFL teachers in Greece, and the classroom practices of these teachers.

In contrast, Mangubhai *et al.*'s (2004) study of one teacher of German in Australia found that she had a sophisticated and well-developed practical theory of CLT and that this was reflected in her classroom practices. Through semi-structured and stimulus recall interviews (see Chapter 7), the study showed how the teacher's understandings of CLT embodied a number of characteristics commonly associated with this approach to language teaching, such as:

- The goal of developing students' communicative competence;
- A commitment to using the foreign language as a medium for classroom communication as much as possible;
- A greater emphasis on fluency and appropriateness in the use of the target language than structural correctness;
- Minimal focus on form with corresponding low emphasis on error correction and explicit instruction of language rules or grammar;
- Use of authentic materials;
- Students being actively involved in interpretation, expression and negotiation of meaning.

The relationship which emerges here between cognitions and practices is markedly different to that in the previous study. Of course, differences in the characteristics of the samples studied may account for some of these differences; Sato and Kleinsasser (1999) studied ten teachers of Japanese (nine of whom were Australians) having between 0.75 and 13 years' teaching experience; Mangubhai *et al.* (2004) studied one native-speaking teacher of German with over 30 years' experience. The use of stimulus recall interviews (i.e. interviews based on the analysis of video recorded practices) in the latter study compared to the use of observations after interviews in the former may have also had some bearing on the respective findings to emerge here. This is another example of how the findings of teacher cognition research are sensitive to the research methods used. These are important methodological issues that I will return to later.

Theme 6: Narrative studies of teacher cognition

The last two studies I will comment on in this section (Golombek and Johnson, 2004; Hayes, 2005) approach the study of experienced language teachers' thinking and action more holistically than those discussed so far in this chapter.

Golombek and Johnson (2004) analyse narratives written by three experienced language teachers (these narratives, and others, appeared in Johnson and Golombek, 2002). Their key arguments are that such narratives can provide insight into teacher knowledge and its development and that by writing narratives teachers come to transform their understandings of themselves and their work. Drawing on sources such as Clandinin and Connelly (2000) and grounding their ideas in sociocultural notions of teacher learning, they argue that 'two decades of educational research argues that teachers' knowledge is largely structured through stories and that story, for many, is epistemologically the most authentic way to understand teaching from the view point of the teacher' (p. 308). They propose a notion of narrative inquiry as 'systematic exploration that is conducted *by* teachers and *for* teachers through their own stories and language' (p. 309). They illustrate their arguments with reference to the narratives of three teachers and point to the manner in which these teachers came to better understand their work. One of the teachers, for example, came to understand the contradiction between his dominant classroom behaviours and his desire to encourage quiet students to participate more in class, while another explored and addressed her misgivings about her approach to the teaching of literature.

One key issue to emerge from the analysis of these narratives is the role of emotions in stimulating cognitive change:

> Our analysis supports a view of teacher development that is socially situated and socially mediated, non-linear, dialogic, and without an endpoint (Bullough, 1989; Clandinin, 1986; Clandinin & Connelly, 1991, 1992, 2000; Grossman, 1990). It suggests an interwoven connection between cognition and emotion, which drives teachers to search for mediational tools to help them externalize their experiences throughout their careers. For these teachers, their emotional dissonance initiated the recognition of cognitive dissonance, a recognition of contradictions in their teaching context . . . we argue, based on our analysis, that emotions are actually a driving factor in teacher development. The

catalytic role of emotions in the process of transformation is an aspect that is not typically highlighted in other models of internal cognitive development.

(Golombek and Johnson, 2004: 323–4)

As Golombek and Johnson argue, emotions have not typically been given much attention in the study of language teacher cognition (more recently, though, see Andrews, 2003a); their work does suggest though that emotions play an important role in stimulating cognitive change. The manner in which narratives provided a space in which teachers could draw on various sources of knowledge to explore their practices was also highlighted here; in particular, the interaction between expert knowledge and experiential knowledge seemed crucial to the cognitive change these teachers experienced:

expert knowledge provided both a discourse through which to name experiences and a basis upon which teachers were able to ground their internal rationale for alternative ways of understanding themselves and the activities of teaching. These teachers used 'expert' knowledge as a tool to restructure themselves in an active way. Although teachers use expert knowledge to understand and name their practice, they still must work through the transformative process in a personally meaningful way that enables them to change their teaching activities.

(*ibid.*, p. 324)

Hayes (2005) shares the above concerns for holistic, narrative ways of exploring language teachers' lives; it merits a comment here both for its focus on language educators in Sri Lanka as well as for its use of a life history approach to studying language teachers – this is not an approach that has been widely used in language teaching, though it has a strong tradition in educational research more generally (see, for example, Carter and Doyle, 1996). Hayes tells the stories of three Sri Lankan English language educators, describing their entry to the profession and professional growth over the years and exploring these experiences in relation to a range of social and personal factors. Two points highlighted in the analysis are of particular relevance to this discussion. Firstly, the manner in which these teachers were heavily influenced in their own early practices by models of teaching inherited from their own teachers:

> Krishnan, for example, gives an instance of using the common technique of reading aloud which he had himself experienced as a school student and Bandara states explicitly that his initial methods 'came from the way my teachers taught me'. Continuing, he notes 'At the back of my mind would have been the way I learnt English and how I developed a liking for English' indicating that methods we now consider outmoded and unproductive were still able to engender positive attitudes towards English as a subject at that time and, in the case of our interviewees, produced successful language learning.
>
> (Hayes, 2005: 182)

Hayes notes, though, that the influence of their teachers on the early practices of the individuals studied here was perhaps not surprising given that entry to the profession was not preceded by any formal teacher-training (the apprenticeship of observation is believed to be particularly powerful where teachers join the profession without formal training). The second point which is relevant to an understanding of how experienced teachers' cognitions may evolve relates to the role of peers; the teachers in this study stressed the role which their peer group played as a learning resource during teacher education courses, to the extent that this form of learning was perceived as being much more beneficial than the input the teachers received during such courses. This suggests, Hayes argues, the potential that collaborative peer learning in teacher education contexts can have for promoting teacher learning (particularly in the case of language teacher education for non-native speakers of English). This study is also valuable in that by examining a hitherto unexplored context it highlights particular issues relevant to cognitive change and professional growth among teachers which have not emerged from studies conducted, for example, in the USA. There is clearly a need for further research in under-studied language education contexts of this kind.

The six themes I have discussed here reflect key concerns in the study of practising language teachers' cognitions and practices. As noted earlier, while the studies within each theme cohere to a certain extent, this work is characterized by individuality and diversity rather than common ground. Across the different themes, it becomes even harder to discern specific features in common. This body of work is a good example of the need, within language teacher cognition, for a unifying investigating framework which will allow research in this field to go forward with a greater sense of coherence. I return to this point in Chapter 10.

Comparisons of novice and expert language teachers

In the final section of this chapter I will focus on studies which have compared the cognitions and practices of more and less experienced language teachers. The small number of studies relevant to this topic are listed in Table 3.5 (additionally, Cumming, 1990, which I discuss in Chapter 5, compared the decision-making of novice and experienced ESL teachers in rating written compositions). There is a tradition of such research in mainstream education and perhaps the individual whose name is most associated with such work is Berliner (e.g. 1987, 2001).

Studies comparing experienced and less experienced language teachers shed light on transformations in teacher cognition which may occur over time (though the majority of these studies lack the longitudinal dimension required to trace such development). Nunan (1992), for example, found that experienced language teachers' decisions showed greater attention to language issues than those of less experienced teachers, who were more concerned with classroom management. This suggests that with experience teachers learn to automatize the routines associated with managing the class, and can thus focus more attention on issues of content. Richards (1998) also found that experienced teachers engaged in more improvisational teaching than inexperienced teachers (see Borko and Livingston, 1989 for a study in the field of mathematics which focuses on improvisation). He argues that

> this suggests that as teachers develop their teaching skills, they are able to draw less on preactive decision-making (the type of

Table 3.5 Expert-novice comparisons in language teacher cognition research

Source	Focus	Context
Johnson (2003)	how novice and experts design language teaching tasks	16 language teachers (8 novice task designers and 8 expert) in the UK
Mok (1994)	experienced and inexperienced teachers' reflections on their work	12 ESL teachers in the USA
Nunan (1992)	experienced and inexperienced ESL teachers' interactive decisions	9 ESL teachers in Australia
Richards (1998)	preactive and interactive decisions of experienced and less experienced ESL teachers	16 ESL teachers in Hong Kong
Richards et al. (1998)	(a) novice and experienced teachers' approaches to reading; (b) literature teaching by teachers with different levels of subject-matter knowledge	(a) 10 trainee teachers, 10 graduate TESL teachers in Hong Kong; (b) 12 practising teachers in Hong Kong
Tsui (2003)	the development of expertise in ESL teachers	4 novice ESL teachers in Hong Kong

planning that occurs prior to teaching) and make greater use of interactive decision-making as a source of their improvisational performance.

(Richards, 1992: 117–18)

In comparing novice and experienced teachers' approaches to a reading lesson and to teaching literature, Richards, Li and Tang (1998) also identified four areas of language teaching which novice teachers were less skilled at: (a) thinking about the subject matter from the learner's perspective; (b) having a deep understanding of the subject matter; (c) knowing how to present subject matter in appropriate ways and (d) knowing how to integrate language learning with broader curricular goals. In a further study of teachers' interactive decisions, Richards (1998) found some differences in the maxims referred to by less and more experienced teachers in explaining their choices. Maxims used more frequently by less experienced teachers were 'cover your lesson plan' and 'fit your plan to match the time available'; more experienced teachers made more frequent reference to maxims such as 'build on students' difficulties', 'maintain active student involvement' and 'develop a language learning focus for the lesson'. There were also some maxims which both groups referred to (e.g. 'maintain a communicative focus to the lesson'). These two studies highlight two ways, then, in which novice and experienced language teachers can be compared; one is by assessing the aspects of their work they are more and less skilled at; the other is by comparing the maxims they refer to in justifying their instructional decisions. These are but two of several possibilities which exist in comparative studies of this kind.

Another option is illustrated by Mok (1994), who compared changes in the cognitions of experienced (more than three years' experience) and inexperienced teachers, using journal entries, practicum reports and interview data collected over a period of 6–30 months (the period varied across participants). Five categories of concern were reported by the teachers in this study: self-concept (e.g. teacher role); attitudes (e.g. towards learners); teaching strategies (in relation to decision-making); materials used (what and how) and expectations (e.g. in relation to classroom behaviour). Though a broader range of issues was mentioned by the inexperienced group, no significant differences were found in the quantity of reflections on these issues in the data for the inexperienced and experienced groups. Mok observes that

> Since the number of issues addressed by the . . . two complete beginners in the inexperienced group was not so outstandingly different compared to the more experienced teachers, it is

impossible to therefore conclude that beginning teachers have more uncertainties or problems about teaching than experienced teachers.

(Mok, 1994: 102)

This quantitative view of the cognitions of more or less experienced teachers, though, is somewhat limited in its ability to discern differences which undoubtedly exist, as the other studies I discuss here indicate. The author claims that following their practicum, inexperienced teachers were able to think about instructional decision-making in a much broader manner than they had previously been able to. Practical experience, it is implied, contributed to changing the cognitions about teaching held by the less experienced teachers more than it did for the more experienced group. It must be remembered, though, that the evidence for these claims comes from reflective writing and interviews rather than observation and analyses of practice.

Despite its limitations, one strength of Mok's study is that it attempted to study cognitive change over time. Without a longitudinal perspective, research is able to comment on differences between more and less experienced teachers without, however, providing insights into the processes through which expertise is acquired or through which experienced teachers' cognitions develop in the way they do. In this respect, Tsui (2003) makes a major contribution to the study of language teachers.

Tsui presents case studies of four ESL teachers – one expert, two experienced and one novice – working at the same secondary school in Hong Kong. Observations and interviews over a period of a year and half were used to understand their expertise. The study identified several differences between the expert teacher studied (Marina) and the other three:

> The knowledge held by Marina is much richer, more elaborate, and more coherent. She was able to see ESL teaching not as the teaching of discrete skills but as all interrelated in using language for communicative purposes. Her ESL teaching was also coherently related to the specific context of situation, and she was able to see and exploit the possibilities for ESL teaching and learning.

Compared with Marina, Ching and Eva's knowledge were less rich and, most important, less integrated. They tend to dichotomize different aspects of teaching that are inextricably linked, such as fun and learning, student interest and learning objectives. They were also more constrained by the limitations presented to them by their specific contexts. Another qualitative difference among the four teachers is that Marina was able to clearly articulate her principles and criteria for making curricular judgement, and the curricular decisions that she made were often conscious decisions. Her principles and criteria were based not only on her personal experience, but also on the theoretical input that she was able to interiorize and realize in the teaching act.

(Tsui, 2003: 223–4)

On the basis of the comparisons between the teachers in this study, three critical differences between expert and novice teachers are posited:

1 the extent to which various aspects of teaching and the knowledge embedded in the teaching act as an integrated whole;

2 the extent to which teachers are able to see possibilities for learning presented by the contexts they work in;

3 the extent to which the practical knowledge gained through experience can be made explicit and to which formal knowledge can be transformed into practical knowledge.

A number of further points about the nature of expertise in ESL are also raised; the development of expertise is a dynamic process which involves 'constant engagement in exploration and experimentation, in problematizing the unproblematic, and responding to challenges' (pp. 277–8). Another conclusion to emerge here is that teachers may achieve expertise in some aspects of their work but not in others (a point which I make in Borg, 2001b, where a teacher who lacked expertise in teaching grammar was quite expert at reading instruction). Tsui's work provides a solid basis for continuing studies of what it means to be an expert language teacher (see also Tsui, 2005 for a very useful discussion of the nature of expertise in teaching generally).

An interest in expertise also underpins Johnson (2003), which compared the ways that specialists and non-specialists designed language-teaching tasks. Specialists had at least five years' experience of task-design as a key part of their job and were or had worked as professional materials writers; non-specialists were second-language teachers with at least five years' experience, with task-design being an occasional focus of their work. On the basis of data collected through think-aloud tasks (see Chapter 7), the study identified a number of characteristics of good task designers and grouped these under two general headings: *logistical control,* which includes procedures and strategies for handling task-design, and *enrichment,* which 'covers everything to do with how designers ensure their design is sufficiently detailed and rich' (p. 128). Examples of characteristics of good task designers from the first of these categories are that they tend to do one thing at a time and they spend time analysing the design problem they face. Examples from the second category are that good task designers are sensitive to learners and to their context, and they are aware of the mechanics of setting up and conducting class activities. Overall, this study highlights the complexity of the behaviours and thinking that specialist task designers engage in and shows that, despite their higher level of expertise in task-design, the specialists were typically those who invested most effort in the process. Their resultant designs are 'richer, more complex than those of the NS/Ts [non-specialists]. They cover more variables, they visualise more concrete detail. And they seem to create or invent issues to complexify far beyond what is necessary' (p. 127). A number of these findings, Johnson concludes, support those from research into teacher expertise in other domains (in particular Bereiter and Scardamalia, 1993).

On the basis of the available evidence, then, there are a number of ways in which the cognitions of more or less experienced and expert teachers would seem to differ. These relate to the content of these cognitions – that is the particular issues which teachers think about – and to their quality – that is the manner in which they function as an integrated system. It is also possible to distinguish between the cognitions of teachers at different developmental or career stages by examining the preactive and interactive phases of teaching (i.e. novices tend to plan in a more structured way and to make fewer improvisational decisions during lessons). The nature of such differences, and of the factors which shape them (an issue we know much less about), is a key area for continuing research to address as we deepen our understandings of the cognitive development of language teachers.

Summary

One obvious characteristic of the work I have discussed in this chapter is its diversity. I have attempted to impose some coherence on my analysis of this work by grouping studies together according to their particular focus or orientation to the study of teacher cognition, and these categories provide some indication of the range of possibilities which exist for continuing work of this kind. In essence, though, the issues which have been examined can be reduced to six overall concerns:

- the cognitions (concerns, maxims, beliefs, knowledge, understandings, theories) that novice and experienced language teachers hold about specific aspects of their work and the origins of these (e.g. in life generally, through schooling and pre- and in-service teacher education);
- the congruence between these cognitions and those held by students or implied in curricula and educational systems;
- the relationship of teachers' cognitions to their instructional practices;
- the internal and external situational factors which underlie language teachers' instructional practices (preactive and interactive, planned and improvised) and which mediate and shape teachers' cognitions;
- the characteristics of expert/experienced teachers' cognitions and practices compared to those with less expertise/ experience;

- the development of teachers' cognitions and practices over time (through teacher education, experience, reflection and narrative inquiry).

The research reviewed in this chapter sheds light on these issues, although the wide range of findings emerging do not lend themselves to neat conclusions. It is clear that practising language teachers hold cognitions about all aspects of their work and that there are several perspectives from which these cognitions can be conceptualized and studied. It also clear that these cognitions are shaped by the totality of teachers' lived experience and that professional development experiences (such as teacher education) may account to greater or lesser extents for what novices actually do in the classroom. It is also clear that teachers' cognitions may assume different forms depending on the manner in which they are elicited; that is teachers may express a particular belief when responding to a survey but state an apparently contradictory view when talking about actual examples of their practice. In the past such incongruence was explained in terms of inconsistency or perhaps even lack of honesty on the teacher's part. We now acknowledge, though, that there may be differences between cognitions elicited theoretically and those generated in relation to practice. We also accept that instructional practices are defined through complex interactions among teachers' cognitions and situational factors both inside the classroom and in the wider institutional and social context. We are only just starting to understand this complexity, but once again an awareness of the many influences on what teachers do has enabled us to make sense of what would otherwise appear to be practices which refute the beliefs teachers say they hold. It is also clear that changes in teachers' cognitions do occur over time, and that there are qualitative and substantive differences in the nature of the thinking and knowledge of more and less experienced and expert teachers. In relation to this point, an important distinction is that between experience and expertise; the two are not synonymous and caution should be exercised in assuming that studies of experienced teachers do in fact shed light on the cognitions and practices of expert language teachers. Notable developments signalled in this body of work are a growing awareness of the need for longitudinal studies of cognitive change in language teachers (as opposed to cross-sectional comparisons of teachers at different stages of their careers), a concern for collective, rather than individual, cognitions and practices (Shulman and Shulman, 2004 also acknowledge that teacher cognition research generally has focused perhaps too much on individuals, thus ignoring the communal dimension of teaching) as well as the use of narrative inquiry and life history in making explicit and deepening our understandings of what experienced language teachers think and do.

4

Teacher cognition in grammar teaching

The research on language teacher cognition discussed so far has been concerned with generic processes such as the impact of teacher education, interactive decision-making and the nature of expertise. There is also, however, a significant body of work which has examined language teacher cognition in relation to specific curricular domains. For example, Lam (2000) and Lawrence (2001) have considered teacher cognition in relation to language teachers' beliefs about and uses of technology; Cathcart and Olsen (1976) focused on teachers' and students' preferences for the correction of classroom conversation errors – this focus on teacher cognition in relation to oral skills is rare and the only other relevant item I am aware of is Cohen and Fass (2001), which examined teachers' beliefs about students' oral production in the classroom. Konopak and Williams (1994) studied teacher cognition in relation to vocabulary instruction, while Zacharias (2005) surveyed English language teachers' beliefs about internationally published materials. In all of these specific areas, attention to teacher cognition has been very limited (a point I return to in the final chapter of this book). In contrast, however, two curricular domains have attracted significant research attention vis-à-vis teacher cognition: grammar teaching and literacy instruction. In this chapter I will focus on the first of these, dealing with literacy in Chapter 5.

The analysis in this chapter uses a framework from Borg (2003b) which divides studies of language teacher cognition in grammar teaching into three groups. The first group examines teachers' declarative knowledge about grammar, the second their stated beliefs about teaching grammar and the third teachers' cognitions as expressed through their grammar teaching practices. I will now discuss each group in turn.

Teachers' knowledge about grammar

In this section I discuss studies which have examined potential and practising language teachers' explicit or declarative knowledge about language. As Table 4.1 shows, most of this work has been conducted with potential and prospective language teachers in the United Kingdom. In an early study, Bloor (1986) used a questionnaire to assess the metalinguistic knowledge of 63 students entering modern language or linguistics courses at two British universities. The questionnaire aimed 'to give students the opportunity to display their familiarity with grammatical terms and concepts and related linguistic issues' (p. 158). Key findings were that the only grammatical terms successfully identified by all students were verb and noun, and that students demonstrated 'fairly widespread ignorance' (p. 159) on the questions asking them to identify functional elements such as subject and object.

In the context of debates about the role of knowledge about language (KAL) in the UK National Curriculum, Wray (1993), Williamson and Hardman (1995) and Chandler, Robinson and Noyes (1988) studied the KAL of prospective teachers. Wray assessed the KAL of a group of student teachers at the start of a primary postgraduate training course. Trainees were asked questions about grammatical forms, the changing nature of grammatical rules, the nature of spoken and written language, geographical and cultural language variation, and literary language. Overall, students achieved a mean score of 42.3 per cent on this test. With respect to the section on grammatical forms, Wray echoes the findings by Bloor (1986), reporting that 'the level of grammatical knowledge of these student-teachers was not particularly high' (p. 55). For example, respondents achieved only a mean success rate of 30 per cent in identifying adverbs, 23 per cent for pronouns and less than 10 per cent for prepositions. Williamson and Hardman (1995) assessed 99 trainee teachers at the start of their programme. On a question asking

Table 4.1 Studies of language teachers' declarative knowledge of language

Source	Focus	Context	Stage[a]
Andrews (1994)	grammatical knowledge of trainees	82 EFL teacher trainers	P
Andrews (1999a)	teachers' knowledge of grammar and grammatical terminology	20 practising and prospective ESL teachers in Hong Kong, 20 native English speaker undergraduates in the UK	P/I
Bloor (1986)	language awareness of university students	63 undergraduates in modern languages or linguistics and 175 2nd year students from other departments in the UK	P
Chandler, Robinson & Noyes (1988)	levels of awareness and linguistic knowledge among trainee teachers	917 primary trainees in the UK	P
Williamson & Hardman	levels of grammatical knowledge in trainee primary school teachers	99 trainee teachers in the UK	P
Wray (1993)	effect of training course on trainees' knowledge and beliefs about language	primary trainees in the UK	P

[a] In this and all subsequent tables in Chapters 4 and 5 the 'Stage' column indicates whether the study focuses on pre-service (P) or in-service (I) teachers. This allows readers with a specific interest in either of these to consider the relevant studies in addition to those covered in Chapters 2 and 3.

them to name parts of speech, trainees obtained a mean score of 5.6 out of 10, performing weakest on items asking them to label different kinds of clauses. In reflecting on their findings, the authors acknowledge that their study reveals significant gaps in trainee teachers' knowledge about grammar, misconceptions about language and a lack of a metalanguage for analysing language use. In their study of 917 student teachers, Chandler *et al.* (1988) found similar inadequacies, though the authors here concluded that, overall, their findings were less negative than suggested by debates at the time about the lack of metalinguistic knowledge in prospective language teachers in the United Kingdom.

The above studies reflect general concerns with the grammatical knowledge of prospective and practising English or Modern FL teachers in the United Kingdom. Andrews (1994, 1999a) examined similar issues in EFL contexts. His 1994 study used a questionnaire to ask 82 trainers on initial TEFL training courses to rate the grammatical knowledge/awareness of the trainees they had worked with. The key finding here was that, according to the trainers, more than 50 per cent of the trainees they had encountered had inadequate levels of grammatical knowledge/awareness (which the trainers described in terms of knowledge of grammar, the ability to reflect on and analyse it and skill in handling grammar in the classroom). Although, as the author acknowledges, this study amounts to little more than a 'collation of impressions' (p. 79) trainers had of their trainees, the findings do once again suggest perceived deficiencies in the grammatical knowledge of prospective language teachers.

Andrews (1999a) extended his work in this field. Using a 60-item test, he compared the explicit knowledge of grammar and grammatical terminology of four groups: non-native speaker (NNS) teachers of English, NNS prospective teachers of English, English native-speaker (NS) prospective teachers with a background in English Studies and English NS prospective teachers of modern languages. Andrews found that the non-native teachers of English (with a total mean score of around 70 per cent) did significantly better on the test than the other groups. In comparing NS and NNS overall, he found that the latter outperformed the former on the test. The NS group studying English studies performed worse of all with an overall average score of less than 41 per cent, a finding which reflects the low levels of KAL reported in UK studies reviewed above.

As a group, the studies in this section were similar in both purpose and method; they all focused on measuring, mainly through tests, the knowledge about language of groups of potential or practising teachers. A trend emerging from these studies is a concern for the generally inadequate levels of grammatical knowledge held, especially by potential language teachers. On the assumption that an explicit understanding of language plays a major role in the effectiveness of the work of language teachers, these findings suggested the need for language teacher preparation programmes to dedicate substantial time to the development of trainees' declarative knowledge about language. As research I review later suggests, though, such knowledge is but one component of the more global knowledge a language teacher must call on in teaching grammar.

Teachers' beliefs about grammar teaching

This second group of studies has focused on teachers' beliefs about formal instruction. In contrast to the previous group, most of these studies have been conducted in L2 and FL contexts. The studies in this group are listed in Table 4.2.

Within the context of the UK National Curriculum, Chandler (1988) used a postal questionnaire to examine practising English teachers' attitudes to language work. On the basis of 50 responses, Chandler reported that although 84 per cent of the teachers taught some grammar, many of these said their own language learning experiences at school were their main source of grammatical knowledge (and hence, Chandler concluded, of their inevitably outdated practices). On the basis of teachers' responses to questions about the importance of knowing about language for their work, Chandler was also very critical of teachers' lack of awareness of the role of language understanding in all facets of their work, leading him to describe the attitude of the teachers in his study as one of 'confident ignorance' (p. 23).

Another analysis of teachers' perspectives on grammar teaching was conducted by Eisenstein-Ebsworth and Schweers (1997), who used questionnaires with a total of 60 university teachers of ESL

Table 4.2 Studies of language teachers' beliefs about grammar teaching

Source	Focus	Context	Stage
Andrews (2003)	cognitions and practices in teaching grammar	170 secondary school EFL teachers in Hong Kong	I
Berry (1997)	teachers' awareness of learners' metalinguistic knowledge	372 undergraduates in Hong Kong and 10 of their English teachers	I
Burgess & Etherington (2002)	teachers' beliefs about grammar and grammar teaching	48 teachers of English for Academic Purposes in the UK	I
Chandler (1988)	teachers' practices in teaching grammar and their grammatical knowledge	50 teachers of English in the UK	I
Chia (2003)	beliefs about grammar teaching	96 primary teachers in Singapore	I
Eisenstein-Ebsworth & Schweers (1997)	teachers' views on conscious grammar instruction	60 University teachers of ESL – 30 in New York, 30 in Puerto Rico	I
Schulz (1996)	student and teacher perceptions of the role of grammar and correction in language learning	824 FL students and 92 L2 and FL teachers	I
Schulz (2001)	student and teacher perceptions of the role of grammar and correction in language learning	607 Colombian FL students; 122 of their teachers	I

in New York and Puerto Rico, and informal interviews with eight of these, to explore their views about conscious grammar instruction. The majority of the teachers felt grammar should be taught at least sometimes, with the Puerto Rico teachers more in favour of conscious instruction than the New York group. This was explained partly in terms of the more traditional approach to language teaching generally advocated in Puerto Rico; as one teacher in the latter group explained, 'grammar has always been part of our language learning experience. We see no reason to abandon it totally' (p. 247). Forty-one of the teachers reported having a well-defined approach to teaching grammar that they were confident in. In a tone strikingly more positive than Chandler (1988), the authors report that 'teachers' ideas regarding grammar were generally well developed. This was confirmed by their abilities to express clear and coherent rationales for their approaches to curriculum and pedagogy' (p. 251). In articulating their rationales, teachers referred to various factors shaping their views, such as student wants and syllabus expectations. However, it was their experience as teachers and learners which emerged as a particularly powerful influence on their views about grammar teaching, and the study concludes that 'it is interesting that our participants rarely justified their approaches by referring to research studies or any particular methodology' (p. 255).

Further insight into teachers' beliefs about formal instruction is provided by two large-scale studies by Schulz (1996, 2001). The first study compared the attitudes to grammar teaching and corrective feedback of 92 FL teachers and 824 language learners at an American university. Supporting the findings of Cathcart and Olsen (1976) and McCargar (1993), this study revealed significant mismatches between teachers' and students' views about error correction. For example, 94 per cent of the students disagreed with the statement 'teachers should not correct students when they make errors in class', while only 48 per cent of the teachers did. Of the students, 90 per cent also said they would like to have their spoken errors corrected, compared to 42 per cent of the teachers who agreed that this was desirable. Schulz (2001) replicated this study with 122 FL teachers in Colombia, together with 607 of their students. The results were consistent with those in the original study.

In addition to comparing teacher and student views on error correction, Schulz also explored respondents' views about how FLs are learned. Her US study revealed 'perturbing differences' (p. 348) between student and teacher opinions on this issue. For example, while 80 per cent of the students believed that 'the formal study of grammar is essential to the eventual mastery of the language', only 64 per cent of the teachers shared this view. In the follow-up study with Colombian participants, the differences in teacher and student opinion about how FLs are learned were even more pronounced. For example, while 76 per cent of the students said they liked grammar, only 30 per cent of the teachers felt students did. On the basis of these findings, it was argued that these mismatches between teacher and student views about the role of formal instruction and error correction may reduce the 'pedagogical face validity' (Schulz, 1996: 349) of instruction in the eyes of the learners, impinge negatively on student motivation and consequently be detrimental to learning.

Also concerned with this need for congruence between teacher and student cognitions, Berry (1997) used a 50-item questionnaire to measure the knowledge of grammatical terminology of 372 undergraduate students in Hong Kong, and also asked ten of these students' English teachers to indicate whether they felt the students knew the terminology covered in the questionnaire. He found 'wide discrepancies between students' knowledge of metalinguistic terms and between this and the teachers' estimation of it' (p. 143). In fact, teachers overestimated students' knowledge of terminology on 16 out of the 50 items on the test. Again, Berry concludes that this mismatch between student knowledge and teachers' assumptions about it could cause serious problems in the classroom. While this hypothesis is plausible, empirical evidence supporting it is not available and this does thus suggest itself as a useful focus for continuing research.

Burgess and Etherington (2002) used a questionnaire to examine the beliefs about grammar and grammar teaching held by 48 teachers of English for academic purposes (EAP) in UK universities. Overall, the teachers in this study reported positive attitudes towards formal instruction; they felt it had a contribution to make to the development of their (normally advanced) EAP students' proficiency and that conscious knowledge of grammar played a role in these students' use of language (as the authors note, the absence of detailed qualitative data precluded further insight into these views). Over 90 per cent of the teachers in this study felt that their students expect them to present grammar points explicitly. In contrast to Schulz's findings (where, however, students themselves responded), the teachers here generally agreed with this expectation. Among other findings, the study concluded that the teachers were more inclined to favour an integrated, focus-on-form approach to teaching grammar, in which it was dealt with reactively as required (no observation of teaching was however conducted). Another conclusion was that teachers' views about appropriate approaches to grammar were influenced by their awareness of student variables, such as past experience of language learning. A similar approach to investigating teachers' beliefs about grammar teaching – this time among 96 primary school teachers in Singapore – was adopted by Chia (2003); in common with other research conducted in this context and which I discuss below, this study found that teachers reported a preference for formal instruction based on explicit, deductive teaching in which drilling played a central role. The nature of the instrument used in this study (a very short questionnaire), though, does limit the scope of these findings.

The studies I have discussed in this section are less homogeneous than those which have studied teachers' declarative knowledge of grammar. Nonetheless, three main conclusions can be identified from this research on teachers' beliefs about grammar:

1 There is no suggestion in any of these studies that formal instruction is becoming less prevalent in language classrooms. Teachers (mostly in L2 and FL contexts) generally reported that attention to grammar was something they valued and promoted in their work.

2 In reporting their beliefs about grammar teaching, teachers commonly refer to the impact on their views of their prior language learning experiences; there is evidence that these may exert a more significant impact on teachers' views than the results of formal research into grammar teaching. This is

not wholly surprising; an apparent lack of impact of formal theory on teachers' cognitions has also been reported in mainstream education (e.g. Crawley and Salyer, 1995).

3 Teachers' and students' views about aspects of grammar teaching may differ considerably and, though there is no evidence to support this claim, it is suggested that such differences can be detrimental to the effectiveness of the formal instruction teachers provide.

Practices and cognitions in teaching grammar

None of the studies discussed so far in this chapter involved the analysis of teachers' cognitions and of their actual classroom practices; there have, though, been a number of such studies, particularly since the late 1990s, and such work is the focus of this section (see Table 4.3 for a summary). Given the number of studies involved I will discuss these in a number of sub-sections.

Early research in the United Kingdom

Early examples of this type of work are provided by Brumfit, Mitchell and Hooper (Brumfit *et al.*, 1996; Mitchell *et al.*, 1994a, 1994b; Mitchell and Hooper, 1992). They noted that, in the United Kingdom, theoretical debate about the rationales and models for developing knowledge about language (KAL) in the classroom had been informed by little empirical evidence regarding teachers' actual beliefs and classroom practices. Against this trend, they used classroom observations and interviews to describe KAL practices in secondary English and modern FL classrooms and to document teachers' beliefs about language and about the role of explicit KAL in language education. This research highlighted significant differences between English and FL teachers; FL teachers viewed KAL largely in terms of sentence-based explicit grammar work, something they felt made a 'direct contribution . . . to the development of pupils' target language proficiency' (Brumfit *et al.*,

Table 4.3 Studies of language teachers' practices and cognitions in relation to grammar teaching

Source	Focus	Context	Stage
Andrews & McNeil and (2005)	declarative knowledge about language in 'good' teachers	3 experienced teachers of English, 2 in Hong Kong and 1 in the UK	I
Andrews (1997)	teachers' metalinguistic awareness and explanations	5 practising English teachers and 9 prospective teachers in Hong Kong	P/I
Andrews (1999b)	teachers' metalinguistic awareness	17 secondary school teachers of English in Hong Kong, 3 of which are reported on	I
Andrews (2001)	impact of teacher language awareness on pedagogy	17 EFL teachers in Hong Kong	I
Basturkmen, Loewen & Ellis (2004)	beliefs and practices about incidental focus on form	3 ESL teachers in a private language school in New Zealand	I
Bigelow & Ranney (2005)	impact of grammar classes on content-based teaching practices	20 pre-service ESL teachers on MA in USA	P
Borg (1998a)	talk about grammar in the FL classroom	2 EFL teachers in Malta	I
Borg (1998b)	cognitions and practices in teaching grammar	1 experienced EFL teacher in Malta	I
Borg (1999a)	teacher cognition in L2 grammar teaching	5 EFL teachers in Malta	I

(Continued)

Table 4.3 (Continued)

Source	Focus	Context	Stage
Borg (1999b)	use of grammatical terminology in classrooms	4 EFL teachers in Malta	I
Borg (1999c)	teachers' personal theories in teaching grammar	2 EFL teachers in Malta	I
Borg (2001b)	teachers' self-perceptions of their knowledge of grammar	2 EFL teachers in Malta	I
Borg (2003)	teachers' practices and rationales in teaching grammar	5 EFL teachers in Malta	I
Borg (2005b)	impact of KAL on classroom practices	2 EFL teachers in Malta and Hungary	I
Brumfit et al. (1996)	teachers' theories about the place of KAL in language education	Teachers of English, French, Spanish and German in 3 secondary schools in the UK	I
Burns & Knox (2005)	the impact of a course on systemic functional linguistics on teachers' practices	2 in-service ESL teachers in Australia	I
Farrell & Lim (2005)	beliefs and practices of primary school teachers	2 experienced primary school teachers in Singapore	I
Farrell (1999)	student teachers' prior beliefs about teaching grammar	34 pre-service ESL teachers in Singapore, 5 of which are reported on	P
Hislam & Cajkler (2005)	primary trainees' use of KAL in their practices	4 primary trainees on a PGCE in the UK	P

Table 4.3 (Continued)

Source	Focus	Context	Stage
Johnston & Goettsch (2000)	teacher knowledge in explaining grammar	4 experienced university ESL teachers in the USA	I
Mitchell & Hooper (1992)	teachers' views about KAL and strategies for developing it	7 state secondary school heads of English and 7 of Modern Foreign Languages in the UK	I
Mitchell et al. (1994a, 1994b)	teachers' models of knowledge about language	7 teachers of English, French, German, and Spanish in the UK	I
Ng & Farrell (2003)	congruence among beliefs and practices in teaching grammar	4 beginning secondary school teachers of English in Singapore.	I
Popko (2005)	the impact of a KAL course on teachers' practices	4 MATESOL students in the USA	P

1996: 77). This was reflected in their classroom practices; for example, in the case of one teacher of French, 23 out of 30 observed episodes of language work focused on language as a system. English teachers, in contrast, adopted a text-based, functional approach to language work, rarely conducting explicit grammar work and reporting that this was of marginal relevance to the development of students' overall linguistic ability (Mitchell et al., 1994b; Mitchell and Hooper, 1992).

Apart from highlighting these differences in the way KAL was being interpreted and implemented by FL and English teachers, these studies also concluded that teachers' own KAL was in general 'patchy and idiosyncratic' (Brumfit et al., 1996: 86) and that these limitations constrained the effectiveness of the KAL work teachers conducted in the classroom. Such findings support concerns emerging from the studies of teachers' declarative knowledge of grammar reviewed earlier, where low levels of knowledge were seen to be an impediment to effective teaching. The work of Brumfit, Mitchell and Hooper also suggested that teachers' understandings of KAL, and hence their practices, had not been shaped in any significant way by curriculum debates about KAL. FL teachers in particular, had been 'influenced relatively little by those theories of second-language acquisition that downgrade the role of explicit, form-focused instruction in the learning of a foreign language' (Mitchell et al., 1994a: 197). This echoes the earlier finding from Eisenstein-Ebsworth and Schweers (1997) regarding the minimal role which an awareness of research in second language acquisition seems to play in FL teachers' rationales for their approach to explicit language work.

Teachers' language awareness

A programme of research on teachers' metalinguistic awareness (TMA) and teachers' language awareness (TLA) by Andrews (1997, 1999b, 2001; Andrews and McNeil, 2005) has also shed light on connections between teachers' cognitions and practices in teaching grammar. In his 1997 study, he explored the role TMA played in explanations of grammar by asking practising and prospective teachers of English in Hong Kong to participate in a controlled role play (simulated, rather than actual, teaching) in which, individually, they were given texts with obvious formal errors in them and asked to identify these and to act out in front of the researcher the subsequent explanation they would give learners. Although the study highlighted weaknesses in the participants' KAL, Andrews argues that 'many of the apparent weaknesses in the performances . . . seem to relate to metalinguistic awareness *in operation* rather than to problems with the underlying declarative KAL' (p. 160). For example, some teachers who identified errors in the text were subsequently unable to formulate explanations of them in language their learners would find helpful. Andrews concludes that discussions of teachers' metalinguistic awareness should account for both its declarative and procedural dimensions, and that 'assessing teachers' metalinguistic awareness solely by focusing on declarative language awareness may miss out on procedural problems' (p. 160). This is an important observation which implies that increasing language teachers' explicit knowledge about grammar through teacher education will not automatically lead to more effective instruction. As research on teacher knowledge has argued (e.g. Grossman, 1989, discussed in Chapter 3) teachers also need to know how to transform this knowledge into effective pedagogy.

Extending this work, Andrews (1999b) argued that TMA might be 'a specifically language-related facet of L2 teacher competence' (p. 176) which affects teachers' ability to transform language from, for example, instructional materials, into appropriate linguistic input for learners. Thus one teacher in this study demonstrated inadequate TMA by adopting 'an unaware, uncritical, diffident acceptance of all that the materials say' (p. 175) with the result that such materials, despite obvious deficiencies in their presentation of language, became learner input without any modification by the teacher. In contrast, a second teacher with a more developed TMA recognized and filtered such deficiencies, transforming the materials in such a way that the input learners received was more effective.

Points from his earlier studies are expanded on in Andrews (2001), where it is argued that teachers' explicit grammar knowledge is but one component of the complex concept which Andrews calls teachers' language awareness (TLA) and which, as with TMA, plays a key role in shaping the effectiveness with which teachers can provide appropriate linguistic input to learners. Effective deployment of TLA in practice, though, also depends on personality factors (e.g. teachers' alertness), attitudinal factors (e.g. willingness to engage with grammar) and contextual factors (e.g. time) which may constrain what teachers can do in the classroom. Similar conclusions are confirmed in Andrews and McNeil (2005), which focuses on both knowledge of grammar and of vocabulary and which suggests a number of characteristics that 'good language teachers' have in relation to TLA:

> the study has revealed a number of other characteristics of language-aware behaviour which might be hypothesised as generalisable in relation to the teacher language awareness of 'Good Language Teachers' worldwide: willingness and ability to engage with language-related issues; self-awareness (with particular reference to awareness of the extent of their own subject-matter knowledge)

accompanied by a desire for continuing self-improvement of their teacher language awareness; willingness and ability to reflect on language-related issues; awareness of their own key role in mediating input for learning; awareness of learners' potential difficulties; and a love of language.

(Andrews and McNeil, 2005: 174)

Andrews' work has made an important contribution to our understandings of the components of teachers' language awareness; clearly there is more to this than a declarative knowledge of grammar. It would be interesting to see some of this work replicated in language education contexts other than Hong Kong and to consider the wider applicability of the ideas Andrews has developed.

Naturalistic studies of grammar teaching

A number of studies of teacher cognition in grammar teaching reflect a desire to observe teachers in naturally occurring contexts, to describe in detail what teachers actually do in teaching grammar, and to explore their thinking through a discussion of these observed practices. This tradition of work is perhaps most clearly illustrated in a series of papers by Borg (1998a, 1998b, 1999a, 1999c, 1999d, 2001b, 2003a, 2005b).

In response to 'a large volume of research on formal instruction which paradoxically fails to contribute at all to an understanding of the process of grammar teaching as it is perceived by teachers' (Borg, 1999a: 21), Borg studied five EFL teachers in Malta, providing insight into the complex, personalized pedagogical systems which teachers draw on in teaching grammar. For example, the data suggest that the decision to conduct explicit formal instruction does not necessarily imply a belief on the teacher's part that such instruction promotes language learning; the teacher in Borg (1998b) was, for example, not convinced this was the case but integrated some explicit work into his teaching because he felt the students expected and would respond positively to it. Another key finding was that in teaching grammar teachers do draw on approaches traditionally considered to be exclusive; one of the teachers in Borg (1999c), for example, employed both deductive and inductive strategies in teaching grammar, justifying these with reference to interacting and sometimes conflicting beliefs based on her own teaching and learning experience.

The approach to meta talk (instructional talk about language) adopted by two teachers in grammar teaching was examined in Borg (1998a). The teachers' practices were analysed in terms of five features: how a focus for meta talk was defined, the modes of interaction used during such talk, the procedures followed in examining language, the occurrence of metalanguage, and the nature of the outcomes of meta talk. An analysis of these practices and of the psychological, pedagogical and situational factors shaping them supported the claim that 'meta talk in the FL classroom is by no means a monolithic phenomenon' (Faerch, 1985: 197). One specific aspect of meta talk, the use of grammatical terminology – another issue widely debated in the language learning literature without any reference to teachers' actual practices and cognitions – was investigated in more detail in Borg (1999d). A comparison of the role of terminology in the work of four teachers highlighted not only a variety of practices but also personalized stances towards the use of terminology shaped by unique educational biographies. The teachers' decisions about terminology were not related directly to beliefs they held about one particular issue; rather, once again, instructional decisions in this aspect of L2 teaching were influenced by the interaction of a range of cognitions, such as beliefs about the best way to learn grammar, the value of talk about language and students' knowledge of and experience of terminology (these are summarized in Table 4.4). This study also provided some support for the possibility (supporting an earlier finding by Brumfit *et al.*, 1996) that teachers' own knowledge of terminology was a factor shaping their instructional decisions (Andrews, 2003a, which I discuss below, also posits a relationship between explicit knowledge of grammar and pedagogical practice). These connections between what teachers know about grammar and their approach to formal instruction were explored further in Borg (2001b), where two experienced EFL teachers were compared. One teacher was generally confident in his own knowledge about grammar, and this was reflected in his willingness to conduct impromptu grammar work and to use students' questions as the springboard for unplanned class discussions of grammar. The second teacher rarely conducted

Table 4.4 Cognitions influencing L2 teachers' use of grammatical terminology (Borg, 1999c: 120). By permission of Oxford University Press.

Cognitions about	Terminology minimized	Terminology promoted
What promotes communicative ability in the L2	Using the language	Using the language and learning *about* the language
Best way to learn grammar	Implicitly	Explicitly
Value of talk about language	Low	High
Contribution of terminology to L2 learning	Non-facilitative	Facilitative
Students' knowledge of terminology	Undeveloped	Sophisticated
Students' experience of terminology	Limited	Extensive
Students' attitudes to metalinguistic discussion	Negative	Positive
Students' learning styles	Responsive to communicative teaching	Responsive to traditional and communicative teaching
Teachers' roles in the L2 classroom	Promoting communicative ability	Displaying metalinguistic knowledge

grammar work and never did so unless he was prepared. A fear of not knowing the answer, triggered by a negative experience much earlier in his career, was the main influence behind this stance. These data suggested that teachers' self-perceptions of their knowledge of grammar motivates their pedagogical decisions. The experiential influences (e.g. prior experience of language learning and teaching) on the self-perception of this same teacher and another EFL teacher in Hungary (who had a markedly more positive outlook on her knowledge about language) are illustrated and compared in Borg (2005b); this work reinforces, with reference to grammar, the generally accepted idea that teachers' educational biographies can impact on all aspects of their cognitions and practices and suggests the value of developing pedagogically-oriented understandings of grammar among teachers as opposed to conceptions of grammatical knowledge in which it is disconnected from teachers' preactive and interactive pedagogical concerns.

Borg (2003a) compares the practices and rationales for grammar teaching of the five EFL teachers discussed with reference to specific aspects of their work in earlier papers. One point to emerge from this analysis was the variety of reasons why teachers stated that they engaged in grammar teaching. Five categories of rationale are presented in Figure 4.1. This indicates that teachers may teach grammar for any combination of acquisition-related, awareness-raising, diagnostic, psychological and classroom management factors. These findings confirm what a growing body of evidence now suggests: that grammar teaching is shaped by the interactions of a complex range of factors and that teachers' rationales for engaging in particular practices may not always be those most obviously suggested. For example, as noted earlier, teachers may engage in grammar teaching not because they feel it enhances language acquisition but because they feel it is something their students expect.

Another perspective on the relationship between cognition and practice in formal instruction is provided by Farrell (1999), who asked 34 pre-service teachers of English in Singapore to write about their past experience of learning English and about their personal views about teaching grammar, to decide whether to approach a grammar lesson inductively or deductively, and to implement and reflect on their chosen approach. Reporting on five of the teachers, this paper highlights the manner in which students' choices were influenced by their own language learning experiences. Thus, for example, some students wrote that as teachers they rejected the deductive system for learning grammar they had experienced themselves because it had not worked for them as learners; others were inclined to approach grammar in the way they had been taught it themselves (inductively or

1. *Acquisition*
    - It enhances the accuracy of students' communicative ability.
    - It enhances students' fluency.
    - It enables students to communicate with greater economy of expression.
    - It enables students to discern, remember and use generative patterns in the language.
2. *Awareness-Raising*
    - It deepens students' explicit understanding of the rules underlying language they use naturally.
3. *Diagnostic*
    - It makes students aware of language areas they need to work on.
    - It provides teachers with indications of students' linguistic needs.
4. *Psychological*
    - It fulfils students' expectations about L2 learning.
    - When based on errors students make during fluency work, it validates the latter in the students' eyes.
    - It provides concrete evidence of instruction which is reassuring to both the teacher and the students.
5. *Classroom Management*
    - Within the context of high-energy interactive learning, grammar analysis work provides opportunities for some quiet reflective time in the classroom.
    - Oral grammar drills provide the teacher with a strategy for rapidly raising energy levels in the classroom.

FIGURE 4.1 *Reasons for teaching grammar*
(Borg, 2003a: 158–9)

deductively), because it was effective (even though in some cases it may have been boring). Such findings once again highlight the impact on what teachers think and do of their educational biographies.

Congruence in beliefs and practices

Another major study of teacher cognition in grammar teaching is Basturkmen, Loewen and Ellis (2004). The particular focus of this study was teachers' beliefs and practices in relation to incidental focus on form – instances within communicative, message-oriented teaching where, either in response to a perceived problem (reactive focus on form) or in anticipation of one (pre-emptive focus on form), learners' attention is drawn to some aspect of grammar. Again, observations and different forms of interview were used to elicit teachers' beliefs about focus on form and to understand their practices in relation to this approach to grammar teaching. The picture to emerge here indicated degrees of both congruence and incongruence in the stated beliefs and actual practices of each teacher. For example, one of the teachers believed that his role in the classroom was to be a resource for the learners, not to direct the lesson; this was reflected in his observed practices, where students spent a significant amount of time working in groups. However, the same teacher expressed the view that students should be encouraged to self-correct when they committed errors and that communicative activities should not be interrupted to deal with errors unless these interfered with meaning; in this case, the teacher's observed practices were at odds with these beliefs. Similar incongruence between beliefs and practices was evident in the work of the other two teachers in this study. In attempting to account for this finding, the researchers draw on distinctions between technical knowledge and practical knowledge (Eraut, 1994) and between espoused theories and theories in use (Argyris and Schön, 1974). When teachers are asked to comment on their beliefs abstractly, that is, without reference to concrete events or experiences, it may be that they draw primarily on their technical (i.e. theoretical or propositional) knowledge and articulate their espoused theories; however, in response to concrete classroom events, it may be that teachers draw on their practical knowledge – their experiential understandings of teaching – and in doing so articulate their theories in use. In this study, the least experienced teacher was the one who exhibited most inconsistency in his beliefs and practices; it was suggested that his technical and practical knowledge might not be as well aligned as they were for more experienced teachers. This connection between experience and the alignment of propositional and practical knowledge in language teachers suggests an interesting avenue for further research.

An interest in comparing stated beliefs and practices in grammar teaching is also evident in Ng and Farrell (2003) and Farrell and Lim

(2005), which examined the congruence between the beliefs and practices in grammar teaching of teachers of English in Singapore. On the basis of observations and interviews, these studies highlighted varying levels of congruence between teachers' stated beliefs and their actual classroom practices. Ng and Farrell (2003), for example, found a lack of congruence between teachers' stated belief that explicit correction of all student errors should be minimized and the amount of explicit correction teachers actually engaged in. In both studies, a lack of congruence between beliefs and practices was explained in relation to the contextual factors which exerted a powerful influence on what teachers did in the classroom; these included time (i.e. deductive explanations were less time-consuming), the need to prepare students for examinations (a high priority in the Singapore context) and institutional policy (the management in these schools placed great emphasis on teaching grammar). Interestingly, such factors seemed less influential in the Basturkmen *et al.* study in accounting for differences in teachers' stated beliefs and actual practices, reminding us once again of the importance of context in studying and understanding teachers' cognitions and practices.

Content and pedagogical knowledge in teaching grammar

In the same naturalistic vein as the work of Borg above, Johnston and Goettsch (2000) examined the knowledge base underlying the grammatical explanations of four experienced ESL teachers in the USA. Conceptually, this study draws on the work in teacher knowledge of Shulman (1987) and focuses specifically on teachers' content knowledge (i.e. knowledge of subject matter), pedagogical content knowledge (i.e. subject-specific instructional techniques) and knowledge of learners in relation to grammar teaching. Although they discuss content knowledge, pedagogical knowledge and knowledge of students separately, Johnston and Goettsch acknowledge that, while this discreteness is analytically convenient, 'in reality, these categories are melded together in complex and indeed inextricable ways' (p. 461).

Defining content knowledge in this study as teachers' declarative knowledge of language, the authors examined the sources of such knowledge in the four teachers' work, finding that, in common with other studies reviewed earlier, education and experience were the two major influences on the development of teachers' content knowledge. In addition, the dynamic nature of the teachers' knowledge about language was also highlighted; that is the understandings of language teachers had were constantly changing as they stored, processed, reflected on, added to and modified what they already knew (see also Borg, 2005b for insights into the development of a teacher's knowledge of English grammar).

Although, as discussed in Chapter 3, the applicability of the notion of pedagogical content knowledge (PCK) to language teaching has been questioned, Johnston and Goettsch argue that 'the way experienced teachers give explanations of grammar points in class . . . is pedagogical content knowledge par excellence' (p. 449). Thus they analysed teachers' explanations in order to shed light on the concept of PCK in an ESL context. Their analysis showed that grammatical rules did not feature prominently in the explanations of any of the teachers (this contrasts quite strongly with observational data on EFL grammar teaching from Hong Kong and Singapore); rather, the teachers placed much more emphasis on using examples during explanations and on 'the importance of student input in facilitating their explanations' (p. 451). Another characteristic of explanations shared by all teachers was encouraging student questions and devoting significant time to student-initiated discussions. This stance was based on the general belief that such active student involvement supported the processes of understanding language. The teachers varied in their views about the role of metalanguage in grammatical explanations, with two of the teachers more supportive of it (particularly at lower levels) and two (teaching higher levels) not feeling it was particularly important.

In analysing teachers' explanations, the study also found that 'teachers' beliefs about how learners learn and what they know affect their pedagogical strategies' (p. 455). Teachers' commentaries revealed complex and multifaceted understandings of student knowledge; learning involved 'grasping conceptually the form and especially the meaning of grammatical constructions' as well as 'accurate production in terms of both form and meaning' (p. 456).

Extending his earlier programme of work, Andrews (2003a) also focused on language teachers' subject-matter knowledge in grammar teaching. He drew on a range of test, survey, interview and observation data in examining the beliefs about grammar pedagogy held by 170 teachers of English in Hong Kong and the relationships among these cognitions, teachers' background variables and teachers' subject-matter knowledge in relation to their explicit knowledge of grammar and grammatical terminology. Little statistical evidence was found that teacher background factors such as years of experience or nature of first degree were associated with the teachers' beliefs about teaching and learning grammar. Relationships were found, however, between levels of proficiency and explicit grammar knowledge on the one hand and beliefs about grammar and language pedagogy on the other:

> teachers who prefer an inductive approach to grammar teaching tend to have higher levels of explicit grammar knowledge, while those who favour a deductive approach tend to have lower levels of explicit grammar knowledge. Also, support for CLT principles appears to be associated with higher levels of language proficiency.
>
> (Andrews, 2003a: 361–2)

These associations between language proficiency and language teaching pedagogy merit much further investigation; they may imply, albeit partly, why the introduction of CLT in contexts such as Hong Kong has had mixed success in terms of its adoption in the classroom.

Seventeen of the teachers in this study were studied in more depth through interviews and classroom observations. Reflecting Breen et al.'s (2001) interest in teachers' collective cognitions, the analysis of the qualitative data from these teachers searched for general patterns in their cognitions about grammar teaching and for associations between these cognitions and teachers' classroom practices. Clear patterns of cognition emerged here which were also associated with particular patterns of practice. For example, it was generally felt by these teachers (and, they reported, by their students) that grammar teaching is 'a boring necessity' (p. 370); in terms of practice, a presentation-practice-production approach was predominant, and marked by a deductive approach to the presentation of new grammar. It was also generally found that while some elements of CLT had influenced the teachers' beliefs about L2 learning (e.g. grammar is needed primarily as a tool for communication) there was little evidence of the principles of CLT in the teachers' practice (see Richards and Pennington, 1998; Sato and Kleinsasser, 1999 in Chapter 3 for similar findings). In considering the general patterns of cognitions and practices found here, and the relationships among them, Andrews concluded that 'the teachers' feelings, beliefs, and understandings about grammar and grammar teaching within their particular field of operations combine to inform what these teachers consider to be necessary, feasible, and desirable in relation to grammar pedagogy' (p. 370). The reference to the affective side of grammar teaching is worth noting here (see Golombek and Johnson, 2004 in Chapter 3 for a discussion of the emotional dimension of teacher cognition). The reference to teachers' 'particular field of operations' is also important, for despite the global patterns of cognition and practice found, there was here, as in Breen et al. (2001), an element of individuality in the teachers' responses. These individual differences among the cognitions and practices of the teachers are partly accounted for by the variations in their individual teaching conditions – the micro-cultures of the schools they work in. The example is given of one teacher, for example, whose cognitions and practices in relation to grammar had changed markedly as a result of her transfer from a traditional secondary school to a less traditional college.

Teacher education and grammar pedagogy

One final set of studies to discuss here appeared together in a volume concerned with the role of applied linguistics in language teacher education (Bartels, 2005b). A common theme in these papers is the connection between, on the one hand, university courses about language knowledge (primarily grammar) and grammar teaching and, on the other, what teachers, both pre-service and in-service, do in practice (these studies, then, are also relevant to themes in teacher education discussed in Chapters 2 and 3). A shared finding in these studies is that the anticipated transfer from course input to practice does not always occur, that it occurs in a variable manner among different teachers and trainees on the same course and that language teaching demands of teachers much more than a knowledge about language. I will consider some examples to illustrate these points.

Hislam and Cajkler (2005) examined the knowledge about grammar of primary trainee teachers on a PGCE programme in the United Kingdom and the challenges these trainees faced in attempting to develop their own learners' knowledge about language. The study highlighted problems new teachers face in learning and teaching grammatical terminology (e.g. the need for teachers themselves to know and feel confident about using terminology). This study also argued for the time that trainees require to explore, work through, and revise the ingrained but often inadequate notions of grammar which they bring with them to their training (e.g. definitions of parts of speech such as 'a verb is a doing word').

In a North American context, both Bigelow and Ranney (2005) and Popko (2005) experienced similar difficulties in enabling trainees to apply in pedagogical contexts theoretical knowledge about grammar learned through teacher education. The results of these studies highlight the variable ways in which the expected transfer of knowledge from theory to practice occurs. For example, in the first of these studies, trainees took an English grammar course, then worked on developing lesson and unit plans for content-based language instruction (CBI) – the expectation was that in developing these plans (which require language and academic content to be integrated), trainees would draw on the knowledge of grammar acquired through their course. On the basis of the plans produced by the trainees, though, the study concluded that the findings

> lend doubt to the assumption that it is enough to provide separate instruction on grammar and instruction on pedagogy with the expectation that preservice teachers will then be able to put the two together. Even with a grammar course that was especially designed to make these connections, the issue of how to apply the knowledge to teaching was the major concern that participants expressed.
>
> (Bigelow and Ranney, 2005: 194)

Distinctions already made between content and pedagogical content knowledge once again seem relevant in accounting for the results of this study; trainees here reported being less concerned at having to master grammatical knowledge (the content); what they found most challenging was how to transform that content into pedagogical material.

Further insights into the transfer of course input to classroom practice in relation to teaching grammar is provided by Burns and Knox (2005). In this case the study examined the teaching of two teachers who had taken an MA course on systemic functional linguistics (SFL). The researchers found that the teachers' practices were characterized by more traditional approaches to grammar teaching and reported that they were struck by 'the enormity of the assumptions we had made about the uptake by the teachers of the SFL grammar component of the course' (p. 255). Through the research process, as observed lessons were collaboratively analysed and discussed, the teachers in the study did come to incorporate SFL principles into their pedagogy; however, the paper suggests that this might not have occurred without the intervention provided by the research. This is further evidence, then, of the challenges which teacher educators face in facilitating productive connections between course input and classroom practice in teaching grammar. Burns and Knox (2005) provide a summary of the range of factors which, interactively and in complex ways, shaped teachers' classroom practices in this study (see Figure 4.2). Teachers' work cannot be related in a linear manner to any one of these factors; rather, 'teachers' classroom decision making is a perpetual and dynamic process, constantly interacting with a vast array of immediate and distant factors (spatial, temporal, and conceptual) at a level of complexity which defies neat description' (p. 254).

Overall, this large group of studies of teachers' practices and cognitions in grammar teaching highlight much more than the previous two groups discussed in this chapter the complex nature of instructional decision-making in formal instruction and the many factors which shape these. Teachers' subject-matter knowledge (and their perceptions of it) can have a clear impact on how they teach grammar. Teachers' understandings of their learners and of

Institutional	Pedagogical	Personal	Physical
exam pressures; timetabling and time pressures; course aims and syllabus requirements; required materials; course focus on tertiary entry/study; time available for preparation	previous lesson(s); student needs; student skills/language ability; newsness of student; experiences of tertiary study; online classroom decision-making; student age; teacher-student relationships; focus of the research project	language learning experiences; previous training as (language) teacher; previous teaching experience; existing practices; theories of teaching; theories of learning; recent study (of SFL); current study; commitments; personal lives and realtionships	heat physical size and layout of class; changes of rooms; student movement in and out of class; presence of researchers in class room

FIGURE 4.2 *Factors mediating classroom practices in teaching grammar (Burns and Knox, 2005: 254). With kind permission of Springer Science and Business Media.*

the classroom environment also influence what teachers do. And while there is also evidence that teachers do teach grammar in a way that reflects their stated beliefs, it is also clear that beliefs and practices are often not congruent. This does not mean that teachers are consciously misrepresenting their real beliefs; rather, such results may be the product of the manner in which beliefs are elicited (i.e. abstractly or with reference to actual examples of teaching). I return to this important methodological issue in Chapter 6. Studies of congruence between beliefs and practice have also shown, once again, that contextual factors in schools and classrooms may have a more powerful impact on what teachers do than their beliefs about effective pedagogy. And also, once again there was ample evidence here of how prior experiences as learners and teachers shape what teachers believe and do in teaching grammar. Noteworthy substantive developments highlighted here in relation to grammar teaching – and which merit continuing study – are the attention to collective principles and practices among teachers in a similar context and the study of how grammar-related input in teacher education is transferred into practical teaching activities.

Summary

As the studies reviewed in this chapter show, various substantive, methodological and conceptual perspectives have been applied to the study of what teachers know, believe and do in relation to grammar and grammar teaching. Language teachers' awareness of grammar has been equated with their performance on various tests of explicit metalinguistic knowledge. These have generally pointed to basic gaps in prospective teachers' understandings of grammar. Comparisons of teacher and student views about aspects of formal instruction have also highlighted discrepancies between these, particularly in relation to students' positive attitudes to formal instruction and regular, explicit error correction, compared to teachers' less favourable attitudes towards these aspects of language teaching. Studies exploring both teachers' beliefs about grammar teaching and the bases for these have pointed towards the powerful role which teachers' prior experiences as language learners have on their own understandings of and beliefs about grammar and grammar teaching. Finally, studies of grammar teaching grounded in classroom practices and teachers' rationales for these have elaborated a multifaceted conception of teacher thinking and teacher knowledge in which teachers' understandings of language, pedagogy and learners, shaped by the teachers' educational and professional biographies, interact in complex ways with macro and micro contextual factors to define instructional decisions and practices in formal instruction.

This body of work is indicative of changing perspectives about how best to understand and to research teaching. For over 25 years the predominant source of knowledge about grammar teaching had been studies of second language acquisition (SLA), where the focus was on learners and learning outcomes; in the work reviewed here, we see evidence of a conceptual shift which acknowledges teacher cognition as a key source of data in attempts to make sense of formal instruction. It is the studies where cognitions are explored with direct reference to teachers' actual classroom practices that this shift is most obvious, and continuing work of this kind is required in a greater range of language teaching contexts. Further research into language teachers' knowledge of grammar and of the effects of this on their practice is also required, as, despite the valuable work highlighted here, our understandings of the relationships between declarative subject-matter knowledge and practice in language teaching are still relatively undeveloped. At the same time, existing work both here and outside the field of language teaching reminds us that subject-matter knowledge is but one of several kinds of knowledge which teachers need to draw on in their work. Further studies into the full range of teacher knowledge that informs grammar teaching practices are thus also required.

Research on teacher cognition in grammar teaching is characterized by one particular gap (and this applies to language teacher cognition research generally): the relationships among teacher cognition, classroom practice and learning have not been studied. Addressing this issue calls for the merging of hitherto separate lines of inquiry into teacher cognition and SLA, and ways of promoting this rapprochement should now be awarded greater attention (I discuss this in more detail in Chapter 10). In the meantime, however, it is clear that the study of teacher cognition in grammar teaching is a well-established and expanding domain of inquiry with potential to provide further insights into this important area of language pedagogy. Given the volume of work now available, and its relevance to the field, the lack of any reference to it in a major recent handbook of research in second language teaching and learning (Hinkel, 2005) which contains three chapters dedicated to grammar teaching is both puzzling and disappointing. This is perhaps indicative of the work which remains to be done in reconciling the long-standing interest in grammar *learning* with the attention to grammar *teaching* and *teachers* illustrated in this chapter.

5

Teacher cognition in literacy instruction

A second major curricular area which has been widely researched from a teacher cognition perspective is the teaching of literacy. In this chapter I will discuss the work available in this area and analyse what it tells us about language teachers' cognitions and practices. One characteristic of this body of work is that, in contrast to the material reviewed in the previous chapter, much of it comes from first language education contexts. In fact, while the study of teacher cognition in L1 literacy instruction (especially reading) stretches back almost 30 years and has generated a significant body of research, there has been relatively little research on teacher cognition in reading and writing instruction in L2 and FL contexts.

I will first consider studies of reading instruction in L1 contexts, then examine similar work in FL contexts. The discussion of teacher cognition in writing instruction will be organized in the same way. Finally, I will consider research which has examined literacy instruction generally without particular attention to either reading or writing.

First language reading instruction

Given the centrality of L1 reading to learning generally, it is not surprising that a significant body of work examining teacher cognition in reading instruction has accumulated in the past 30 years. This has been conducted almost exclusively in the USA (see Table 5.1).

Table 5.1 Studies of teacher cognition in first language reading

Source	Focus	Context	Stage
Beach (1994)	beliefs, practices and context in teaching reading	4 elementary teachers in USA	I
Davis et al. (1993)	beliefs and practices in reading instruction	2 elementary teachers in USA	I
Duffy (1977)	teachers' conceptions of reading	350 teachers initially; 37 with strong orientations did repertory grids; and 8 of these were then observed 10 times each	I
Grisham (2000)	pre-service teachers' beliefs and classroom practices in reading	12 pre-service trainees followed into their first 2 years of teaching	P/I
Hulshof & Verloop (2002)	the use of analogies in the teaching of reading comprehension	8 experienced teachers of L1 Dutch	I
Johnston (2001: 333)	beliefs and practices in teaching spelling	elementary teachers (Grades 2–5) in the USA	I
Kinzer (1988)	beliefs about reading of pre- and in-service teachers	83 undergraduate and 91 practising teachers in the USA	P/I
Maloch et al. (2003)	beliefs and reported practices of beginning reading teachers	101 beginning teachers in the USA	I
Meloth et al. (1989)	teachers' and students' concepts of reading	18 elementary teachers and 60 students in the USA	I

Table 5.1 (Continued)

Source	Focus	Context	Stage
Olson & Singer (1994)	theoretical beliefs and classroom practices in reading instruction	20 teachers in the USA and their students	I
Richardson et al. (1991)	beliefs and practices in reading instruction	39 teachers in Grades 4, 5 and 6 in the USA	I
Wilson, et al. (1992)	theoretical beliefs and classroom practices in reading instruction	1 high school teacher of English in the USA	I
Wray (1988)	impact of psycholinguistic theories of reading on views of teacher trainees	Same UK teacher trainees in 2nd and 4th year of study (33 2nd year, 27 4th year)	P

A dominant focus in this work has been teachers' theoretical orientations to reading (though some early work also examined teacher judgements and planning in relation to reading instruction – Borko and Niles, 1982; Borko et al., 1981). The notion of theoretical orientations was promoted by Harste and Burke (1977), who defined this concept as the knowledge, beliefs and philosophical principles which guide teachers' expectations and decisions in teaching reading.

Their argument was that it is possible to identify the theoretical orientations to reading adopted by teachers and that these orientations underpinned the approach to reading instruction teachers adopted in practice. A clear connection between cognition and practice in reading instruction was thus being posited.

This tradition of research into teachers' theoretical conceptions of reading remains popular today. It is a domain of inquiry characterized by a wide range of instruments which have been developed for accessing teachers' beliefs about reading and reading instruction. DeFord's (1985) Theoretical Orientation to Reading Profile (TORP) – a 28-item Likert-scale instrument – is one of the most widely used;

the profiling instruments developed by Kinzer (1988, 1989; Kinzer and Carrick, 1985; Leu and Kinzer, 1987) have also been widely adopted. These consist of two belief inventories and sample lesson plans for respondents to indicate a preference for. The TORP classifies teachers in terms of three orientations to reading – phonics, skills or whole-language; Kinzer's instruments classify teachers in terms of their views about how reading takes place (text-based, reader-based or interactive processes) and about how reading ability develops (whether it involves the development of specific skills, of holistic language or whether it is a case of differential acquisition – i.e. one where different behaviours are required at different stages of development). In addition to these written instruments, interview-based strategies for eliciting teachers' theoretical orientations to reading have also been developed, such as the Conceptual Framework of Reading Interview (Gove, 1983). The work I discuss below draws frequently on these kinds of profiling instruments (I discuss these in more detail in Chapter 6). Most of the studies I comment on here do not involve the study of actual classroom practices. One criticism which has been made about research into teachers' theoretical orientations to reading is in fact that it lacks ecological validity (Kinzer, 1988; Richardson *et al.*, 1991); that is, the absence of observations of what teachers actually do in such studies limits the nature of the claims which can legitimately be made about the relationship between cognition and practice in reading instruction.

Relationship between beliefs and practices

The study of beliefs and practices in L1 reading instruction is characterized by two positions; some studies have shown a lack of congruence among teachers' stated beliefs and their practices, while others have provided evidence that such consistency does in fact exist. Such differences in findings are often a product, at least in part, of the research methods that have been used.

A significant early contribution to research on teachers' theoretical orientations to reading was made by the Conceptions of Reading Project at Michigan University. The researcher most associated with this programme of work is Duffy (e.g. Duffy, 1977; Duffy and Anderson,

1984; Duffy and Ball, 1986; Duffy and Metheny, 1979; Duffy, 1982). In Duffy (1977), five conceptions of reading were initially defined (basal text, linear skills, natural language, interest, integrated whole) and the theoretical orientations of 350 teachers assessed against these. A subset of eight teachers with a strong orientation were then observed and their practices compared to their theoretical position; four of the teachers were found to teach in ways which were consistent with their orientations, while the other four did not. In explaining the inconsistencies between stated beliefs and actual practices highlighted in this study, the influence of intervening contextual factors was highlighted – mandated curricula, resources, time and student abilities were all seen to be factors which impinged on the extent to which teachers taught reading in a manner aligned to their theoretical beliefs. Duffy and Anderson (1982) reported similar findings at the end of a three year project; they found that teachers' classroom decisions in teaching reading were not influenced predominantly by their theoretical orientation but by pressures in the instructional context; for example, maintaining a smooth activity flow emerged as a main concern. It is worth noting here that despite an initial interest in teachers' beliefs, it was *knowledge structures* that emerged in time as the focus of the work on reading instruction of Duffy and colleagues. See, for example, Roehler *et al.* (1988), who argue that

> we moved from the study of beliefs and implicit theories to a study of knowledge structures because there appears to be a difference between how beliefs and theories influence practice and how knowledge structures influence practice. Our research, as well as other research on teacher-thinking (Clark and Peterson 1986), indicates that beliefs and theories influence what teachers say in discussion *outside* the helter-skelter world of classroom life. When they are engaged in the real world of classroom teaching, however, teachers appear to filter their beliefs and theories through their interpretation of the experiences encountered 'in the trenches' (Duffy and Anderson 1984). Knowledge structures, we believe, are the representative products of teachers' attempts to make sense of the experiences they encounter in classrooms. Consequently, in real classrooms it is how the context shapes teachers' organization of knowledge, rather than the teacher's

beliefs or theory, which most immediately influences teacher thought and decision-making.

(Roehler *et al.*, 1988: 160)

This distinction between beliefs and knowledge structures, then, provides another way for us to consider the fact that teachers' stated beliefs and their classroom practices are not always congruent. I return to the study of knowledge structures in Chapter 9 where a research method called concept mapping will be discussed.

Returning to the focus of this section, several other studies have reported a lack of consistency among the beliefs and practices of teachers in reading instruction. Davis, Konopak and Readence (1993), for example, investigated the beliefs and practices in reading instruction of two elementary-school teachers in the USA. They collected data through the profiling instruments of Kinzer, described above, but supplemented these through observations, document analysis and interviews. The relationship found between the two teachers' beliefs and instructional practices varied significantly; although they shared a reader-based view of reading (i.e. one that emphasized the use of students' prior knowledge in constructing meaning), in one case the teacher's practices were not aligned with this theoretical orientation, focusing more on activities which reflected a text-based orientation. Thus, in this study, although the teachers' beliefs did affect their decision-making, other factors often exerted a stronger influence on these decisions. The environmental realities of the school and classroom were, once again, seen to militate against teachers' personally held belief systems. Factors influencing instructional practices were state and local district requirements (e.g. official reading tests), colleagues and 'varying social, psychological and environmental realities of the participants' respective schools that either created an opportunity for or constrained the two teachers from implementing their reader-based beliefs about reading' (p. 117). Beach (1994) also explained differences in the practices of teachers with similar beliefs in terms of the differing instructional contexts the teachers worked in. Wilson, Konopak and Readence (1992) also found inconsistencies in the theoretical beliefs and practices in reading instruction of a teacher. They suggested that in reporting their theoretical beliefs, teachers are expressing a view of what reading instruction *should* be like, rather than what actually occurs. This distinction reminds us of that made in Basturkmen *et al.* (2004), who explained inconsistencies between the beliefs and practices of teachers in grammar teaching in terms of tensions between their theoretical and practical knowledge (see Chapter 4). It is clear that, where cognitions are being assessed through surveys and similar instruments, caution is required in assuming that teachers are providing an account of actual instructional processes; arguably, the only satisfactory way for teachers to do this is through the act of teaching itself (i.e. practical knowledge may not lend itself to codification in the form of responses to theoretical profiles).

In contrast to the conclusions cited so far here, there is also evidence that teachers' theoretical orientations to reading are consistent with their classroom practices. Olson and Singer (1994) used a set of self-report instruments — including the TORP and Conceptual Framework of Reading Interview described above — together with classroom observations to analyse the beliefs and practices in teaching reading of 20 teachers in the USA. Their conclusion was that 'teachers have belief systems that influence their teaching and those beliefs are generally consistent with classroom practice' (p. 106). Richardson *et al.* (1991) also present evidence to counter the generally prevalent view that beliefs and practices in reading instruction are not congruent. They studied 39 elementary school teachers in the USA using interviews and observations. They focused their attention on four specific aspects of reading: teachers' use of basal readers, their consideration of students' background knowledge, their use of oral or silent reading and the teaching of vocabulary. Through ethnographic interviews and classroom observations, the researchers found that they were able to establish connections between teachers' beliefs about reading and these teachers' actual classroom practices. For example, most teachers were found to believe in a skills-oriented text-based orientation to reading and implemented such an orientation in practice. The study concluded that 'for most cases, practices could be quite accurately predicted from belief interviews' (p. 575). This study stands out in its rejection of the profiling instruments which have dominated research in reading instruction in the USA. (Muchmore, 1994 is another example of such work, surveying over 1,200 reading teachers.) In fact, it is argued that these instruments may be partly the cause of the lack of congruence between beliefs and practices reported in the studies that utilize them. This reflects the view that beliefs may not lend themselves to accurate study via paper and pencil measures and that, as Richardson et al. argue, 'an understanding of a teacher's practices, and potential changes in those practices, is enhanced by observations of the teacher in combination with the elicitation of the teacher's verbal commentary on beliefs and practices' (p. 561).

Overall, then, when we consider research on the relationship between beliefs and practices in L1 reading instruction, the picture, as reviews by Fang (1996a) and Cummins, Cheek and Lindsey (2004) have concluded, remains unclear. It would seem, though, given our current understandings of teacher cognition, that studies of theoretical orientations which rely exclusively on profiling instruments are unlikely to provide significant insights into the relationship between teachers' cognitions and practices in reading instruction; similarly, studies relying on such instruments which conclude that teachers are inconsistent (often in a negative sense) should also be viewed critically. What such studies are unable to capture is the manner in which instruction is shaped through the interaction between cognition and context; in some cases, the latter may outweigh the former (this can cause a lack of consistency among beliefs and practices), while at other times, the former prevails or the two are aligned (and teaching is thus seen to be consistent with theoretical orientations). Another key issue to emerge here concerns the nature of the beliefs that teachers report in response to different instruments; theoretical profiling instruments may elicit beliefs about what should be the case, while less structured interviews, perhaps grounded in concrete classroom events, may be better able to elicit beliefs about instruction as it actually unfolds.

Other concerns in research on teacher cognition in L1 reading

While the study of theoretical orientations and practices dominates teacher cognition research in L1 reading, a small number of studies with an alternative focus merit comment here. Wray (1988), Grisham (2000) and Maloch et al. (2003) examined the impact of teacher education on the beliefs about reading instruction of pre-service teachers, while Meloth *et al.* (1989) examined relationships between teachers' and students' conceptions of reading.

Wray (1988) used a beliefs inventory consisting of 12 statements which expressed a view of reading not supported by a psycholinguistic perspective (e.g. 'Discourage guessing. Be sure the children read carefully'). The same pre-service trainees completed this inventory in their second and fourth year of study. In the intervening period they had been exposed to psycholinguistic theories of reading in their coursework. The results were that students generally *agreed* with the statements (i.e. their beliefs were at odds with psycholinguistic theories) and a comparison of results in the second and fourth year suggested that during that time their views actually moved away from psycholinguistic theories. This was unexpected given that this theoretical position was one promoted on the course. A number of reasons were suggested to account for this lack of impact: the trainees' lack of practical teaching experience, the difficulty of translating psycholinguistic theories into statements for practice, trainees' own experiences of learning to read, and the manner in which they had observed reading being taught. Collectively, these factors may have outweighed any influence theoretical input on the course might have had (contemporary understandings of teacher cognition and teacher learning, of course, make the lack of impact found here less surprising than it was felt to be at the time; this was, though, an early study of this kind).

In contrast, Grisham (2000) used the TORP, interviews, observations and a technique called teacher storylines to study the conceptions of reading and practices of 12 pre-service teachers in the USA during their teacher education programme and into their first two years of teaching. The study found that this programme, which promoted in a coherent manner a constructivist view of reading instruction, did influence teachers' conceptions of reading in that direction. The teachers were asked, at intervals, to rate how far their beliefs and practices reflected the constructivist philosophy of the teacher education programme. The results showed that these ratings became higher (i.e. more aligned with constructivism) as the programme progressed. When the practices of these teachers were studied, it was found that the impacts of teacher education were sustained, but mitigated by the teaching culture each teacher worked in. In some cases, teachers were not able to teach reading in a manner that reflected their beliefs; influential factors in such cases were the teaching environment, students and teachers' self-confidence (a factor also highlighted in Chapter 4 in relation to the teaching of grammar). The contrasts between Wray (1988) and Grisham (2000) capture well conceptual and methodological advances in the study of the relationship between teacher education and teachers' cognitions about reading instruction; while both were interested in cognitive change over time, the latter study – with a number of data collection strategies (including observation) deployed at intervals, provides a much richer understanding of the relationships among teacher education, teacher cognition and classroom practice than the former – based on a pre-post questionnaire focusing on theoretical beliefs – was able to.

Grisham's findings about beginning teachers' experiences and cognitions in reading instruction were reflected in Maloch et al. (2003). Telephone interviews were used with 101 teachers at three points during their first year of teaching to elicit these teachers' beliefs about how best to teach reading, their students' progress and the relationship of their teacher education course and their classroom practices. Graduates from programmes recognized for their excellence in reading teacher education differed in their beliefs and reported practices to those from teacher education programmes which did not provide specialized preparation for reading instruction. In fact, graduates from the former programmes reflected in their responses characteristics generally associated with effective reading teachers, such as an understanding of their students' abilities, enthusiasm, commitment and high expectations of themselves and their students. Such characteristics were less evident in the responses of graduates from non-specialist programmes. On the basis of these findings (and while acknowledging the limitations of findings based solely on interviews), the study concludes that 'quality reading teacher preparation likely affects beginning teachers' perceptions and understandings of what it means to teach reading' (p. 450). A comparison of responses from the different interviews also suggested that the effects on beginning teachers of high-quality teacher education in reading instruction were stable over their first year of teaching.

The study by Meloth *et al.* (1989) considered not just teachers' conceptions of reading and their practices, but also the relationship between the conceptions of reading held by 18 teachers and 60 students. Through interviews, these four questions were asked to both teachers and students: (a) what does a good reader do? (b) what is the first thing you do when you read an article or a book? (c) what do you do when you do not understand a word in an article or book? and (d) what do you do when you do not understand an article, book or study? On the basis of the answers to these and other questions (teachers were asked nine additional questions), ten dimensions of reading were identified (e.g. reading involves intention/planning; reading involves effort; reading is systematic). Correlations were computed for student and teacher conceptions of reading using these dimensions and no significant relationships were found. One explanation for this finding was that teachers were not effective in communicating their concept of reading to students. Once again, therefore, as indicated by studies of grammar in Chapter 4, teachers' conceptions of an aspect of language instruction were not found to be aligned with those of their students.

Second and foreign language reading instruction

The volume of research into teacher cognition in L2/FL reading instruction (I will use FL here to refer to both of these) has, in contrast to that reviewed above, been minimal (see Table 5.2). It is difficult to find an immediate explanation for this; reading instruction is an important facet of FL learning and teaching, and it has been the focus of extensive theoretical and methodological discussion over the years; there is also, as we have seen, a strong tradition of teacher cognition research in L1 reading instruction for FL researchers to draw on. It may be the case that the teaching of reading is seen to be (in comparison, say, to teaching grammar) unproblematic and thus not a suitable object of study from a teacher cognition perspective; any such notions, though, are clearly misguided. The teaching of FL reading and the cognitions which underpin them are worthy

Table 5.2 Studies of teacher cognition in foreign language reading

Source	Focus	Context	Stage
Collie Graden (1996)	beliefs and practices in FL reading instruction.	6 secondary French and Spanish teachers in the USA	I
El-Okda (2005)	beliefs about reading	57 pre-service teachers in Oman	P
Johnson (1992b)	teachers' beliefs and practices in literacy instruction	30 ESL teachers in elementary secondary, adult and college settings in the USA	I
Meijer et al. (1999)	teachers' practical knowledge in teaching reading comprehension	13 teachers in the Netherlands – 4 mother-tongue Dutch, 3 English, 3 Latin, 2 French, 1 German	I
Meijer et al. (2001)	similarities and differences in teachers' practical knowledge about reading comprehension	69 language teachers in the Netherlands – 26 Dutch, 21 English, 9 Latin/Greek, 8 German, 5 French	I
Richards et al. (1988)	novice and experienced teachers' approaches to reading	10 trainee teachers, 10 graduate TESL teachers in Hong Kong	P/I
Tercanlioglu (2001)	pre-service teachers' views of themselves as readers and future reading teachers	132 pre-service EFL teachers in Turkey	P

issues of inquiry, and the limited amount of work available in this area is undeniably a clear gap in our understandings of FL teaching. A similar situation pertained in relation to grammar teaching until the late 1990s, yet less than a decade later a substantial body of teacher cognition research in this area now exists. It is to be hoped that similar progress in relation to the study of FL reading instruction can in time be achieved.

Turning now to the research which is available, Johnson (1992b) examined the cognitions and actual practices of ESL teachers. Drawing on the tradition of research into theoretical orientations to reading, she examined the extent to which ESL teachers possessed theoretical beliefs which reflect the methodological divisions of skill-based, rule-based and function-based approaches towards L2 teaching. She also analysed the extent to which teachers' theoretical beliefs were consistent with their practices. On the basis of theoretical profiling instruments completed by 30 teachers, she found that '. . . the majority of these ESL teachers (60%) possess clearly defined theoretical beliefs which consistently reflect one particular methodological approach to second language teaching' (p. 93). A function-based orientation towards reading instruction – emphasizing authentic language, situational contexts and meaningful communication – emerged here as the most commonly held. Both quantitative and qualitative analyses of the data obtained from the profiles and classroom observations showed that

> ESL teachers who possess clearly defined theoretical beliefs provide literacy instruction which is consistent with their theoretical orientation . . . the study supports the notion that ESL teachers teach in accordance with their theoretical beliefs and that differences in theoretical beliefs may result in differences in the nature of literacy instruction.
> (Johnson, 1992b: 101)

The study also found a relationship between years of teaching experience and teachers' theoretical orientation, with the less experienced teachers embracing the most recent, chronologically speaking, theoretical stance (i.e. functional) and the more experienced aligning themselves with the least recent (i.e. skill-based). These findings suggest that teachers' beliefs are resistant to theoretical shifts in the field and that 'the sources of ESL teachers' theoretical beliefs may stem from the methodological approaches that were prominent when they began teaching ESL' (pp. 93–4).

Collie Graden (1996) also examined the consistency between teachers' reported beliefs and their observed practices in reading instruction. Overall, her findings reflected Johnson's in that practices and beliefs were generally consistent; however, this study did highlight instances of inconsistency with regard to three beliefs the teachers held: (a) that students need frequent opportunities to read; (2) that the use of students' L1 should be minimized during reading instruction and (3) that reading aloud interferes with comprehension. Practices opposed to these beliefs were observed for each of the teachers. An analysis of teachers' comments on these practices showed that

> the most significant influence that led the teachers to compromise their beliefs on instructional decisions was the day-to-day necessity of planning activities for students who did not or could not perform according to the teachers' expectations. Other factors, although less often cited, were time constraints and lack of appropriate materials. The relative impact of the three factors on the teachers' instructional decisions was extrapolated from the comparative number of instances recorded in the data base: 24 recorded instances deal with the issue of time, 30 with materials, and 166 with concerns about students.
> (Collie Graden, 1996: 390)

In shaping the actual practices adopted in the classroom, the teachers' beliefs about the ability and motivation of their students, then, appeared to be more powerful than the beliefs held by the teachers about effective reading instruction.

Unrelated to either of the above studies on reading instruction, Tercanlioglu (2001) examined pre-service teachers' views of themselves as readers and future reading teachers. In terms of self-perception as readers, 'results revealed that respondents here are not very confident that they have the capability to read effectively' (p. 12). Moreover, this finding was stable for students at different stages of their teacher education programme (despite explicit emphasis during the programme on students' self-development as readers). With respect to self-perceptions as future teachers of FL reading, the study reports that the pre-service teachers themselves were not very motivated to teach reading. This work signals once again the role which self-perception and confidence may play in influencing teachers' work (though in this case actual teaching practices were not examined). This paper is also one of the few that consider FL reading in a pre-service context. El-Okda (2005) is another; in eliciting student teachers' beliefs about reading, he found that these reflected positions not in keeping with contemporary understandings of reading instruction. For example, the trainees believed that reading aloud was a useful strategy because it developed children's pronunciation and that the role of modelled reading by the teacher was also to help children improve their pronunciation. Making these beliefs explicit through teacher education, it was argued here, was an important first step in enabling student teachers to modify these.

As part of a paper I discussed earlier in relation to comparisons between more and less experienced teachers, Richards, Li and Tang (1998) compared how trainee and graduate ESL teachers with on average five years' experience approached the planning (but not the teaching) of a reading lesson using a provided text. A number of generic pedagogical differences were found in terms of, for example, the time spent planning (about one hour for the novices, 40 minutes for the graduates). With specific reference to the teaching of reading, though, the novices were characterized by a narrow conception of reading (e.g. focused on understanding vocabulary), while the graduates demonstrated through their planning a broader view of what reading and teaching reading involve (e.g. by encouraging learners to think about the content of the text and the characters in it). It is difficult to draw any generalizations about less and more experienced teachers of reading from this study, though it is clear from this work that experience enabled the graduates to discern learning potential in instructional materials in a way that the novices were not able to.

Important insights into teacher cognition in reading instruction to 16–18-year-olds come from the work in the Netherlands of Meijer, Verloop and Beijaard (1999, 2001) (the majority of the teachers in these studies taught foreign languages, though some teaching mother-tongue Dutch also participated). Using the notion of practical knowledge as the conceptual basis of their work, and through concept mapping and interview techniques, the researchers identified six categories of teachers' practical knowledge about reading comprehension, shown in Table 5.3 (these categories overlap in many ways with those originally proposed by Shulman, 1987). By examining patterns among these

Table 5.3 Categories of teachers' practical knowledge about teaching reading comprehension (adapted from Meijer, 1999: 49)

Category	Description
Subject-matter knowledge	Knowledge of reading comprehension in the specific language-subject, not directly related to teaching
Student knowledge	Knowledge about 16–18-year-old students in general, not directly related to reading comprehension
Knowledge of student learning and understanding	Knowledge of the learning and understanding of 16–18-year-old students with respect to reading comprehension
Knowledge of purposes	Importance of, and goals for teaching reading comprehension
Curriculum knowledge	Texts and materials used in lessons on reading comprehension
Knowledge of instructional techniques	Design, preparation and structure of lessons in reading comprehension

categories in teachers' concept maps and interview responses, they defined a theoretical typology which describes three types of practical knowledge about teaching reading comprehension (Meijer et al., 1999). The first type is characterized by a focus on subject-matter knowledge (i.e. the other categories of knowledge are defined with reference to the subject matter of reading comprehension); the second by a focus on student knowledge and the third by a focus on knowledge of student learning and understanding. Each position reflects a distinct orientation to the way reading instruction to 16–18-year-olds is conceived of by teachers.

Building on this work, these researchers conducted a quantitative study of similarities and differences in teachers' practical knowledge about reading: 69 teachers of reading comprehension to 16–18-year-olds completed a questionnaire in which they expressed their degree of agreement/disagreement with 167 statements. The statements in the questionnaire were based on data emerging from the earlier qualitative study and related to the categories of practical knowledge identified there. A statistical analysis of the results showed that only 22 items on the questionnaire (13.1 per cent of the total) could be identified as shared knowledge among the teachers, leading to the conclusion that 'no large shared-knowledge base could be found in the teachers' practical knowledge' (p. 177).

Subsequent analyses of the patterns in these differences in teachers' practical knowledge, however, suggested there were four clusters of teachers with relatively similar practical knowledge. The largest of these, called the *segmental view on teaching reading comprehension* (accounting for 25 of the 69 teachers) was characterized by teachers' concerns for the difficulties students encountered while reading and with the small elements of reading comprehension. The *low appreciation for reading comprehension* was the second most common cluster (20 teachers, who generally questioned the importance of reading comprehension); the *large element view on reading comprehension* and *teaching reading comprehension by relating texts and students* clusters each contained 11 teachers. These clusters pointed to the existence of some shared knowledge among the teachers, despite the large differences overall in their practical knowledge (as defined by their questionnaire responses) about reading comprehension. This study again points to the potential which the analysis of collective cognitions among teachers may have for expanding our understandings of what teachers think and do (see also Andrews, 2003a; Breen *et al.*, 2001, discussed earlier, for similar attention to shared cognitions). It must be pointed out, though, that neither of the two Netherlands studies discussed here report on teachers' actual practices, and the relationship between teaching behaviour and practical knowledge as elicited in these studies was not examined. This work, though, did have an observational element focusing on teachers' interactive cognitions in teaching reading comprehension and which is described in detail in Meijer (1999).

Overall, then, there is a marked difference in the volume of research available on teacher cognition in L1 and FL reading instruction. The former comprises a tradition stretching back some 30 years; it is marked by a well-defined research agenda – in particular in relation to the congruence between teachers' beliefs and practices in reading instruction and to the impact of teacher education on reading instruction – and by a recurring set of methodological tools, especially in relation to the measurement of teachers' theoretical orientations to reading (although the ecological validity of the profiling instruments used to measure these orientations has been questioned). In contrast, the limited number of studies in FL contexts marks this out as an underdeveloped domain of inquiry in which substantive findings are scarce and methodological debate non-existent. The work available, though, does illustrate ways in which concepts (e.g. teacher knowledge) and methods (e.g. theoretical profiling instruments) developed in L1 contexts can be usefully applied to study of teacher cognition in FL reading instruction. Much more work of this kind is required.

First language writing instruction

Teacher cognition in writing instruction has been the focus of less research than reading in both L1 and FL contexts. Table 5.4 lists studies of teacher cognition in L1 writing. These fall into two groups; the larger group of six studies represent a key research concern in this line of inquiry – pre-service and in-service teachers' conceptions of writing in the context of teacher education (see also Lapp and Flood, 1985, for another study in this vein); the remaining study considers the relationship between teachers' conceptions of writing and those of their learners. All have been conducted in the USA.

In the context of pre-service teacher education, Norman and Spencer (2005) analysed autobiographies written by 59 teachers to investigate the conceptions these teachers held of themselves as writers. Four themes emerged here. Firstly, most teachers had positive views of themselves as writers. Secondly, there was a general preference among the teachers for personal and creative forms of writing (e.g. poetry). Thirdly, respondents identified several characteristics of teachers and instruction which had contributed positively to their own development as writers, and to their current beliefs about writing:

> Former teachers who used positive reinforcement to motivate were consistently credited with building preservice teachers' positive

Table 5.4 Studies of teacher cognition in first language writing

Source	Focus	Context	Stage
Fang (1996)	teachers' and students' conceptions of writing	1 elementary teacher in the USA and 15 students	I
Chambless & Bass (1996)	student teachers' attitudes to writing	pre-service teachers in the USA	P
Florio-Ruane & Lensmire (1990)	pre-service teachers' views of writing instruction	6 pre-service teachers on a writing methods course in the USA	P
Gomez (1990)	learning to teach writing	Prospective secondary English teachers on teacher education programmes in the USA. 31 surveyed, 8 interviewed	P
McCarthey (1992)	influence of staff development programme on teachers' conceptions of writing	3 elementary teachers in the USA	I
Mosenthal (1995)	impact of an in-service course on teacher's views of writing and writing instruction	1 teacher on in-service writing instruction programme in the USA	I
Norman & Spencer (2005)	pre-service teachers' views of themselves as writers	59 pre-service elementary school teachers on a teacher education programme in the USA	P

self-concepts. Additionally, they held that writing instruction should provide students with choice, that writing assignments are more meaningful when connected with students' interests and backgrounds, and writers and their writing should be supported with positive feedback. The powerful role of teachers and their instructional decisions in shaping writers' self-perceptions was consistently recognized across the participants.

(Norman and Spencer, 2005: 36)

The fourth theme to emerge here was the interplay between the beliefs held by pre-service teachers about the nature of writing and their beliefs about the value of writing instruction. Thus, the many teachers who believed that writing was a talent that not everyone had or could develop were less inclined to believe that instruction could have a positive influence on writing development. For these teachers, effective writing instruction consisted of providing learners with opportunities to write and encouragement to do so.

Both Gomez (1990) and Florio-Ruane and Lensmire (1990) examined changes in conceptions of writing instruction among prospective teachers of English. In the first of these studies, the participants were found to have positive initial beliefs about writing and about themselves as writers; however, it also emerged that such positive dispositions were

> not sufficient to bridge the gap between knowing the discipline of English and sharing one's understanding with diverse secondary school students. It is clear that personally valuing writing in different modes of discourse and for different audiences than one's peers is not sufficient to enable prospective teachers to create classrooms where they enable diverse secondary learners to have similar experiences.

(Gomez, 1990: 11)

A positive attitude to writing, then, though clearly desirable, was not itself facilitative of writing instruction. Prior to becoming engaged in classroom instruction, these pre-service teachers were characterized by a range of other cognitions; they embraced the idealistic notion that all learners could and would want to learn to write; they held a conception of writing as a process involving writing and rewriting; and their main concern earlier in their programmes was with developing the subject-matter knowledge (e.g. of grammar) which they felt was required for them to teach writing effectively.

Over a period of around eight months, though, evidence of significant changes in the pre-service teachers' conceptions of writing instruction emerged. Two main changes were identified. Firstly, their concerns shifted from subject-matter knowledge to knowledge of discipline and classroom management; many of the teachers had not anticipated that these issues would be central to their ability to teach writing effectively. Secondly, the teachers' previously clear belief that all learners can benefit from writing instruction based on a process model was shaken by their experiences of having to cope with a wide range of learners, including groups who were not motivated or easy to manage.

In analysing these changes the paper concludes that 'a set of interrelated features of the school context and features of the teacher education programme combined to alter or challenge the teachers' beliefs' (Gomez, 1990: 19). For example, beginning teachers were subject to performance measurement evaluations which may have encouraged them to teach in a manner that was at odds with the process approach to writing advocated by their teacher education programme. This study illustrates clearly that, even when teacher education promotes a consistent pedagogical message which teachers embrace, factors in institutions and classrooms, such as learners and policies, exert an extremely powerful influence on what teachers do and on how their beliefs develop. This study also offers further evidence of the particularly powerful impact that the practicum experience can have on pre-service teachers' cognitions.

Florio-Ruane and Lensmire (1990) tried to modify the conceptions of writing and writing instruction held by pre-service teachers on a writing methods course. At the start of this course the authors found that the teachers' understandings of writing and how it is learned and taught were very limited and the course tried to challenge these conceptions and to promote change in relation to three key issues. The first was a move from formal to functional notions of writing. Teachers' prior conceptions of writing instruction were that it involved the teacher in explaining and modelling correct text structures, which students would then imitate. The course tried to replace this view with one that stressed writing functions – the idea that, driven by a purpose, students were to be encouraged to discover the structure of texts themselves. The second issue where change was promoted related to a move from individual to cooperative work in learning to write. The course promoted the view that writing is best learned and practised in contexts which encouraged the sharing of written drafts. This idea was at odds with the conventional, teacher-centred notions of classroom organization held by the teachers. The third area targeted for change concerned teachers' understandings of how children learn to write (e.g. promoting the view that children attempt to make meaning through text).

Of the three areas where change was promoted, success was registered only in one; the teachers resisted both a move towards functionally oriented writing and the introduction of collaborative learning. They did, however, develop and embrace alternative conceptions of how children learn to write. In reflecting on these outcomes, the authors note that resistance to change was greatest where the teachers felt that the changes being promoted would, by suggesting changes to conventional classroom roles and relationships, make it harder for them to control instruction. The changes which were resisted also related to aspects of writing instruction where teachers' apprenticeship of observation would have had a powerful effect on their prior notions; this study then, provides further evidence of the challenges which altering such notions through teacher education poses. In contrast, the fact the teachers accepted new ways of thinking about children learning to write suggests that strong notions related to this issue had not been developed through their prior experience. Also, accepting new ways of thinking about children perhaps represented less of a threat to these teachers than did changes to their own roles in teaching writing. Overall, then, the course had mixed success in impacting on teachers' conceptions of writing and writing instruction, though it was successful in enabling them to revise their understandings of how children write. The experiences of this study can be contrasted with those of Chambless and Bass (1996), who found that, by providing student teachers with both formal instruction in process writing and positive experiences in planning and implementing process writing activities, they were able to bring about positive changes in the trainees' attitudes towards writing.

McCarthey (1992) and Mosenthal (1995) were also interested in the effects of teacher education on the conceptions of writing held by teachers, this time in an in-service context. McCarthey used semi-structured interviews with three elementary teachers who had attended a particular staff development programme – the Teachers College Writing Project. This programme consisted of workshops and classroom-based training over the course of a year and reflected the following views:

> Writing is assumed to be purposeful in the Teachers College Writing Project; students should be involved in what real authors do, including choosing their own topics to write about, recording their ideas, and making plans. The Writing Project emphasizes introducing children to different genres of literature and providing anecdotes about authors to provide models for students' own writing. Writing is considered a process of drafting ideas, revising and rethinking, sharing the drafts with others, and editing for publication. Very young children are involved in the process of writing through drawing pictures and labelling those pictures; the project encourages invented spelling and writing sounds as they are heard. The major goals of the Project include getting students to communicate through writing, to become empowered through writing, and to develop an appreciation for literature.
>
> (McCarthey, 1992: 2)

The main finding of this study was that teachers' conceptions of writing showed definite changes in the direction promoted by the programme. These changes were specifically apparent in relation to teachers' conceptions of teacher-student relationships, their views of the goals of writing instruction, and in their classroom practices. Thus all teachers embraced the notion that children, rather than teachers, should be in control of the writing process. In terms of goals for writing, one teacher, for example, at the start of the programme held a clear product orientation to writing in which the goal was to produce accurate text on a set topic; through the programme, this teacher 'came to embrace a process approach to writing in which she focused on ideas, clarity of written expression, and the importance of the writer communicating with an audience. Her conception also included an aesthetic appreciation for literature' (p. 11). There was also evidence of a movement in the direction promoted by the programme in the teachers' classroom practices. For example, one teacher who initially conducted explicit whole-class instruction on the use of apostrophes changed her views and practices about this aspect of writing, limiting attention to it to individual student conferences and to students who she felt were developmentally ready to focus on language in this manner. Her general view at the end of the programme was that students would learn apostrophes through reading and exposure to literature.

The same teacher development programme was the context for Mosenthal's (1995) study of the changes in conceptions of writing and writing instruction of one teacher. Once again, interviews were used, this time at the start and end of the programme. Developments in the teacher's conceptions and practices were, also once more, reported in the direction promoted by the training programme. In this case, at the start of the programme the teacher was struggling with, but still not free of, notions of writing which emphasize products and textual accuracy. Following the training programme, the teacher embraced the notion of genre in writing and used it to define the purposes of writing; writing was subsequently conceived of as the process of identifying one's intentions and working to close the gap between these and written expression. This study again highlights how changes in conceptions of writing and in pedagogical practices may be closely aligned.

In addition to the studies of conceptions of writing in L1 settings already discussed here, Fang (1996b) examined the relationship between teachers' and learners' conceptions of good writing. One elementary teacher and 15 students participated in the study, which collected data through interviews. The teacher's view of good writing was that it

> should simultaneously address substance, mechanics, and style. According to her, a good piece of writing uses transitional words, sequences right . . . has extended vocabulary, is not mundane or

sloppy, contains no misspelt words, and paints a vivid picture. In addition, it must show effort and be able to jump out at you.

(Fang, 1996b: 251–2)

The students' views were closely aligned to those of the teacher; all 15 stated that a good piece of writing should be detailed, neat, correct and be interesting. In highlighting the similarity between the views of the teacher and the students, Fang notes that 'the vocabulary these pupils used in describing the criteria of good writing bears striking resemblance to that of their teacher's' (p. 253). This study concluded that teachers' beliefs on writing have a considerable impact on the way writing is perceived by learners. The similarities found here between teacher and student cognitions contrast with findings of similar studies in the context of grammar teaching; as we saw earlier (see Chapter 4), in that context teachers and students have been found to hold quite different beliefs.

Second and foreign language writing instruction

Table 5.5 lists studies which have investigated teacher cognition in writing instruction in foreign language teaching. The range of studies available here is again limited, though there is some overlap in the themes explored.

Burns (1992) studied the beliefs and writing instruction practices of six teachers in beginning ESL classes in Australia. She found 'an extremely complex and interrelated network of underlying beliefs, clustering around five major areas which appeared to influence the instructional practices and approaches adopted by the teachers' (p. 59). These were (1) the nature of language as it relates to beginning language learning; (2) the relationship between written and spoken language; (3) the nature of beginning language learning and strategies relevant to language learning at this stage; (4) learner characteristics, their ability to learn and their ability to learn English and (5) the nature of the language classroom and the teacher's role within it. Differences

Table 5.5 Studies of teacher cognition in foreign language writing

Source	Focus	Context	Stage
Burns (1992)	teacher's beliefs and practices in writing instruction	6 teachers in beginning ESL classes in Australia	I
Cumming (1990)	decision-making of novice and expert teachers in rating written compositions	7 novice and 6 expert ESL teachers in Canada	P/I
Diab (2005)	teachers' and student beliefs about feedback on writing	1 university ESL teacher and 2 students	I
Scott (1995)	changes in attitudes to writing instruction	7 Spanish and French high school teachers in the USA	I
Sengupta & Xiao (2002)	development of personal theories of ESL writing	3 teachers in Hong Kong	I
Shi & Cumming (1995)	post-lesson thinking and beliefs about ESL writing instruction	5 experienced university ESL instructors in Canada	I
Tsui (1996)	change in a teacher's approach to writing instruction	1 ESL teacher in Hong Kong	I

in the beliefs teachers held about these issues were reflected in differences in their practices in teaching writing.

Sharing this interest in cognitions and practices in L2 writing instruction, Shi and Cumming (1995) conducted an extensive study of the post-lesson thinking and beliefs of five experienced university ESL instructors in Canada through a series of 48 interviews over two years.

These were supplemented by classroom observations. The study also examined the manner in which three of the five teachers introduced an innovation into their practices for teaching writing – a strategy called 'thinking prompts' which consisted of a set of questions which students can use to guide themselves while they are writing (e.g. 'Is this the right word for this expression? Possible words are . . .' or 'How do I say it in my language? Does it make sense in English?').

The post-lesson interviews examined (a) the aspects of writing the teachers focused on in the lesson, (b) the organization of the class, (c) students' performance and (d) the teachers' evaluation of the lesson. All the teachers commented mostly on the first of these categories, although there was variation among the teachers in terms of which particular aspect of writing they referred to most – language use, rhetorical organization, composing processes or ideas and content. However, the teachers using the innovation of thinking prompts emphasized composing processes more than those who did not. The authors are careful not to imply that the innovation was the cause of this attention to composing processes; in fact they admit that 'the extent to which the instructors did or did not attend to composing processes in their interviews may relate more distinctly to their existing pedagogical beliefs . . . than to the nature of our experimental intervention' (p. 96).

In terms of the teachers' conceptions of writing, the study suggests that each teacher displayed a distinct set of personal conceptions about second language writing pedagogy. These are defined in terms of core beliefs reiterated by teachers throughout their interviews, typical pedagogical practices that they tended to reflect on during the interviews and the criteria that the teachers said they used to evaluate their students and the effectiveness of their teaching. Teachers' conceptions of writing in relation to these issues demonstrated stability over the course of this study.

The way teachers reacted to the innovation they were encouraged to implement also varied. Two of the teachers had reservations about the thinking prompts and were guided in their teaching more by their existing beliefs about writing than by the innovation; in one case, the teacher resisted the prompts to the extent that these often did not feature in her lessons at all; in a second case, the teacher used a form of the prompts which she felt was more useful but which did not follow the pattern suggested in the innovation (i.e. she changed the way the guiding questions were worded). The third teacher implementing the innovation did not attempt to accommodate them within her existing writing practices, as the other two did; rather she set aside specific time during the lesson to implement the innovation, treating it as a kind of subject matter which needed to be covered.

Two implications arising from this study are worth highlighting here. One is that it provides support for the view that the knowledge underpinning writing instruction is most appropriately conceived of in personal practical terms. Secondly, the study sheds light on the processes of innovation in writing instruction. The teachers who were implementing the innovation interpreted and responded to it in individual ways which related to their existing beliefs and practices. One teacher accepted it more than others because it seemed to fit in with her existing stance; another teacher accepted those aspects of the innovation which were aligned with her beliefs but ignored others; and the third teacher resisted the innovation because she found it hard to accommodate it within her existing, textual accuracy orientation to writing instruction. On the basis of these findings, the introduction of innovation in writing instruction, then, 'is not a uniform process but rather is construed uniquely by individual instructors, who may accommodate or resist it in terms of their personal beliefs, founded on years of previous experience, reflection, and information' (p. 104).

The introduction of an innovation in writing instruction was also studied by Tsui (1996). She examined the experience over two and a half years of an EFL teacher in Hong Kong who, dissatisfied with a product approach to writing instruction, introduced process writing into her classroom. Despite the positive reactions of the teacher and the students to this innovation, process writing was problematic because students were writing fewer compositions than other classes (process writing was more time-consuming) and students were making more grammatical mistakes than before. (This concerned the teacher because accuracy was important in the public examinations students would be sitting.) Wider support for the process approach was also not provided by the teacher's head of department. Consequently, the teacher reverted to a product approach, although in time she eventually implemented a modified version of process writing which was not as time-consuming as the one she had first tried to use. This study illustrates changes in the teacher's cognitions and practices over time, and further highlights the manner in which institutional and curricular factors can constrain teachers' capacity to implement practices they feel are desirable.

Yet a further perspective on teacher cognition in foreign language writing instruction is provided by Scott and Rogers (1995), who measured change in teachers' conceptions of writing by administering an 20-item attitude survey before and after a nine-week training programme. The participants, seven Spanish and French high-school teachers in the USA, were also asked to score sample compositions during the first and last of the three workshops which made up the programme; in between workshops the teachers tried out in their classrooms ideas related to process writing and holistic writing assessments which were being promoted on the course. A comparison of the results on the attitude surveys showed that in the first set of responses 58.5 per cent of the attitudes expressed were aligned with the principles and practices promoted on the course, while the corresponding figure at the end of the programme was 89 per cent. Changes in the way teachers assessed the sample compositions before and after the course were also noted, with a move towards the implementation of a more holistic approach. The authors concluded that these findings represented a significant change in teachers' conceptions of writing. As always, caution is required in interpreting these findings, as questionnaire responses may not always be good indicators of changes in practices and/or of deep, long-lasting cognitive change.

An interest in how teachers assess L2 writing is also reflected in the work of Cumming (1990), who compared the decision-making processes of novice and experienced raters of ESL compositions. The comparisons were based both on the actual ratings the teachers gave the compositions as well as on think-aloud protocols of the processes the teachers engaged in while making their decisions (see Chapter 6 for think-aloud protocols). In terms of the actual ratings, there was a statistically significant difference between the novices and the experts in relation to the criteria of rhetorical organization and content (in both cases the novices' ratings were higher); there was no such difference, however, in the way the two groups rated language use.

Twenty-eight distinct decision-making behaviours were identified from the raters' verbal reports of their thinking and these were classified into two broad strategies – *interpretation strategies* used in reading the text (e.g. scan whole text to obtain initial impression) and *judgement strategies* used to evaluate the text (e.g. assess coherence). Significant differences were found among novices and experts in relation to some specific strategies; for example, experts paid more attention than novices to analysing the rhetorical structures of the texts. Overall, though, there was no significant difference in the frequencies with which these strategies were used by novice and expert raters. Thus, any overall differences in the rating behaviours of the two groups were qualitative rather than quantitative. As Cumming explains,

> expert teachers appear to have a much fuller mental representation of 'the problem' of evaluating student compositions, using a large number of very diverse criteria, self-control strategies, and knowledge sources to read and judge students' texts. Novice teachers tend to evaluate compositions with only a few of these component skills and criteria.
>
> (Cumming, 1990: 42)

There were clear differences in the way novices and experts responded to and made use of language errors in reaching a judgement about the quality of the writing. Novices focused more on such errors in isolation of other components such as overall meaning and rhetorical structure. Novices (in five cases) also made widespread use of editing strategies, actually correcting the language errors they noticed (there was no need for this, as the writers were not going to receive feedback). The experts, in contrast, noticed errors and classified them to inform their overall judgements about the writing; they did so, however, while retaining a focus on the content and organization of the text. This study is another example of the contribution which teacher cognition research can make to a better understanding of language education; it targets a specific task common to the work of language teachers worldwide (i.e. rating written work) and investigates the cognitive processes teachers engage in while completing this task. The context of this study is more closely aligned with that which pertains where written work is being marked anonymously (for a similar study in the context of large-scale testing, see Lumley, 2002); additional factors, though, will certainly come into play in situations where teachers are assessing the written work of students that they know personally. Further research of this kind in such contexts is thus needed.

The research on L1 and FL writing instruction I have considered here reflects distinct areas of concern. The L1 research has focused almost exclusively on teachers' conceptions of writing, in pre-service and in-service contexts, and on how these conceptions develop during teacher education programmes. The results point to varying degrees of success in promoting change in the desired direction, although there is evidence that programmes with a coherent perspective and which provide opportunities for teachers to explore writing instruction in their own classroom may be more successful in this respect. Even where such conditions apply, though, we have also seen that teachers may resist change if it threatens to disturb ingrained notions of what writing instruction, and indeed teaching more generally, involves. The L1 studies have also highlighted a range of writing-related cognitions which impinge on teachers' pedagogy; conceptions about the nature of writing, its role in life generally, its forms, functions purposes, how it is learned and how it is taught all interact – as always, with contextual factors in schools and classrooms – to shape what teachers do.

The FL research shows limited attention to the development of cognitions about writing instruction during teacher education (Sengupta and Xiao, 2002, though, discuss the development of teachers' personal theories about writing); it has focused, rather, on teachers' decision-making in rating written compositions, the nature of teachers' practices and cognitions in writing instruction, and on the implementation of pedagogical innovations in teaching writing (additionally Diab, 2005 has compared ESL teacher and student beliefs about feedback on writing, reporting a degree of mismatch between the two). These studies highlight a range of orientations to writing instruction which may shape what teachers do; they also highlight the challenges involved in implementing innovations in the writing classroom; even where the teacher is committed to the innovation, pressures from students and the educational system more generally (e.g. exam requirements) may limit the degree to which innovative practices can be sustained. In the case of in-service teachers who are being asked to adopt an innovation in teaching writing, uptake may vary from general rejection to modified forms of acceptance depending on the extent to which the new practices are seen by teachers to be compatible with their current beliefs and practices.

Teacher cognition in literacy

In the third and final section of this chapter I will consider studies of language teacher cognition which define their focus as being on literacy, rather than specifically on reading or writing. The studies I include here are listed in Table 5.6. They were all conducted in L1 English language education contexts and all but one of these studies

Table 5.6 Studies of teacher cognition in literacy

Source	Focus	Context	Stage
Linek et al. (1999)	beliefs about literacy of teachers in different teacher education programmes	case studies of 3 pre-service programmes in the USA (7, 25 and 8 participants respectively)	P
McCutchen et al. (2002)	teacher knowledge, classroom practice and student learning in beginning literacy	44 teachers and 779 kindergarten and first-grade students in the USA	I
Muchmore (2001)	practices and beliefs in literacy instruction	1 experienced high-school teacher of English in the USA	I
Poulson et al. (2001)	teachers' theoretical orientations towards literacy	225 British primary-school teachers	I
Wing (1989)	teachers' and pupils' conceptions of reading and writing	2 directors of preschool programmes and 10 children from each programme in the USA	I

took place in the USA. There is little here in terms of overlap and replication; each study has specific orientations and concerns, as the discussion below illustrates.

Wing (1989) compared the conceptions of literacy held by directors of two preschool programmes and those of ten children from each programme. Through interviews, observations and the analysis of literacy materials, the study highlighted how each school had a particular philosophy regarding reading and writing. In one school this was a mastery of skills/text-based orientation and in the other a holistic/reader-based orientation. Interviews indicated that these philosophies were reflected in the ways the children in each school talked about reading and writing. For example, in the school which embraced a mastery of skills and text-based view of reading, children talked about reading as 'sounding out words' and writing as 'copying letters'. Children in the school which promoted a holistic/text-based view of reading and writing, in contrast, talked about reading as 'looking at books' and writing as 'writing a story'. The conclusion of the study was that 'teachers' beliefs and instructional decisions also influence preschool-age children's conceptions of reading and writing' (p. 71). Fang (1996b), which we discussed above, reached similar conclusions in relation to the teaching of writing (Meloth *et al.*, 1989, though, did not).

A very different investigation of teacher cognition in literacy instruction is provided by Muchmore (2001), who conducted a narrative study of one high-school English teacher's beliefs and practices over a five-year period. Using interviews, observations and conversations with the teacher and her acquaintances, the study highlighted the manner in which the teacher's beliefs about literacy 'stemmed from her personal life experience and from her career-long observations of children and how they learn – rather than directly from formal theories of literacy' (p. 103). There is no suggestion here, though, that formal theory did not play a role in shaping the teacher's beliefs. Earlier in her career, she had been influenced by theories learned through teacher education. However, the study found that 'many of these beliefs were superficial and short-lived. She discarded them rather quickly after trying to put them into practice and not being satisfied with the results' (p. 103). Formal knowledge about literacy acquired early in the teacher's career, then, (e.g. regarding a mastery of skills approach to literacy) was in time replaced by insights developed through experience. Her key beliefs about literacy at the time of the study were that it was a tool for communication, a means of self-discovery, and that children should have some say in the choice of topics for literacy work. These beliefs were reflected in the literacy practices observed during the study. This study also argues for the importance of narrative approaches to studying beliefs about literacy, in contrast to the survey methods which dominate, as we have seen in this chapter, research into this issue. In this sense, this work echoes the methodological concerns raised earlier by Richardson *et al.* (1991), who also argued for the need for more qualitative understandings of teachers' practices and beliefs in literacy instruction.

In the context of teacher education, Linek *et al.* (1999) examined the literacy beliefs of pre-service teachers on different types of programmes. Three types of programmes were compared: a wholly campus-based course with no field experience; a course combining campus based work and unsupervised field experience; and a field-based course which involved two full days of teaching each week. Data were collected through interviews at the start, middle and end of the semester during which each course was taught.

These data pointed to widespread changes in teachers' beliefs about literacy, literacy instruction and assessment. For example, literacy was initially viewed as a set of skills to be learned hierarchically (e.g. letter, word, sentence); after the courses literacy was viewed as the process of engaging in reading and writing and the development of appropriate strategies for doing so. To take another example, while the predominant view of assessment at the start of the course was a means of identifying deficits in knowledge and understanding, at the end of the course assessment was seen as an opportunity to demonstrate progress. Shifts in pre-service teachers' beliefs were also evidenced in relation to a range of other issues in literacy, such as teachers' theories of instruction (from teacher-centred to learner-centred) and instructional strategies (from rote learning to strategic learning).

This study also examined the factors which the pre-service teachers felt had promoted changes in their beliefs about literacy. While some common influences on all three courses were identified, in the course having no field experience cognitive and affective factors from in-class activities were the greatest influence on teachers' beliefs. In the two other programmes field experience was the most influential factor. Thus, while the study provides evidence that all three programmes impacted on the teachers' beliefs, those involving field experience – hands-on planning, teaching and being part of a school – seemed to provide greater opportunities for these beliefs to be challenged and tested and, according to the researchers, to

> provide the critical follow-up needed to actually transform preservice teachers' beliefs in the longer term. Applying beliefs and practices in authentic settings allows preservice teachers to confirm and strengthen the philosophies that they begin to develop in university-based methods courses.
> (Linek, 1999: 381)

The conclusion of this study is that field experience, given its potential to impact on beliefs in the manner shown here, is a vital component of pre-service teacher education programmes.

Continuing the tradition of research into theoretical orientations discussed earlier, Poulson *et al.* (2001) used an instrument derived from the TORP (DeFord, 1985) to measure the orientations towards literacy of 225 British primary school teachers identified as successful in teaching literacy. The instrument elicited both theoretical views and views about the utility of different types of literacy activities. The literacy teachers were

> more positively oriented to whole language theoretical positions which promoted the creation of meaning in reading and writing in the following ways: a strong emphasis on helping learners to understand text; the use of authentic texts and activities in teaching reading; a focus on process in writing; and developing children's understanding of a range of text forms and structures, and their ability to write for a range of purposes.
> (Poulson *et al.*, 2001: 288)

The authors summarized this position as fundamentally constructivist, 'prioritizing pupils' ability to make sense of, and produce, written texts in a range of contexts and for authentic purposes' (p. 288). In contrast, the teachers were negative towards theoretical positions which stressed technical accuracy over meaning. When theoretical orientations and preferred activities were compared, the literacy teachers in the study showed a substantial level of consistency.

Finally, McCutchen *et al.* (2002) is an important study of teacher cognition because it studies the links among teacher education, classroom practice and student achievement. It thus addresses one ongoing critique of teacher cognition research – the lack of findings which demonstrate a connection between particular cognitions and learning outcomes. The focus of this study was beginning literacy, specifically phonological and orthographic awareness in kindergarten and Grade 1 classes in the USA. The teachers in the study received input on instruction in phonological and orthographic awareness over the course of year (through a combination of intensive courses and school-based support). The subject matter and general knowledge of participating teachers were assessed through tests of linguistic knowledge and culture. The classroom practices of experimental and control groups of teachers were studied for a year and their students' learning was also assessed through multiple measures of phonological and orthographic awareness over that period. Three major findings are reported by this study. Firstly, that teachers' knowledge of phonological awareness can be deepened through ongoing collaborative in-service professional development (i.e. the training intervention resulted in increases in teachers' knowledge in this respect); secondly, that teachers can use that knowledge to change their classroom practices (i.e. the experimental teachers modified their classroom practices to reflect their deepened knowledge of effective instruction in promoting phonological awareness – e.g. more explicit instruction of word sounds) and thirdly, that changes in teacher knowledge and classroom practice can improve student learning (i.e. students' phonological awareness in the experimental groups showed greater gains than those in control groups). Methodologically, this study was sophisticated, combining multiple interventions and measures longitudinally, and subjecting the data to complex statistical analyses. Nonetheless, this work does demonstrate that it is possible to examine links between teacher cognition (or at least teacher knowledge) and learning.

The individuality of the five studies of teacher cognition in literacy discussed here makes it difficult to extract any common trends from their findings. This work does, however, reflect concerns illustrated elsewhere in this chapter for the congruence between teachers' and students' conceptions, the impact of teacher education on teachers' cognitions and practices, teachers' theoretical orientations and instructional preferences and for the need for in-depth qualitative analyses of what teachers do and think. These studies provide insights into each of these issues. The work that stands out most here, in my view, is that discussed last; in linking teacher cognition, teachers' practices and children's learning, it suggests one way, methodologically and conceptually, in which the division between teacher cognition research and that on language acquisition can be bridged. This is a clear issue for further work as the field of language teacher cognition continues to move forward.

Summary

No consistent substantive focus emerges from the body of work I have discussed in this chapter. Studies of L1 reading represent a significant research tradition characterized by theoretical profiling work and by concerns about the relationship between teachers' beliefs and reported practices; there is also an interest here in the knowledge structures that underpin reading instruction. The work in L2 contexts is, in comparison, very limited, and it is difficult to offer an explanation as to why this is the case – reading has certainly attracted substantial attention in the methodological literature on language teaching. L2 reading instruction is thus clearly an area where a gap exists between our understandings of methodological and theoretical principles on the one hand, and what we know about teachers' actual practices and cognitions in teaching reading on the other. In writing, L1 studies have focused almost exclusively on changes in teachers' conceptions of writing during teacher education, while in L2 contexts the most prominent (but by no means dominant) focus has been on the practices and cognitions of in-service teachers. In both cases here, though, the volume of literature remains too small to support a meaningful discussion of emergent substantive frameworks; rather, what these studies of writing (in both L1 and L2 contexts) do is to signal some of the perspectives from which teacher cognition can be studied (e.g. the everyday work of practising teachers, the conceptions of pre-service teachers, the decision-making of expert and novice raters, the process of innovating in writing instruction). These and undoubtedly several other perspectives on writing instruction present themselves as legitimate foci for further research in this domain. The L1 literacy studies, as noted above, reflect many of the themes covered by the specific research on reading and writing.

6

Self-report instruments

In this and subsequent chapters our focus moves onto the ways in which language teacher cognition has been and can be studied, drawing on the research discussed earlier to illustrate various methodological options. Given that teacher cognition research is interested in phenomena which are not directly observable, a key challenge for researchers has been to identify data collection strategies through which these phenomena can be elicited. Taxonomies of the methods used for this purpose have been presented both in education generally (Calderhead, 1996; Clark and Peterson, 1986; Kagan, 1990; Shavelson and Stern, 1981; Shavelson et al., 1986; Shulman and Elstein, 1975), as well as in the field of applied linguistics and teacher education more specifically (Bartels, 2005a). Earlier classifications reflected concepts and terminology – such as *policy capturing* and *lens modelling* – imported into educational research from the field of psychology. There is, however, little evidence of such terms in methodological discussions of language teacher cognition today, so I will not use them here; similarly, there is little evidence in the work I have reviewed here of controlled laboratory tasks which characterized teacher cognition research (particularly studies of planning) during its early phase. A methodological analysis of language teacher cognition research suggests that the approaches commonly adopted in such work can be classified into four groups as described in Table 6.1. This classification provides the basis of this and the subsequent three chapters.

Table 6.1 Data collection methods in language teacher cognition research

Category	Goal	Methods
Self-Report Instruments	to measure teachers' theoretical orientations, beliefs or knowledge about an aspect of language teaching	• questionnaires • scenario rating • tests
Verbal Commentaries	to elicit verbal commentaries about teachers' beliefs, attitudes, practical theories and related mental constructs	• structured interviews • semi-structured interviews • scenario-based interviews • repertory grids • stimulated recall • think-aloud protocols
Observation	to collect descriptions of real or simulated planning and teaching which can be compared to previously stated cognitions and/or provide a concrete context for the subsequent elicitation of cognitions	• unstructured observation • structured observation
Reflective Writing	to elicit through writing tasks teachers' perceptions of their experiences, beliefs and knowledge of the concepts they associate with particular aspects of language teaching	• journal writing • biographical accounts • retrospective accounts • concept maps

The categories specified here operate at the level of methods of data collection rather than more broadly as approaches to research, such as ethnography or case study. Particular research approaches are of course often associated with particular strategies for data collection, and in selecting which methods to adopt in collecting data about teacher cognition researchers may want to consider how far these choices are consistent with the broader approach and research tradition (e.g. interpretive) a study is being located in. An analysis of these wider issues is, though, beyond the scope of the current discussion and readers are referred to the literature on research methodology more generally (e.g. Babbie, 2003; Cohen *et al.*, 2000; Creswell, 2003; Ernest, 1994; Robson, 2002). My focus throughout this and the three chapters that follow is on specific strategies for collecting data in the study of language teacher cognition – what they entail, how they have been used and their strengths and weaknesses in providing insights into teachers' mental lives. I will begin by discussing self-report instruments.

Three common types of self-report instruments are evident in the literature on language teacher cognition: questionnaires, scenario-rating tasks and tests. What these strategies have in common is that they elicit beliefs, knowledge and attitudes through instruments, typically consisting of a series of questions or tasks, which require a written response. These written responses are then used as evidence of the respondents' cognitions. Below I will describe and analyse examples of these three strategies in the study of language teacher cognition and highlight key considerations which should govern their use in this field of inquiry. One important goal here is awareness-raising; it will become clear in the course of the chapter that a wide range of self-report instruments for studying language teacher cognition exist, particular in terms of questionnaires, and it is important for researchers in the field to be aware of these before deciding that additional instruments need to be designed. This is another example of the rationalization – in this case methodological – which I feel is needed to allow the study of language teacher cognition to assume a greater sense of coherence and common purpose.

Questionnaires

There is a vast methodological literature on the design, administration and analysis of questionnaires in educational research (e.g. Aldridge and Levine, 2001; Brown, 2001; Dörnyei, 2002; Fowler, 2002; Oppenheim,

1992); I will not provide a general discussion of the issues involved here, but an awareness of these issues is obviously a prerequisite for the effective use of this research strategy in the study of language teacher cognition.

In this field, questionnaires have been widely used to study teachers' beliefs about language learning and teaching, both generally and in relation to specific curricular domains such as reading. Table 6.2 lists examples of such work and I will now discuss these.

Horwitz (1985, 1988) developed the BALLI – Beliefs about Language Learning Inventory – to examine beliefs about five areas of foreign language learning: difficulty of language learning, foreign language aptitude, the nature of language learning, learning and communication strategies and motivation and expectations. Examples of statements on the BALLI are:

- It is easier for children than adults to learn a language.
- It is important to speak a foreign language with an excellent accent.
- It is OK to guess if you don't know a word in the foreign language.
- It is easier to speak than to understand a foreign language.
- People who speak more than one language are very intelligent.

The BALLI is a Likert-scale instrument, and answers to each statement on it are indicated on a scale of possibilities, such as from *strongly disagree* to *strongly agree*. The BALLI has been widely used to study learners' beliefs (for reviews, see Barcelos, 2003; Bernat and Gvozdenko, 2005; Horwitz, 1999), but variations of this instrument have also been used in studying language teachers' beliefs. Peacock (2001), for example, administered the BALLI at different points in a three year teacher education programme to assess change in ESL pre-service teachers' beliefs about second language learning. Kern (1995) also used the BALLI to examine the beliefs about university language teachers and to compare these to those of their students.

Table 6.2 Questionnaires in language teacher cognition research

Source	Focus	Instrument
Allen (2002)	teachers' beliefs about foreign language learning	Foreign Language Education Questionnaire (FLEQ)
Burgess & Etherington (2002)	teachers' beliefs about grammar and grammar teaching	questionnaire
Flores (2001)	beliefs and reported practices of bilingual educators	Survey of Bilingual Teachers Epistemology and Teaching Practices (SBTETP)
Johnson (1992b)	teachers' theoretical beliefs about L2 learning and teaching and their practices during literacy instruction	beliefs inventory
Karavas-Doukas (1996)	teachers' attitudes to communicative language teaching	attitude scale
Kern (1995)	teachers' and students' beliefs about language learning	BALLI
Kinzer (1988)	beliefs about reading of pre- and in-service teachers	beliefs inventory
Linek et al. (1999)	changes in the beliefs about literacy of teachers in different pre-service teacher education programmes	Philosophical Orientations to Literacy Learning (POLL)
MacDonald et al. (2001)	influence of a course in SLA on beliefs about English language learning	Statements from Lightbown & Spada (1993)

(*Continued*)

Table 6.2 (Continued)

Source	Focus	Instrument
Peacock (2001)	changes in trainees' beliefs about L2 learning	BALLI
Poulson et al. (2001)	teachers' theoretical orientations towards literacy	TORP
Sato & Kleinsasser (1999)	teachers' understandings and practices in relation to CLT	Foreign Language Attitude Survey for Teachers (FLAST)
Schulz (1996; 2001)	student and teacher perceptions of the role of grammar and correction in language learning	questionnaires
Westwood et al. (1997)	teachers' beliefs about literacy instruction	teachers' beliefs about literacy questionnaire (TBALQ)

Not all questionnaire-based studies of teacher cognition, however, use the BALLI. Schulz (1996, 2001), whose work focused specifically on beliefs about grammar teaching and error correction held by foreign language teachers and students, developed two Likert-scale questionnaires for this purpose. Different versions of this instrument were prepared for teachers and students; two further versions in Spanish were also prepared for the Colombian participants in this study (the 2001 paper lists the alternate forms of question wording which were used for the four different groups of respondents). Another self-report instrument used in the study of language teacher cognition is a list of statements about second and foreign language learning from Lightbown and Spada (1993) (see Figure 6.1). This has been used in studying changes in beliefs over time, particularly in teacher education contexts.

MacDonald et al. (2001), for example, administered these statements to students on a course about second language acquisition; by comparing students' levels of agreement with them

> 1. Languages are learned mainly through imitation.
> 2. Parents usually correct young children when they make grammatical errors.
> 3. People with high IQs are good language learners.
> 4. The most important factor in second language acquisition success is motivation.
> 5. The earlier a second language is introduced in school programmes, the greater the likelihood of success in learning.
> 6. Most of the mistakes which second language learners make are due to interference from their first language.
> 7. Teachers should present grammatical rules one at a time, and learners should practice examples of each one before going on to another.
> 8. Teachers should teach simple language structures before complex ones.
> 9. Learners' errors should be corrected as soon as they are made in order to prevent the formation of bad habits.
> 10. Teachers should use materials that expose students only to those language structures which they have already been taught.
> 11. When learners are allowed to interact freely (for example in group or pair activities), they learn each others' mistakes.
> 12. Students learn what they are taught.

FIGURE 6.1 *Statements about second language learning*
(Lightbown and Spada, 1993: xv)

before and after the course the authors drew conclusions about the impact their course had on changing these students' beliefs. As I noted in Chapter 2, though, caution is required when comparisons of pre- and post-measures of this kind are used as indications of cognitive change; if the material covered on the course is still fresh in the students' minds then there is a danger that their responses may only reflect the views promoted on the course rather than what they actually believe themselves.

In the field of reading instruction, a widely used questionnaire for profiling teachers' theoretical orientations is the TORP – Theoretical Orientation to Reading Profile, developed by DeFord (1985) and adopted or modified in a number of subsequent studies (e.g. Grisham,

2000; Olson and Singer, 1994; Poulson *et al.*, 2001). It consists of 28 statements which reflect beliefs associated with three orientations to reading instruction – phonics, skills and whole language – and which can be scored in order to provide a measurement of where, in terms of these three orientations, a respondent lies. Sample statements from the TORP are presented in Figure 6.2. DeFord (1985) explains in detail the manner in which the instrument was developed and validated, and how it is scored. Evidence is also provided that TORP scores can be used to predict teachers' actual reading instruction practices; the ability of theoretical measurements of teachers' beliefs to predict behaviour is of course an important measure of their validity and DeFord does make claims for the TORP in that respect.

Further examples of Likert-scale questionnaires in the study of language teacher cognition are the teachers' beliefs about literacy

---

1. A child needs to be able to verbalize the rules of phonics in order to assure proficiency in processing new words.
2. An increase in reading errors is usually related to a decrease in comprehension.
3. Dividing words into syllables according to rules is a helpful instructional practice for reading new words.
4. Fluency and expression are necessary components of reading that indicate good comprehension.
5. Materials for early reading should be written in natural language without concern for short, simple words and sentences.
6. When children do not know a word, they should be instructed to sound out its parts.
7. It is a good practice to allow children to edit what is written into their own dialect when learning to read.
8. The use of a glossary or dictionary is necessary in determining the meaning and pronunciation of new words.
9. Reversals (e.g. saying 'saw' for 'was') are significant problems in the teaching of reading.
10. It is a good practice to correct a child as soon as an oral reading mistake is made.

FIGURE 6.2 *Sample statements from Theoretical Orientation to Reading Profile*
(DeFord, 1985)

questionnaire (TBALQ) developed by Westwood *et al.* (1997) and the Foreign Language Education Questionnaire (FLEQ), developed by Allen (2002) for use in the USA. Questionnaires of this type have been used in the study of beliefs about grammar teaching too (Burgess and Etherington, 2002; Chia, 2003; Eisenstein-Ebsworth and Schweers, 1997; Ng and Farrell, 2003) and in the study of the beliefs of bilingual educators (Flores, 2001). In their study of communicative language teaching, Sato and Kleinsasser (1999) used a modified version of the Foreign Language Attitude Survey for Teachers (FLAST) while Karavas-Doukas (1996), also focusing on communicative language teaching, used an attitude scale. There are clearly a wide number of questionnaires available for researchers in language teacher cognition to draw on (though, apart from the BALLI, there is little evidence of repeated use in a range of contexts of any of the instruments I have mentioned so far).

Not all questionnaires used in the study of language teacher cognition follow the Likert-scale model. This is particularly true in the study of reading instruction, as illustrated by the work of Kinzer (1988; Leu and Kinzer, 1987). In this case two questionnaires were used. The first focuses on beliefs about how one reads and provides a measure in relation to three possible orientations to the process of reading – text-based, reader-based or interactive. The second questionnaire (see Figure 6.3) focuses on beliefs about how reading ability develops and provides a measure in relation to three possible orientations to the process of reading development – through mastery of specific skills, holistically or differentially (i.e. different processes at different stages). Each questionnaire consists of 15 statements, five for each of the three orientations being examined and respondents are requested to choose in each case five statements from the 15 which reflect their views (respondents are not told in advance which statements relate to which orientations). Respondents' orientations to reading are defined according to the kinds of statements they selected. These instruments for profiling teachers' beliefs about reading instruction have been utilized in a number of studies (e.g. Wilson *et al.,* 1992) and modified to examine beliefs in vocabulary instruction (Konopak and Williams, 1994) and second language learning (Johnson, 1992b). In the latter case, the 15 statements used covered three methodological approaches to second language learning – skill-based (e.g. language learning as

1. It is important for teachers to provide very clear, precise presentations during reading instruction.
2. Children should receive many opportunities to read materials unrelated to specific school learning tasks.
3. In deciding how to teach reading, one should carefully consider the nature and abilities of the children.
4. Reading, writing, speaking and listening are closely related learning tasks.
5. Children learn reading best when the task is broken down into specific skills to be taught by the teacher.
6. Children should be tested frequently to determine if they have learned what was taught. These tests should match very closely the nature of the instruction.
7. Some children learn to read best by reading widely and often; others learn best through direct instruction.
8. Children should be frequently read to while they are young so they acquire a 'feel' for what reading is like.
9. Opportunities should be created in the classroom to provide children with a reason to read.
10. Less proficient readers often benefit from more direct and structured learning experiences.
11. Teachers should have a list of separate reading skills appropriate for their grade level and make certain that each student masters these skills, and only these skills.
12. Much of what children learn about reading can be attributed directly to what a teacher taught in the classroom.
13. It is important to individualize reading instruction as much as possible by taking into consideration the children's reading abilities.
14. Children learn a great deal about reading by watching their parents at home.
15. A teacher should generally spend greater time in the classroom with less proficient readers than with more proficient readers.

(Mastery of specific-skills statements: 1, 5, 6, 11, 12. Holistic statements: 2, 4, 8, 9, 14. Differential acquisition statements: 3, 7, 10 13, 15.)

FIGURE 6.3 *Beliefs about how reading ability develops (Kinzer, 1988: 374). Reproduced with permission of the National Reading Conference.*

habit formation) rule-based (e.g. language learning as rule-governed activity) and functional (e.g. language learning as communication). The congruence between the statements and the different theoretical orientations they are meant to represent was validated by three expert raters. That is, the raters examined the different statements and agreed that each set of five did relate to a distinct theoretical orientation. Validation is an important stage in the process of devising instruments of this kind and I comment on this further in the next section.

Questionnaires continue to be a strong feature of research on language teacher cognition. They allow large amounts of data to be collected quickly, economically, and without significant effort on the researcher's part (although questionnaire design itself is a demanding process). Questionnaire data, though, are obviously limited in their ability to capture the complex nature of teachers' mental lives. I comment further on these limitations at the end of this chapter.

In terms of questionnaire administration, one development in recent years has been the use of web-based mechanisms (for a discussion see, for example, Couper, 2000). To date, there is little evidence of this trend in the study of language teacher cognition, though in a current project I am involved in a web-based survey is being used to study teachers' beliefs about the integration of grammar in adult ESOL classrooms in a range of contexts around the world.

Scenario rating

I use the term *scenario rating* here to refer to strategies for eliciting self-reported measures of language teacher cognition which ask teachers to assess exemplars of practice, such as hypothetical teacher-student interactions and lesson plans. These have not been widely used in the study of language teacher cognition. An early example is Cathcart and Olsen (1976) who, as part of their study of ESL teachers' and students' preferences for correction, asked teachers to rate a list of possible responses by a teacher to a student's error. Figure 6.4 is the version of the scenarios presented to students; for the teachers' version, the scenarios were the same but the instruction was for teachers to

5. Look at the grammar corrections below. Rate them as very good, good, not very good or bad.
Example: Teacher says: 'Where did you go yesterday!'
Student says: 'I go to the bank.'

Corrections:	Very good	good	not very good	bad
a. 'Don't say go; say went.'				
b. 'I went to the bank.'				
c. 'Yesterday, I ...'				
d. 'Go is in the present tense. You need past tense here.'				
e. 'What's the second word?'				
f. 'Students?' (class gives answer)				
g. 'Mmmmmmm' (disapproval)				
h. 'Please repeat the sentence.'				
i. 'What?'				
j. 'Again. Where did you go?'				
k. 'Really? Did you make a deposit?'				
l. 'When you went to the bank, what did you do?'				

FIGURE 6.4 *Scenario analysis for error correction in ESL (students' version) (Cathcart and Olsen, 1976: 43). Reproduced with permission of TESOL.*

indicate whether they used each type of correction often, sometimes or never. This technique allows teachers to express their views in relation to concrete examples of instruction, though it is important to remember that even in such cases the preferences teachers express may not reflect what they actually do in the classroom. (This study did in fact report that correction strategies some teachers said they never used were actually observed in their teaching.)

Another form of scenario rating (often used in conjunction with questionnaires) is based on the analysis of lesson plans (Johnson, 1992b; Kinzer, 1988; Wilson et al., 1992). The aim here is to go beyond the brief, abstract and normally decontextualized statements which questionnaires contain and to provide teachers with a more realistic stimulus; the assumption here is that the beliefs elicited in this way will reflect more closely those that teachers draw on in practice (as opposed to their theoretical beliefs). In Kinzer (1988), nine lesson plans in total (three each focusing on vocabulary, comprehension and syllabication) were produced (see Figure 6.5 for an example). In each set of three, one lesson reflected a text-based/mastery of specific skills approach to reading, one a reader-based/holistic orientation, and one an interactive/differential orientation. Respondents were asked to choose three lessons – one each for vocabulary, comprehension and syllabication – which they would choose for a group of average second-grade students. Teachers' orientations were classified in terms of their choices. Johnson (1992a) adapted this idea for use in her study of literacy instruction in ESL. In this case, only three lesson plans were used, one each to reflect rule-based, skill-based and function-based orientations to second language teaching, and teachers had to select the one which best reflected their own beliefs about second language learning.

In constructing instruments of this type, distinct theoretical orientations (e.g. to reading instruction) must first be identified, then lesson plans reflecting those orientations written and validated to ensure they do reflect the orientations they purport to. The validation process in Johnson (1992b), for example, is described as follows:

> The lesson plans designed for this task were validated as reflecting one of the three methodological approaches by two expert raters. The expert raters were two university professors, one in the field of Teaching ESL and the other in the field of Applied Linguistics. Raters were asked to code each lesson plan according to one of the three methodological approaches. Raters were also given the option of rating the lesson plans in another category if they felt the design of the lesson did not reflect any of the approaches. All three lesson plans received 100% agreement by both raters and were incorporated into this task without modification.
>
> (Johnson, 1992a: 88)

> The words to be taught in this lesson have been identified by the basal reader teacher's guide as being new words that will appear in a story about a shipwreck and how a family solved the problem of *getting off* the ship and onto a nearby island. The words are:
>
> crash lifeboat float shelter waves jammed
>
> The teacher has decided on the following procedure to teach the words.
>
> 1. Before the children read the story, they are told that there may be some words in what they are about to read that they may not know. Write the vocabulary words on the chalkboard and read them to the students. Stop after each word and ask the students to use the word in a sentence, if they know the meaning.
> 2. For each word, ask students if they have had any experiences where the word can be used as a descriptor. For example, ask if they have been to a lake, swimming pool, or ocean. Ask *if* they have had a water toy that can float. Can they float? Have children name things that can *float*. What might happen if a person couldn't float or swim?
> 3. Ask students what a *lifesaver* might be. You might be told it is a piece of candy. If so, why might a piece of candy be called a *lifesaver*? Encourage students to think of people who might be called lifesavers (police, firefighters, etc.); ask students if they can think of things that work as lifesavers. Give hints such as What might be a lifesaver if a person is in a car wreck? (safety belt) A plane? (parachute) A ship?
> 4. Discuss how *lifeboats* are small boats which are placed on large ships and are used when the ship is in danger of sinking, that is, when the large ship can no longer float. Continue to use the children's knowledge and experiences to build connections between what they already know and the vocabulary words.
> 5. After each of the new words have been discussed in this way, have the students write a story either collectively or individually, using all of the words. Encourage them to illustrate their stories. Stories might also be read by students and tape recorded for later discussion.
>
> After students have read the reading selection:
>
> 1. Select the sentences which contain the words from the story. Write these sentences on the board and have students read the sentences, then make up new sentences in ways that show each word's meaning.
> 2. Have the class make up another story containing the words. Write this story on the board.
> 3. Students copy their made-up story into their notebooks. After they have copied the whole story, they go back and underline the vocabulary words.
> 4. The next day, a quiz is given on the meanings. Students are given a sheet with the words on it. They are to write a sentence appropriately using the word such that its meaning is shown.

FIGURE 6.5 *Example of reader-based/holistic vocabulary lesson (Kinzer, 1988: 376). Reproduced with permission of the National Reading Conference.*

El-Okda (2005) used scenarios in the form of vignettes to elicit student teachers' beliefs about reading instruction in EFL. The vignettes depicted situations where a teacher made an instructional decision while teaching reading; student teachers had to indicate if they agreed with the decision and then to indicate the reasons for their choice. While the use of vignettes is certainly a useful strategy in eliciting teachers' cognitions, in this case the instrument may have imposed too much structure on student teachers' responses; for example, the instructional decision described in each vignette was followed by this question: 'Do you think that her decision was right or wrong?' The dichotomous nature of the choice available here would have undoubtedly constrained the ways in which the trainees were able to respond.

A further variation on the use of scenarios comes from my current work on research engagement by English language teachers (Borg, in press). To elicit teachers' conceptions of research, I devised a series of research scenarios (see Figure 6.6 for examples) and asked teachers to rate each according to the extent to which they were seen to be examples of research. The piloting of these scenarios with 50 teachers of English as a foreign language in Turkey suggests that these scenarios provide an internally consistent measure of respondents' conceptions of research (Cronbach's alpha = 0.82).

Tests

Tests are obviously suited to the measurement of teachers' factual knowledge and it is no surprise to find that they have been used in the study of language teacher cognition, particularly in relation to teachers' linguistic knowledge (see Chapter 4 for a discussion of this work). A number of examples occur in studies of UK teacher trainees' knowledge about language (Bloor, 1986; Chandler *et al.*, 1988; Hislam and Cajkler, 2005; Williamson and Hardman, 1995; Wray, 1993). These studies have generally been motivated by concerns that trainees lack the knowledge about language required for them to promote such knowledge among learners as specified by the UK National Curriculum. There is less evidence of this strategy for studying teacher cognition in L2 and FL contexts (where, perhaps, it is often

This section presents ten brief descriptions. Read each and choose ONE answer to say to what extent you feel the activity described is research.

1. A teacher noticed that an activity she used in class did not work well. She thought about this after the lesson and made some notes in her diary. She tried something different in her next lesson. This time the activity was more successful.

Definitely not research ☐	Probably not research ☐	Probably research ☐	Definitely research ☐

2. A teacher read about a new approach to teaching writing and decided to try it out in his class over a period of two weeks. He video recorded some of his lessons and collected samples of learners' written work. He analysed this information then presented the results to his colleagues at a staff meeting.

Definitely not research ☐	Probably not research ☐	Probably research ☐	Definitely research ☐

3. A teacher was doing an MA course. She read several books and articles about grammar teaching then wrote an essay of 6,000 words in which she discussed the main points in those readings.

Definitely not research ☐	Probably not research ☐	Probably research ☐	Definitely research ☐

4. A university lecturer gave a questionnaire about the use of computers in language teaching to 500 teachers. Statistics were used to analyse the questionnaires. The lecturer wrote an article about the work in an academic journal.

Definitely not research ☐	Probably not research ☐	Probably research ☐	Definitely research ☐

5. Two teachers were both interested in discipline. They observed each other's lessons once a week for three months and made notes about how they controlled their classes. They discussed their notes and wrote a short article about what they learned for the newsletter of the national language teachers' association.

Definitely not research ☐	Probably not research ☐	Probably research ☐	Definitely research ☐

FIGURE 6.6 *Scenarios for eliciting teachers' views of research*
(Borg, in press)

assumed that teachers have had a thorough grounding in the study of language), though the work of Andrews (1999a, 2003b; Andrews and McNeil, 2005) is an exception here. From a different perspective, in their study of knowledge and practices in initial literacy instruction in the USA, McCutchen et al. (2002) administered the *Informal Survey of Linguistic Knowledge* (Moats and Lyon, 1996) to collect data about teachers' knowledge of phonology and orthography and of their role in literacy instruction. This test measures the ability to identify sounds within words (e.g. to identify the third sound in a word or the number of syllables and morphemes in it).

If we consider the kinds of test items included in the instruments which focus on L1 and FL teachers' grammatical knowledge of English, the range is finite. This is in part due to the fact that much of this work builds on Bloor's (1986) SPAM questionnaire (Students' Prior Awareness of Metalinguistics). Two examples of the items in the SPAM are given in Figure 6.7. Williamson and Hardman (1995) developed Bloor's test further. Respondents were asked to describe the function of words highlighted in sentences, to comment on the grammatical accuracy of examples of children's writing (see Figure 6.8), to define parts of speech and to answer questions about English usage, such as 'List three common uses for commas'. Wray's (1993) test, also used with trainee teachers, was broader in scope, asking not just about grammatical items but also about the nature of spoken and written language, geographical and cultural language variation and literary language.

In FL studies, the instrument used by Andrews (1999a) to assess teachers' explicit knowledge of English grammar and grammatical terminology draws on earlier work by Alderson, Clapham and Steel (1996), in itself influenced by Bloor (1986). Andrews' test consisted of four sections, the first two similar to those from Bloor in Figure 6.7, while two further sections focused on error identification and the explanation of grammar rules. For example, respondents were presented with sentences such as 'I walk to work very quick' and asked to explain the nature of the error.

Overall, then, the range of items appearing in tests of linguistic knowledge used with teachers is not very broad: finding examples of parts of speech in given sentences, stating what part of speech highlighted words in sentences are, defining grammatical terms and

> From the sentence below give ONE example of each of the grammatical items requested and write it in the space provided. NB You may select the same word(s) more than once if appropriate.
>
> Materials are delivered to the factory by a supplier, who usually has no technical knowledge, but who happens to have the right contacts.
>
> verb
> noun
> countable noun passive verb
> adjective
> adverb
> definite article
> indefinite article
> preposition
> relative pronoun
> auxiliary verb
> past participle
> conjunction
> finite verb
> infinitive
>
> *In the following sentences underline the item requested in brackets.*
>
> 1. Poor little Joe stood out in the snow. (subject)
> 2. Joe had nowhere to shelter. (predicate)
> 3. The policeman chased Joe down the street. (direct object)
> 4. The woman gave him some money. (indirect object)

FIGURE 6.7 *Sample test items*
(Bloor, 1986: 158)

giving examples of them, identifying errors (in sentences or examples of writing) and correcting these and/or explaining why they are incorrect. The test used by McCutchen *et al.* (2002) contains different kinds of items given its focus on phonological and orthographical awareness.

One issue to keep in mind regarding the use of tests of linguistic knowledge is that practising teachers may be less willing to take these than novices. Tests may represent a threat to one's self-esteem and the prospect of embarrassment can be a powerful disincentive.

Each of the extracts below is taken from a child's writing. Please comment briefly in the space provided on what you think, if anything, is grammatically wrong with the piece of writing and what has been successfully achieved by the child.

(a) One day Mel and me took the dog for a walk and the dog ran away and David ran after it and caught it and we went home and had our tea.

(David – aged 7)

Comments

_____

(b) When the box and polystyrene which kept it neatly packaged there in front of us stood a six foot robot, he shrunk without the packing.

(James – aged 10)

Comments

_____

(c) We walk for three mile and didn't see nothing bigger than a dog.

(Karen – aged 9)

Comments

_____

FIGURE 6.8 *Evaluating the grammaticality of children's writing* (Williamson and Hardman, 1995: 132)

An extreme case of poor judgement on a researcher's part would be asking experienced teachers whose own confidence or explicit knowledge in the language was known not to be high to complete a test of proficiency or grammatical knowledge (perhaps even with the aim of demonstrating how low the knowledge of these teachers was). This would be highly inappropriate, even if teachers were willing to consent to the exercise. Tests, then, need to be used very sensitively in the study of what teachers know about language.

Given these points, it is not surprising that most work involving tests has been conducted in the context of teacher education courses where respondents are in a sense captive or where perhaps the tests are used as part of some form of assessment. Andrews (2003a) is at first a striking exception in that he was able to obtain the participation of 170 practising teachers of English in Hong Kong on a wide range of measures, including tests of language knowledge and proficiency. This is an usually high number of participants for a study of this kind; however, it is explained in the study that these teachers were all applicants to a course taught at the author's institution and that the teachers were required to respond to various tests and surveys as part of the application or joining process. In McCutchen *et al.* (2002), the teachers participating in the study were paid to do so.

Summary

In this chapter I have illustrated key data collection strategies available to researchers whose aim is to study language teacher cognition using self-report instruments. To conclude this chapter I will review a number of issues which researchers must be mindful of in utilizing these strategies.

1. Theoretical measures of teacher cognition cannot be used as measures of actual practices. This is a fundamental principle in teacher cognition research. Even where teachers report on their teaching, it is essential that these data be treated as reports. When such data are written up, the difference, linguistically, between 'teachers taught grammar regularly' and 'teachers said they taught grammar regularly' is small; in substance, though, the former claim is unwarranted. Theoretical measures of language teacher cognition, then, whether based on questionnaires, scenarios or tests, constitute a record of what teachers say they believe, do or know. I am not suggesting such insight into teacher cognition is trivial; in terms of what such data tell us about teaching, though, it is important to recognize their limitations. A key issue here is ecological validity (Kinzer, 1988; Richardson *et al.*, 1991): the measures discussed in this chapter are low on ecological validity because their findings cannot be

extrapolated with confidence to real teaching situations. For example, teachers might respond differently to the kinds of lesson plan selection tasks we have discussed if they were choosing a lesson they were actually going to teach to a group of students they actually knew, and in a particular context familiar to them. As noted in Chapter 5, one explanation for the mismatch between teachers' reported cognitions and their actual practices which has been identified in studies of reading instruction is that when presented with theoretical statements or hypothetical situations to comment on, teachers' responses may reflect their views of what *should* be done rather what they actually do. Self-report instruments may, then, reflect teachers' *ideals*. For this reason they are inadequate, on their own, in situations where there is an interest in real classroom practices, and need to be supplemented with additional forms of data such as observations and interviews.

2 Although questionnaires and tests can be an efficient means of collecting large amounts of data, the limitations of such instruments must also be acknowledged (see, for example, Dörnyei, 2002; Oppenheim, 1992 for a discussion of disadvantages of questionnaires). Kagan (1990) highlights potential problems of short-answer self-report scales in studying teacher cognition:

> Any short-answer, self-report scale of teacher thinking has certain inherent limitations. First, teachers' responses may be influenced by social desirability (i.e., a teacher might be reluctant to endorse a professionally unpopular belief). Similarly, some might feign endorsement of items perceived to be 'correct'. In addition to conscious dishonesty, all self-report scales are vulnerable to the possibility that much teacher belief is unconsciously held. A teacher may not recognize a statement as his or her own belief because of the language in which the statement is couched. Any researcher who uses a short-answer test of teacher belief (i.e., an instrument consisting of prefabricated statements)

runs the risk of obtaining bogus data, because standardized statements may mask or misrepresent a particular teacher's highly personalized perceptions and definitions.

(Kagan, 1990: 427)

In the same vein, it must be noted that in self-report instruments of teachers' beliefs, such as Likert-scale questionnaires, the statements included are defined by the researcher. They, thus, may not cover the full range of beliefs that respondents have or want to talk about; additionally, teachers' responses may not reflect their own beliefs, but those which they have chosen from among those identified by the researcher (my earlier comments on El-Okda, 2005 illustrate this point – trainees could only choose 'right' or 'wrong'). The above concerns have been reflected in the methodological choices made by a number of researchers (e.g. Basturkmen et al., 2004; Richardson et al., 1991) who have purposefully avoided the use of 'pencil and paper measures' of teacher cognition in the belief that these are inadequate in their ability to capture the complexities of the phenomena under study.

3   Self-report instruments need to be subject to adequate development, piloting and validation procedures. DeFord (1985) and Westwood et al. (1997), for example, detail at length the manner in which the TORP and TBALQ respectively were validated, covering key concerns in questionnaire and test design such as construct validity, concurrent validity and reliability. Though few sources discuss their validation procedures in such detail, studies which use self-report instruments do commonly include a reference to the manner in which they verified that the instruments being used do actually measure what they claim to. Many studies will draw on instruments that have been previously validated, in which case a reference to the original source often suffices; this is the case with studies that use the TORP; Andrews (1999a) also justifies the adoption of a test from Alderson et al. (1996) on the basis that it had been thoroughly validated in their work. A key question for researchers who use self-report

instruments in studying language teacher cognition, then, is 'what evidence do you have that your instruments provide a credible account of the phenomena they claim to portray?' Evidence of careful design, including attention to wording, organization and layout, piloting and revision as necessary, together with a justification for the choice of items in an instrument, would seem to be minimum requirements in providing a positive answer to this question. These issues are covered thoroughly in the general methodological literature on questionnaire and test design.

4 When used longitudinally, self-report instruments may provide evidence of change, but there are a number of issues to consider in making claims about such change. Firstly, change measured in this way is theoretical and cannot be used to make claims about changes in what teachers do in the classroom. Secondly, a judgement needs to be made about whether the change – especially when it refers to beliefs – represents real change or whether it is an artefact of some other factor. For example, if a questionnaire is used at the end of a course, participants may feel the need to select answers which match the views promoted on the course. In such cases, the degree of real cognitive change occurring may be questionable. And thirdly, it is very difficult, on the basis of self-report instruments administered at different points in time, to draw conclusions about the causes of any changes which emerge. Concluding, for example, that differences in pre- and post-questionnaires used on a teacher education course are indicative of the impact of the course, is not necessarily warranted. In the absence of opportunities to track classroom practices over time, the repeated administration of a questionnaire contributes little to an understanding of the factors which are promoting or hindering teacher change. It is also worth noting that when two or more administrations of a self-report instrument over time do not reveal changes (e.g. Peacock, 2001), this too does not necessarily mean that respondents' cognitions have remained static over that time.

Finally, it is very important for researchers to award due attention not only to the construction of instruments but also to the nature of the respondents who will be involved and to the contexts they work in. As suggested above, there will be differences in the ways that pre-service and in-service teachers respond to invitations to complete different types of self-report instruments, with tests having the most potential for arousing distrust. Much research on language teacher cognition is done with captive audiences on teacher education programmes; in such cases, high response rates are more likely even when the instruments being used are lengthy; the survey used with pre-service EFL teachers in Hong Kong by Urmston (2003), for example, contains 55 questions stretching over more than ten pages; it is unlikely that many practising teachers not enrolled on a formal course and who receive such an instrument in their schools would complete it. Self-report instruments, then, need to be chosen and designed with a clear understanding of the target audience in mind.

7

Verbal commentaries

Verbal commentaries – getting teachers to talk about their beliefs, thoughts and similar mental constructs – is another widely used strategy in the study of language teacher cognition. It can assume a number of forms, but the options available and which I discuss here are all essentially (with arguably one exception) forms of interview. In this chapter I will describe and illustrate these options and analyse their value and limitations in the study of language teacher cognition.

There are a number of methodological texts dedicated to the use of interviews in educational research (e.g. Drever, 1995; Fontana and Frey, 1994; Gillham, 2005; Holstein and Gubrium, 1997; Kvale, 1996; Measor, 1985; Oppenheim, 1992; Powney and Watts, 1987; Rubin and Rubin, 2004) and all standard research textbooks will dedicate space to this widely used data collection strategy. Familiarity with the broader principles which govern the design, implementation, analysis and interpretation of specific kinds of interview more generally is, of course, important for researchers of teacher cognition; however, I will not dwell at length on such generic issues here, focusing more specifically on the ways that verbal commentaries have been elicited in the study of language teacher cognition.

One background point which is worth highlighting here, though, is that various types of interviews do exist; a common way of distinguishing among these is to locate them along a continuum ranging from more structured to less structured. *Structured* interviews are characterized by an agenda which is predetermined by the researcher (e.g. through specifically worded and sequenced questions), which is applied in a standardized manner with all respondents, and which allows the researcher to retain tight control over the course of the interview (particularly when the range of possible responses has also been fixed in advance). *Unstructured* interviews (perhaps more appropriately called *non-structured,* for arguably an interview must always have a structure of some kind), in contrast, unfold much like conversations rather than following a pre-set course. Along the continuum just referred to, interviews may also be *semi-structured*. This kind of interview is directed by a set of general themes, rather than specific questions, and researchers have a great deal of flexibility in the manner in which they encourage the interviewee to talk about these themes.

The choices made by researchers from among these interviewing strategies will typically reflect the methodological principles and the empirical goals of a study; thus in interpretive research, where a smaller number of respondents are interviewed in-depth and where the interaction between researcher and respondent aims to capture some elements of natural conversation, semi-structured or non-structured interviews are more common; where responses from a larger group of respondents need to be collected in a standardized and efficient manner, then structured interviews are more appropriate. I will now illustrate these different approaches to eliciting verbal commentaries (including variations such as repertory grid and stimulated recall interviews) with reference to studies of language teacher cognition. I will also discuss think-aloud protocols here; though this is not strictly speaking a form of interview, it is clearly a research strategy for studying language teacher cognition that relies on the elicitation of verbal commentaries. I should also point out here that I am not aware of any examples of unstructured interviews in the study of language teacher cognition. Hayes (2005), perhaps, comes close in his life history study of language educators in Sri Lanka (see Chapter 3). This is how he describes the interviewing strategy he used:

> There was no specific interview schedule though I had written out a list of general topic areas which I wanted at some stage to cover in the interviews. I thought it more important to let the

interviews take a course dictated by the connections made by the interviewees themselves with the topic areas.
(Hayes, 2005: 173)

Structured interviews

Structured interviews are characterized by an element of standardization in the questions asked; that is all respondents will be asked the same questions in the same order. The questions themselves may be open-ended (allowing for a range of possible responses formulated in the interviewee's words) and/or closed (allowing a limited choice of answers from among those defined in advance by the researcher). In research on language teacher cognition, the open-ended approach to structured interviewing seems more prevalent. For example, in their study of communicative language teaching, Sato and Kleinsasser (1999) used a standardized open-ended interview protocol consisting of 12 questions (though their schedule of questions is not presented). Shi and Cumming (1995) describe their approach to interviewing as non-directive and open-ended, but based on a standard schedule of questions. Meloth *et al.* (1989) also report that teachers were asked a set of 13 questions about their conceptions of reading and reading instruction. From the examples they provide, these questions appeared to be open-ended; for example, teachers were asked 'What does a good reader do?' and 'What is the most important thing you communicate to students about reading?' Also in the field of reading, Gove (1983) developed the Conceptual Framework of Reading Interview (Figure 7.1 for sample items). This consists of 11 open-ended items which aim to elicit teachers' beliefs about reading and reading instruction. The fact that it can also be administered and responded to in writing reflects its structured nature. Structured open-ended interviews were also used by Meijer *et al.* (1999) in their study of teachers' practical knowledge in teaching reading comprehension. In all of the cases cited here, interviews were conducted face-to-face; although this is the most common mode for the conduct of interviews, these can also be carried out over the telephone, as in Maloch *et al.*'s (2003) study of the cognitions and reported practices of beginning reading teachers.

> In answering each of these questions, think of what you would do in your classroom.
> 1. Describe the reading instruction in your classroom on a typical day.
> 2. Of all the reading instructional goals you have in mind, which one (ones) do you think you've made pretty good progress towards accomplishing this year?
>   What do the students do that shows you they're doing a good job of _____?
>   What did you do as a teacher to get your students to _____?
> 3. What do you do when a student is reading orally and makes an error? [If a conditional answer is given] What practice do you follow under what conditions?
> 4. Is it a good practice to correct a child as soon as an oral reading error is made? Why or why not?
>   [If a conditional answer is given] When is it good practice and when is it not good practice?
> 5. What do you do when a student is reading orally and does not know a word? Why?
>   [If a conditional answer is given] Which practice would you use under what conditions?
>
> [The full interview contains 11 items]

FIGURE 7.1 *Conceptual Framework of Reading Interview* (Gove, 1983)

Scenario-based interviews

One problem with interviews which aim to elicit mental constructs such as beliefs is that they can often be abstract – that is lacking in reference to the concrete contextual detail which is arguably essential if teachers are to be able to discuss their conceptions of their work in ways which have practical meaning. It has also been argued that directly asking teachers about their beliefs is not a productive elicitation strategy:

> teachers are often unaware of their own beliefs, they do not always possess language with which to describe and label their beliefs,

and they may be reluctant to espouse them publicly. Thus a direct question such as 'What is your philosophy of teaching?' is usually an ineffective or counterproductive way to elicit beliefs.

(Kagan, 1992b: 66)

One response by interviewers to these challenges has been the use of structured interviews based on scenarios (e.g. brief descriptions of hypothetical instructional events) which teachers are invited to respond to orally through a series of prompts. The large-scale Teacher Education and Learning to Teach study (TELT) carried out by Michigan State University in the late 1980s utilized this interviewing strategy in studying teachers' conceptions of their work. McDiarmid and Ball (1989) outline the rationale for using scenarios in this project as follows:

> After a series of questions in which we ask teachers and prospective teachers about their experiences as learners of math and writing, we present them with a series of scenarios that describe typical instructional situations. We developed these scenarios around common teaching tasks such as deciding what to teach, responding to student errors, and determining what students have learned. In responding to these scenarios, teachers reveal how they weigh and blend their knowledge and understandings of the various dimensions of knowledge. One of the questions that follows these scenarios asks practicing and prospective teachers what they would do in the situation; we thereby get a glimpse of their dispositions – that is, how they are inclined to act in circumstances common to classrooms.
>
> (McDiarmid and Ball, 1989: 10)

Drawing on data from this project, Mosenthal (1995) examined the work of a teacher of writing, and in doing so provided an example of the kinds of scenarios which were used:

> Here is a paper a fourth-grade student wrote in response to an assignment that asked him to read about dolphins and fish and to write a report about them. How would you respond to this student?
>
> (Mosenthal, 1995: 268)

McCarthey (1992) also drew on data from the TELT project in her study of teachers' conceptions of writing. Her report illustrates further examples of the scenarios used in eliciting teachers' verbal commentaries (I have inserted numbers here to mark out the different examples):

> [1] The teacher was asked to respond to a scenario in which the principal comes in at the beginning of the year to ask about her goals for writing . . . [2] about what she would do if a third grader had trouble with apostrophes . . . [3] the scenario in which the teacher is asked to respond to a text written by a third grader, Jessie, containing many spelling and punctuation errors; and . . . [4] the one asking the teacher to explain what she would do if a child asked her if he should use the grammatical construction 'is' or 'are' in a particular sentence.
> (McCarthey, 1992: 5)

A more recent example of the use of scenarios in interviews is Basturkmen *et al.* (2004), who used what they call *cued response scenarios*. In this study, the researchers were interested in ESL teachers' beliefs about focus on form. As part of the study, teachers were given descriptions of typical classroom situations and asked to comment on what they felt should be done in each situation and why. An example of a scenario from this study is given in Figure 7.2. It must be acknowledged, as the authors in this case do, that while scenarios

---

Below are a number of possible situations that can occur in communicative activities. For each situation, please state *what* you think you should do and *why*.

1. The class is working in small groups exchanging information about their future plans. One student turns to you and asks – In the far *future, is this correct?*
   What should I do?
   Why?

FIGURE 7.2 *Cued response scenario*
(Basturkmen *et al.*, 2004: 270)

can make the discussion of teachers' beliefs more concrete, they are unable to capture all the factors which influence teachers' decisions in actual teaching, such as their knowledge of the learners or their assessment of the mood of the class at any particular point in time. Additionally, as McDiarmid and Ball (1989: 12) acknowledge, while through scenarios

> we can simulate actual teaching situations in an interview, such inquiry remains hypothetical. We do not learn whether respondents are actually inclined to do what they describe, nor how competently they could carry out their plans.

This is in fact a limitation of verbal commentaries generally; they may reveal teachers' stated beliefs and intentions, but, on their own, do not allow us to draw conclusions about what teachers actually do. It is for this reason that interviews are often combined with classroom observation (see Chapter 8) in studies of language teacher cognition.

Repertory grid interviews

Repertory grid interviews are another structured approach to eliciting verbal commentaries in the study of language teacher cognition. Before considering examples of its use, I will provide some background to the procedures involved as some understanding of these is needed to make sense of the studies I will subsequently refer to.

The repertory grid is a data collection strategy associated with Kelly's personal construct theory (Kelly, 1955). A full discussion of personal construct theory is beyond our scope here (but see, for example, Bannister and Fransella, 1986; Pope and Keen, 1981), but in essence it is a personality theory which accounts for the way individuals perceive and make sense of their experiences. According to this theory, individuals exercise choices in assigning meanings to their lives and these meanings are embodied in personal constructs. Applied to education, this implies that understanding teachers involves eliciting their personal constructs, and repertory grid interviews are a strategy for achieving this. It is a form of structured interview which generates data suitable for statistical analysis. It been applied widely (and, according to Pope and Denicolo, 1993, frequently misused) in the study of teacher cognition generally (e.g. Ben-Peretz, 1984; Munby, 1982), but used in a much more modest fashion in the study of language teacher cognition (Bodycott, 1997; Murray, 2003; Sendan and Roberts, 1998).

Figure 7.3 can be used to highlight the basic characteristics of repertory grid interviews (though, as Cohen *et al.*, 2000 explain, a number of variations of this technique have been developed since Kelly originally introduced it). There are two basic components in such interviews. Firstly, there are the elements. In this example the elements are the people who are going to be talked about in the interview (e.g. mother, father, etc.). Elements can be any phenomenon, such as events, objects, ideas, in addition to people. It is essential that these are representative of the area to be studied. For example, if the focus is on individuals who have had a significant influence on teachers' beliefs, then elements might include former teachers, colleagues, teacher educators and parents. The second component consists of the constructs – the conceptualizations which are applied to the elements. Constructs are the ways in which elements are similar or different and, as this example shows, are expressed in bipolar form (e.g. quiet-talkative). In a repertory grid interview, elements are typically arranged into groups of three (these

---

A person is asked to name a number of people who are significant to him. These might be, for example, mother, father, wife, friend, employer, priest. These constitute the elements in the repertory grid.

The subject is then asked to arrange the elements into groups of threes in such a manner that two are similar in some way but at the same time different from the third. The ways in which the elements may be alike or different are the *constructs*, generally expressed in bi-polar form (quiet – talkative; mean – generous; warm – cold). The way in which two of the elements are similar is called the *similarity pole* of the construct; and the way in which two of the elements are different from the third, the *contrast pole* of the construct.

A grid can now be constructed by asking the subject to place each element at either the *similarity* or the *contrast* pole of each construct. Let x = one pole of the construct, and blank = the other. The result can be set out as follows:

CONSTRUCTS	ELEMENTS						
	A	B	C	D	E	F
1 quiet – talkative	x	x	x			x
2 mean – generous	x			x	x	
3 warm – cold			x		x	

It is now possible to derive different kinds of information from the grid. By studying each *row*, for example, we can get some idea of how a person defines each construct in terms of significant people in his life. From each *column*, we have a personality profile of each of the significant people in terms of the constructs selected by the subjects. More sophisticated treatments of grid data are discussed in examples presented in the text.

FIGURE 7.3 *Example of repertory grid*
(Cohen *et al.*, 2000: 338)

are called triads) and respondents are asked to comment on the ways in which two elements in each group are both similar as well as different to the third. On the basis of the interviewee's responses, a grid can be constructed, as shown in Figure 7.3. The grid lists all the elements and all the constructs.

The grid is completed by recording on it the way each element is evaluated by the respondent in relation to each construct. In this example, a dichotomous approach to rating elements is adopted; that is, responses are either marked with a cross (e.g. in this example, element A is judged to be quiet) or left blank (e.g. element D is judged here to be talkative). Ranking and rating scales are two other ways in which judgements about elements may be expressed (see Cohen et al., 2000: 339–40 for examples). In the former, elements are ranked in relation to the similarity pole of each construct (e.g. different individuals will be ranked in terms of how *quiet* they are). In the latter (which, according to Beail, 1985 is the most popular method of completing grids), elements are rated in relation to each construct (e.g. on a five-point scale, individuals who are very quiet are rated as a 5, individuals who are very talkative are rated as 1).

Once grids have been constructed, they can then be inspected manually or analysed using computers (there are a number of free programmes for analysing repertory grids). The purpose of the analysis will generally be to reveal patterns of relationships among the constructs and the elements, though the precise nature of the analyses conducted will depend on the research questions being investigated; Pope and Denicolo (1993) mention different types of analyses which are possible: content analysis, hand sort, cluster analysis and principal component analysis, while Beail (1985) explains different ways in which associations among constructs and elements can be computed. The choice of particular analytical methods, their implementation and interpretation assume a certain level of technical understanding; this requirement may be one reason for the limited use to date of repertory grids in the study of language teacher cognition. It is clear that researchers wanting to adopt this methodological strategy will need to undergo a certain amount of theoretical and practical training before they are ready to do so. To fully understand published studies using repertory grids, readers, too, will require some background knowledge of how the grids are generated and what they mean. Without this understanding, the grids presented in studies such as Sendan and Roberts (1998), for example, cannot be fully interpreted.

In addition to decisions about how to construct grids and about the form of analysis to adopt, researchers using repertory grid interviews need to consider at least two more central issues. One is whether to administer the interview once or on repeated occasions. The former option provides a snapshot of the personal constructs held at a particular time; the latter allows the analysis of changes in personal constructs over time. A second issue relates to the origins of the constructs and elements used in the repertory grid interviews. Constructs and elements can be elicited from respondents themselves, as in the example in Figure 7.3; here respondents are first asked to name people who are significant to them (in this way elements are elicited) and then asked to describe similarities and differences between these (in this way the constructs are elicited). The elicitation of constructs and elements in this manner was what Kelly originally proposed. However, varieties of repertory grid interviews also exist in which constructs are provided for respondents to comment on. Pope and Denicolo (1993) argue for the use of free elicitation of both elements and constructs on the basis that this approach provides insight into the personal perspectives held by respondents. Figure 7.4 is a summary of the process of eliciting constructs and constructing repertory grids. This assumes that elements and constructs are being elicited and that a rating scale approach is being used to evaluate elements.

With this background in place, let us now consider the use of repertory grid interviews in the study of language teacher cognition. Bodycott (1997) studied the constructs of the ideal teacher held by 12 pre-service teachers preparing to teach Malay, Tamil, Chinese or English in primary schools in Singapore. In this study, the elements were provided rather than elicited – they were derived from a previously published study and through consultations with professionals in the context studied. The elements were presented to respondents in randomly chosen triads (this suggests that the respondents were not selecting the triads themselves) and the teachers were asked to distinguish two elements in each case from the third. In terms of how the constructs were devised, we read that 'participants responded [to the triads] through the elicitation of

VERBAL COMMENTARIES

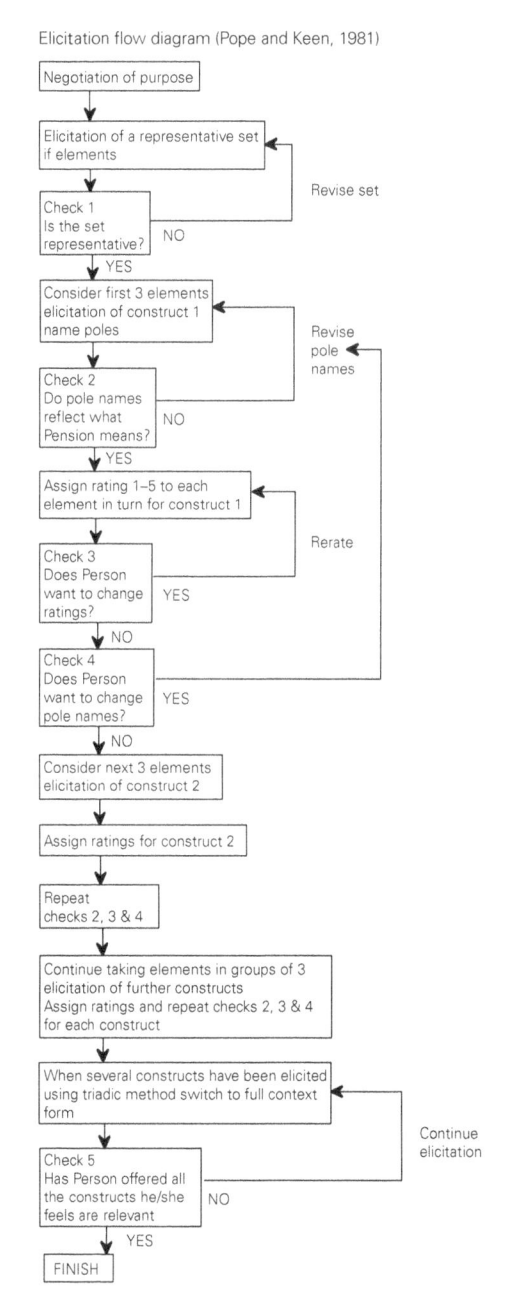

Elicitation flow diagram (Pope and Keen, 1981)

```
Negotiation of purpose
        │
        ▼
Elicitation of a representative set ◄──── Revise set
if elements
        │
        ▼
Check 1
Is the set
representative?  NO ──┐
        │ YES          │
        ▼              │
Consider first 3 elements ◄──────┐
elicitation of construct 1        │ Revise
name poles                        │ pole
        │                         │ names
        ▼                         │
Check 2
Do pole names
reflect what
Pension means?  NO ───────────────┘
        │ YES
        ▼
Assign rating 1–5 to each ◄─────┐
element in turn for construct 1  │
        │                        │ Rerate
        ▼                        │
Check 3
Does Person
want to change
ratings?  YES ───────────────────┘
        │ NO
        ▼
Check 4
Does Person
want to change
pole names?  YES ────────────────┘
        │ NO
        ▼
Consider next 3 elements
elicitation of construct 2
        │
        ▼
Assign ratings for construct 2
        │
        ▼
Repeat
checks 2, 3 & 4
        │
        ▼
Continue taking elements in groups of 3
elicitation of further constructs
Assign ratings and repeat checks 2, 3 & 4
for each construct
        │
        ▼
When several constructs have been elicited ◄──┐
using triadic method switch to full context    │
form                                           │ Continue
        │                                      │ elicitation
        ▼                                      │
Check 5
Has Person offered all
the constructs he/she
feels are relevant  NO ────────────────────────┘
        │ YES
        ▼
      FINISH
```

FIGURE 7.4 *Repertory grid elicitation process (Roberts, 1999: 142)* © *1999 Edward Arnold Publishers*

personal anecdotes and re-counts of past experience. It was from these that personal constructs or views of the ideal language teacher were derived' (pp. 59–60). A list of the constructs elicited, though, is not reported. The study does, however, explain that a seven-point rating scale was used to rate the elements once the constructs had been elicited and that these were subject to cluster analyses using the FOCUS program. FOCUS is a common form of computerized analysis which rearranges the constructs and elements in a grid so that those that are most similar are grouped together. On the basis of these analyses (and combined with data in the form of written biographies and further interviews), the repertory grid data revealed the constructs which were core in the teachers' views of the ideal teacher. These constructs, for example, related more to personal characteristics (e.g. patience and empathy) than to matters of instructional technique.

Sendan and Roberts (1998) used repertory grids in the study of student teachers' personal theories about effective teachers. They argue that personal construct theory provides an appropriate way of studying conceptual change in student teachers because it can provide access to the *structural* dimension of such change rather than, as in most existing studies, only considering the *content* of student teachers' thinking (see Chapter 2 for further discussion of this study). The full study from which this paper is drawn consisted of a cross-sectional component in which repertory grids were completed by 48 student teachers (12 from each year of a four-year teacher education programme) as well as a longitudinal component in which six additional student teachers completed repertory grids on three occasions in years 3 and 4 of their programme. For these six student teachers, in-depth interviews were conducted after each repertory grid elicitation to explore their interpretations of the patterns found in their grids when these had been analysed (see Roberts, 1999: 143 for the interview schedule used). In the repertory grids, the elements consisted of nine English language teachers (three effective, three typical and three ineffective) chosen by each respondent as well known to them. (Details of the elicitation procedures used in this study are supplied in Roberts, 1999 but these essentially followed those outlined in Figure 7.4.) The repertory grid data were subjected to FOCUS and Exchange grid analyses (see Pope and Keen, 1981 for a discussion of these and other forms of repertory grid analysis).

Through an analysis of the repertory grids for one particular student teacher, this study was able to demonstrate evidence of conceptual development in his thinking about effective teaching and in particular to focus on the structural dimension of such development. An analysis of three repertory grids over time by this student and the study of the way his constructs related to effective teaching were organized and reorganized over this time revealed a developmental pattern which, the authors argue, a focus limited to the content of the student teachers' thinking would not reveal.

The final example of the use of repertory grids in the study of language teacher cognition I will discuss here is Murray (2003), who used this interviewing strategy as part of her investigation into the development of the language awareness of pre-service teachers of English as a foreign language. Murray (pp. 109–10) provides the following reasons for her choice of repertory grid interviews:

- There was evidence in teacher thinking research that it was a suitable way of studying teachers' conceptual development.

- She saw development in teacher trainees' language awareness as a process of changing personal conceptualizations; repertory grid interviews were conducive to studying such change.

- It allowed respondents to express their language-related concepts using their own metalanguage.

- It combined the openness of a semi-structured interview with the element of standardization provided by the use of similar stimuli (i.e. elements in the repertory grid) in eliciting constructs from respondents.

In relation to this final point (and given that I am discussing repertory grids here as a form of structured interview), Murray does in fact comment in various places on the flexibility of repertory grid interviews, arguing that the technique is not necessarily as rigid and structured as often seems to be the case.

The elements for this study were derived from an analysis of the types of language which underpin language teacher decision-making. Three types of language were identified – learner language, native-speaker language and coursebook language. Accordingly, the elements for this study consisted of written and/or transcribed spoken texts, chosen by the researcher, illustrating each of these types. Figure 7.5, for example, shows elements which illustrate learner written language and learner spoken language.

Written Learner Language

Two students have been asked to write about being alone on an island.

A
I am alone on an island. When I got up I was on a beach. I was all wat and I was very hungrey too. So I walked toward a forest. I saw there was many fruit trees.

B
I am alone on an island. I don't know where I am, but I can hear birds calling in the distance. I arrived here last night, washed up on the beach after days on a board that swam. There are a lot of fruit trees nearby, which is good because I have the hunger of a wolf.

Spoken Learner Language

Two students are telling a story based on pictures.

C:
'He fell down. He lied on a floor and per'aps uh uh uh yes 'e broked 'is airm an' 'e was browt to da 'ospital.'

D:
'He .... felt ... no fell on .. on. .onto…the….flower?..floor?.. Oh..
I uh.... onto the floor.... The arm .... His arm .... was break broke broken… urn his arm was broken.'

FIGURE 7.5 *Learner language elements in the study of pre-service teachers' language awareness (Murray, 2003: 112–14). Reproduced with kind permission of the author.*

In the repertory grid interviews in this study, respondents were asked about the similarities and differences between the two elements in each set with a view to eliciting the constructs which would reflect on their language awareness. In contrast with the common approach of using triads of elements, then, in eliciting constructs, this study used pairs (i.e. dyads) (according to Beail, 1985, this is acceptable practice). Respondents were also given the elements to think about one day before the interview. There was also a longitudinal dimension to this study, with repertory grids being completed by the teachers in the first, fourth and seventh months of a seven-month teacher education programme. Interestingly, though, the use of the same elements in successive interviews was not positively received by all respondents:

> The trainees were not told after the first interview that they would be given the same elements for the second interview because it was feared they might try to recall them or be tempted to discuss them with the others. Unfortunately, a number of them expressed strong disappointment in the second interview to find that they were asked to construe elements they had already compared in the first. Despite the fact that three months had passed, they claimed they could remember what they had said the first time and found it boring to say 'more or less the same thing' again.
>
> (Murray, 2003: 118)

In response to this reaction, the researcher included some additional elements in the third wave of repertory group interviews, acknowledging that although the introduction of new elements midway through the study was not wholly desirable, it was important to take into the consideration the interests and motivation of the respondents.

Methodologically, this study is also interesting in that it does seem to have applied statistical analysis to the repertory interview data. In fact, repertory grids themselves were not constructed. Rather, interviews were transcribed, the transcripts were analysed for concepts, and changes in constructs were noted in the successive data sets. A detailed description of the procedures followed is included in an appendix to this study (Murray, 2003: 326–8).

In concluding this section, some potential problems with repertory grid interviews should be highlighted. Firstly, as already noted, their design, implementation, analysis and interpretation require a certain amount of technical skill; training, practice and time for piloting are thus essential if this strategy is to be used successfully in the study of language teacher cognition. Secondly, as highlighted in the final study discussed here, respondents may not react positively to being asked to analyse the same set of elements on more than one occasion; this is an issue which researchers using repertory grids longitudinally need to take into account. Thirdly, effective repertory grid interviewing is a sophisticated skill (an art not just a science, as Pope and Denicolo, 1993 say) and researchers need to be aware (especially where constructs are being elicited) of the danger that they might be imposing constructs on respondents (putting words into respondents' mouths, so to speak). Cohen et al. (2000) also note that questions have been raised about the extent to which repertory grids, with their emphasis on measurement and statistical analysis, are actually compatible with the constructivist-interpretive theoretical base they stem from. A final observation about repertory grids is that they 'impose a simple bipolar structure on knowledge, which some have argued may misrepresent its nature' (Calderhead, 1996: 722). These are certainly issues for language teacher cognition researchers interested in exploring repertory grid interviews to consider; Fransella and Bannister (1977) provide a useful discussion of these and other difficulties associated with the technique.

Semi-structured interviews

As noted earlier, semi-structured interviews are typically based around a set of topics or a loosely defined series of questions; they are flexible, allowing the conversation a certain amount of freedom in terms of the direction it takes, and respondents are also encouraged to talk in an open-ended manner about the topics under discussion or any other matters they feel are relevant. Semi-structured interviews are widely used in educational research generally and several advantages claimed for them are listed in Table 7.1.

Table 7.1 Advantages of semi-structured interviews

- Semi-structured interviewing enables the researcher to develop a relationship with the participants. Given the dialectic nature of knowledge construction in such interviews, establishing rapport (what Miller and Glassner, 1997: 669: 106, call 'intersubjective depth') is fundamental to the quality of the inquiry (Fontana and Frey, 1994).

- It allows the interview to proceed as a conversation (Kvale, 1996) rather than as a formalized exchange in which the interviewer imposes his or her authority on the interviewee. The effects of the asymmetrical relationship between interviewer and interviewee can be minimized if the interview is conducted in true interpretive spirit as a two-way conversation rather than a researcher-dominated activity (Woods, 1986).

- It allows the researcher to explore tacit and unobservable aspects of participants' lives (Glesne and Peshkin, 1992).

- By avoiding forced-choice responses (those where the respondent must choose one of the responses provided by the interviewer), it facilitates the researcher's task of interpreting participants' experiences from their point of view (Ely, 1991) and of representing these experiences in participants' own language (Kvale, 1996).

- By relying predominantly on open-ended questions, it has the potential to generate data which are more elaborate and qualitatively richer than those generated by closed questions (Anderson and Burns, 1989).

- It provides the researcher with a flexible tool for data collection in that the direction of the conversation is not predetermined but responsive to the specific contributions the interviewee makes. This reflexive approach to interviewing also makes it possible for the researcher to make and explore unexpected discoveries (Cohen, Manion and Morrison, 2000).

- It encourages interviewees to play an active part in the research, rather than being passive objects to be studied (Holstein and Gubrium, 1997). This form of interviewing solicits the active involvement of individuals in communicating the sense-making processes through which they interpret their own experiences.

The strategy is also widely used in language teacher cognition research; the justification for using semi-structured interviews provided by Mangubhai *et al.* (2004) highlights the value it is seen to have in eliciting verbal accounts of teachers' cognitive processes:

> First, this method has a long and successful tradition in teacher thinking research dating back two decades . . . It gives teachers the opportunities and time to detail fully and freely the bases for their approaches to teaching, without the constraints of a set schedule of invariant questions. Moreover, this approach allows prominence to be given to the voice of teachers rather than that of researchers, an important consideration for ensuring fidelity of accounts of practice and their rationales . . . Second, practical theories are considered to be largely implicit (Clark and Peterson, 1986; Gage, 1977) because they tend to build up in teachers' minds in the absence of a formal process of theory construction and because teachers are rarely invited to make them explicit. For these reasons, articulation of implicit theories by teachers can pose difficulties. These difficulties can be assuaged to an extent within the context of an in-depth interview by creating a climate conducive to teacher reflection and disclosure of details of their practical theories. Teacher engagement in these introspective processes can be encouraged by interviewers being empathic, supportive and nonevaluative, asking open-ended questions, seeking clarification and extension of the teachers' remarks and using the language of the teachers where possible.
>
> (Mangubhai *et al.*, 2004: 294)

These points are echoed in a number of studies which have examined teacher cognition, partly or exclusively, through semi-structured interviews. Table 7.2 lists examples, and I will now comment on some of these.

Borg (1998b) explored teachers' cognitions in relation to grammar teaching through semi-structured interviews. These were of two types; background interviews, which took place prior to any classroom observations, and stimulated recall interviews conducted after teaching had been observed (I discuss stimulated recall interviews overleaf). Figure 7.6 is an example of a background interview schedule

Table 7.2 Semi-structured interviewing in language teacher cognition research

Source	Description of interview	Characteristics
Basturkmen et al. (2004)	in-depth interview	used some closed but mainly open questions; avoided direct questioning about beliefs in favour of indirect items
Borg (1998b)	semi-structured interview	flexible focus on particular themes; open-minded exploration of meaning assigned to teacher's educational and professional experiences
Mangubhai et al. (2004)	semi-structured in-depth interview	free from constraints of set schedule; gives prominence to teacher's voice; empathic and supportive interviewer required
Richardson et al. (1991)	ethnographic belief interview	inductive discovery of beliefs through elicitation; adaptation of heuristic elicitation technique used in anthropology; both open and closed questions
Tsui (2003)	semi-structured interview and conversation	progressive focusing, moving from general background issues to sharper focus on issues and themes arising in previous interviews and observations
Warford & Reeves (2003)	long interview	questions designed to cover analytical categories derived from the literature; 'grand tour' (i.e. general), tone setting and background questions followed by more specific prompts

from this study. Although the list of questions may appear structured, these were more a guide to the range of issues which the researcher was interested in discussing with teachers; the wording of questions in the actual discussion varied from that on the schedule, as did the order in which different themes were covered; additionally, questions

Section 1: Education

1. What do you recall about your experiences of learning English at school?
   - What approaches were used?
   - Was there any formal analysis of language?
2. Did you study any foreign languages? What do you recall about these lessons?
   - What kinds of methods were used?
   - Do you recall whether you enjoyed such lessons or not?
3. What about post-secondary education? University? Did the study of language play any role there?
4. Do you feel that your own education as a student has had any influence on the way you teach today?

Section 2: Entry into the Profession and Development as a Teacher

1. How and why did you become an EFL teacher?
   - What recollections do you have about your earliest teaching experiences?
   - Were these particularly positive or negative?
   - What kinds of teaching methods and materials did you use?
2. Tell me about your formal teacher training experiences.
   - Did they promote a particular way of teaching?
   - Did they encourage participants to approach grammar in any particular way?
   - Which aspect(s) of the course(s) did you find most memorable?
3. What have the greatest influences on your development as a teacher been?

Section 3: Reflections on Teaching

1. What do you feel the most satisfying aspect of teaching EFL is, and what is the hardest part of the job?
2. What do you feel your strengths as an EFL teacher are, and your weaknesses?
3. Can you describe one particularly good experience you've had as an EFL teacher, and one particularly bad one? What's your idea of a 'successful' lesson?
4. Do you have any preferences in terms of the types of students you like to teach?
5. What about the students? Do they generally have any preferences about the kind of work they like to do in their lessons?

Section 4: The School

1. Does the school you work for promote any particular style of teaching?
2. Are there any restrictions on the kinds of materials you use or on the content and organization of your lessons?
3. Do students come here expecting a particular type of language course?

FIGURE 7.6 *Example of pre-observation semi-structured interview schedule (Borg, 1998: 35–6). Reproduced with permission of TESOL.*

not on the schedule were asked in the course of the unfolding discussion between the researcher and the respondent. These are typical characteristics of semi-structured interviews.

A similar example comes from the work of Lam (2000) who conducted semi-structured interviews with ESL teachers to explore their beliefs about technology. Once again, an interview guide consisting of a range of potential questions was developed (these are reported on page 419) but this was used flexibly, despite its apparent structure:

> the questions were by no means limited to the list, which allowed me to follow the flow of conversation and to ask for elaboration of certain points or probe other issues that were not mentioned by the participant. As a result, questions were not asked in the same order for each participant, nor were exactly the same questions asked.
>
> (Lam, 2000: 398)

The interview guide used by Richardson *et al.* (1991) illustrates another way of devising a semi-structured interview schedule (see Figure 7.7 for an extract). This is organized around a series of headings, within which there are set questions and probes to guide the researcher. This particular approach to interviewing is called by the authors an ethnographic belief interview, through which beliefs are elicited inductively. Interviews were specifically chosen in this study in the belief that they were more suited to capturing beliefs than questionnaires (see Chapter 5).

While semi-structured interviews are widely used in the study of language teacher cognition, extended extracts from these do not commonly appear in published studies. Even when they do, it is generally the case that the focus is on what respondents' say without reporting the specific prompts used by researchers. While limitations of space often do preclude the inclusion of extended interview extracts, in such cases readers have to assume that the semi-structured interviews being reported on were conducted in a manner which reflects the principles underpinning their use (see Table 7.1). Achieving this consistency between methodological principles and practice, though, is not always straightforward, and may be particularly

> Reading Instruction:
>
> Could you describe the way you teach reading comprehension? Probe–typical day? reading out loud? Objective–vocabulary? remembering ideas? memorizing facts? Questioning students–why? what is a good response? what is a poor response? what is a creative response? Where did you learn to teach reading that way? Have you ever had in-service/graduate courses on how to teach it? Have you ever tried something different? Why? What happened? Have you ever wanted to do something different? Grouping: on what basis? why? Probe–do you change the groups? why? Have you ever tried to teach the whole group? Under what conditions would you do so? Do you do different things in the different groups? Why? What indicates to you that a lesson is going poorly? How is teaching reading different from teaching math? from teaching science or social studies? from teaching writing? Probe–more/less difficult? less clarity about objectives? Do you ever feel like you are getting behind in reading?

FIGURE 7.7 *Extract from a semi-structured interview guide* (Richardson *et al.*, 1991: 580)

hard for novice researchers to achieve. Consider the following extract (supplied by a research student and used here with their permission):

(I is the interviewer, T the teacher. This is a post-lesson interview which aims to explore the teacher's rationale for their instructional choices in the observed lesson).

I: What is your focus in this activity?
T: To identify the meaning of the title. I introduce to the student what they are going to study in the unit.
I: What is your goal in this introduction?
T: To make the student understand what they are going to deal with and study in the unit, so the title becomes clearer for the student. I explain the title. It is like pre-reading activity OK so the students know what the unit is about.
I: Can you explain why you used the picture in your introduction of the unit?
T: OK the picture simplifies the unit for the student. The picture introduces the lesson so the students can understand what

	the unit is about. This is better than to start the reading passages directly like we did in the previous curriculum.
I:	There are some discussion questions about the picture. In your opinion how do the students interact with these questions?
T:	It depends on the level of the students. Frankly there is not too much response. For example in this class you find two, three, four students only. Because the students have complexity speaking in English. It is known that our students come to the school with having complexity in speaking.
I:	When you deal with discussing the picture, which skill are you focusing on?
T:	Speaking. It is not important even if the explanation of the picture is wrong. The important thing is that they express themselves. Any sentence, the important thing is to speak. I try to encourage them to speak.
I:	How do you form the discussion in the class?
T:	I give the students some time to think, and then I select one of the students who raise their hands. I do not use pair or group discussion.
I:	Why don't you use pair or group discussion?
T:	Because it will become chaotic and noisy. Students are not used to pair or group discussion. They will waste the time. I think individually is better.
I:	What is your role when the students start the discussion?
T:	I ask a student. They answer. I correct their word. For example, I explain a sentence. I give a word to help them in the discussion.
	They are the ones who discuss.

This interview clearly does not read like it is semi-structured. The interviewer's questions sound terse (e.g. there is no social interaction and questions are very direct) and opportunities to build on and explore the teacher's responses are not seized (e.g. the teacher's views on pair and group work could have been explored further). This is part of a longer interview which followed a similar pattern, but even from this brief extract one gets the feeling that the interviewer was focusing more on the questions they wanted to ask than on listening to the teacher and responding thoughtfully to them. This undoubtedly contributed to the brevity of most of the teacher's answers. The point to make here, then, is that interview skills, generally but perhaps more particularly those required for semi-structured interviews, may require conscious study and training, and definitely require practice and reflection, if such interviews are to reflect in practice the principles which underlie them. Woods (1996: 41) reflects on this very point with reference to his early attempts at interviewing teachers; one transcript, he recollected, 'looked more like a game of 'Twenty Questions' than a narrative'.

Stimulated recall interviews

A further technique for eliciting verbal commentaries on teachers' cognitions is stimulated recall. According to Calderhead (1981: 212)

> the term 'stimulated recall' has been used to denote a variety of techniques. Typically, it involves the use of audiotapes or videotapes of skilled behaviour, which are used to aid a participant's recall of his thought processes at the time of that behaviour . . . It is assumed that the cues provided by the audiotape or videotape will enable the participant to 'relive' the episode to the extent of being able to provide, in retrospect, an accurate verbalised account of his original thought processes, provided that all the relevant ideas which inform an episode are accessible.

The assumption that stimulated recall interviews can capture interactive thought processes retrospectively is one which has been questioned and which I comment on later; in terms of its procedures, though, this form of interview involves the use of a stimulus (most often a video recording) to elicit verbal commentaries about the cognitions (typically thoughts or decision-making) occurring during previously performed behaviours. Typically, then, teachers watch video recordings of themselves in class, then comment on what they were thinking or doing at the time.

Stimulated recall dates back to the 1950s, though its use in the study of teaching first appeared in the mid-1970s. From then onwards, stimulated recall was widely applied to the study of teachers' interactive decision-making. Teachers cannot teach and talk about their thoughts at the same time (i.e. concurrent verbalization is not possible) and thus retrospective verbal accounts are required to examine interactive thinking. Stimulated recall was seen to be an effective way of eliciting these accounts, to the extent that in the mid-1980s Yinger (1986: 267) described it as 'the primary source of data for interactive thought'.

Stimulated recall may assume a more or less structured nature depending on decisions the researcher makes about three issues:

> replaying only researcher-selected portions of the recording versus replaying the complete tape; researchers asking prespecified questions each time the tape is stopped versus soliciting open-ended commentary from the teacher; and researcher control of when to stop the tape versus teacher control or shared control.
> (Clark and Peterson, 1986: 259)

It is clear, then, that a stimulated recall interview where the research decides which specific stimuli to use, where predetermined questions are asked and where the researcher retains control over when recall comments are made is substantially different in nature to one where the respondent has a greater role in determining what is said, when and in relation to which stimuli. Whereas stimulated recall in early research on interactive decision-making was predominantly more structured in nature, today the strategy appears most commonly as part of interpretive work where it provides teachers with the opportunity to verbalize their thinking, in a relatively free and open-ended manner.

Before discussing some examples of stimulated recall from the field of language teacher cognition, it is also important to note that this technique has been the subject of much methodological debate, focusing in particular on the validity of the data which it generates. Yinger (1986), for example, argues that 'there is good reason to doubt the validity of stimulated recall as a means for accurately reporting interactive thinking' (p. 268) and that 'the data generated during stimulated recall interviews may at best be only tangentially related to actual thinking during the recorded event and at worst be entirely fabricated' (p. 273). Such views (also discussed in Calderhead, 1981,

1996; Lyle, 2003; Shavelson et al., 1986) are grounded in concerns about

- the adequacy with which teachers can accurately report information (e.g. thought processes) that is no longer in their short-term memory;
- the extent to which stimulated recall can generate a complete account both of teacher thinking (much of which may be tacit) and teacher behaviour (which will often be automatized and thus not subject to explicit description);
- the extent to which teachers, under pressure to explain their actions in stimulated recall interviews, may provide post-hoc rationalizations for them – that is explanations made up at the time of the interview rather than accounts of the thinking underpinning the events they are asked to reflect on;
- the possibility that the stimulus itself (e.g. video) may supplement teachers' incomplete memories, thus generating comments on what the video suggests rather than on prior thinking processes;
- the manner in which the video presents the events under study from a different perspective for the teacher, creating a new experience which does not allow teachers to recall the original one;
- the extent to which the prompts used to assist teachers' recall may influence the way in which they report their thinking.

A useful summary of principles for introspective work developed in response to these limitations, based on the work of Ericsson and Simon (1993), is provided by Brown and Rodgers (2002) (see Figure 7.8).

It is clear from these concerns, then, that stimulated recall, though widespread in the study of teacher cognition, is not unproblematic. Carefully structured designs, as Gass and Mackey (2000) argue, are required to minimize many of the threats which are associated with the data this elicitation technique produces; one key issue that seems generally accepted, for example, is that stimulated recall will generate more valid data when the time between the event under analysis and the subsequent interview is minimized. This is particularly the case if the aim of the stimulated recall is to elicit the precise thoughts teachers had at particular points in a lesson; stimulated recall, though, as we see below, has also been used with the more general purpose of facilitating the discussion and analysis of teachers' actions and rationales, and in these circumstances not all of the concerns raised above will apply; certain dangers, however, such as those associated with post-hoc rationalizations, remain.

Turning now to the study of language teacher cognition, Table 7.3 lists ten studies which have utilized stimulated recall. It also states for each study what the stimulus used was and quotes an extract which describes some facet of the procedures used. Seven of these studies used video as the stimulus, two used lesson transcripts and one

---

1. Time intervening between mental operations and report is critical and should be minimized as much as possible;
2. Verbalization places additional cognitive demands on mental processing that requires care in order to achieve insightful results;
3. Verbal reports of mental processes should avoid the usual social conventions of talking to someone;
4. There is a lot of information in introspective reports aside from the words themselves. Researchers need to be aware of these parallel signal systems and be prepared to include them in their analyses;
5. Verbal reports of automatic processes are not possible. Such processes include visual and motor processes and low-attention, automatized linguistic processes such as the social chat of native speakers; and
6. Research should be based on a model of mental processes that allows predictions about how mental operations will be organized under various conditions.

(Based on Ericsson and Simon, 1993)

FIGURE 7.8 *Verbal reports of mental operations*
(Brown and Rodgers, 2002: 55)

Table 7.3 Stimulated recall interviews in language teacher cognition research

Source	Stimulus	Description
Andrews & McNeil (2005)	video	'Each subject was shown a videotape of herself teaching. As soon as practicable . . . the interviewer and subject sat together and watched the videotape of that lesson. The subjects were invited to comment on the lesson at any point, pausing the videotape as necessary. On occasions, a pause led to an extended interchange. The interviewer also posed spontaneous questions relating to incidents in the lesson' (p. 163).
Basturkmen (2004)	audio and transcript	'The aim of the stimulated recall was to provide the teachers with the opportunity to verbalize their thoughts about their interactive decisionmaking. We wanted to find out whether the episodes reflected what the teachers felt they should have done in these events' (p. 251).
Borg (1998b)	transcript	'In order to gain access to the teacher's thoughts about the issues included in these categories, I presented him with key episodes from his lessons and prompted him to elaborate on these through a form of stimulated recall' (p. 13).
Breen et al. (2001)	video	'Teacher and researcher viewed the video recorded lesson during which the teacher indicated a number of key features or incidents. As the lesson proceeded or at moments the teacher wished to highlight, the researcher explored further those aspects of the lesson that may have been typical of the teacher's usual ways of working and/or may have illustrated the principles on which the work was based' (p. 481).

Table 7.3 (Continued)

Source	Stimulus	Description
Burns & Knox (2005)	transcript	'All the data were transcribed in preparation for stimulated recall interviews . . . Before the interviews the teachers were sent the lesson transcripts so that they could check their accuracy. We asked the teachers to comment on any parts of the transcript they wished to discuss and we also selected segments for discussion ourselves. Such an approach overcomes the difficulties of short-term memory as the participants can focus back on the actual discourse at the time, and both participants and researchers can offer interpretations of the events that can be directly linked back to specific points in the lesson' (p. 242).
Gatbonton (1999)	video	'Each teacher was asked to view one hour of his or her video recorded lessons . . . While viewing, the teachers were asked to recollect aloud (into an ongoing tape recorder) what they were thinking while teaching the particular segment being viewed' (p. 37).
Golombek (1998)	video	'Teachers were asked to consider their decisionmaking processes and evaluate their instructional decisions' (p. 451).
Johnson (1994)	video	'Teachers were asked to view their own lessons and provide stimulus recall comments . . . that detailed the nature of their instructional thoughts and decisions while watching themselves teach. They were asked to stop the videotape at points where they recollected their instructional decisions and explain why they chose to make those decisions' (p. 442).

(Continued)

Table 7.3 (Continued)

Source	Stimulus	Description
Mangubhai et al. (2004)	video	'In re-play sessions, the teacher was to be asked to stop the videotapes where aspects of a CLT approach were in evidence and explain the rationale for those classroom events' (p. 296).
Woods (1996)	video	'By pressing a remote pause button to stop the video and then making the comment, the teacher provided unstructured commentary regarding thoughts, plans and decisions that were related to the classroom events on tape' (p. 28).

used audio recordings and transcripts. The implementation of video stimulated recall (VSR) in these studies highlights both common practices and variety. For example, while in most cases recordings seemed to have been made by the researcher, in Johnson (1994) the recordings were made by the colleagues of the teachers being studied and in Breen et al. (2001) teachers recorded their own lesson and viewed this before the interview. Also, while teachers generally seemed to have been given a remote control and invited to pause the tape at places they wanted to comment on, not all studies explicitly report using this strategy; the extract from Gatbonton (1999) cited in Table 7.3, for example, suggests that teachers' verbalizations were collected in the form of a running commentary (i.e. without pausing the video recording). Another area of commonality in these examples of VSR is that teachers were asked to respond in a largely unstructured manner (see, for example, Andrews and McNeil, 2005 in Table 7.3; Woods, 1996) rather than being given specific prompts to respond to (it is difficult to comment precisely on this as the exact prompts used by the researchers are rarely stated in the published reports – Meijer, 1999 is an exception – see Figure 7.9). Overall, the evidence suggests that the VSR in the study of language teacher cognition has been characterized by the less structured approach in which teachers are encouraged to take the initiative in identifying which

> We are going to watch a video recording of the lesson you have just given. The purpose of this interview is to stimulate you to remember what you were thinking, or what was 'on your mind', during this lesson. Of course, in a 50-minute lesson, a lot of thoughts have gone through your head, and it would be impossible to remember them all without some help. I hope that the video-recording of the lesson will help you to recall what was on your mind during the lesson. Try to 'relive' the lesson when watching the videotape. Stop the videotape every time you recall what you were thinking during the lesson, or what was on your mind. Try to say everything you can remember thinking during the lesson, without asking yourself whether these thoughts are important, 'strange', etc. To illustrate what I expect you to do, I will first show you a short videotape with some examples of what teachers say while watching.
>
> So, I want you to tell your thoughts while you were teaching this lesson. I want you to clearly distinguish these thoughts from the ones you will have while watching the videotape. These last thoughts are not the focus of this interview. Of course, sometimes it is hard to distinguish between these two kinds of thoughts. In case I have doubts about whether a thought you report concerns one you had during the lesson, or one which arises now that you are watching the videotape, I will ask, 'Were these your thoughts during the lesson, or are you thinking this right now, while you are watching the videotape?'
>
> Sometimes teachers become absorbed in watching the videotape of their own lesson and forget to report their thinking during the lesson. In case this happens, and you let the videotape run for more than 45 seconds without reporting your thoughts, I will stop the tape, and ask whether you can recall your thoughts at that moment in the lesson. In case you cannot recall your thoughts, you can say so, and start the tape again. In general, however, I will not interfere during the interview: You will be the only one talking. I will just listen and write something down every now and then. Perhaps I will ask some short questions.
>
> It absolutely does not matter whether the lesson we are about to watch was a 'good' one or not, whether there was a marvelous atmosphere or not, etc. For this interview, which is focused on what you were thinking during the lesson, this is not of any interest. I do not intend to evaluate the lesson. This videotape and everything you say is confidential. Outside the context of my study, nobody will have access to this information.
>
> Do you have any questions?

FIGURE 7.9 *Stimulated recall interview instructions (Meijer, 1999: 67). Reproduced with kind permission of the author.*

aspects of their teaching to comment on and what precisely to say (though, as Woods, 1996 notes, teachers vary in the extent to which they can take such initiative and where they do not prompts from the researcher are necessary, such as 'what were you doing here?'). The researcher's role in this teacher-centred approach to VSR is thus 'facilitator . . . to assist teacher disclosure . . . by listening carefully to the teacher, seeking clarification or elaboration where necessary, and reacting supportively but not judgmentally' (Mangubhai *et al.*, 2004: 296). In this sense, there is little distinction between semi-structured and stimulated recall interviews.

Borg (1998b) and Burns and Knox (2005) both used transcripts of lessons as the basis of their stimulated recall interviews. In the former, key instructional episodes (in this case related to grammar teaching) from audiotaped lessons were transcribed and used to generate interview questions; during the interview, the transcripts were presented to the teacher and the questions used to explore the teachers' beliefs and rationales in relation to the specific issues the transcript highlighted. Figure 7.10, for example, illustrates an episode related to the teacher's use of students' L1 and translation in teaching grammar, and lists the questions this episode generated. Generally in this study, when the teacher was given transcripts from his lessons he was asked to respond in a number of ways:

- by commenting on what he was trying to do at a particular stage of the lesson, and why;
- by responding to assertions the researcher made about the teacher's practice on the basis of what had been observed in the classroom;
- by talking about how a particular episode fitted into the structure of his lesson;
- by explaining his decisions to make use of particular instructional activities and materials in his work.

Burns and Knox (2005) used transcripts in a different way; in advance of the stimulated recall interviews, they sent teachers transcripts of lessons which had been observed and asked them to identify parts of

> Students' L1 and Translation
>
> The teacher calls on students to refer to their L1 many times during the lessons:
>
> S3 says she has a problem using a particular structure, 'Have been, continuous present, is it?'. 'The name doesn't matter', says the teacher, and he proceeds to write the following on the board:
> Je suis ici depuis deux jours
> Ich bin hier seit zwei Tage
> Sono qui da due giorni
> I came here two days ago
> I _____ 2 days.
> The teacher asks, 'Can you complete the sentence?' S2 says 'I have been here for two days'. 'In many European languages', the teacher explains, 'a present tense is used where in English the present perfect is used. We can say "I am here for two weeks", but it has a different meaning, it means "now and in the future."' (EO.1: 98–133)
>
> - What contribution to EFL can the students' L1 make?
> - With specific reference to grammar, how does reference to the L1 help?
>
> During the same lesson, when he tells them to analyse the transcript, the teacher asks the students to tick grammatical structures which are 'the same in my language' or to put a question mark next to items which look 'very different to my language'. Students are asked to write translations of words they don't know. The use of bilingual dictionaries is encouraged.
>
> - What beliefs underlie the teacher's position here?

FIGURE 7.10 *Example of lesson transcript stimulus (Borg, 1998b: 37). Reproduced with permission of TESOL.*

the transcript they wanted to discuss. The researchers also selected extracts from the transcript they wanted to discuss. While there may be an inherent methodological appeal in asking teachers to read transcripts and to identify issues for subsequent discussion in this way, this option must be exercised with caution. Not all teachers will have the time and be sufficiently enthusiastic about the research or committed to it to engage in this process in the manner envisaged by the researcher. Teachers may also feel uncertain about what precisely it is they are expected to do with the transcript and researchers need to ensure that instructions are clear and, more importantly, that realistic demands are being made of the teachers.

Basturkmen *et al.*'s (2004) use of audio recordings and transcripts reflects a more structured approach to stimulated recall interviews. They identified four extracts from the lessons of each teacher in their study, then used the audio recordings of these together with transcripts of them to elicit teachers' commentaries on the classroom events being described. Figure 7.11 is an example of stimulated recall from this study. Both the selection of teaching episodes and the prompts are controlled by the researchers here, providing a contrast

---

In this final part of the interview I am going to ask you about what actually happened during communicative lessons in your classroom and your role as the teacher. We will listen to a number of episodes (short pieces on interaction) recorded from your teaching.
For each episode, please comment on what this is about. Then state if this is how you prefer to deal with this kind of event.

Episode 1

In this episode, a student makes a linguistic error and you respond to it.

T: have you ever betrayed China
S: no, never
T: never
S: yeah I'm a patriost
T: a patriot
S: yeah
S: not like this, like this.
T: yes, a patriot.

1. Can you tell me what this is about?
2. Is this how you prefer to deal with linguistic errors? if not – why not?

FIGURE 7.11 *Example of audio-based stimulated recall* (Basturkmen *et al.*, 2004: 270–1)

to the more open-ended approaches to stimulated recall discussed so far.

The studies I have considered here show some awareness of the methodological problems associated with stimulated recall which were discussed earlier. For example, a number of studies comment on the need to conduct stimulated recall interviews as soon as possible after the events under study (e.g. a lesson) have been completed. Andrews and McNeil (2005: 163), for example, note that their stimulated interviews were conducted 'as soon as practicable' following observations while Mangubhai *et al.* (2004: 297) also explain that 'stimulated recall interviews were conducted on the same day as the videotaping, with preferred times being immediately after the lesson was videotaped or as close as possible there-to'. Not all studies were this explicit in describing how long after observed events the stimulated recall took place. In any case, while in theory the gap between events and their recall should be kept short, teachers will often have their own schedules to follow and researchers will need to accommodate these. This was the case in Gatbonton (1999), who noted that

> Ideally, the teachers should have viewed each videotaped lesson right after teaching it, but it was often not possible to schedule this because some had teaching commitments in regular programs. For one or two teachers, the delay in viewing time ranged from a few days to 3 weeks long.
>
> (Gatbonton, 1999: 37)

Immediate stimulated recall interviews will also not be possible where transcripts are used, given that some time will be required to produce these. In Borg (1998b), for example, there was a gap of one week between the completion of observations and the stimulated recall interview.

One other widely debated issue in the use of stimulated recall, as indicated earlier, is the extent to which it can adequately capture earlier interactive thought processes. In most research on language teacher cognition, though, researchers do not seem to be using stimulated recall to elicit teachers' interactive thoughts; stimuli, whether video, audio or print, are in contrast being used more as the basis of concrete discussions of what the teachers were doing, their interpretations of the events represented in the stimuli and of their reasons for the instructional decisions they were taking. This orientation is implied in many of the extracts quoted in Table 7.3; elsewhere it is made very explicit:

> the goal was not to find out specifically about what the teacher was thinking at that particular moment, but rather to use the moment as a concrete point to elicit talk about the teaching in general. In fact, many of the subsequent verbalizations of the teachers expanded into discussions of other lessons, other studies, their planning, their beliefs, and so on. The specific moment at which the tape was stopped, therefore, is not a crucial element of the research.
> (Woods, 1996: 28)

The nature of the prompts in Basturkmen *et al.* (2004) (see Figure 7.11) also reflects this orientation; teachers were not asked about their thinking during the lesson extracts under discussion, but about what was happening and about whether the instructional strategy described was their preferred one. In fact, a closer look at the description of the purpose of stimulated recall given in this study reveals that it was to provide teachers 'with the opportunity to verbalize *their thoughts about their interactive decision-making*' (my italics). This is different to claiming that the stimulated recall elicits an account of the interactive thinking itself. Of the studies under discussion here, only Johnson (1994) (in addition to Meijer, 1999) suggests that her focus was at least partly on eliciting teachers' instructional thoughts and decisions while teaching. Technically speaking, then, the purposes for which stimulated recall has been utilized in language teacher cognition research seems somewhat different to that for which it had originally been used in the study of teacher thinking; this is not a criticism of research in language teacher cognition; however, the distinction between the recall of interactive or concurrent thought processes and the recall of events to facilitate a discussion of the factors influencing them (such as beliefs) is an important one. This distinction is often reflected in the prompts using during stimulated recall interviews; 'what were you paying attention to, what was on your mind' (Meijer, 1999: 84) reflect an interest in eliciting interactive cognitions; questions which ask teachers for the reasons behind their interactive decisions, in contrast, are not focusing on concurrent thoughts.

One final point to make about the use of stimulus recall interviews relates to the preparation of teachers for this activity. Most studies do not comment on this issue; in some cases mentioned above teachers are asked to view or read data in advance, but otherwise teachers receive little support in preparing for the task of analysing and commenting on the cognitions underlying their teaching. Johnson (1992a) is an exception here. The stimulated recall procedures followed in this study were identical to those in her 1994 paper included in Table 7.3. Additionally, though, in this earlier paper she also explained how the participants in her study were prepared to conduct stimulated recall:

> To familiarize the teachers with these procedures, a demonstration videotaped lesson from a pilot study was shown and sample audiotaped stimulus recall reports were played at predetermined decision points identified on the videotape. Four to six segments of the demonstration videotape were played for each teacher. The teachers were given ample opportunity to ask questions about the stimulus recall procedures.
>
> (Johnson, 1992a: 512)

Training may have been needed in this study because the teachers were, it seems, asked to view their videotaped lessons and to audiotape their comments on these without the researcher being present; if this were indeed the case, stimulated recall procedures were applied, but not in the form of an interview. Johnson's work, then, highlights both the role that the training of respondents may play in stimulated recall work, as well as suggesting that this can be conducted by respondents independently. Again, though, this latter option would need to be applied judiciously. Johnson was working with pre-service teachers on their practicum; asking practising teachers, though, to record their own lessons and to provide the audio commentary on these without the researcher being present would in many cases not be a feasible strategy given the time and effort it would demand of the teachers.

Think-aloud protocols

Stimulated recall interviews require teachers to verbalize or comment on their cognitions with reference to prior behaviours; they are thus retrospective. In contrast, think-aloud protocols are a written record of thoughts verbalized while a task is being performed; they are thus introspective.

Good quality think-aloud protocols will have two key characteristics. One is that they will be as *accurate* as possible – that is represent actual thoughts during a task. Second, they will be as *complete* as possible – that is they will include the full range of thoughts which occur during a task. According to Gilhooly and Green (1996), the approach to thinking aloud which addresses these two criteria most effectively is that which requests from respondents a straightforward description of ongoing thought, without elaboration and explanation of it. The quality of think-aloud protocols is also enhanced when social interaction between the researcher and the respondent is minimized; at the start of the process it is extremely important for instructions to be relayed very clearly by the researcher so that respondents are able to produce rich verbal reports; subsequent interventions by the researcher (even in the form of facial expressions) during the think-aloud may, though, influence the verbalizations produced; for this reason, respondents in think-aloud studies are often encouraged to verbalize their thoughts as if they were alone (Gilhooly and Green, 1996).

As a research strategy in the study of teacher cognition, then, thinking aloud elicits verbal commentaries from teachers about what they are doing while they are engaged in particular tasks. Of course, these must be tasks which can be completed while teachers are verbalizing their thoughts. For this reason, teachers' interactive thinking is not an issue which can be studied using think-aloud protocols. In contrast, planning is an activity where the concurrent articulation of thoughts is less likely to interfere with the satisfactory completion of the task, and this was in fact the focus of several early think-aloud studies in mainstream educational research (see Shavelson and Stern, 1981 for a summary of such work). In such studies (often conducted in contrived rather than naturally-occurring contexts), teachers were typically given a set of new instructional materials and asked to verbalize their thoughts as they set about the task of planning lessons using them. These verbalizations were recorded, transcribed and subsequently analysed in order to shed light on the nature and focus of teacher thinking during planning. One criticism of this approach to the study of planning was, of course, that related to its ecological validity – the extent to which conclusions about actual planning practices could be derived from research conducted in settings artificially created for the purposes of research.

Although thinking aloud has been widely used in studies of teacher cognition in education more generally (see Clark and Peterson, 1986), and in the study of language learning (e.g. Faerch and Kasper, 1987), examples of it in the study of language teacher cognition are not common. There has been some research using this technique into the decisions and criteria used by raters of written compositions in ESL; thinking aloud has also been applied in the study of how language teachers design pedagogic tasks; and there has also been a study of teachers' orthographic awareness.

In this latter study, Xiao (2005) asked six teachers of Chinese as a foreign language (CFL) to complete and audio record two think-aloud tasks. In the first task respondents were asked to comment on a pedagogy course in CFL they had recently completed (e.g. which parts were most helpful). In the second think-aloud task, participants were presented with a list of 50 Chinese characters and asked to identify and correct errors in these. While doing this, respondents were asked '(1) to tell everything in his/her mind, and (2) answer questions to him/herself such as "How should I help the students correct this error? What should I do in the future to help prevent such errors"' (p. 225). The analysis of the recorded protocols provided insights into the extent to which explicit knowledge about Chinese orthography taught on the earlier pedagogy course had been utilized by the teachers.

In the field of language assessment, Lumley (2002) used think-aloud protocols to examine the manner in which raters of written compositions interpret the rating scales they are asked to use. In this study, four trained and experienced raters of a high-stakes test used in Australia marked 24 scripts; 12 were marked under normal operational conditions, while for the second 12 scripts, raters were asked to think aloud about the rating process. The instructions for think-aloud which raters received are reproduced in Figure 7.12. The resultant verbal protocols were transcribed and analysed; in particular the analysis focused on raters' interpretations of the standard rating scale that they used. On the basis of his analysis of the think-aloud protocols, Lumley concluded 'that although there appears to be some evidence that the raters understand the rating category contents similarly in general terms, there is also evidence that they sometimes apply the contents of the scale in quite different ways' (p. 266). This study suggests that think-aloud protocols can make a contribution to our understandings of the cognitions of language teachers while they are engaged in the process of assessing written work.

> I am now going to ask you to rate a second set of 12 writing scripts. I would like you to rate them as far as possible in the usual way, that is, just as you have just rated the previous 12. However, there will be one important difference with this second batch: as I have previously mentioned, I am conducting a study of the processes used by raters when they rate writing scripts, and I would now like you to talk and think aloud as you rate these 12 scripts, while this tape recorder records what you say. First, you should identify each script by the ID number at the top of the page, and each task within each script by number as you start to read and rate it. Then, as you rate each task, you should vocalise your thoughts, and explain why you give the scores you give. It is important that you keep talking all the time, registering your thoughts all the time. If you spend time reading the script or the rating scale, then you should do that aloud also, so that I can understand what you are doing at that time. In order to make sure there are no lengthy silent pauses in your rating, I propose to sit here, and prompt you to keep talking if necessary. I will sit here while you rate and talk. I will say nothing more than give you periodic feedback such as 'mhm', although I will prompt you to keep talking if you fall silent for more than 10 seconds.

FIGURE 7.12 *Instructions for think-aloud protocols*
(Lumley, 2002: 274)

In a similar vein, though with a different focus, Cumming (1990), used think-aloud protocols to examine the decision-making processes of novice and expert raters of ESL written compositions (see Chapter 5). One aspect of this study to note was that the teachers were given 'thinking-aloud demonstrations and training with arithmetic problems' (p. 34). This is a sensible strategy to adopt in ensuring that participants understand what is required of them (thinking aloud is, after all, not generally a normal or natural process and Green and Gilhooly, 1996 do recommend that an appropriate warm-up task always precede the think-aloud task proper). A further methodological feature of this study was that participants were given the option of performing their think-alouds alone or in the presence of the researcher (two out of 15 individuals requested the latter option, both novices who wanted immediate feedback on their performance as raters). This study again highlights the value of think-aloud protocols in making explicit the decision-making of raters (and in particular of raters marking work anonymously and without any information about the writers).

Finally, think-aloud protocols have been applied in the study of pedagogic task design in language teaching (Johnson, 2003; Samuda, 2005). In this research, novice and expert task designers were asked to report their concurrent thoughts as they responded to a design brief (see Figure 7.13). These verbal reports, which lasted approximately two and a half hours for each of the sixteen participants, were video and audio recorded. The qualitative analysis of these data allowed comparisons of the task design processes engaged in by experts and novices (see Chapter 3 for a summary of the findings). In reflecting on the use of thinking aloud in this study, Johnson (2003) reviews the pros and cons of this technique. The main advantage highlighted was that it allows the study of processes which are normally covert. A number of criticisms of thinking aloud are also discussed. One is that the technique is often used in conditions especially created for the purposes of research (i.e. not naturally occurring). This was the case in this study – the novice and experts who participated did not think aloud in the course of everyday task design behaviours. Johnson (2003) justifies this decision by arguing that collecting such naturalistic data would have taken a very long time, presented serious logistical difficulties and not have generated comparable data from the different participants. Other challenges Johnson highlights in relation to thinking

> **Design Brief:**
>
> You are asked to imagine that you have been teaching, or writing materials for an adult, monolingual group of students at intermediate level. The group is studying a general English course in their own country meeting for a two-hour class once a week. There are approximately 15–20 students in the class.
>
> In recent lessons you have been dealing with the general functional area of *describing people*. This has included simple descriptive statements of the *He/she is very tall/short* sort, but also more complex descriptions of character as well as physical appearance.
>
> You now wish to give these learners a 'communicative activity' to practise this area further. You want the students to interact as much as possible and involve as many different members of the class as possible. Although reading and writing may be involved, you are most concerned to provide opportunities for speaking skills. You want the activity to last roughly between 15 and 30 minutes.
>
> The materials you produce are to be used on the next day or so, and your activity needs to be worked out in sufficient detail for this to happen. This should include preparation of any worksheets. It would be useful for us if you were to include clear written instructions on how to use the activity. If you are a teacher, you might imagine these instructions to be for a colleague who is to teach the activity. If you are a materials writer, the instructions might take the form of Teachers' Notes.

FIGURE 7.13 *Task design brief for think-aloud protocols*
(Samuda, 2005: 240)

aloud is that respondents vary significantly in how well they can do it; that the warm-up task used (in this study, solving an anagram) may cause anxiety in respondents who are unable to complete it; and that respondents may tend to explain their thoughts to the researcher rather than providing a verbal report of their thinking. In response to this latter issue, two strategies were used in Johnson's study; one was that the instructions were explicit about the roles of the respondent and the researcher ('while you're doing your thinking aloud on designing tasks I'm going to be taking notes, but I'm not going to be looking at you and you're not talking to me OK. You're just thinking out aloud', p. 39).

A second strategy used to discourage respondents from explaining their thoughts to the researcher was to ensure that the latter was not an expert, or perceived to be an expert, in language teaching (piloting for this study showed that respondents tended to explain their thoughts if they felt the researcher was an expert). Overall, this study provides much practical insight into the use of think-aloud protocols to study language teacher cognition.

Summary

This chapter has focused on the use of a range of structured and less structured techniques for eliciting verbal commentaries in the study of language teacher cognition. I have commented in some detail on each technique, and so a lengthy review of the issues involved is not required here. Overall, though, it is clear from the examples considered that these investigative strategies are valued because they allow tacit and unobservable aspects of teachers' mental lives to be made explicit. At the same time, this analysis has highlighted both strengths and criticisms of different elicitational strategies. Overall, semi-structured and stimulated recall interviews appear to be the strategies most commonly adopted for eliciting verbal commentaries in the study of language cognition; there is adequate evidence here, though of the contribution that elicitation based on structured interviews, scenarios, repertory grids and thinking aloud can also make to our understandings of what language teachers think, know, believe and do. Particularly where there is keen interest in what teachers do, the value of verbal commentaries emerges even more clearly when they are combined with data collected through observation, which is the focus of the next chapter.

8

Observation

Can language teacher cognition be usefully studied without reference to what happens in classrooms? Personally I am sceptical, though it is clear that where large numbers of teachers are being studied and/or ideal typologies are being developed, analyses solely of teachers' reported cognitions can provide a useful basis for further inquiry. Ultimately, though, we are interested in understanding teachers' professional actions, not what or how they think in isolation of what they do.

(BORG, 2003c: 105)

My position on this matter remains unchanged and thus it is positive to note that observation is an increasingly common data collection strategy in studies of language teacher cognition. Before considering specific studies in detail, I will outline some of the methodological options and issues which are associated with the use of observation in the study of teachers.

Dimensions of observation

Many textbooks on doing social science research include a chapter on the use of observation as a data collection strategy, in both qualitative and quantitative work (e.g. Babbie, 2003; Cohen *et al.*, 2000; Richards, 2003; Silverman, 2001). Collectively, these sources highlight both strengths and weaknesses of observation; on the one hand, it provides direct evidence of behaviour, is (in theory) non-interventionist and allows large amounts of descriptive data to be collected; on the other hand, though, observation is a time-consuming activity and the presence of observers does inevitably have an effect on (and hence alters) the situation being observed. There are clearly, therefore, arguments both in favour and against the use of observation in the study of teachers, and I refer to these in more detail throughout this chapter.

Another point which emerges from the literature on research methods is that there are several methodological dimensions to observation which researchers must consider and make decisions about. Five of these are summarized by Patton (1990: 217), who says that observation may vary in terms of (1) the role of the observer, (2) the extent to which those observed know that observation is taking place, (3) the extent to which those observed know the purpose of the observation, (4) the duration of the observations and (5) the focus of the observation.

With reference to the way the observer's role can be defined, several typologies exist but, according to Burgess (1984), these generally draw on the four-way distinction introduced by Gold (1958) and which is summarized in Table 8.1. This characterizes the observer's role in terms of how overt the observer dimension is and how much the observer participates in the settings under study (Patton describes these two dimensions separately). A simpler, two-way distinction between participant and non-participant observation is also commonly cited in research on teachers (I discuss this further below).

Further dimensions of observation as a research strategy can be added to the five mentioned above. One relates to the authenticity of the settings under observation – are they naturally occurring or created especially for research purposes? The manner in which observational data are recorded, coded and analysed is also a central issue for researchers to consider; a common distinction in relation to these issues is that between structured and unstructured approaches

Table 8.1 Field roles in observational research (based on Burgess, 1984: 80–2)

Observer role	Description
complete participant	conceals the observer dimension and observes covertly
participant-as-observer	the researcher participates as well as observes by developing relationships with informants
observer-as-participant	contact with informants is brief, formal and openly classified as observation
complete observer	eavesdropping and reconnaissance in which the researcher is removed from sustained contact with the informant

to observation (see, for example, Cohen *et al.*, 2000). Structured observation will have the following characteristics:

- the categories of behaviour to be observed are defined in advance;
- an observation schedule based on these categories – typically a checklist or rating scale – is devised;
- the observer is trained, if required, in the use of the observation schedule;
- the observer completes this schedule while conducting the observation (either in real time or using a video or audio recording);
- the result of the observation is a completed schedule in which behaviours have been categorized, counted or rated;
- these data are then analysed quantitatively.

Evertson and Green (1986) describe observation where categories are defined in advance as *closed*; they define systems for coding data which use categories, checklists and rating scales as *categorical*.

Structured observation, then, is typically closed and categorical (for a detailed discussion of this approach to observation, see Bryman, 2001; Robson, 2002).

In unstructured observation

- a full account of the events under study is collected, typically through fieldnotes, audio recordings or video;
- the data are written up to produce narrative observation transcripts;
- these are analysed and categories identified from the data themselves;
- the result of this analysis is typically qualitative, though quantification is also possible.

Evertson and Green (1986) describe an approach to observation which has no preset categories or which at least allows additional categories to be added to any defined in advance as *open*. They also define *narrative* approaches to recording observations as those which use diaries, journals, fieldnotes and similar forms of non-categorical representations. Unstructured observation, then, is typically open and narrative.

In terms of how data are analysed, although it is commonly the case that open observations recorded narratively are analysed inductively (i.e. analytical categories are derived from the data) it is also possible to apply existing frameworks to narrative data (and for this reason in describing the dimensions of observational research it is helpful to distinguish between how data are recorded and the origins of the analytical categories). Also, while unstructured observation often leads to qualitative analysis, it is possible for data recorded narratively to be subject to quantification (so again, it is useful to distinguish between how data are recorded and the kind of analysis they are subjected to). I illustrate these points below.

Table 8.2 presents a list of nine dimensions of observation derived from the above discussion. Each dimension is briefly defined and the poles of the continuum along which the dimensions can vary are also indicated. The fact that these dimensions constitute continua is important to note (i.e. intermediate positions on each dimension are possible). These dimensions will now be used to discuss observational research in the study of language teacher cognition.

Table 8.2 Dimensions of observational research

Dimension	Description	Options (from/to)
Participation	The extent to which the observer participates in the settings under study	Participant/Non-participant
Awareness	The extent to which those observed know they are being so and by whom	Overt/Covert
Authenticity	The extent to which the settings under observation are naturally occurring	Real/Contrived
Disclosure	The extent to which the purposes of the observation are explained to those being observed	Full/Minimal
Recording	How a record of the observation is made	Manual/Technological
Structure	The extent to which data are recorded against predetermined analytical categories	Closed/Open
Coding	The extent to which data are coded according to existing frameworks	Deductive/Inductive
Analysis	The role of quantification in the analysis	Quantitative/Qualitative
Scope	The extent to which a range of individuals, events and times are studied	Limited/Extended

Observation in language teacher cognition research

In the previous chapter I examined a number of studies of language teacher cognition which make use of observation data as the basis of stimulated recall interviews; Table 8.3 lists a further selection of

Table 8.3 Observational data in language teacher cognition research

Source	Role	Awareness	Authenticity	Disclosure	Recording	Structure	Coding/Analysis	Scope
Andrews (1997)	non-participant	overt	simulated	?	video	open	inductive/qualitative	14 teachers; 2 role plays each
Bailey (1996)	non-participant	overt	real	?	audio	open	inductive/qualitative	6 teachers, 1 lesson each
Borg (2005b)	non-participant	overt	real	partial	fieldnotes	open	inductive/qualitative	2 teachers, at least 5 lessons each
Collie Graden (1996)	non-participant	overt	real	?	audio	open	inductive/qualitative	57 reading lessons by 6 teachers
Farrell & Lim (2005)	non-participant	overt	real	?	audio	open	inductive/qualitative	2 observations with 2 teachers over 3 months
Farrell (2003)	non-participant	overt	real	yes	audio	open	abductive/qualitative	10 classes over one semester

Freeman (1993)	non-participant	overt	real	?	?	open	inductive	4 teachers over 18 months
Hulshof & Verloop (2002)	non-participant	overt	real (using test chosen by researchers)	partial	video	open	deductive/ quantitative	1 lesson each for 8 teachers
Johnson (1992a)	non-participant	overt	real	?	video	open	deductive/ quantitative	1 lesson each for 6 teachers over a semester
Johnson (1996)	participant	overt	real	?	video	open	inductive/ qualitative	1 teachers weekly for 15 weeks
Johnston & Goettsch (2000)	non-participant	overt	real	?	audio	open	inductive/ qualitative	2 classes each for 4 teachers
McCutchen et al. (2002)	non-participant	overt	real	?	fieldnotes	open	inductive/ qualitative	44 teachers observed several times across the school year

(Continued)

Table 8.3 (Continued)

Source	Role	Awareness	Authenticity	Disclosure	Recording	Structure	Coding/Analysis	Scope
Muchmore (2001)	participant	overt	real	yes	audio	open	inductive/qualitative	55 classroom visits over 5 years
Nunan (1992)	non-participant	overt	real	?	audio	open	inductive/both	1 lesson each for 9 teachers
Richards & Pennington (1998)	non-participant	overt	real	?	fieldnotes	open	inductive/qualitative	11 observations each with 5 teachers over 9 months
Sato & Kleinsasser (1999)	non-participant	overt	real	?	fieldnotes	open	inductive/qualitative	2–3 lessons each for 8 teachers
Tsang (2004)	non-participant	overt	real	yes	video	open	inductive/qualitative	10–15 lessons for 3 teachers over 28 weeks
Tsui (2003)	non-participant	overt	real	?	video	open	inductive/qualitative	1 of 4 teachers, every day for 1–2 months

studies which draw on observational data (some of these studies, it is worth noting, also use the observations as the basis of stimulated recall interviews – e.g. Hulshof and Verloop, 2002; Tsang, 2004). Each study in this table is described using the dimensions from the classification defined above (question marks indicate that I was unable to retrieve a particular item of information in a source). All of the studies included here were open in their structure and in all cases those observed knew they were being so and were aware of the identity of the observer. In all of these studies, too, it is important to note that observation was not the only data collection strategy employed. This is to be expected in studies of language teacher cognition as observation on its own permits inferences about cognitive processes but is insufficient as a means for exploring these processes in more depth and ascertaining the validity of the inferences made. For such purposes different forms of verbal commentaries (Chapter 7) or written reflections (Chapter 9) are typically utilized. Observation, though, clearly has a central role to play in the study of language teacher cognition by providing a concrete descriptive basis in relation to what teachers know, think and believe can be examined. I will now discuss various dimensions of observational research with reference to the studies in Table 8.3.

Observer role

There is a very clear preference in language teacher cognition research for non-participant observation – that is where the researcher in the classroom typically sits at the back, makes notes and avoids interacting with teacher or students during the events being observed. Not all studies in Table 8.3, though, describe the role of the researcher as non-participant. Muchmore (2001), for example, describes his role during a five-year life history study of a high-school teacher of English as that of a participant observer; Johnson (1996) also says she followed participant-observation procedures. The terminology used by researchers to describe their observer roles, though, does not necessarily imply similarities or differences in practice; to ensure the precise nature of their role in observational studies is made explicit, researchers should supply not only a label but also explain their interpretation for it. This is because the notion of 'participation' may refer solely to the degree to which the researcher actively takes part in the events under study or also encompass the extent to which positive relationships between researcher and those observed were fostered (see the definition of participant-as-observer in Table 8.1).

On occasion a conflict may arise between the non-participant role envisaged for themselves by the researcher (who does not want to be actively involved in classroom events) and an invitation to participate from the teacher or students. Such invitations take several forms; you may be asked by the teacher to answer a student question they are not sure about; students may come up to you with their written work and ask you to mark it; or teachers may even ask you to teach or co-teach a lesson. The researcher's response to such situations cannot be governed simply by a determination not to participate; ethical concerns also come into play here. In the first of the situations just described, for example, it might possibly be embarrassing for the teacher if the researcher were simply to ignore the request for fear of having an influence on the lesson; my response in such situations has been to provide a brief answer and to allow the teacher to resume with the lesson as quickly as possible. An example of the researcher being invited to teach is provided by Sato and Kleinsasser (1999), who observed teachers of Japanese in order to look for evidence of a communicative approach to language teaching. One of the researchers was a native-speaker of Japanese and two of the teachers in the study who were not native-speakers of Japanese wanted to use this researcher as a native-speaker informant in their lessons. The researcher agreed to this request, but acknowledged that 'in these classrooms it was not possible to observe a typical class session. However, the interactions in these particular classes were recorded as participant observations' (p. 500).

I have had this experience myself too, though I was actually asked to teach a lesson. The context for this was a study of the cognitions and practices of an experienced teacher of English as a foreign language to young learners in Spain. I had been with the teacher for a week in a non-participant observer role (i.e. sitting at a desk of my own and making notes about lessons) and during this time the pupils had been working on a project which involved thinking about travelling to another country and deciding what to pack in their cases. For my final day there the teacher asked if I would lead an activity in which the pupils had to guess what items I had packed in my suitcase. I therefore came to class that day with my hand-luggage packed with suitable items and the children proceeded to try to guess what items I had. I made notes about this lesson afterwards and I was able to use it to inform my understanding of the kind of practices the teacher used, but I could not of course use the data as evidence of what the teacher did. In this situation, refusing to teach a lesson because I was determined to remain in a non-participant role would have been wrong.

Authenticity

Most studies of language teacher cognition using observation have examined naturally occurring teaching – that is instruction conducted by teachers in their usual classrooms, with learners they normally teach, and using materials that are part of the curriculum they follow (where trainees are involved, the degree of authenticity is perhaps somewhat lessened, as in Tsang, 2004, for example, where some of the observations were based on microteaching). Intervention by researchers – for example in asking teachers to teach a particular lesson – has generally been minimal. Two exceptions here can be highlighted though. In Andrews (1997), a controlled environment in which teachers role-play grammar teaching was created. This was the task set for the participating teachers:

> You are the teacher of a Form 3 class of average ability. You recently gave your students a composition concerned with sport. You have corrected your students' compositions and are going over some of their mistakes in class.
>
> (Andrews, 1997: 150)

Teachers were given composition extracts 'concocted for the purposes of the study' (p. 150). They were then asked to role-play how they would respond to the grammatical errors in these compositions.

There were no learners present and the researcher was the sole audience. Each teacher did two role-plays; in the first they had no opportunity to prepare other than being given one minute to look through the composition they had been given. Overall, then, the instructional situation being studied here was highly contrived, a point the researcher acknowledges:

> It would be unjustified to assume that behaviour manifested under such stressful and unfamiliar conditions reflected what happens in the classroom. Many aspects of subject behaviour could be artefacts of the video-based task and the fact that there were no students present.
>
> (*ibid.*, p. 151)

The study of teachers' use of analogy by Hulshof and Verloop (2002) also controlled the instruction observed, but to a much lesser extent than the role-play just described. In this case, all teachers in the study had to base a reading comprehension lesson on a particular text, chosen by the researchers. No constraints were placed on how the lesson was conducted; the only requirement was that the set text be used.

These examples aside, though, there is a clear trend in language teacher cognition research to study naturally occurring teaching. Of course, the concept *naturally occurring* merits critical attention itself; for example, it should not imply that those being observed have not altered their behaviours in any way in response to the observer's presence as some degree of reactivity is inevitable. In fact, I would suggest that it is not uncommon for observational studies to report as natural behaviour classroom events which are anything but natural; the problem is that, barring a lucky break, as researchers we may have no way of identifying the extent to which what is observed is typical of normal practice. An example of such a break comes from the work of a research student of mine who recently conducted observations in an EFL classroom; at the end of the first observed lesson he overheard the students complaining to the teacher that they had not been able to understand him because he had – uncustomarily – spoken English for most of the lesson. This was a clear signal that the teacher had adjusted his behaviours in response to the researcher's presence. Reactivity of this kind will be more likely under certain conditions, such as where

- the teacher is not aware of the nature and purposes of educational research;
- the observation of teachers is associated with teacher appraisal and inspection;
- the teacher is suspicious of the researcher's motives;
- the teacher is not committed in any way to the research;
- the researcher is seen to be in a position of authority or power in relation to the teacher being observed;
- the teacher believes they understand what the researcher wants to see and tries hard to provide this;
- the teacher is concerned about losing face in front of the researcher.

Observation needs to be planned and conducted very sensitively where conditions such as these are likely to exist.

Disclosure

Covert observation in educational research is generally considered to be unethical; thus it is not surprising to note in the studies of language teacher cognition I have reviewed that the individuals being observed have been aware of this and have also known who the observer was. In most research reports, though, it is difficult to ascertain how much prior information was disclosed to teachers about the purposes of the observations. For example, Bailey (1996) explains that 'in gathering information from the teachers, I requested appointments for classroom observations, and the teachers chose whether or not they wished to participate in the study' (pp. 24–5). It is impossible to know from this account what precisely the teachers were told. In studies where observations follow interviews, it is possible that the interviews will make teachers aware of the focus of subsequent observations. Sato and Kleinsasser (1999), for example, first interviewed teachers about communicative language teaching, then observed these teachers for evidence of the instructional approaches they used. Even here, though, it is not clear whether teachers were aware that interview and observational data were going to be compared in order to assess the consistency between teachers' stated beliefs and their actual practices.

Disclosure is in fact a matter of degree. Deception – that is misrepresenting the purposes of the observation – is unethical (though some ethical codes of practice may allow it if justified, e.g. AERA), but it is clearly possible to disclose the purposes of observation – or of a study more generally – in more or less explicit ways. Denscombe (2002) reflects on this issue as follows:

> From the researcher's point of view, decisions need to be made about *how much information to supply.* Not enough information and the researcher can stand accused of not providing the basis for a fully 'informed' agreement. Too much information and the researcher can unintentionally contaminate the data by 'leading' the participant's responses. If participants know exactly what is being investigated, this might influence the replies they give.
> (Denscombe, 2002: 189)

Thus within the general principle of informed consent and honest disclosure about the purposes of the researcher, there is scope for decisions about how much detail research participants need to receive. Whereas in many cases, revealing the purposes of classroom observations will not be problematic, in others it will be. This may be particularly true when the purpose of the observation is to study the frequency with which particular behaviours occur. Hulshof and Verloop (2002), for example, wanted to understand the extent to which teachers used analogies during reading comprehension instruction. They report that

> The teachers were told that we were observing lessons in order to learn how teachers usually develop reading comprehension. Nothing was said beforehand about the use of analogies and

we did not indicate that we were interested in seeing how the teachers used examples and analogies to make difficult concepts easier to understand.

(Hulshof and Verloop, 2002: 83)

In this case, full disclosure may have influenced teachers' behaviours (i.e. they may have made a greater effort to use analogies); the information provided was, thus, a generalized but arguably not untrue statement about the focus of the research (Fine and Sandstrom, 1988 describe this degree of disclosure as *shallow cover,* contrasting it with *deep cover* – i.e. covert observation – on the one hand and *no cover* – complete openness – on the other). The explicit nature of Hulshof and Verloop's (2002) comment on this matter is a rare example in the research on language teacher cognition and most reports are silent on issues of disclosure. In my study of grammar teaching in EFL classrooms in Malta, I described my position on these issues as follows:

> Before starting any fieldwork, I also provided each teacher with a description of the research. Although I specified that the study was interested in the relationship between teachers' beliefs and practices, I did not reveal my specific interest in grammar teaching until the post-observation interviews in which the teachers discussed their work with me. My decision here was based on my understanding of the Maltese educational context. Teachers in Malta often respond to classroom researchers by trying to give them what they would like to see. Two examples will illustrate this point. One teacher who I had asked to participate in this study (but who eventually did not) responded to my request by saying that if I told her what I was after, she would do her best 'to act accordingly'. Another teacher, who did participate in this study, taught very little grammar, yet admitted that he had tried harder than usual to include some formal instruction in his work because I was present. Both these incidents support my decision not to reveal my specific objectives to the teachers until the observations had been completed.
>
> (Borg, 1999b: 30–1)

Muchmore (2001), in contrast, reports that at the start of his observations he introduced himself to the class, 'telling them exactly who I was and why I was there' (p. 92). The account provided by Tsang (2004) (e.g. her use of words such as 'informed' and 'warned') also raises interesting questions about handling disclosure in pre-service teacher education contexts, where data collection is built into course procedures and where the academic may feel less of a need to explain in detail the purposes of any research:

> I informed the participants at the beginning of the courses that interviews, observations and taping would take place as standard routines built into the course. I obtained their consent to use the data collected in writing an academic paper about teachers' decision making. I warned them of further contact with them to validate my interpretation of the data, including video-recordings of two lessons taught during microteaching.
> (Tsang, 2004: 169)

For a fuller discussion of the ethical and practical arguments both in favour of and against decisions not to reveal the specific purposes of research, see, for example, Punch (1986), Deyhle, Hess and LeCompte (1992) and Cohen *et al.* (2000). A comment on the position adopted by the researcher in respect to such issues would seem important to include in any study of language teacher cognition which is based on observational data.

Recording observations

Observational data need to be recorded in some way. Researchers may use manual (e.g. completing a checklist or writing narrative fieldnotes) and technological means (e.g. video, audio, photographs). Artefacts (e.g. teaching materials, students' work) may also be collected as part of the observational record. Table 8.3 shows that both manual and technological records are widely used in language teacher cognition research (I have only listed the primary means of recording for each study; where audio and video are used, these are commonly accompanied by fieldnotes).

Reliance on handwritten fieldnotes may seem an outmoded practice given the technological means available today for recording observations. However, decisions about the recording options which are adopted will need to reflect both the resources available to the researcher and, often more importantly, what is appropriate and permissible in the context under study. Video recording, for example, while valued for its ability to capture both vision and sound, is also the most intrusive of recording devices and one therefore that may generate most reactivity among the individuals under observation. It is also possible that teachers may not grant permission for researchers to video record them. Decisions about how to record observations, then, need to made not only on methodological grounds but with an appreciation of the context in which the observations will occur.

Decisions about how to record observations will also have implications for the manner in which these can be later reported. Sato and Kleinsasser (1999), for example, collected written fieldnotes and reported these in continuous prose, as in the following example:

> At the beginning, she handed out quiz sheets to everyone. She gave students 10 minutes to complete the quiz. While students were working on the quiz, she wrote grammatical points on the board. After the quiz, she started to explain the grammar (passive form) by using English sentences as examples. Then, she explained it with Japanese sentences. While she explained verb conjugations, students wrote them down in their notebooks. After that, she showed verb cards and made students say passive forms. It was like drills. Then, she asked students to open the textbooks, and they did exercises that transformed active sentences into passive ones. She called on each student individually and let him or her answer. Finally, she asked students to create their own sentences by using passive forms. After a few minutes, the bell rang.
>
> (Sato and Kleinsasser, 1999: 505–6)

Borg (2005b) also collected descriptive fieldnotes, but reported these in a more extended way (see Figure 8.1), while Burns (1996) audio recorded the observations in her study and reported these as a transcript in direct speech (Figure 8.2). The level of detail which can be attained in reporting observations, then, is limited by the detail of the original recording and where, for example, it is important to be able to report precisely what a teacher and/or students said, fieldnotes alone are unlikely to be adequate. A sole source of audio recording can also be problematic when there is a need to identify and track the contributions of individual students in a class.

Zsanna – Perfect Tenses

1. For homework, the teacher had asked the students to write sentences using present perfect tenses related to some photos of people they had used in the previous lesson.

    Examples of the sentences the students report are:
    She has been sunbathing.
    She has just put on her new contact lenses.
    She has just combed her hair.
    She has worn her bracelet since her boyfriend gave it to her.

2. The teacher has written out different functions of present perfect tenses in English on individual sheets of paper. She now sticks these up around the classroom (numbered 1–7) and asks the students to move round the room, to read the functions and to decide which function each sentence they wrote for homework goes with.

    The functions were as follows:
    Actions/events that have already happened.
    Actions/events that have happened for the first, second, last time.
    Actions/events that have been happening for some time.
    Actions/events that have just happened.
    Actions/events that have been happening since a particular time or event.
    Actions/events that have happened in a period of time that links the present to the past.
    Actions/events that have not happened yet.

    The students move around for a few minutes trying to match their sentences to these functions.

3. Then they sit down for a general discussion in which the teacher elicits an example of each function. The students do not suggest an example for function 2, so the teacher writes on the board:

    This is the first time she has driven a car.
    That's the tenth time she has visited London.

4. The teacher now draws a map of the perfect tenses in English on the board, eliciting from the students the information to place in it. The completed diagram looks like this:

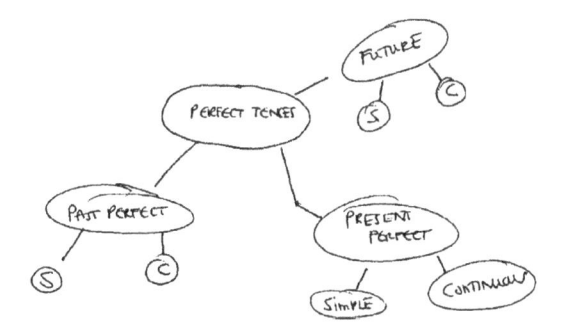

```
                    FUTURE
                       |
         PERFECT TENSES─(S)─(C)
        /        |         \
   PAST PERFECT  |        PRESENT
                |         PERFECT
     (S) (C)    |        /      \
                |    Simple    Continuous
```

5. The teacher now gives the students a list of sentences (e.g. By this time next week I'll have been studying for my exams for two months) and asks them to match them to this diagram. The students work on this in groups, identifying which of the perfect forms each sentence illustrates. They take a few minutes to do this.

6. In groups, the students are then asked to compile everything they know about perfect tenses in English. The teacher elicits from the students what this will involve and together they establish that students should think about the form, when to use it, examples, and common expressions or related words. The students engage in this task, and the teacher circulates and discusses with them as they do.

7. For homework, the students are asked to look at pp. 71–2 of their course book, where a summary on perfect tenses is given, and to compare the notes they made during today's lesson to the information provided there. The teacher asks the students to make a note of any questions they want to ask and to bring them back next lesson.

FIGURE 8.1 *Lesson description (Borg, 2005a: 330–1).*
With kind permission of Springer Science and Business Media.

Transcript 2: I did some ironing.
T: Susanna, what about you?
Su: Uh?
T: What did you do at the weekend?
Su: Weekend........stay oos.
T: Sorry, I don't understand. (laughs) Say that again please.
Su: Oos . . . I can't say. Oos.
T: At home. AT home, yeah, stayed at home.
Su: Yeah. Yeah, cook.
T: Really? What?
Su: Biscuit . . .
T: Biscuit. Everybody understand? Biscuit. Biscuit (writes 'biscuit' on board.)
S: Biscuit. Yeah.
T: Cook. Cook biscuits.
S: Ah, yeah. Cook.
T: You like biscuits . . . Tan?
Su: Ah, food . . . food.
T: Food . . . yes. Lunch, dinner, yes. (Susanna makes ironing motion and giggles) What's that? What's this? (T also motions ironing. Some learners discuss in first language. Lian looks up her dictionary.) In English? (Lian laughs and so does T.)
Li: Oh . . .
T: What is it?
Li: Ironing.
T: Ironing. Right . . . do the ironing. Yeah. (T writes 'iron' on board and draws a picture of an iron. Beneath iron she writes 'ironing' and beneath this 'I did some ironing'.) Yeah. OK. Iron (Learners speak in first language and copy words as teacher writes.)
S: Ironing.
T: Ironing. So you can say, 'On the weekend, I did some ironing. I did some ironing.'

FIGURE 8.2 *Lesson transcript (based on audio recording)*
(Burns, 1996: 165)

Coding and analysing

In terms of coding and analysis, Evertson and Green (1986) note, as explained above, that a key difference between open and closed approaches to observation lies in the point at which a coding system is developed. For open observation, it is developed retrospectively; for closed observation, it is defined in advance. They also note that with closed systems coding takes place while lessons are being observed (in real time or on video) and that the observer ignores behaviours or events not covered by the structured observational schedule they are using. With open observation, coding may take place retrospectively, allowing categories to be influenced by what is found in the data.

So there are two questions here. One is whether data are being analysed into a predefined coding system. As Table 8.3 suggests (under the heading of 'structure'), there is little evidence of this in the study of language teacher cognition. The ease with which technological records of observations can today be obtained (e.g. video and audio recording devices are now portable and relatively inexpensive compared to 10–15 years ago) explains at least partly the reduced use of *a priori* schemes for coding observations in educational research (i.e. data can be recorded and taken away for analysis at leisure). Also, while the use of structured (also called *systematic*) observation schedules characterized research on classroom interaction in language teaching in the 1970s and 1980s (see Allwright and Bailey, 1991; Chaudron, 1988 for examples), the use of such schedules has been criticized (see, for example, Seedhouse, 2004) because they attend solely to discrete surface behaviours in the classroom. They may also imply that exclusive attention to these observable behaviours can allow us to fully understand teaching (of course, this is an assumption which stands in opposition to the fundamental bases of research on teacher cognition). And there is also the danger that tight prespecifications of what to observe may lead researchers to ignore unanticipated but potentially insightful classroom events and behaviours. These criticisms of structured observation schedules explain to some extent why less structured, more open approaches to observation are today more prevalent in language teacher cognition research.

The second question relates to the origins of the categories used to analyse the data. These may be based on an existing framework or developed inductively from the observational data collected. A range of options are evident in the studies in Table 8.3 (under 'coding'), although the bulk of observational work in language teacher cognition research involves inductive analysis. A typical example of the procedures involved is provided by Collie Graden (1996), who explains that

> To analyze the data, transcriptions of the 12 teacher interviews and the 57 classroom observations were entered into a word processor. Data were organized by looking for salient or recurring themes (Marshall and Rossman 1989). Patterns were then organized around 11 structural categories. Further coding of the structural categories resulted in 76 thematic and 17 subthematic categories. A database was created containing 1,179 records coded with one or more thematic categories.
> (Collie Graden, 1996: 388–9)

Farrell (2003) similarly collected narrative written field notes in his study of a novice teacher's socialization processes and subsequently derived analytic categories from them. In this case, though, an existing framework (based on Pennington and Urmston, 1998, discussed in Chapter 2) was initially used to guide the coding of the data. This framework served as a heuristic – it suggested themes which could be used to classify teachers' work and experiences – but did not limit the emergence of additional categories during the analysis. This study illustrates how existing analytical frameworks can play an important supporting role in the analysis of narrative observational data (see also Mangubhai et al., 2004, who used a framework from Joyce et al., 1992); this is in contrast to the view that qualitative data analysis must rely entirely and exclusively on the data as a source of categories. In Table 8.3, the approach to analysis in Farrell (2003) is in fact described as *abductive*, rather than inductive or deductive:

> abductive inferences seek to go beyond the data themselves, to locate them in explanatory or interpretive frameworks. The researcher is not content to try to slot them into existing ideas, for

the search includes new, surprising, or anomalous observations. On the other hand, such strange phenomena are not used only to disconfirm existing theories: They are used to come up with new configurations of ideas. There is thus a repeated interaction among existing ideas, former findings and observations, new observations, and new ideas. Abductive inference is thus especially appropriate for qualitative work, in which an open-minded intellectual approach is normally advocated.

(Coffey and Atkinson, 1996: 156)

A similar approach to the analysis of narrative observational data is evident in my own work on grammar teaching; in describing teachers' practices in formal instruction I did consider existing classifications of grammar teaching practices, without, however, letting these constrain the range of practices which were eventually identified (see, for example, Borg, 2003a).

Another approach to the analysis of observational data is illustrated by Johnson (1992a) (whose treatment of observations I have classified as deductive/quantitative). She drew on a coding scheme from the mainstream educational literature which provided a way of classifying teaching and analysing teachers' decision-making. She found, though, that this needed to be modified for use in the context of L2 teaching. The narrative observational data she collected were retrospectively coded using this modified framework. Hulshof and Verloop (2002) followed a similar approach, analysing their observations of reading lessons by using existing classifications of analogies.

Open/inductive observational studies typically analyse data qualitatively, while the closed/deductive approach often generates quantitative data. Here, too, though, variations are possible. McCutchen et al. (2002), for example, devised a systematic coding scheme on the basis of extensive fieldnotes (i.e. inductively) and subsequently applied this scheme to their observational data, reducing them to quantifiable measures. Nunan (1992) audiotaped and transcribed lessons from ESL teachers, then on the basis of his analysis of these lessons and of subsequent interviews identified three categories for describing the teachers' instructional teacher-making (pedagogical, interpersonal and evaluative). In this case, the data were analysed quantitatively and qualitatively.

This brief discussion highlights the variety of options available to researchers in relation to how observational data can be coded and analysed. Although the general distinction between structured and unstructured observation will capture many of the options highlighted here, it is important for researchers to be explicit about which precise aspects of the observation these labels apply to, as data recorded in an unstructured manner may clearly be analysed using a structured framework.

Scope of observations

What I refer to here as the *scope* of observations covers several issues. One (which is not summarized in Table 8.3) is the specificity of the substantive issue the observation is concerned with. For example, Hulshof and Verloop (2002) had a very specific interest in analogy; Bailey's (1996) concern with teachers' interactive decisions was less specific. Studies can thus be described as having a broad or narrow focus. In describing the scope of observations we are also concerned with how many individuals were observed, how many times and over what period of time. As Table 8.3 indicates, a wide range of practices are evident in research on language teacher cognition. In some studies, several teachers were observed once (e.g. Bailey, 1996; Hulshof and Verloop, 2002); in contrast, Muchmore (2001) conducted 55 observations over five years with one teacher; Collie Graden (1996) also reported analysing 57 lessons by six teachers, while Tsui (2003) visited one of the four teachers in her study every day for two months.

There is obviously no 'correct' figure to aim for in making decisions about the number of observations which are required in a study of language teacher cognition. However, given that reactive behaviours by teachers and students are likely to decrease over time, observational data collected on several occasions and over a period of time may be more valid. If necessary, prestudy observations, as described by Johnson (1992a) can also be built into a study to allow participants to become accustomed to the observer and any equipment before the observational study proper commences. Studies which base their conclusions about what teachers do on a substantial volume of observational data will carry greater evidentiary warrant. Studies involving the observation of one teacher conducting one lesson will be obviously limited in the claims they can make about the nature of that teacher's work more generally. We must also remember that decisions about how many observations to conduct and for how long will also be influenced by practical issues such as the time available to the researcher and the availability of teachers. Unforeseen circumstances can also intervene in shaping the scope of an observational study – for example, a teacher's illness, resignation from a job, transfer to another school, unexpected timetable changes and withdrawal from the study are just some of the issues that may constrain what can be achieved. Farrell and Lim (2005) do not specify which particular problem they encountered (which suggests it was something quite sensitive), but they do report that 'we had hoped for more classroom observations but circumstances beyond our control prevented further classroom observations' (p. 4).

Summary

One clear issue which emerges from the discussion in this chapter is the complex nature of observation as a multi dimensional research strategy. I have suggested nine dimensions along which observational practices can vary, and the careful attention researchers must pay to these should dispel any notions that observation in the study of language teacher cognition requires less planning and skill than, for example, interviewing. In fact, because observation is the research method that has most potential for creating discomfort among teachers, its planning and implementation may call for especially high levels of skill and sensitivity.

Observation is a valuable strategy in the study of language teacher cognition because it provides evidence of what happens in classrooms. In this respect it is superior as a data collection strategy to both self-report instruments and interviews, as these can only capture teachers' reports of what they do. Observation, on its own, though, provides an inadequate basis for the study of what teachers think, know and believe. Researchers may draw inferences about cognitions from what is observed, but verification for these must be sought through further sources of data. This is also necessary because, as Kagan (1992b) notes, teachers may adopt similar practices for very different reasons. Observation, in the study of language teacher cognition, is thus never the sole form of data, but is commonly combined with interviews and/ or self-report data. These additional forms of data can be collected prior to observations (in which case comparisons between stated beliefs and actual practices can be made); interviews also commonly take place subsequent to observations, either through stimulated recall or in semi-structured form (in which case interviews aim to elicit the thinking or rationale behind the observed practices). A three-stage sequence of initial background interview, classroom observation and follow-up interview is a further option commonly used. Various methodological combinations are clearly possible here.

I have highlighted in this chapter several practical and theoretical threats to the effective use of observation in the study of language teacher cognition. Two critical qualities researchers can benefit from in dealing with the practical challenges are anticipation and sensitivity. Although we cannot foresee every problem that arises during fieldwork, it is possible to develop the anticipatory mindset which envisions potentially difficult situations, and considers ways of minimizing or avoiding these. A prior analysis of the observation setting, for example, is one simple way of identifying potential problems earlier on – for example finding out whether researchers have visited the school before, what teachers' experiences of them were, whether observation plays any role in the teachers' professional lives and what kinds of attitudes to research generally and observation specifically exist. Being upfront about your requirements early on (e.g. how many lessons you would like to observe, if you want to record them and how) can also avoid difficulties further down the line. Sensitivity is also essential in observational work, in particular an awareness of the fact that we are indebted to the teacher who has allowed us into their classroom, and not the other way round; sensitivity to potential sources of anxiety among those being observed and a willingness to adjust our observation plans so that they minimize the inconvenience for the teachers are two further examples of dispositions that can facilitate observational research.

From a theoretical point of view, we must also be mindful of the threats that exist to the reliability and validity of observational data. Obvious threats are the influence the researcher has on the settings being observed, the possibility that those observed might modify their behaviours to assist or obstruct the researcher and the danger that tacit assumptions held by the researcher may colour what they attend to during observation and during the analysis of the data. We must always acknowledge, too, that observation will provide a particular and partial perspective on a phenomenon (as it is not possible to observe everything that happens in a setting, all the time and from all different angles). Where structured observation is being used, a particular threat will relate to the reliability with which the observation schedule is being applied. The general literature on research methods discusses such threats in detail and suggests a number of strategies for addressing them, such as training observers to use structured instruments, prolonged engagement (conducting observation over an extended period of time) and reflexivity (which involves the researcher making explicit and monitoring potential sources of researcher bias) (for extended discussions of these issues, see Creswell, 2003; Evertson and Green, 1986; Maxwell, 1996; Robson, 2002).

9

Reflective writing

Reflective writing is used here to refer to strategies which require teachers to express in written form their thoughts, beliefs and attitudes, typically in relation to particular topics or experiences. I will consider four types of reflective writing here: journals, autobiography, retrospective accounts and concept maps. The use of reflective writing has a long tradition in education generally, particularly in the field of teacher education, where journals and autobiography in particular have been widely employed to support and study teachers' understandings of their own learning and practices (e.g. Connelly and Clandinin, 1990; Francis, 1995; Holly, 1989a; Thomas, 1995b; Witherell and Noddings, 1991). Reflective writing, particularly journals, has also been used in the field of language learning to study the processes of acquiring a second language (e.g. Bailey and Ochsner, 1983) and in teacher education to document teacher development, encourage reflection and as a tool for collecting feedback on teacher education courses (e.g. Appel, 1995; Bailey, 1990; Brock *et al.*, 1992; Jarvis, 1992; Porter *et al.*, 1990). A particular form of journal writing, the research journal, has also been used to document and study individuals' experiences and development as researchers (Borg, 2001a; Janesick, 1999). My focus here, though, is specifically on studies which have engaged teachers in reflective writing as a research strategy for studying language teacher cognition.

Journal writing

Table 9.1 lists studies of teacher cognition which have drawn on data from journals. Two issues of terminology need to be addressed before I proceed to discuss this work. Firstly, Holly (1989b) distinguishes between journalistic writing (which is descriptive), analytical writing (which focuses on specific events), reflective writing (which is retrospective) and introspective writing (which examines thoughts and feelings). The use of the term journal writing in the study of language teacher cognition, though, blurs these distinctions; in this context, it involves writing where events are described and analysed, both retrospectively and introspectively. Secondly, Holly (1989b) also

Table 9.1 Journal writing in language teacher cognition research

Source	Description	Details
Bigelow & Ranney (2005)	Reflective comments written by pre-service teachers at the end of taught classes	20 teachers, 6 journal entries each during a course
Johnson (1994)	Journals written by pre-service teachers during a practicum	4 teachers during a 15-week practicum
Mok (1994)	Journals written by teachers during a practicum	12 teachers during a practicum
Numrich (1996)	Diaries written by pre-service teachers during a practicum	26 teachers, 20 entries each over a semester
Sakui & Gaies (2003)	Journal entries written by a teacher investigating her own practices and cognitions	1 teacher, 20 entries over an academic term
Woods (1996)	Logs written by teachers about the planning and teaching of their courses	8 teachers during courses lasting 6–13 weeks

distinguishes between three forms of reflective writing – logs, diaries and journals – as follows:

> the log is an objective record of information (pages read, attendance, activities, lesson plans); the diary is a personal document in which the author can record log-type information but is primarily a book for expressing the author's thoughts, reactions, ideas, and feelings related to everyday experiences; and the journal is a document that includes both the objective data of the log and the personal interpretations and expressions of experiences of the diary, but which moves beyond these to intentional personal and professional reflection, analysis, planning, and evaluation.
>
> (Holly, 1989b: 25–6)

Once again, though, these distinctions are not strictly applied in the studies I discuss here and I will use the term *journal* to cover these various possibilities. Terminology apart, different forms of introspective writing are valued in teacher cognition research for their ability to make tacit mental processes explicit and hence available for examination.

Two general points can be made at the outset about the six studies in Table 9.1. Firstly, they use journal writing in conjunction with data collected from other sources, typically observations and interviews. Journal writing, then, can in isolation provide insights into teachers' cognitive processes, though on the basis of the work available here the trend is for these insights to be complemented by findings from additional data sources. Secondly, while these studies are united by their use of journal writing, methodologically they highlight a range of options available to researchers. I will now illustrate these options by considering these six studies more closely.

Mok (1994) studied the perceptions of teaching of more and less experienced teachers by analysing the journals written by these teachers during the teaching practice component of a teacher education programme. In this study, though, teachers were not writing these journals specifically for the purposes of the research being conducted; rather, these journals were written by teachers while they were on teaching practice, presumably as part of the requirements of their programme, then a decision was subsequently made by the author to utilize them as data for the study. The author's justification for proceeding in this manner was 'to eliminate biases resulting from the student teachers' high consciousness of the purpose of the research' (p. 99). The earlier discussion of disclosure in relation to observation is thus clearly relevant here too: if respondents are aware their journals will be used for research purposes and/or that the researcher is interested in a particular issue, what effect might that have on the content of those journals? Where teachers are primarily writing their journals for purposes other than research (e.g. as part of the requirements of a course), it may be feasible to delay any discussion of the use of journals for research until they have been written; where journals are being written primarily for research purposes though, this is not an option.

Another issue to consider in analysing the use of journal writing in language teacher cognition is the extent to which published reports explain the procedures involved in the writing of the journals (e.g. what precisely teachers were asked to write about). Mok (1994) is, quite typically, silent on this matter, though extracts from journal entries quoted in the study do provide some sense of the issues which teachers were focusing on. Here is an example of a novice teacher reflecting on the tension between students' needs and curricular goals:

> I have concerns that I am not addressing the WANTS of my students. I make this comment fully recognizing the difference between Wants and Needs. To this point, J [a tutor?] counsels me not to worry so much about student Wants because their more critical Needs are being met. Still I am uncomfortable because I believe there is not much overlapping here. Because I am teaching more or less on my own this week, this doubt is foremost in my mind. For instance, I had originally planned to take this opportunity to address some student Wants as expressed in their mid-term class evaluation, i.e. grammar, cross-cultural rhetoric and computer tips. My plans were not approved, however, because they were not identified course objectives (Needs). Still, I can't believe that grammar, rhetoric and computer literacy complaints don't have a basis in real problems. This cancellation

of my original plans is perfectly understandable. However, my over zealous agenda would have thrown off curriculum goals as well as the students.

(Mok, 1994: 105)

Johnson's (1994) study also took place in the context of a pre-service teacher education programme. In this case, the nature of the journal writing used in this study was described in detail:

> Each teacher kept a written journal which consisted of open-ended reactions and observations about the practicum. These included comments about the students, the curriculum, the cooperating teacher, and the practicum experience itself. Journal entries also focused on the preparation involved in teaching certain lessons, actual lesson plans, and post-lesson comments and reactions. Teachers also wrote assigned journal entries at the beginning of the practicum in which they were asked to articulate their beliefs about second language learning and teaching, their experiences as second language learners, and their views about the role of the teacher in second language instruction. These assigned entries were also repeated at the end of the practicum. Journals were collected and analyzed at four points throughout the practicum. At the completion of the practicum, Xerox copies of the journals were made and kept for final data analysis.
>
> (Johnson, 1994: 441)

A distinction is made here between open-ended and assigned journal entries; in the former teachers had more freedom in deciding what to focus on, while in the latter they were required to write about specific issues. In utilizing journal writing in the study of language teacher cognition then, researchers need to make decisions about the degree of structure to impose on the task and whether to vary this over time; for example, it is possible to move from less to more structured forms of journal writing, or conversely to start with more structure and to gradually make the task more open-ended. These choices should be determined not only by the purposes for which the journals are being written but also, importantly, by the degree of readiness for journal writing which teachers possess. It is a mistake to assume that all teachers are equally capable of engaging productively in reflective writing and even more of a mistake to assume that teachers can do this in a second or foreign language. Journal writing has associated linguistic, cognitive and socio-cultural demands and simply asking teachers to reflect on and document in writing their thinking and beliefs will often not generate particularly rich data. For example, such a task calls for an ability to stand back from and to objectify one's experience – a skill in itself, which needs to be learned and developed. Where teachers do not possess such prerequisite skills, researchers should consider carefully whether journal writing is the most appropriate strategy to use in studying teacher cognition.

Also in the context of pre-service teacher education, Numrich (1996) analysed diaries written by teachers during a ten-week practicum. Drawing on Bailey and Ochsner (1983), a diary is defined here as 'a first person case-study that is reported in a journal, an introspective account of an L2 experience that reports on affective factors normally hidden from or inaccessible to an external observer' (p. 131). Again here, the author reports concerns about data 'contamination' which may have resulted if the teachers knew in advance that their journals were going to be used for research; thus permission to use the journals for this purpose was not requested until the final day of the course during which they had been written. In this study, the goal of analysing teachers' journals was to identify the issues which were of most concern to novices during their practicum and the range of issues emerging from the study suggest that the use of journals was effective in this respect. For example, the journals highlighted that one early preoccupation novice teachers had during their practicum related to the role of textbooks. Here are two extracts related to this point:

> I think I've come to rely too much on the textbook . . . at first I felt guilty about using the textbook after I had been thinking of my own lesson plans . . . now I seem to have gone the other way. I'm realizing how easy it is just to rely on the textbook. I have to stop myself from doing that.
>
> I found it very difficult and tiring to try and find a way to fit the book into my lesson plan – I felt the book was an added burden rather than a time-saving resource for me and a potentially stimulating

and interesting educational resource for my students . . . Now I almost feel positive about it – like it might be a friendly helper to me in planning my lessons.

(Numrich, 1996: 137)

This study is also instructive in that it reproduces (see Figure 9.1) the directions teachers were given for writing their journals; as already noted, this level of practical methodological detail is typically not reported.

Bigelow and Ranney (2005) used what they call journals as part of their study into the application of knowledge about language to content-based language instruction (CBI). In this case, teachers were given 15 minutes at the end of class time in order to make their journal entries; the prompts used each time varied but generally required the teachers to write about the connections they perceived between the material covered in that day's class and classroom teaching, and to comment on any issues they felt confused about. Given that journals are normally not written under time pressure and in class, the authors correctly note here that they are using the term *journal* loosely to describe the kind of writing completed by their teachers;

---

1. Set aside a regular time and place each day in which to write.
2. Plan on allowing an amount of time for writing . . . at least equal to the period of time spent in the language classroom.
3. Keep your diary in a safe, secure place.
4. Do not worry about your style, grammar, or organization. especially if you are writing in your second language.
5. Carry a small pocket notebook with you so you can make notes about your language teaching experience whenever *you* wish.
6. Support your insights with examples. When you write something down, ask yourself, 'Why do I feel that is important?'
7. Write in the first person. It's more personal.
8. Write anything and everything you feel. When you revise your diary for the 'public version,' the class project, you will be able to edit out anything too personal or embarrassing.

FIGURE 9.1 *Instructions for journal writing*
(Numrich, 1996: 151)

productive journal writing would have necessitated more than the 15 minutes allowed for each entry in this study, a point the authors also acknowledge.

The studies discussed so far took place in the context of pre-service language teacher education; in this context journal writing is in fact widely deployed, most commonly as assigned work intended to promote reflective teaching and teacher development (e.g. Bailey, 1990) and only secondarily as a means of studying teacher cognition (hence the small number of studies discussed here). The journal writing of experienced teachers, in comparison and as noted by McDonough (1994), has in fact been the focus of limited empirical study and I am aware of only two studies where practising teachers' cognitions have been studied using journals. In his study of ESL teachers' beliefs and decision-making, Woods (1996) collected data through 'written logs kept by the teachers about what they carried out related to planning, organizing and teaching their course (including thinking and talking about it)' (p. 28). These logs did not appear to be a major source of data in this study, though, but served to complement interviews conducted with the teachers. More significant evidence of the use of journals in the study of practising teachers' cognitions comes from Sakui and Gaies (2003). In this work, a Japanese teacher of English at a university engaged in the self-study of her beliefs about teaching, learning and writing, and her professional identity, using questionnaire and interview data collected from her students, but drawing on journal entries she wrote over one term of an academic year as the main source of data. An interesting feature of this study was the manner in which the journal writing process was dialogic:

> It was our feeling that self-study by a teacher/researcher of her beliefs could be enhanced by the collaboration of a 'sympathetic outsider.' The second author (Stephen) was the 'audience' for the journal entries that Keiko wrote periodically throughout the semester. We did not determine in advance how often Keiko should send a journal entry, and it was up to Stephen to decide whether and how quickly to respond to a journal entry. Altogether, Keiko wrote more than twenty entries, some of which were quite long. Stephen responded to several of them. Sometimes the response was intended to have Keiko clarify or expand upon some topic

discussed in a journal entry she had just sent; but some responses also aimed at eliciting her beliefs about some topic that she had not explicitly discussed. At times, Stephen described his own learning and teaching experiences. Thus, Keiko's journal entries were not simply a series of monologues, but were often responses to and triggered by what Stephen had written. In this sense, some of Keiko's journal entries were dialogues co-constructed with her research partner.

(Sakui and Gaies, 2003: 159)

Dialogic journals of this type are not unusual in teacher education (where teacher educators often respond in writing to journals written by trainees), but their use here as a purposeful research strategy for investigating teacher cognition is noteworthy and not a feature of any of the other studies I have discussed here.

Overall, then, a number of observations about the use of journals (diaries, logs) in the study of language teacher cognition can be made on the basis of the work analysed here:

1. Data from journals have been used to study language teacher cognition in relation to a variety of issues – course and lesson planning, pedagogical concerns during teaching practice, trainees' understandings of teacher education coursework, and teachers' beliefs and professional identity. Journals are thus a flexible research tool, enabling researchers to study respondents' personal accounts of their thinking and practices over a period of time (e.g. a course, semester, practicum or term – see Table 9.1).

2. Journal writing has been used to study language teacher cognition predominantly in the context of pre-service teacher education. In this context journals can be more easily incorporated into assigned coursework, particularly during the practicum. Studies of journal writing with practising language teachers are rare.

3. Researchers need to make a number of methodological decisions when using journals to study language teacher cognition, and these are summarized in Figure 9.2. The

> 1. Whether journals are an appropriate data collection strategy to use (e.g. Do the teachers have the prerequisite skills?);
> 2. Whether to inform respondents in advance that their journals will be used for research purposes;
> 3. If advance notice is given, how specifically to explain the purposes of the research;
> 4. How much structure to impose on the journal-writing process (e.g. in terms of topic, length and number of entries) and whether to vary this over time;
> 5. Whether to use journals dialogically, or monologically (i.e. where the writer does not receive a written response from a reader);
> 6. In L2 and FL contexts, whether to allow journal writing to be conducted in respondents' first language;
> 7. When and where the journals should be written (e.g. in class or in respondents' own time);
> 8. Whether the journals should be handwritten or word-processed (handwritten data needs converting into an electronic format for qualitative data analysis software to be used);
> 9. What forms of analysis (e.g. qualitative and quantitative) to apply to the data.

FIGURE 9.2 *Methodological decisions in using journal writing to study language teacher cognition*

principled use of journal writing as a strategy in language teacher cognition research should be based on an explicit consideration of the options available in relation to each of these points. This explicitness should also be reflected in the way the study is reported (i.e. readers should be given full details of the procedures that were used).

4   Prior to all these decisions though, researchers need to ascertain whether the targeted respondents have the prerequisite skills and attributes required for productive journal writing. In the absence of such skills, such as the ability to articulate, analyse, evaluate and reflect on experiences and thinking processes, journal writing may not generate more than descriptions of events without any insights into the cognitions which researchers are

interested in studying. In many cases, the absence of these prerequisites will mean that journal writing is not an appropriate research strategy to adopt.

5   In the studies discussed here, limited information is generally given about what precisely participants were asked to do (in only one case were the instructions given to teachers reproduced). A lack of such information limits the extent to which the procedures used in existing studies can be both critiqued as well as replicated in continuing work of this kind. I would recommend that the instructions, rubrics or directions teachers are given be included in all reports of studies which employ journal writing to study language teacher cognition.

Autobiographical accounts

Autobiographical accounts are a form of reflective writing which examine the writer's own professional and broader life experiences. They typically take the form of narratives, presented in extended, continuous text and which have a holistic quality to them (journal writing, in contrast, often consists of a series of discrete entries, not necessarily having a shared focus). The personal focus and reflective narrative nature of autobiographical writing are clearly qualities it shares with journal writing; however, in terms of how journals and autobiographical accounts have been used in the study of language teacher cognition there are clear differences, as I illustrate below, in both the nature of the task respondents are asked to complete and the writing produced.

Though a tradition of narrative autobiographical research exists in education generally (see, for example, Abbs, 1974; Carter and Doyle, 1996; Clandinin and Connelly, 2000a; Cooper, 1991; Knowles and Holt-Reynolds, 1994; Thomas, 1995b; Witherell and Noddings, 1991), there are not many examples of studies where teachers have been asked to write autobiographical accounts in the study of language teacher cognition (see Table 9.2).

As we see from this table, a common feature in research of this kind is for teachers to be asked to write a history of their own language

Table 9.2 Autobiographical writing in language teacher cognition research

Source	Focus of autobiographical writing
Bailey (1996)	language learning history
Bodycott (1997)	personal histories and metaphors of language teaching and learning
Farrell (1999)	experience of learning English and personal approach to teaching English grammar
Golombek & Johnson (2004); Johnson & Golombek (2002)	teachers' classroom practices and their reflections on them
Norman & Spencer (2005)	beliefs about writing and writing instruction
Numrich (1996)	personal language learning history
Tsang (2004)	language learning/teaching history

learning experiences. In Bailey *et al.* (1996), for example, seven teachers plus their professor wrote summaries of their language learning histories in response to the following questions:

1. What language learning experiences have you had and how successful have they been? What are your criteria for judging success?

2. If you were clearly representative of all language learners, what would we have learned about language learning from reading your autobiography? What can be learned about effective (or ineffective) teaching by reading your autobiography?

3. How has your experience as a language learner influenced you as a language teacher?

(Bailey *et al.*, 1996: 12–13)

The assumption behind this kind of work is that, drawing on the notion of the apprenticeship of observation (Lortie, 1975), teachers' experiences as language learners will have an influence, often implicit, on their current beliefs and practices. The writing and analysis of autobiographical accounts of this type, then, can provide insights into the connections between prior learning experience and current beliefs and practices. In this study, for example, it emerged that teachers held implicit teaching philosophies which had been shaped by their prior learning.

While in the above study the autobiographical accounts were the primary data source, in other cases, such as Numrich (1996) and Tsang (2004) language learning histories written by pre-service teachers played a less central role; in the former case, as discussed earlier, diaries were the main source of data, while in the latter case observations and interviews were. In both cases, though, teachers were asked to write autobiographical accounts before embarking on teaching practice; Numrich explained her purpose in doing so as 'for these new teachers to recall the teaching/learning techniques that had been most and least successful in their own learning of an L2 and to begin to identify some of their own values about teaching and learning' (p. 133). Tsang's rationale was similar: the writing in her case would be 'the first attempt at critical reflection on their language learning and teaching experience and on their theories and practices before they began their on-site teaching practice' (p. 169). In both these studies, the autobiographical accounts aim to assist pre-service teachers in understanding their current beliefs about teaching by examining prior language learning experiences. In both cases, too, the accounts were written as part of assigned coursework. The same was true in the work of Farrell (1999), who asked trainees to write about their past experiences of learning English as part of a three-part reflective assignment into the teaching of grammar (see Figure 9.3 for the assignment rubric). The following extract gives a flavour of the kinds of accounts the teachers produced:

> I must admit that her method [overt teaching] of teaching grammar did produce results – my English results were always among one of the top few in my school. On the other hand, her method of instruction also made me feel that grammar is a very boring

> This assignment is in three parts. The first part of the assignment is to write your past experience of learning English in Singapore and your personal approach to teaching English grammar in English lessons in Singaporean secondary schools. Please include references to material we have covered in the course if this was an influence. Second, write a DETAILED lesson plan on any grammar structure and teach it to some secondary students in a school, or elsewhere. Third, the final part of the assignment is to reflect on your class: would you change any of your techniques of teaching grammar? If so, why? if not, why not? Any other reflections you would like to make on your experiences? In other words, I want you to reflect before, during, and after the lesson. The assignment should be a minimum of five double spaced pages with the actual lesson plan and teaching materials in the appendix at the back. Please give references (the rationale for teaching a particular method); these pages are not counted in the five pages.

FIGURE 9.3 *Rubric for reflective assignment*
(Farrell, 1999: 5–6)

> component of English. As a result, my interest in grammar slowly diminished. There was a period of time when grammar became my most hated component in English. However, I still managed to perform quite well in English.
>
> (Farrell, 1999: 7)

Norman and Spencer (2005) also used autobiographical writing as part of assigned coursework. They studied 59 pre-service teachers' experiences and beliefs about writing and writing instruction through accounts of these teachers' lives as writers. This study explains that prior to writing their autobiographies, the teachers engaged in pre-writing activities which aimed 'to activate their recall of previous experiences as writers' (p. 28). One of these was to read an anecdote in which an author provides a vivid account of his own writing process and of the experiences which influenced his views of himself as a writer. The use of such pre-writing activities highlights an element of autobiographical writing not signalled in the other studies of language teacher cognition I am discussing here – preparation. Just as simply asking teachers to write reflectively in their journals may not be productive, requesting that they produce autobiographical accounts without preparation may also fail to generate adequate data for the study of teacher cognition. Researchers need to make an assessment of the extent to which teachers are ready to write autobiographical accounts and, as in this case, to provide appropriate support for the task where required.

This same study also provides insights into the various forms which teachers' autobiographical accounts may take:

> Students' compositions focused on a particular content, yet took different forms. Some provided chronological accounts from early childhood to the present, while others focused on critical incidents. While the assignment elicited a particular response, students were encouraged to respond uniquely to their own experience. The varied responses show that they chose a form that they thought best told their stories.
>
> (*ibid.*, p. 28)

In this case it seems implied that teachers were not advised to follow a particular format in organizing their accounts (the rubric used is not reproduced in the article). However, suggestions for possible formats might certainly be merited in cases where teachers require a greater degree of support to be able to produce their autobiographical accounts. This need for an appropriate level of task structure is the same point that I made in discussing journals and which applies to any form of data collection which requires teachers to generate extended prose accounts

In contrast to the trend illustrated above for using autobiographical writing as assigned coursework on pre-service teacher education courses, Bodycott (1997) and Johnson and Golombek (2002) used it with practising teachers. In the former, teachers were asked to write personal histories of learning and teaching, though detail about the procedures involved is not provided and the focus of the paper is more on the repertory grid interviews also used in this study. In the latter, the cognitions of in-service teachers are illustrated through narratives written by the teachers themselves and where the focus is not on learning and teaching histories but on current classroom practices. The theoretical perspective on teacher cognition which underlies this collection is outlined clearly in its introduction: teachers' narrative accounts acknowledge the socially situated nature of what teachers know and do, recognize teachers as knowledge generators rather than just consumers of others' knowledge, value teachers' explorations of their own ways of knowing and see narrative inquiry not just as a means for documenting and providing insight into teachers' experiences but also as a strategy which promotes professional development. What is also distinct about this collection is that it presents extended accounts of teachers engaged in the study of their own work, written by the teachers themselves for an audience of fellow teachers. Thus, the stories teachers tell in each case are presented without commentary by outside researchers (but see Golombek and Johnson, 2004 for an analysis of three of these narratives). In fact, little information is given about the processes through which these narratives were constructed (the teachers must have been given some kind of brief, no matter how general, to work to). Thus while the resultant narratives provide undoubted insight into teachers' cognitions and practices, and also illustrate the potential formats autobiographical writing can take, guidance on how to stimulate and support the generation of such texts is not provided.

Just as with journals, then, researchers wanting to study language teacher cognition by studying teachers' autobiographical accounts have a number of important decisions to make (and the considerations specified in Figure 9.2 apply to autobiographical writing too). As we have seen, autobiographical writing has been used predominantly with pre-service teachers, where it can be assigned as compulsory course-work (in such cases teachers' permission to use their work for research purposes should nonetheless be sought). Exemplars of autobiographical accounts by practising language teachers are less common in teacher cognition research, a fact which is not particularly surprising given the effort, commitment and support which writing such accounts calls for; the motivation of having an account published in a book, as in Johnson and Golombek (2002), may stimulate practising teachers to write autobiographically, but researchers wanting to study the cognitions of practising language teachers should be wary of asking teachers to produce extended written accounts without ascertaining that the teachers are motivated to engage in the task and ensuring that appropriate support for them to complete it is going to be provided.

Furthermore, we must recognize that reflective writing represents teachers' subjective perceptions of current, recent or more distant events. Particularly in the latter case, questions can legitimately be asked about the accuracy of teachers' written reconstructions of their lives (e.g. there is a danger that in constructing coherent autobiographical narratives teachers may simplify or even distort complex processes and experiences). Thus, where teachers provide extended written accounts of their thinking and professional actions, historical or current, these accounts reflect just one possible perspective – the teachers' – on the experiences being described. Researchers can also not assume that reflective writing – particularly of the narrative form – is generally accepted as a legitimate form of knowledge in research on teacher education; while the epistemological status of written narrative data of this kind has been affirmed in educational research in the last 20 years, it remains the case that this is not a universally accepted position; thus language teacher cognition researchers wishing to use reflective writing as a primary form of data are advised to ground their work in a clearly argued rationale for the value of such data in studying teacher cognition. There is much published work to draw on which can inform such an undertaking, both in education generally (e.g. Carter and Doyle, 1996; Thomas, 1995a) as well as in the field of language teaching (Golombek and Johnson, 2004).

Retrospective accounts

A retrospective account is writing which teachers conduct with the specific purpose of reflecting on a prior, normally recent, experience. If conducted repeatedly over time such writing could arguably be classified as a form of journal writing. Here, though, I want to highlight the way in which one-off retrospective accounts can be used to support the study of language teacher cognition. One example comes from the work of Farrell (1999) which was discussed earlier (see Figure 9.3). In addition to personal histories, the teachers in this study were asked to teach a lesson then to write a retrospective account in which they reflected on their experience. To illustrate the nature of these accounts, here is an extract from one teacher who had planned and implemented an inductive approach to teaching grammar:

> I discovered that this method is more complicated than I thought. I found that I actually had no idea how to conduct a grammar lesson in this manner. In the past, I had always employed the deductive method, giving the rule first, then giving lots of examples and lots of practice. Now I have to come up with the examples. The students did not manage to verbalize the grammar rules. I was made more insecure as I could not tell whether the form and its use had been internalized. All I can say is that after I have tried the inductive method, I am more confident in using it again.
>
> (Farrell, 1999: 11)

Writing of this kind is clearly useful in making explicit the thinking (in this case, post-lesson) of teachers.

Johnson (1992a) also used retrospective written accounts, though here they played a minor role in the overall study by providing confirmation for some of the conclusions suggested through the analysis of observations and stimulated recall interviews. The procedures used in eliciting the written accounts in this study are described as follows:

> Immediately after teaching their lessons, teachers wrote a one-page written retrospective in which they responded to two questions: What was your greatest concern during this lesson? and What influenced your instructional decisions most? A second written retrospective, based on the same questions, was written after the teachers viewed their own videotaped lessons and completed the stimulus recall procedures.
>
> (Johnson, 1992a: 512)

As in Farrell's case, a clear purpose for the retrospective writing was established in the rubric provided to the teachers. Given the one-off nature of these forms of writing, and the specific research purposes for which they are being elicited, this degree of direction would seem necessary. In other words, specific instructions are needed to ensure that the resulting data are relevant to the issues under study. Although it is likely that retrospective writing of this kind occurs quite frequently in teacher education contexts, there is limited evidence of its use as a strategy in the study of language teacher cognition.

Concept mapping

Concept mapping is a research technique through which respondents' understandings of particular concepts and of relationships among them are represented graphically, through a concept map. In constructing a concept map, respondents typically first brainstorm on a particular topic and write down a list of concepts related to it; they then construct a diagram which shows how their understandings of how these concepts are related (see Figure 9.4 for an example). It is also possible for the procedure to be more structured, with an initial list of concepts being supplied to respondents who then have to organize them into a concept map. Thus, although concept mapping is not a form of writing as such, it does involve an element of reflective written output which justifies its inclusion in this chapter (alternatively, concept mapping can be discussed, as Calderhead, 1996 suggests,

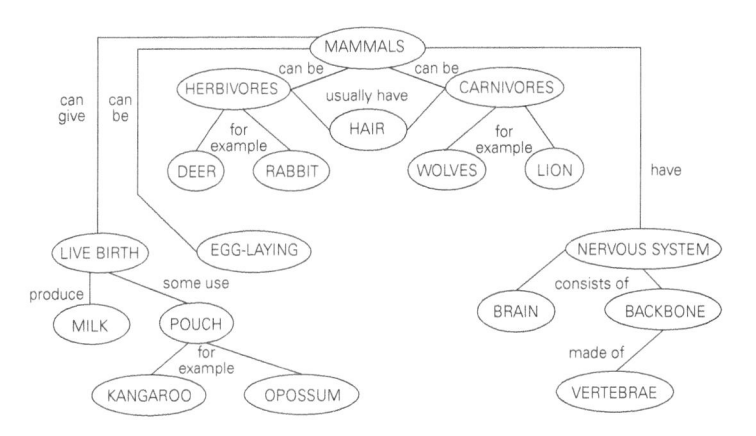

FIGURE 9.4 *Example of a concept map about mammals (Markham et al., 1994: 95). Reproduced with permission of John Wiley & Sons Inc.*

as an example of those research strategies, such as repertory grid interviews, which aim to elicit and represent conceptual structures). In reviewing studies which have used concept maps to study teachers, Mergendoller and Sachs (1994: 589) conclude that the 'results converge in finding that the maps are sensitive to differences between more and less experienced teachers, and that they are useful for measuring cognitive change resulting from participation in academic courses'. In relation to this latter point, concept mapping has been used to study conceptual change in teacher education, typically through the comparison of concept maps produced by pre-service teachers at different points in their studies. Morine-Dershimer (1993) illustrates this use of concept maps:

> On the first day of class in the fall students were asked to make a concept map depicting their view of the important components of teacher planning. All students received the same written directions, together with an example of a concept map on 'leisure activities'. On the last day of class in the spring semester students were again asked to draw a concept map showing their view of the important aspects of teacher planning. The same written directions were provided as a reminder. When the post maps were completed, students were given their pre maps (held by the course instructors during the year), and were asked to compare the two maps. They wrote short descriptions of the changes they saw, noting what they considered to be the reasons for any changes in their thinking about teacher planning.
> (Morine-Dershimer, 1993: 16–17)

The provision of a sample concept map is important here; concept mapping will not be familiar to all teachers and they will thus benefit from an illustration of what is expected. The preparation of clear written instructions is also essential to ensure that all respondents have a comparable understanding of the task they are being asked to complete; if this is not the case (e.g. if vague instructions mean that teachers interpret the requirements of the task in different ways) conclusions based on comparisons across teachers will be questionable.

In the study of language teacher cognition there is limited evidence of the use of concept maps. Roehler and colleagues (e.g. Roehler *et al.*, 1988; Roehler *et al.*, 1989; Roehler *et al.*, 1990) studied teachers' knowledge of reading using what they called ordered trees (a form of concept map); trees produced by novice teachers consisted of fewer concepts and were less coherent than those of experts; novice teachers' trees also developed in the direction of those of the experts over the course of two reading method courses. These findings support the view that concept maps can be useful in tracking conceptual development over time and in capturing differences in conceptual knowledge between novices and expert teachers (expertise does not necessarily equate with years of experience – in Mergendoller and Sachs, 1994 there was no correlation between experience and the quality of the concept maps produced).

Concept maps also played a role in Meijer *et al.* (1999). The focus of this work, which I discussed in Chapter 5, was teachers' practical knowledge about teaching reading comprehension. Thirteen teachers received written instructions on how to construct a concept map and were also given an example. They had to think about 'teaching reading comprehension' with reference to students who were 16–18 years of age. Figure 9.5 is a concept map from this study. This particular map was produced by what is described as a subject-matter oriented

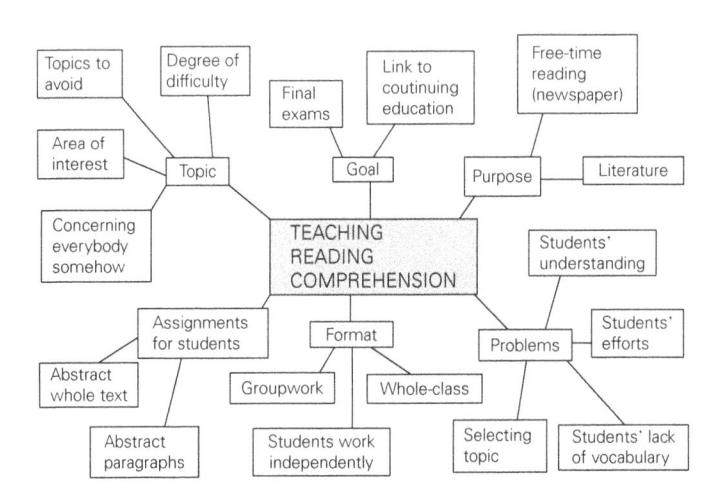

FIGURE 9.5 *Concept map about teaching reading comprehension (Meijer, 1999: 94). With kind permission of the author.*

teacher, that is one whose practical knowledge about teaching reading comprehension was defined by a concern for content, skills, knowledge, assessment and textual analysis, with less attention to issues related to students and learning. The elements in Figure 9.5 reflect this orientation. This study also provides examples of concept maps which illustrate additional orientations to teaching reading comprehension and which are characterized by a focus on students and on student learning and understanding respectively.

A number of interesting reflections on the effectiveness of concept maps in eliciting teachers' practical knowledge are provided in Meijer (1999). Firstly, the researcher found it difficult to make any direct comparisons among the maps. Two reasons for this difficulty were suggested. One is that the concept maps were very different in content and structure (this is not wholly surprising given the open-ended nature of the task). Also, the content of the concept maps was not considered to provide a sound basis for conclusions about the nature of teachers' practical knowledge; the presence of items in the concept maps was indicative of a teacher's awareness of them, but it was not possible to conclude that teachers lacked knowledge of any items that were not mentioned. Given these difficulties, it was not possible to draw conclusions about teachers' practical knowledge from the concept maps alone; such conclusions were, rather, derived from a collective analysis of the concept maps, follow-up explanatory interviews and further semi-structured interviews with the teachers.

This example points to some of the methodological concerns associated with concept mapping. A number of these relate to the way concept maps are analysed. An initial challenge here is ensuring that the concept maps to be compared are in fact comparable. As noted above, clear instructions and an illustration of what is expected may help in this respect. Also, where teachers' pre- and post-course concept maps are being compared, the subject matter of the course (which all teachers will have taken) can ensure a certain level of comparability across the individual concept maps produced. Where, however, concepts maps are being produced on a one-off basis and without reference to a particular body of shared knowledge, the results are likely to be more idiosyncratic and difficult to compare.

In analysing concept maps researchers also need to make decisions about the particular techniques which are to be used. Typically, these are quantitative in nature (see, for example, Markham et al., 1994); one criticism of concept mapping has in fact been related to the complexity of the procedures conventionally involved in reducing the maps to quantifiable measures (Kagan, 1990). In response to such concerns Morine-Dershimer (1993) devised a simplified approach to the analysis of concept maps; this still involves transforming the maps into quantitative measures, but relies less on sophisticated statistics than has often been the case.

In her review of the use of concept mapping in the study of teacher cognition, Kagan (1990) identifies a number of further criticisms of this technique. Two are that concept maps have typically been used with small numbers of participants and that they have assessed conceptual change only in the short term. Kagan also questions the assumption that concept maps are a direct representation of cognitive structures (this claim is implicit in studies which use concept maps as evidence of how knowledge is organized in the mind). A parallel assumption in the field of language teaching would be that learners' explicit explanations of grammar rules are isomorphic with the ways those rules are stored mentally; this is similarly questionable as we have no evidence that this is the case. Finally, Kagan also suggests that where changes in concept maps are identified over time, caution is necessary in interpreting what these changes mean; they may simply reflect a respondent's increased knowledge of a topic rather than any deeper change in their cognitive structures. This reflects a point I made in Chapter 2 about the use of Likert-scale belief instruments before and after teacher education coursework; pre- and post-course differences do not necessarily reflect any deep cognitive change. Morine-Dershimer (1993) acknowledges these criticisms of concept maps and designed her study of concept mapping in pre-service teacher education with them in mind. Thus, she studied 65 pre-service teachers over one year; also 'the maps students produced were considered to be evidence of knowledge growth, rather than reflections of cognitive structure' (p. 15). And, as noted above, she devised a more manageable and less time-consuming system for analysing them.

Summary

This chapter has provided an overview of different forms of reflective writing which can constitute data in the study of language teacher cognition. The number of studies which have utilized the strategies discussed here is small, compared to those using interviews, observations and self-report instruments; one reason for this may be the additional commitment and effort, on the part of respondents, that reflective writing, compared to other forms of data collection, demands. It is because of these additional demands too, perhaps, that reflective writing has been used to study teacher cognition mainly in pre-service contexts, where research data can be collected through compulsory assigned coursework and/or using a captive audience. Despite the challenges that reflective writing presents to teachers, however, the studies reviewed here demonstrate its value to the study of language teacher cognition and its ability to provide insights into teachers' thinking and practices over time.

One key distinction we need to keep in mind is that between reflective writing conducted to promote teacher professional development and that arranged with teacher cognition research purposes in mind. While both purposes may be productively combined, a research dimension demands added rigour in the manner in which the purposes of a study are defined and in which data are collected and analysed. For example, while reflective writing conducted to promote professional development may give teachers freedom in deciding what to write about, how and when, such freedom may not be conducive to the generation of sufficient data about specific research questions in a manner which allows adequate comparisons among data to be made. Similarly, while reflective writing oriented to professional development may benefit from a dialogic perspective, with writers sharing their work with and receiving responses from readers, the implications of such interaction for the nature of the accounts produced clearly need to be carefully considered if these accounts are going to be used as evidence of teachers' cognitions. Also, where reflective writing is being produced, as is often the case, in the context of assessed coursework on teacher education programmes, the implications of this context merits discussion by the researcher.

To what extent, for example, are teachers' accounts being shaped by the knowledge that the work is going to be assessed and by their views about what the assessor – their tutor or lecturer – is looking for? This may be particularly true in the case of concept mapping, where what teachers write may be more a reflection of the input received on a course than of any actual deeper cognitive engagement with that material. These issues, together with the various practical, methodological and conceptual challenges highlighted in this chapter, merit critical consideration by researchers aiming to utilize reflective writing in the study of language teacher cognition.

10

A framework for studying language teacher cognition

The study of language teacher cognition has made a significant contribution to our understandings of how teachers learn, what teachers do, and the cognitive bases for their actions. Although still small compared to the volume of work on teacher cognition in education generally, the material I have discussed in this book constitutes a substantial knowledge base for the field of language education. Professionals in this field – language teacher educators, researchers, policy makers and teachers interested in exploring their own practices and development – can find much that is instructive in this body of work. I will now summarize the salient issues to emerge from my analysis under the following eight headings:

- the nature of language teacher cognition;
- the scope of language teacher cognition research;
- the relationship between language teachers' cognitions and classroom practices;
- the impact of context on language teachers' cognitions and practices;
- the processes of pre-service language teacher learning;

- the relationship between cognitive change and behavioural change in language teachers;
- the nature of expertise in language teaching;
- methodological issues in the study of language teacher cognition.

The nature of language teacher cognition

By the *nature* of language teacher cognition I refer to its key characteristics and the concepts through which it is defined. In terms of its characteristics, earlier, on the basis of mainstream educational research, we saw that teacher cognition has a practical orientation, is personally defined, often tacit, systematic and dynamic. There is evidence of all these qualities in language teacher cognition; in addition, it is clear from the research discussed in this book that teacher cognition is also highly context-sensitive (I discuss the impact of context on teacher cognition separately below). Of these characteristics, that least understood is the manner in which the cognitions of language teachers function as a system. Further research is thus required for us to understand not just what language teachers have cognitions about, but how the different elements in teachers' cognitive systems interact and which of these elements, for example, are core and which are peripheral. A further aspect of teacher cognition which is currently not well understood, but which has been signalled in some research on language teachers, is its emotional or affective dimension. This is an issue which is likely to become more prominent in continuing research as we seek to understand how cognitive and affective factors interact in shaping what teachers do.

In terms of how language teacher cognition is defined, one particular challenge is posed by the array of concepts and terminology this research draws on (see Table 2.2). While terminological proliferation was perhaps a necessary feature of early research, the continued introduction of new terms should, I feel, be strongly opposed. Arguably, one or more of *cognition, knowledge* (and its subtypes), *beliefs, attitudes, conceptions, theories, assumptions, principles, thinking* and *decision-making* should be adequate for most purposes. Rationalization in this respect is one way in which the study of language teacher cognition overall can achieve a greater sense of unity and coherence. In any case, it is important for the continuing development of the field for a shared set of concepts and definitions to be established and consistently used. Until that is the case, individual researchers should continue not only to identify the particular psychological constructs they are drawing on, but also to define these; this is necessary because, in the absence of a shared conceptual and terminological framework, it is likely that similar labels will continue to be used with different meanings, and different terms will be used to refer to the same constructs.

Throughout this book I have used language teacher cognition as an inclusive term referring to the complex, practically-oriented, personalized, and context-sensitive networks of knowledge, thoughts and beliefs that language teachers draw on in their work. The research I have considered examines what language teachers, at any stage of their careers, and in any language education context, think, know or believe in relation to any aspect of their work; the work reviewed has, additionally but not necessarily, also entailed the study of actual classroom practices and of the relationships between cognitions and these practices. My position remains that the study of what teachers do should be integral to the study of language teacher cognition, given that our goal is ultimately to better understand teachers and teaching, not only to describe in theoretical terms what teachers believe and know.

The scope of language teacher cognition research

Under this heading I consider the volume of research available, the contexts it has been conducted in, and the topics it has examined.

Volume

In this book I have drawn on language teacher cognition research from over 180 sources published between 1976 and 2006. The bulk of research in second and foreign language contexts has been published since the mid-1990s. I am also aware of some additional studies which I have not included here (Akyel, 1997; Davis and Wilson, 1999; Palfreyman, 1993; Scharer *et al.*, 1993; Wham *et al.*, 2001; White *et al.*, 2003), either due to difficulties in accessing them or because they came to my attention late in the review process, and I mention them now to enable readers to follow up items which may be of particular interest. These additional studies do not alter, though, the general trends and patterns evident in the work I have discussed here, though the work by White, Sturtevant and Dunlap (2003) is worth noting for its focus on teachers' perceptions of high-stakes tests in the context of literacy instruction. In addition, I am also aware of a number of Ph.D theses on language teacher cognition which are currently being written or which have been recently completed; publications from these theses will undoubtedly enrich the literature in the next few years. Overall, though, I am confident that the material this book is based on represents the field of language teacher cognition comprehensively.

Contexts

Despite the volume of work available, though, it is still vastly unrepresentative of language teaching contexts worldwide and is dominated by research into the teaching of English (as a first, second or foreign language) and conducted largely in the USA, although several other locations, such as Hong Kong, the United Kingdom and Australia have also generated a number of studies. Caution must thus be exercised in generalizing the findings of this existing work to language teaching contexts globally; secondary schools in state sector education, for example, have been the focus of very little attention. Similarly, the surge in interest in teaching languages to young learners in recent years has not been matched by studies of cognitions and practices in this area. Whole areas of language education, such as adult ESOL in the United Kingdom, remain unexplored from a teacher cognition perspective. In terms of the contexts studied, then, geographic, educational and linguistic, there is much scope for expansion in the study of language teacher cognition.

Topics

The material discussed in this book highlights a range of substantive issues which language teacher cognition can shed light on. In Chapters 2 and 3 I considered research which had as its primary focus the generic cognitions of pre-service and in-service teachers respectively. Generic cognitions are those which are studied without attention to a particular curricular area; for example, studies of interactive decision-making and planning are often interested in these processes themselves rather than how those processes are being played out in relation to specific curricular areas. In contrast, in Chapters 4 and 5 I considered research which examines language teacher cognition in relation to specific curricular areas. Grammar, reading and writing emerged here very clearly as the areas which have been awarded substantial attention, even though there are also variations in the extent to which each area has been studied in different language education contexts (the contrast between the study of reading in L1 and L2/FL contexts is particularly evident). The scarcity of research into the teaching of speaking, listening and vocabulary, especially in L2 and FL contexts, is hard to explain and these areas provide obvious foci for continuing research.

The full range of substantive issues teacher cognition research may focus on is arguably infinite, as teachers can have cognitions in relation to any aspect of language teaching and learning. An indication of the scope available to us was provided in Figure 1.5, but even these areas can be broken down further. For example, in relation to language teachers' cognitions about teachers, I have investigated teachers' views of the *defining* characteristics of foreign language teachers (Borg, 2006); this complements but is distinct in focus to existing work on teachers' beliefs about *good* language teachers (e.g. Mullock, 2003). As an example of emergent substantive areas in the study of language teacher cognition I would also include my current work into teachers' conceptions of research (see Chapter 6). The list of substantive areas that language teacher cognition research can focus on is impressive; when multiplied by the range of language education contexts each area can be studied in, the possibilities are clearly unlimited and the work available to date addresses only a small selection from among these.

The relationship between teacher cognition and classroom practice in language teaching

We know that what language teachers do is underpinned and influenced by a range preactive, interactive, and post-active of cognitions which they have. However we also understand that the relationship between cognition and practice in language teaching is neither linear nor unidirectional. It is not linear because cognitions and practices may not always concur, due to the mediating influence of contextual factors (see below); and it is not unidirectional because teachers' cognitions themselves are shaped in response to what happens in the classroom. Language teaching, then, can be seen as a process which is defined by dynamic interactions among cognition, context and experience.

The impact of context on language teachers' cognitions and practices

The social, institutional, instructional and physical settings in which teachers work have a major impact on their cognitions and practices. The study of cognitions and practices in isolation of the contexts in which they occur will inevitably, therefore, provide partial, if not flawed, characterizations of teachers and teaching. Evidence from a range of sources highlights how contextual factors can constrain what teachers do, particularly in the work of novice teachers whose ideals about language teaching may need to, at least temporarily, be put aside while they come to grips with the instructional and social realities they face in schools. The elements which constitute these realities are potentially many, inside the classroom, the school and beyond; some will be temporary (e.g. excessive heat on a particular day), others more permanent (e.g. institutional policy). Contextual factors may interact with teachers' cognitions in two ways; they may lead to changes in these cognitions or else they may alter practices directly without changing the cognitions underlying them. This latter scenario can lead to a lack of congruence between teachers' stated beliefs and actual practices. Attention to the contextual dimension of teaching allows us to interpret such mismatches in more intelligent ways. Superficially, such incongruence is easily dismissed as inconsistency on the teachers' part; such an interpretation, though, reflects a simplistic appreciation of how cognition, context and practice are mutually informing.

The processes of pre-service teacher learning in language teaching

Much of the research I have discussed here was conducted with pre-service language teachers. This is undoubtedly a context that lends itself to being researched, as participants and data are relatively easy to secure. Consequently, we now have a better understanding of the nature of prospective teachers' cognitions and of how these are shaped by their prior schooling, experiences of teacher education and initial teaching. We know that teachers come to pre-service teacher education with established, though often tacit, conceptions of teaching and learning. We also have evidence of the ways in which teachers' experiences as learners contribute to the development of cognitions which may continue to exert an influence on what teachers do throughout their careers. Teachers of foreign and second languages, in particular, possess conceptions of their work which are influenced by their own experiences of language learning. Studying these experiences is important as a means of understanding the factors which shape teachers' mental lives. And because we know that prospective teachers' preconceptions about language teaching may not always be conducive to effective practice, making these preconceptions explicit is an important part of the process of pre-service teacher education.

Pre-service teachers' prior cognitions also act as a filter through which input and experience during teacher education is processed; acknowledging these prior cognitions, making them explicit and providing teachers with opportunities to examine and reconsider these in the light of new information and experience are thus important elements in the process of teacher learning. We also appreciate that the impact of pre-service teacher education on what new teachers learn cannot be taken for granted; individual teachers make sense of and are affected by training programmes in different and unique ways. It is also clear that practice teaching and early classroom experiences are a major influence on the development of teachers' cognitions and that these experiences – which provide first-hand encounters with the realities of life in schools and classrooms from a teacher's perspective – may outweigh input from coursework. There are clear implications here both for the role of practice teaching in pre-service teaching education as well as for the relationship between the experiential and theoretical dimensions of what and how pre-service teachers learn. One variable which is clearly relevant to pre-service teacher learning, but which has yet to receive much empirical attention, is the impact of the duration of the training; this is particularly relevant in the field of language teaching where a qualification to teach can be achieved in anything from four weeks to five years.

The relationship between cognitive change and behavioural change in language teachers

We now possess more sophisticated understandings of the notion of change in language teachers' cognitions and practices. Much work in this area remains to be done; however, it is clear that the distinction between cognitive change and behavioural change is important because one does not necessarily imply the other. Teachers may adopt and display particular behaviours without any accompanying change in their cognitions (e.g. during assessed teaching practice, visits by inspectors or observation by researchers); teachers' cognitions (e.g. their belief in the value of a particular instructional technique) may also change without any obvious change in what they do (due to, for example, situational constraints). Additionally, we know that similar behaviours in different teachers may be underpinned by very different cognitions, and that similar cognitions may be translated into a range of behaviourally distinct practices (further research on communal cognitions and practices has a contribution to make in extending our understanding of these issues). In relation to cognitive change in teachers, there is also value in distinguishing between content, structure and process. The first of these has been that most researched, though the measures used in doing so have often lacked sophistication (e.g. pre- and post-course questionnaires). However, because cognitive change may take the form of a reorganization in content, rather than just changes in the content of what is known, the structure of teacher cognition also merits further attention. Research using repertory grids and concept mapping has potential in this respect. Overall, in studying change in language teachers' cognitions we must also remain aware that different research instruments have different levels of sensitivity in detecting various types of change. Questionnaires, for example, may capture changes in teachers' reported theoretical orientations, but will not be able to track cognitive change in the way that repertory grids or concept mapping can. Conclusions about a lack of change in studies of teacher cognition should always be qualified with reference to how change was actually operationalized. Finally, and distinct from discussions of, for example, what language teachers know and how that knowledge is organized, further attention to the processes of cognitive change is also required.

The nature of expertise in language teaching

Isolated pockets of interest in expertise in language teaching have existed for several years but it is only recently that this topic has established itself more prominently as a key area of research. On the basis of the evidence currently available we are now able to identify some differences in the cognitions of teachers with different degrees of expertise. A key issue in such work is the manner in which expertise is defined; in some studies there is an explicit association between expertise and years of teaching experience, though we now appreciate that the two do not always co-occur. Overall, though, comparisons of novice and experts have highlighted differences in the content and structure of their cognitions. More expert language teachers are characterized by cognitions in which different forms of formal and experiential knowledge function as an integrated whole and which enable such teachers to envision learning potential in instructional contexts, to anticipate problems and to respond (often improvisationally) in ways which are both technically skilled and sensitive to learners. Novices are characterized by a higher degree of compartmentalization in their knowledge, inflexibility in responding to unplanned learning opportunities, a less varied instructional repertoire and difficulties in thinking about learning from the learners' perspective. Longitudinal work examining the processes through which expertise in language teaching develops, though, remains limited.

Methodological issues in the study of language teacher cognition

What counts as evidence of language teacher cognition is a fundamental methodological question in this domain of research. Chapters 6–9 illustrated a diverse range of answers to this question: responses to questionnaires, tests and rating tasks; verbal commentaries elicited through structured, semi structured, stimulated recall and repertory grid interviews; think-aloud protocols; structured and less structured observational data; different forms of narrative and schematic reflective writing: all of these have been cited, individually or in combinations, as evidence of the unobservable psychological context of language teaching. Self-report instruments, semi-structured and stimulated recall interviews and unstructured observation are the strategies most widely used.

A wide range of methodological possibilities are clearly available to researchers studying language teacher cognition, each with its own particular strengths and potential pitfalls. No one approach to studying teacher cognition will be free of problems and this is reflected in the range of studies which have adopted multi-method strategies, combining, for example, self-report instruments, interviews and observations. Assuming the different methods are applied with the requisite level of technical expertise, in combination they may counteract the limitations of any one individual strategy. In any case, acknowledging the methodological problems inherent in the study of language teacher cognition is essential in ensuring that the claims we make are justified.

Different kinds of evidence reflect different assumptions about the nature of teacher cognition itself. An awareness of these is important both in selecting data collection strategies and in understanding the limits of the claims which different methods allow us to make. The exclusive use of self-report instruments, for example, implies that beliefs can be articulated and rated against predefined propositional statements and understood without direct reference to actual instructional practices. Interviews reflect the view that beliefs can be articulated orally and that teachers are able to provide a verbal account of the cognitions underpinning their work. Concept mapping often assumes that internal cognitive structures can be represented in diagrammatic form. Assumptions of this kind are present for every data collection strategy we use in studying language teacher cognition; they should not remain unexplored and unquestioned by researchers.

Another issue to emerge from the methodological analysis presented here is that the nature of the cognitions which are obtained is a product of the elicitational methods used. An important distinction here is between cognitions which are expressed in relation to ideal instructional practices (how things should be) and, in contrast, in relation to instructional realities (how things are). Self-report instruments and verbal commentaries not grounded in concrete examples of real practice may generate data which reflect teachers' ideals; data based on and elicited in relation to observed classroom events may better capture teachers' cognitions in relation to actual practice. This distinction between ideal-oriented cognitions and reality-oriented cognitions is supported by studies which have found discrepancies between what teachers say (e.g. in completing questionnaires) and do (in the classroom). Once again, then, rather than concluding that teachers are inconsistent, we can understand the varying nature of teachers' responses in relation to how they react to different forms of data collection. It is important to clarify that I am not suggesting that ideal cognitions are less important from a research point of view; they do provide insight into the workings of teachers' minds. However, as researchers we must ensure that cognitions expressed theoretically and in relation to ideals are not used as evidence of the practically-oriented cognitions which inform teachers' actual instructional practices. It is also worth noting in the context of this discussion that there is evidence that certain theoretical profiling instruments, such as the TORP, are accurate predictors of classroom practice. Much more work of this kind is required though before we are able to rely on cognitions elicited theoretically for insights into what teachers do in the classroom.

One final point I have stressed throughout the discussion of research methods in the study of language teacher cognition is that choices will often need to be made not just on methodological grounds but also with an awareness of what is practically feasible, acceptable and permissible in the particular context under study.

A framework for language teacher cognition research

The field of language teacher cognition lacks a programmatic research agenda conceived within an overall unifying framework and one of my goals in this book has been to impose some structure on this field in order to allow a fuller appreciation of both the issues it has been concerned with and the methods applied in investigating these. The range of issues summarized above are one contribution in this respect; they provide an orientation to both major themes and gaps in the study of language teacher cognition as well as to some key methodological issues researchers in the field should be aware of (and which were expanded on in detail in Chapters 6–9).

A second way in which I have attempted to make sense of what is a significant and diverse volume of research is reflected in the structure of this book itself. An initial distinction can thus be made between the substantive and methodological dimensions of language teacher cognition research. The former covers *what* is being studied, the latter *how*. Each of these can be further broken down into constituent parts. Substantively, research can be *generic* or *domain-specific*. The former encompasses an interest in the nature and processes of teacher cognition irrespective of the curricular areas involved (e.g. planning, interactive decision-making), while the latter aims to understand cognitions in relation to specific curricular areas (e.g. grammar, writing). Both generic and domain-specific issues can be broken down into progressively smaller elements (e.g. within grammar teaching, there can be a focus on the explanation of grammar rules). Cutting across the substantive elements are variables related to the stage of development teachers are at – typically *pre-service* or *in-service,* but other distinctions we have seen are *novice-expert* and *non-specialist-specialist.* This simple classification allows us to define the substance of language teacher cognition research in relation to two independent variables: topic and participants. This is illustrated in the top part of Figure 10.1. A study of language teacher cognition can be placed in any of the quadrants to reflect its particular mix of topic and participants (two quadrants will be used where both pre-service and in-service teachers participate in a study). Applying this to the material reviewed here, the bulk of it would be on the left-hand side of the diagram (pre-service teachers) with a roughly equal distribution between generic and domain-specific topics. Different distributions might emerge if research in specific domains, such as L1 and L2 contexts, was analysed separately.

Methodologically, I have divided studies of language teacher cognition into four groups depending on their data collection strategies: self-report instruments, verbal commentaries, observation and reflective writing. I have also specified a number of options within each of these broader categories. This classification covers the major strategies researchers will want to consider, though I am aware that other possibilities, not currently illustrated in the research available, exist (e.g. experiments and simulations). The bottom part of Figure 10.1 summarizes the methodological options in language teacher cognition research I have discussed here.

A third tool for conceptualizing the field of language teacher research is Figure 10.2. This represents an update on Figure 1.5 in five particular ways:

- it adds broader experiences early in life to the *schooling* box to reflect the fact that preconceptions about education may also be defined through relationships with influential adults, such as parents;

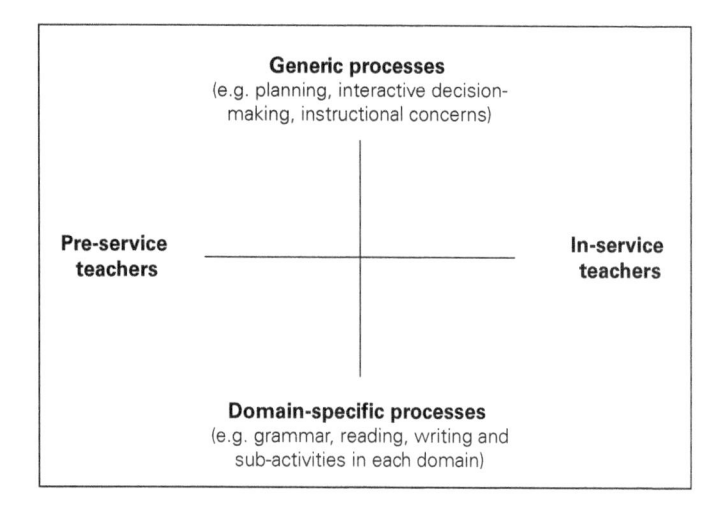

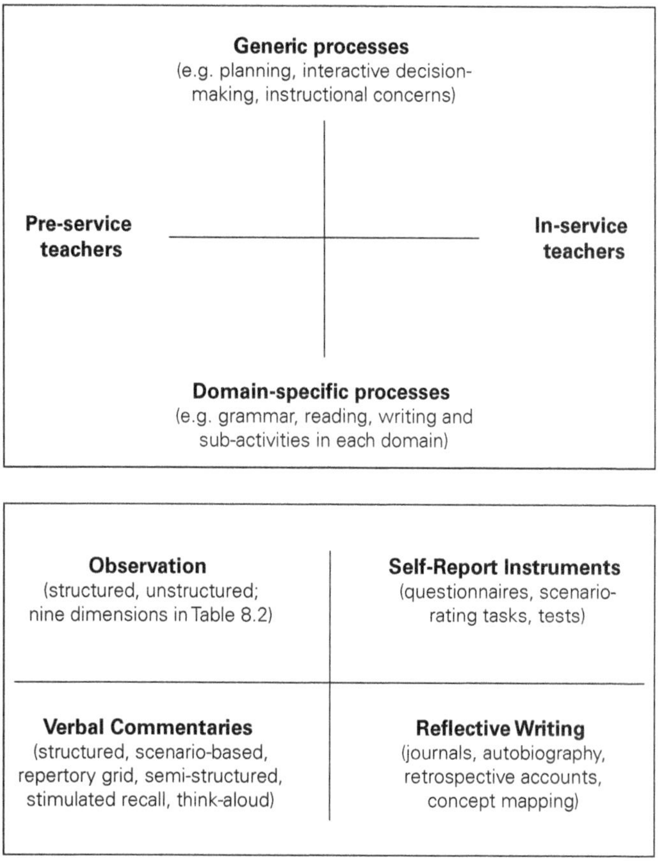

332 TEACHER COGNITION AND LANGUAGE EDUCATION

```
                    Generic processes
                 (e.g. planning, interactive decision-
                  making, instructional concerns)

Pre-service                                            In-service
teachers                                               teachers

                  Domain-specific processes
                 (e.g. grammar, reading, writing and
                  sub-activities in each domain)
```

Observation	Self-Report Instruments
(structured, unstructured; nine dimensions in Table 8.2)	(questionnaires, scenario-rating tasks, tests)
Verbal Commentaries	**Reflective Writing**
(structured, scenario-based, repertory grid, semi-structured, stimulated recall, think-aloud)	(journals, autobiography, retrospective accounts, concept mapping)

FIGURE 10.1 *Substantive and methodological elements in language teacher cognition research*

- it positions contextual factors in teaching *around* classroom practice, rather than just *external* to it, as the earlier diagram suggested; the classroom itself thus becomes part of the context;
- it includes a shorter list of constructs for describing teacher cognition, in line with the need for rationalization in this respect that I argued for earlier in this chapter;

- it adds elements to the issues which teachers can have cognitions about;
- it has *language* teacher cognition at its centre, rather than teacher cognition (the previous diagram was based on the literature in education generally).

This diagram indicates that language teachers have cognitions about all aspects of their work and that these can be described using various psychological constructs which I collectively refer to as teacher cognition. It also outlines relationships among teacher cognition, teacher learning (both through schooling and professional education)

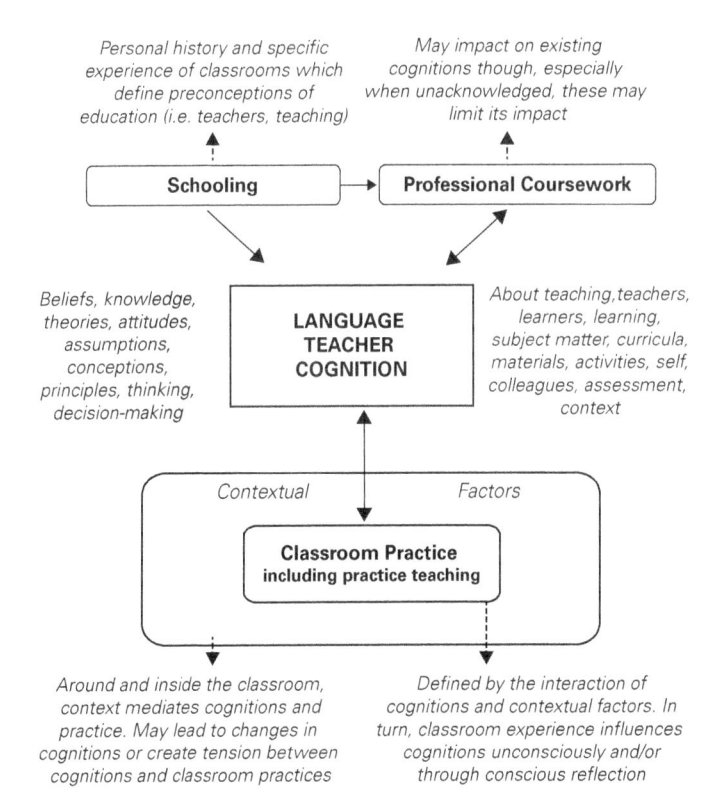

```
Personal history and specific              May impact on existing
experience of classrooms which          cognitions though, especially
   define preconceptions of            when unacknowledged, these may
 education (i.e. teachers, teaching)          limit its impact
                ↑                                   ↑
        ┌───────────────┐              ┌───────────────────────┐
        │   Schooling   │─────────────▶│ Professional Coursework│
        └───────────────┘              └───────────────────────┘

Beliefs, knowledge,        ┌──────────────┐       About teaching, teachers,
 theories, attitudes,      │   LANGUAGE   │        learners, learning,
    assumptions,           │   TEACHER    │       subject matter, curricula,
    conceptions,           │   COGNITION  │       materials, activities, self,
 principles, thinking,     └──────────────┘       colleagues, assessment,
  decision-making                                        context
                                  ↕
          ┌──────── Contextual         Factors ────────┐
          │         ┌──────────────────────┐           │
          │         │  Classroom Practice  │           │
          │         │ including practice teaching │    │
          │         └──────────────────────┘           │
          └─────────────────────────────────────────────┘
                       ↓                        ↓
Around and inside the classroom,        Defined by the interaction of
  context mediates cognitions and      cognitions and contextual factors. In
  practice. May lead to changes in      turn, classroom experience influences
 cognitions or create tension between    cognitions unconsciously and/or
  cognitions and classroom practices      through conscious reflection
```

FIGURE 10.2 *Elements and processes in language teacher cognition*

and classroom practice. As already noted, there is ample evidence that teachers' experiences as learners (and as children generally) can inform cognitions about teaching and learning and that these cognitions may continue to exert an influence on teachers throughout their career; there is also evidence to suggest that although professional preparation does shape trainees' cognitions, programmes which ignore trainee teachers' prior beliefs may be less effective at influencing these; and research has also shown that teacher cognitions and practices are mutually informing, with contextual factors playing an important role in mediating the extent to which teachers are able to implement instruction congruent with their cognitions.

Collectively, the key themes highlighted at the start of this chapter, Figure 10.1 and Figure 10.2 represent my current attempts at defining a framework for language teacher cognition research. Such a framework is necessary for several reasons; it militates against the accumulation of isolated studies conducted without sufficient awareness of how these relate to existing work; it reminds researchers of key dimensions in the study of language teacher cognition; and it highlights key themes, gaps and conceptual relationships and promotes more focused attention to these.

Consolidating and extending language teacher cognition research

There is clearly scope for continuing research into all of the themes in language teacher cognition which I have highlighted in this book. There are also themes which have to date been awarded scant attention, and these have been noted too. To conclude this book, I would like to comment on one issue which continues to challenge researchers in teacher cognition, both generally and in language teaching. This is the relationship between teacher cognition and student learning. I have referred to a number of studies which have compared teachers' and students' cognitions, and while these are based on the premise that a mismatch between the two is undesirable, there is no empirical support for this. The only study I am aware of which explicitly addresses the relationships between teacher cognition and student learning is

McCutchen et al. (2002), discussed in Chapter 5. Otherwise, research on learning and research on teacher cognition have developed in parallel to one another without any signs of converging. I will illustrate this with reference to the study of grammar learning and teaching in second and foreign language (L2) contexts.

Ellis (2001) summarizes the history of research on grammar learning over 40 years by highlighting the changing questions which have been addressed:

- What's the best method for teaching grammar? (1960s–70s)
- Does teaching grammar make a difference? (1970s–80s)
- What interactions take place in language classrooms? (1980s)
- What effect does grammar teaching have on the order and sequence of acquisition? (1980s)
- Does grammar teaching influence learning outcomes? (1980s–90s)
- Do some types of grammar teaching work better than others? (1990s–)

In contrast to this history, the study of L2 grammar teaching from a teacher cognition point of view only emerged in the late 1990s (see, for example, Borg, 1998b).

While there have been an increasing number of descriptive studies of grammar teaching in intact classes, overall a major focus of grammar learning research has been the measurement of learning outcomes in relation to specific instructional strategies; to rule out influences on the results other than the instructional technique, an element of experimental control has often been required in such studies. This approach is reflected in the following extract:

> Because of the large number of teachers who participated in this study it was decided to reduce their influence on the students' performance as much as possible. While this could not be done completely, limiting each approach to a written presentation minimized the teacher factor as much as possible.
> (Shaffer, 1989: 400)

Studies of teacher cognition in L2 grammar teaching, in contrast, have often been based on naturalistic designs, typically drawing on observations and interviews. The goals of these studies have been to describe what teachers do and to understand the cognitive bases for instructional decisions in grammar teaching. Consequently, this research tells us nothing about the effectiveness of what teachers think and do in relation to what students learn.

From a teacher cognition point of view, the dominant paradigm in research on grammar learning is unsatisfactory because the teacher is treated as a variable that needs to be controlled. We know, though, that teachers are a powerful shaping influence on what happens in the classroom. From a language learning point of view, teacher cognition research is unsatisfactory because it neglects the quality of learning; it says nothing about the kinds of cognitions which are likely to enhance learning outcomes.

This example of grammar teaching and learning is quite characteristic of research on language learning and teacher cognition more generally. At the time of writing there is no evidence to suggest that these two lines of inquiry are moving any closer together. The question we are faced with at this point, then, is how to respond to the division in language teaching generally between these two domains of inquiry. I currently see three options:

1. Accept that the study of learning outcomes and teacher cognition are two distinct, irreconcilable domains of research.

2. Acknowledge the strengths of each perspective and look for ways in which they can mutually inform one another.

3. Consider whether, conceptually and methodologically, it is feasible to seek links between teacher cognition and learning outcomes.

The first option argues for the status quo. Second language acquisition (SLA) research is about learners and learning; teacher cognition research is about teachers and teaching. Both positions make a valuable but distinct contribution to our understandings of the processes of language learning and teaching, but they are not reconcilable. This position is not, in my view, acceptable if we are genuinely interested in developing more holistic understandings of language teaching and learning.

In considering the second option, how might the two perspectives inform each other? Ellis (2002) acknowledges that ideas based on SLA research are not necessarily more valid that those based on teachers' experience. He suggests that SLA research provides ideas which teachers need to experiment with in their own classrooms. This is a constructive way of looking at the relationship between SLA research and teaching. Teacher cognition research, then, can be seen, partly, as the study of the sense and use teachers make of theories suggested by SLA. SLA research can also inform teacher cognition research by suggesting substantive issues to focus on, especially in research involving classroom observation. Key topics in SLA research have been, for example, corrective feedback, grammar practice and input enhancement. Teacher cognition can take these topics and explore teachers' cognitions and practices in relation to them. This may shed light on the gap that often exists between what teachers do and what SLA theory suggests (e.g. despite arguments about the inadequacy of traditional production practice in L2 learning, this is still by far the most prevalent form of practice that language learners receive).

Teacher cognition research can also inform the work of SLA researchers. Firstly, it can highlight the many factors in a classroom which impinge on what teachers do (and hence on learning). SLA researchers wishing to conduct controlled studies can benefit from being aware of these factors (e.g. learners' expectations). Secondly, an awareness of teacher cognition research can inform any pedagogical claims that SLA researchers make about their work. Teacher cognition research illustrates the many complexities which influence what teachers do. In making claims about the relevance of their findings to classroom practices, SLA research is likely to be more credible, pedagogically, if it shows an awareness of these factors. Another possible way in which teacher cognition research can inform work in SLA is by highlighting practices which can then be subject to more controlled study. For example, one teacher I worked with believed that learners responded well to fluency work followed by a focus on errors noted during that work. This is an approach to grammar teaching which could then be tested from an SLA point of view to see if there were any benefits to language learning of this strategy.

I believe that mutual informing of this kind is possible. It requires both camps to be aware of and to see value in each other's research. This position, though, still stops short of arguing that teacher cognition researchers need to study the relationship between what teachers know, believe and think, and what students learn. The study by McCutchen *et al.* (2002) approached this task by:

- testing 40 teachers' knowledge of the structure of language.
- conducting an intensive two-week training course for these teachers.
- testing teachers' knowledge again after the training course.
- observing these teachers over a year and documenting the nature of their practices regarding the teaching of initial literacy.
- comparing the knowledge and practices of the teachers in the study to a control group not involved.
- measuring the phonological awareness, spelling, listening comprehension and word-reading of 492 students taught by the participating teachers at various points during the year.

The conclusions reached were that teachers' knowledge can be deepened through training, that teachers can use this knowledge to change their practice and that these changes can improve student learning. A causal link was thus posited between teacher knowledge, classroom practice and learning.

While this is an impressive study, I am not convinced it provides a model that is easy to emulate in the field of language teaching generally. It was a large, funded study (eight researchers; teachers were paid to participate); it relied on expertise in experimental designs and sophisticated statistical analyses (the lead researchers were educational psychologists); it depended on teachers' willingness to take written tests. Apart from the resources and expertise this kind of work requires, there is also an immediate tension between the approach taken here and the generally interpretive nature of research on language teacher cognition. One reason teacher cognition research has been valuable is that it has highlighted the complex nature of teaching. It has used qualitative methods to portray in rich detail what teachers do and the factors behind their work. Viewing teachers, their work and their cognitions as quantifiable phenomena may thus require teacher cognition researchers to adopt an alternative perspective. This may be possible; rather than calling for either SLA researchers or teacher cognition researchers to alter their perspectives on researching language education, though, it is perhaps more realistic and ultimately more productive to combine the expertise of both parties in the collaborative study of ways of linking teacher cognition and learning. Collaborations of this kind would allow both parties to exploit their respective methodological strengths and to recognize more fully the respective value of each other's work. I would see advances in this direction as key to the continued development not only of language teacher cognition research, but of the study of language teaching and learning more generally.

References

Abbs, P. (1974). *Autobiography in Education*. London: Heinemann Educational Books.

Abelson, R. P. (1979). *Differences between beliefs and knowledge systems. Cognitive Science, 3,* 355–66.

Adams, P. E. and Krockover, G. H. (1997). Beginning science teacher cognition and its origins in the preservice secondary science teacher program. *Journal of Research in Science Teaching, 34,* 633–53.

Akyel, A. (1997). Experienced and student EFL teachers' instructional thoughts and actions. *Canadian Modern Language Review, 53,* 677–704.

Alderson, J. C., Clapham, C., and Steel, D. (1996). *Metalinguistic Knowledge, Language Aptitude and Language Proficiency.* Lancaster: CRLE, University of Lancaster Working Papers, 26.

Aldridge, A. and Levine, K. (2001). *Surveying the Social World: Principles and Practice in Survey Research.* Buckingham: Open University Press.

Alexander, P. A., Schallert, D. L., and Hare, V. C. (1991). Coming to terms: How researchers in learning and literacy talk about knowledge. *Review of Educational Research, 61,* 315–43.

Allen, L. Q. (2002). Teachers' pedagogical beliefs and the standards for foreign language learning. *Foreign Language Annals, 35,* 518–29.

Allwright, D. and Bailey, K. M. (1991). *Focus on the Language Classroom: An Introduction to Classroom Research For Teachers.* Cambridge: Cambridge University Press.

Anderson, L. W. and Burns, R. B. (1989). *Research in Classrooms: The Study of Teachers, Teaching and Instruction.* Oxford: Pergamon Press.

Andrews, S. (1994). The grammatical knowledge/awareness of native-speaker EFL teachers: What the trainers say. In M. Bygate, A. Tonkyn and E. Williams (eds), *Grammar and the Language Teacher.* (pp. 69–89). London: Prentice Hall International.

—(1997). Metalinguistic knowledge and teacher explanation. *Language Awareness, 6,* 147–61.

—(1999a). 'All these like little name things': a comparative study of language teachers' explicit knowledge of grammar and grammatical terminology. *Language Awareness, 8,* 143–59.

—(1999b). Why do L2 teachers need to 'know about language'? Teacher metalinguistic awareness and input for learning. *Language and Education*, 13, 161–77.

—(2001). The language awareness of the L2 teacher: Its impact upon pedagogical practice. *Language Awareness*, 10, 75–90.

—(2003a). 'Just like instant noodles': L2 teachers and their beliefs about grammar pedagogy. *Teachers and Teaching*, 9, 351–76.

—(2003b). Teacher language awareness and the professional knowledge base of the L2 teacher. *Language Awareness*, 12, 81–95.

Andrews, S. and McNeil, A. (2005). Knowledge about language and the 'good language teacher'. In N. Bartels (ed.), *Applied Linguistics and Language Teacher Education* (pp. 159–78). New York: Springer.

Angeli, C. and Valanides, N. (2005). ICT-Related Pedagogical Content Knowledge: A Model for Teacher Preparation. *Technology and Teacher Education Annual*, 5, 3030–37.

Anning, A. (1988). Teachers' theories about children's learning. In J. Calderhead (ed.), *Teacher's Professional Learning*. (pp. 128–45). London: The Falmer Press.

Appel, J. (1995). *Diary of a Language Teacher*. Oxford: Heinemann.

Argyris, C. and Schön, D. A. (1974). *Theory in Practice: Increasing Professional Effectiveness*. San Francisco: Jossey-Bass.

Babbie, E. (2003). The Practice of Social Research (10th edn). Belmont: Thomson/Wadsworth.

Bailey, K. M. (1990). The use of diary studies in teacher education programs. In J. C. Richards and D. Nunan (eds), *Second Language Teacher Education* (pp. 215–26). Cambridge: CUP.

—(1996). The best laid plans: teachers' in-class decisions to depart from their lesson plans. In K. M. Bailey and D. Nunan (eds), *Voices From the Language Classroom* (pp. 15–40). Cambridge: Cambridge University Press.

Bailey, K. M., Bergthold, B., Braunstein, B., Jagodzinski Fleischman, N., Holbrook, M. P., Tuman, J., Waissbluth, X., and Zambo, L. J. (1996). The language learners' autobiography: examining the 'apprenticeship of observation'. In D. Freeman and J. C. Richards (eds), *Teacher Learning in Language Teaching* (pp. 11–29). New York: Cambridge University Press.

Bailey, K. M. and Ochsner, R. (1983). A methodological review of the diary studies: Windmill tilting or social science? In K. M. Bailey, M. H. Long and S. Peck (eds), *Second Language Acquisition Studies* (pp. 188–98). Rowley, M.A.: Newbury House.

Ball, D. L. and McDiarmid, G. W. (1990). The subject-matter preparation of teachers. In W. R. Houston (ed.), *Handbook of Research on Teacher Education* (pp. 437–49). New York: Macmillan.

Bannister, D. and Fransella, F. (1986). *Inquiring Man: The Psychology of Personal Constructs* (3rd edn). London: Routledge.

Barcelos, A. M. F. (2003). Researching beliefs about SLA: a critical review. In P. Kalaja and A. M. F. Barcelos (eds), *Beliefs about SLA: New Research Approaches* (pp. 7–33). Dordecht, Netherlands: Kluwer.

Bartels, N. (1999). How teachers use their knowledge of English. In H. Trappes-Lomax and I. McGrath (eds), *Theory in Language Teacher Education* (pp. 46–56). London: Prentice Hall.

—(2005a). Researching applied linguistics in language teacher education. In N. Bartels (ed.), *Applied Linguistics and Language Teacher Education* (pp. 1–26). New York: Springer.

Bartels, N. (ed.). (2005b). *Applied Linguistics and Language Teacher Education*. New York: Springer.

Basturkmen, H., Loewen, S., and Ellis, R. (2004). Teachers' stated beliefs about incidental focus on form and their classroom practices. *Applied Linguistics*, 25, 243–72.

Beach, S. A. (1994). Teacher's theories and classroom practice: beliefs, knowledge, or context? *Reading Psychology*, 15, 189–96.

Beail, N. (1985). An introduction to repertory grid technique. In N. Beail (ed.), *Repertory Grid Technique and Personal Constructs: Applications in Clinical and Educational Settings* (pp. 1–24). London: Croom Helm.

Ben-Peretz, M. (1984). Kelly's theory of personal constructs as a paradigm for investigating teacher thinking. In R. Halkes and J. K. Olson (eds), *Teacher Thinking* (pp. 103–11). Lisse, Netherlands: Swets and Zeitlinger.

Ben-Peretz, M., Bromme, R., and Halkes, R. (1986). *Advances of Research on Teacher Thinking*. Lisse: Swets and Zeitlinger.

Bereiter, C. and Scardamalia, M. (1993). *Surpassing Ourselves: An Inquiry into the Nature and Implications of Expertise*. Chicago: Open Court.

Berliner, D. C. (1987). Ways of thinking about students and classrooms by more and less experienced teachers. In J. Calderhead (ed.), *Exploring Teachers' Thinking* (pp. 60–83). London: Cassell.

—(2001). Learning about and learning from expert teachers. *International Journal of Educational Research*, 35, 463–82.

Berliner, D. C. and Calfee, R. C. (eds). (1996). *Handbook of Educational Psychology*. New York: Macmillan.

Bernat, E. and Gvozdenko, I. (2005). Beliefs about language learning: Current knowledge, pedagogical implications, and new research directions. *TESL-EJ*, 9, 1–21.

Berry, R. (1995). Grammar terminology: is there a student-teacher gap? In D. Nunan, R. Berry and V. Berry (eds), *Language Awareness in Language Education* (pp. 51–68). Hong Kong: Faculty of Education, University of Hong Kong.

—(1997). Teachers' awareness of learners' knowledge: The case of metalinguistic terminology. *Language Awareness*, 6, 136–46.

REFERENCES

Bianchini, J. A., Johnston, C. C., Oram, S. Y., and Cavazos, L. M. (2003). Learning to teach science in contemporary and equitable ways: The successes and struggles of first-year science teachers. *Science Education*, 87, 419–43.

Bigelow, M. and Ranney, M. (2005). Pre-service ESL teachers' knowledge about language and its transfer to lesson planning. In N. Bartels (ed.), *Applied Linguistics and Language Teacher Education* (pp. 179–200). New York: Springer.

Bloor, T. (1986). What do language students know about grammar? *British Journal of Language Teaching*, 24, 157–60.

Bodycott, P. (1997). The influence of personal history on preservice Malay, Tamil and Chinese teacher thinking. *Journal of Education for Teaching*, 23, 57–68.

Borg, M. (2004). The apprenticeship of observation. *ELT Journal*, 58, 274–276.

Borg, M. (2005a). A case study of the development in pedagogic thinking of a pre-service teacher. *TESL-EJ*, 9, 1–30.

Borg, S. (1998a). Talking about grammar in the foreign language classroom. *Language Awareness*, 7, 159–75.

—(1998b). Teachers' pedagogical systems and grammar teaching: A qualitative study. *TESOL Quarterly*, 32, 9–38.

—(1999a). Studying teacher cognition in second language grammar teaching. *System*, 27, 19–31.

—(1999b). The use of grammatical terminology in the second language classroom: A qualitative study of teachers' practices and cognitions. *Applied Linguistics*, 20, 95–126.

—(1999c). Teachers' theories in grammar teaching. *ELT Journal*, 53, 157–67.

—(2001a). The research journal: a tool for promoting and understanding researcher development. *Language Teaching Research*, 5, 156–77.

—(2001b). Self-perception and practice in teaching grammar. *ELT Journal*, 55, 21–29.

—(2003a). Second language grammar teaching: practices and rationales. *Ilha do Desterro*, 41, 155–83.

—(2003b). Teacher cognition in grammar teaching: a literature review. *Language Awareness*, 12, 96–108.

—(2003c). Teacher cognition in language teaching: a review of research on what language teachers think, know, believe, and do. *Language Teaching*, 36, 81–109.

—(2005b). Experience, knowledge about language, and classroom experience in teaching grammar. In N. Bartels (ed.), *Applied Linguistics and Language Teacher Education* (pp. 325–40). New York: Springer.

—(2006). The distinctive characteristics of foreign language teachers. *Language Teaching Research*, 10, 3–31.

—(in press). *Research engagement in English language teaching. Teaching and Teacher Education.*
Borko, H. and Livingston, C. (1989). Cognition and improvisation: Differences in mathematics instruction by expert and novice teachers. *American Educational Research Journal, 26,* 473–98.
Borko, H., Livingston, C., McCaleb, J., and Mauro, L. (1988). Student teachers' planning and post-lesson reflections: Patterns and implications for teacher preparation. In J. Calderhead (ed.), *Teacher's Professional Learning* (pp. 65–83). London: The Falmer Press.
Borko, H. and Niles, J. (1982). Factors contributing to teachers' judgments about students and decisions about grouping students for reading instruction. *Journal of Reading Behavior, 14,* 127–36.
Borko, H. and Putnam, R. (1996). Learning to teach. In D. C. Berliner and R. C. Calfee (eds), *Handbook of Educational Psychology* (pp. 673–708). New York: Macmillan.
Borko, H., Shavelson, R., and Stern, P. (1981). Teachers' decisions in the planning of reading instruction. *Reading Research Quarterly, 16,* 449–66.
Breen, M. P. (1991). Understanding the language teacher. In R. Phillipson, E. Kellerman, L. Selinker, M. Sharwood Smith and M. Swain (eds), *Foreign/Second Language Pedagogy Research* (pp. 213–33). Clevedon, UK: Multilingual Matters.
Breen, M. P., Hird, B., Milton, M., Oliver, R., and Thwaite, A. (2001). Making sense of language teaching: Teachers' principles and classroom practices. *Applied Linguistics, 22,* 470–501.
Brock, M. N., Yu, B., and Wong, M. (1992). 'Journalling' together: Collaborative diary-keeping and teacher development. In J. Flowerdew, M. Brock and S. Hsia (eds), *Perspectives on Second Language Teacher Education* (pp. 295–307). Hong Kong: City Polytechnic of Hong Kong.
Brookhart, S. M. and Freeman, D. J. (1992). Characteristics of entering teacher candidates. *Review of Educational Research, 62,* 37–60.
Brousseau, B. A., Book, C., and Byers, J. L. (1988). Teacher beliefs and the cultures of teaching. *Journal of Teacher Education, 39,* 33–39.
Brown, H. D. and Rodgers, T. S. (2002). *Doing Second Language Research.* Oxford: Oxford University Press.
Brown, J. and McGannon, J. (1998). What do I know about language learning? The story of the beginning teacher. *23rd ALAA Congress.* Retrieved 17 February, 2006, from http://www.cltr.uq.edu.au/alsaa/proceed/bro-mcgan.html
Brown, J. D. (2001). *Using Surveys in Language Programs.* Cambridge: Cambridge University Press.
Brown, S. and McIntyre, D. (1986). How do teachers think about their craft? In M. Ben-Peretz, R. Bromme and R. Halkes (eds), *Advances of Research on Teacher Education.* (pp. 36–44). Lisse: Swets and Zeitlinger.

Brumfit, C., Mitchell, R., and Hooper, J. (1996). Grammar, language and classroom practice. In M. Hughes (ed.), *Teaching and Learning in Changing Times* (pp. 70–87). Oxford: Blackwell.

Bryman, A. (2001). *Social Research Methods*. Oxford: Oxford University Press.

Bullough, R. V., Jr. (1989). *First-Year Teacher: A Case Study*. New York: Teachers College.

Burgess, J. and Etherington, S. (2002). Focus on grammatical form: explicit or implicit? *System*, *30*, 433–58.

Burgess, R. G. (1984). *In the Field: An Introduction to Field Research*. London: Routledge.

Burns, A. (1992). Teacher beliefs and their influence on classroom practice. *Prospect*, *7*, 56–66.

—(1996). Starting all over again: From teaching adults to teaching beginners. In D. Freeman and J. C. Richards (eds), *Teacher Learning in Language Teaching* (pp. 154–77). Cambridge: Cambridge University Press.

Burns, A. and Knox, J. (2005). Realisation(s): Systemic-functional linguistics and the language classroom. In N. Bartels (ed.), *Applied Linguistics and Language Teacher Education* (pp. 235–59). New York: Springer.

Cabaroglu, N. and Roberts, J. (2000). Development in student teachers' preexisting beliefs during a 1-Year PGCE programme. *System*, *28*, 387–402.

Calderhead, J. (1981). Stimulated recall: A method for research on teaching. *British Journal of Educational Psychology.*, *51*, 211–17.

—(1987). Introduction. In J. Calderhead (ed.), *Exploring Teachers' Thinking* (pp. 1–19). London: Cassell.

—(1988a). The development of knowledge structures in learning to teach. In J. Calderhead (ed.), *Teachers' Professional Learning* (pp. 51–64). London: The Falmer Press.

—(1989). Reflective teaching and teacher education. *Teaching and Teacher Education*, *5*, 43–51.

—(1991). The nature and growth of knowledge in student teaching. *Teaching and Teacher Education*, *5*, 531–5.

—(1996). Teachers: Beliefs and knowledge. In D. C. Berliner and R. C. Calfee (eds), *Handbook of Educational Psychology* (pp. 709–25). New York: Macmillan.

Calderhead, J. (ed.). (1988b). *Teachers' Professional Learning*. London: The Falmer Press.

Calderhead, J. and Gates, P. (eds). (1993). *Conceptualizing Reflection in Teacher Development*. London: The Falmer Press.

Calderhead, J. and Robson, M. (1991). Images of teaching: Student teachers' early conceptions of classroom practice. *Teaching and Teacher Education*, *7*, 1–8.

REFERENCES

Carlgren, I., Vaage, S., and Handal, G. (eds). (1994). *Teachers' Minds and Actions: Research on Teachers' Thinking and Practice*. London: The Falmer Press.

Carter, C. and Doyle, W. (1996). Personal narrative and life history in learning to teach. In J. Sikula, T.J. Buttery, and E, Guyton (eds), *Handbook of Research on Teacher Education* (2nd ed., pp. 120–42). New York: Macmillan.

Carter, K. (1990). Teachers' knowledge and learning to teach. In W. R. Houston (ed.), *Handbook of Research on Teacher Education* (pp. 291–310). New York: Macmillan.

Carter, K. and Doyle, W. (1987). Teachers' knowledge structures and comprehension processes. In J. Calderhead (ed.), *Exploring Teachers' Thinking* (pp. 147–60). London: Cassell.

Cathcart, R. and Olsen, J. E. W. B. (1976). Teachers' and students' preferences for the correction of classroom conversation errors. In J. Fanselow and R. H. Crymes (eds), *On TESOL '76* (pp. 41–53). Washington, DC: TESOL.

Chambless, M. S. and Bass, J. A. F. (1996). Effecting changes in student teachers' attitudes toward writing. *Reading Research and Instruction*, 35, 153–9.

Chandler, P., Robinson, W. P., and Noyes, P. (1988). The level of linguistic knowledge and awareness among students training to be primary teachers. *Language and Education*, 2, 161–73.

Chandler, R. (1988). Unproductive busywork. *English in Education*, 22, 20–28.

Chaudron, C. (1988). *Second Language Classrooms: Research on Teaching and Learning*. New York: Cambridge University Press.

Chia, S. C. C. (2003). Singapore primary school teachers' beliefs in grammar teaching and learning. In D. Deterding, A. Brown and E. L. Low (eds), *English in Singapore: Research on Grammar*. (pp. 117–27). Singapore: McGraw Hill.

Clandinin, D. J. (1986). *Classroom Practice: Teacher Images in Action*. London: The Falmer Press.

Clandinin, D.J. and Connelly, F.M. (1987). Teachers' personal knowledge: What counts as personal in studies of the personal. *Journal of Curriculum Studies*, 19, 487–500.

—(2000). *Narrative Inquiry: Experience and Story in Qualitative Research*. San Francisco, CA: Jossey Bass Publishers.

Clark, C. and Yinger, R. (1977). Research on teacher thinking. *Curriculum Inquiry*, 7, 279- 304.

Clark, C. M. (1980). Choice of a model for research on teacher thinking. *Journal of Curriculum Studies*, 12, 41–7.

—(1986). Ten years of conceptual development in research on teacher thinking. In M. Ben-Peretz, R. Bromme and R. Halkes (eds), *Advances of Research on Teacher Thinking*. (pp. 7–20). Lisse: Swets and Zeitlinger.

—(1988). Asking the right questions about teacher preparation: contributions of research on teaching thinking. *Educational Researcher*, 17, 5–12.

Clark, C. M. and Peterson, P. L. (1986). Teachers' thought processes. In M. C. Wittrock (ed.), *Handbook of Research on Teaching* (3rd edn, pp. 255–96). New York: Macmillan.

Cochran, K. F. and Jones, L. L. (1998). The subject matter knowledge of preservice science teachers. In B. Fraser and K. Tobin (eds), *International Handbook of Science Education* (pp. 707–18). Dordrecht, The Netherlands: Kluwer.

Coffey, A. and Atkinson, P. (1996). *Making Sense of Qualitative Data: Complementary Research Strategies*. London: Sage.

Cohen, A. D. and Fass, L. (2001). Oral language instruction: Teacher and learner beliefs and the reality in EFL classes at a Colombian university. *Íkala (Journal of Language and Culture, Universidad de Antioquia)*, 6, 43–62.

Cohen, L., Manion, L., and Morrison, K. (2000). *Research Methods in Education* (5th edn). London: Routledge.

Collie Graden, E. (1996). How language teachers' beliefs about reading are mediated by their beliefs about students. *Foreign Language Annals*, 29, 387–95.

Connelly, F. M. and Clandinin, D. J. (1988). *Teachers as Curriculum Planners, Narratives of Experience*. New York: Teachers College Press.

Connelly, F. M. and Clandinin, D. J. (1990). Stories of experience and narrative inquiry. *Educational Researcher*, 19, 2–14.

Connelly, F. M., Clandinin, D. J., and He, M. F. (1997). Teachers' personal practical knowledge on the professional knowledge landscape. *Teaching and Teacher Education*, 13, 665–74.

Cooper, J. E. (1991). Telling our own stories: The reading and writing of journals and diaries. In C. Witherell and N. Noddings (eds), *Stories Lives Tell: Narrative and Dialogue in Education* (pp. 96–112). New York: Teachers College Press.

Couper, M. P. (2000). Web surveys: a review of issues and approaches. *Public Opinion Quarterly*, 64, 464–81.

Crawley, F. E. and Salyer, B. A. (1995). Origins of life science teachers' beliefs underlying curriculum reform in Texas. *Science Education*, 79, 611–35.

Creswell, J. (2003). *Research Design: Qualitative, Quantitative, and Mixed Methods Approaches* (2nd ed.). Thousand Oaks, CA: Sage.

Crookes, G. and Arakaki, L. (1999). Teaching idea sources and work conditions in an ESL program. *TESOL Journal*, 8, 15–19.

Cumming, A. (1989). Student teachers' conceptions of curriculum: Towards an understanding of language teacher development. *TESL Canada Journal*, 7, 33–51.

REFERENCES

—(1990). Expertise in evaluating second language compositions. *Language Testing*, 7, 31–51.

Cummins, C. L., Cheek, E. H., and Lindsey, J. D. (2004). The relationship between teachers' literacy beliefs and their instructional practices: a brief review of the literature for teacher educators. *E-Journal of Teaching and Learning in Diverse Settings*, 1, 175–88.

da Silva, M. (2005). Constructing the teaching process from inside out: How pre-service teachers make sense of their perceptions of the teaching of the four skills. *TESL-EJ*, 9, 1–19.

Davis, M. M., Konopak, B. C., and Readence, J. E. (1993). An investigation of two Chapter I teachers' beliefs about reading and instructional practices. *Reading Research and Instruction*, 33, 105–18.

Davis, M. M. and Wilson, E. K. (1999). A Title I teacher's beliefs, decision-making, and instruction at the third and seventh grade levels. *Reading Research and Instruction*, 38, 289–300.

Davson-Galle, P. (2004). Understanding: 'Knowledge', 'belief' and 'understanding'. *Science and Education*, 13, 591–8.

Day, C., Calderhead, J., and Denicolo, P. (eds). (1993). *Research on Teacher Thinking: Understanding Professional Development*. London: The Falmer Press.

Day, C., Pope, M., and Denicolo, P. (eds). (1990). *Insights into Teacher Thinking and Practice*. London: The Falmer Press.

DeFord, D. (1985). Validating the construct of theoretical orientation in reading instruction. *Reading Research Quarterly*, 20, 351–67.

Denscombe, M. (2002). *Ground Rules for Good Research*. Buckingham: Open University Press.

Deyhle, D. L., Hess, G. A., Jr., and LeCompte, M. D. (1992). Approaching ethical issues for qualitative researchers in education. In M. D. LeCompte, W. L. Millroy and J. Preissle (eds), *The Handbook of Qualitative Research in Education*. (pp. 597–641). San Diego, CA: Academic Press.

Diab, R. L. (2005). Teachers' and students' beliefs about responding to ESL writing: A case study. *TESL Canada Journal*, 23, 28–43.

Dirkx, J. M. and Spurgin, M. E. (1992). Implicit theories of adult basic education teachers: How their beliefs about students shape classroom practice. *Adult Basic Education*, 2, 20–41.

Dörnyei, Z. (2002). *Questionnaires in Second Language Research: Construction, Administration and Processing*. New York: Lawrence Erlbaum.

Drever, E. (1995). *Using Semi-Structured Interviews in Small-Scale Research. A Teacher's Guide*. Edinburgh: Scottish Council for Research in Education.

Duffy, G. (1977). *A study of teacher conceptions of reading*. Paper presented at the National Reading Conference., New Orleans.

—(1982). Fighting off the alligators: What research in real classrooms has to say about reading instruction. *Journal of Reading Behaviour*, *14*, 357–73.

Duffy, G. and Anderson, L. (1982). *Final Report: Conceptions of Reading Progress*. Research Series No. 111. East Lansing, Michigan: Institute for Research on Teaching, Michigan State University.

Duffy, G. and Anderson, L. (1984). Teachers' theoretical orientations and the real classroom. *Reading Psychology*, *5*, 97–104.

Duffy, G. and Ball, D. (1986). Instructional decision making and reading teacher effectiveness. In J. Hoffman (ed.), *Effective Teaching of Reading: Research and Practice*. Newark, DE: International Reading Association.

Duffy, G. and Metheny, W. (1979). *Measuring Teacher's Beliefs about Reading*. Research Series No. 41. East Lansing, Michigan: Institute for Research on Teaching, Michigan State University.

Dunkin, M. J. (1995). Synthesising research in education: a case study of getting it wrong. *The Australian Educational Researcher*, *22*, 17–33.

Dunkin, M. J. (1996). Types of errors in synthesizing research in education. *Review of Educational Research*, *66*, 87–97.

Dunkin, M. J. and Biddle, B. J. (1974). *The Study of Teaching*. New York: Holt, Rinehart and Winston.

Dunkin, M. J., Precians, R. P., and Nettle, E. B. (1994). Effects of formal teacher education upon student teachers' cognitions regarding teaching. *Teaching and Teacher Education*, *10*, 395–408.

Eisenhart, M. A., Shrum, J. L., Harding, J. R., and Cuthbert, A. M. (1988). Teacher beliefs: Definitions, findings and directions. *Educational Policy*, *2*, 51–70.

Eisenstein-Ebsworth, M. and Schweers, C. W. (1997). What researchers say and practitioners do: Perspectives on conscious grammar instruction in the ESL classroom. *Applied Language Learning*, *8*, 237–60.

El-Okda, M. (2005). EFL student teachers' cognition about reading instruction. *The Reading Matrix*, *5*. Retrieved 20 February 2006, from http://www.readingmatrix.com/articles/okda/article.pdf

Elbaz, F. (1981). The teacher's 'practical knowledge': A report of a case study. *Curriculum Inquiry*, *11*, 43–71.

Elbaz, F. (1983). *Teacher Thinking: A Study of Practical Knowledge*. New York: Nichols Publishing.

Ellis, R. (2001). Investigating form-focused instruction. *Language Learning*, *51*, 1–46.

Ellis, R. (2002). Methodological options in grammar teaching materials. In E. Hinkel and S. Fotos (eds), *New Perspectives on Grammar Teaching in Second Language Classrooms* (pp. 155–79). Mahwah, New Jersey: Lawrence Erlbaum.

Ely, M. (1991). *Doing Qualitative Research: Circles Within Circles*. London: The Falmer Press.

Eraut, M. (1994). *Developing Professional Knowledge and Competence*. London: Falmer.

Ericsson, K. A. and Simon, H. A. (1993). *Protocol Analysis: Verbal Reports as Data* (2nd edn). Cambridge, MA.: MIT Press.

Ernest, P. (1994). *An Introduction to Research Methodology and Paradigms*. Exeter: School of Education, University of Exeter.

Evertson, C. M. and Green, J. L. (1986). Observation as inquiry and method. In M. C. Wittrock (ed.), *Handbook of Research on Teaching*. (Third edn, pp. 162–213). New York: Macmillan.

Faerch, C. (1985). Meta talk in FL classroom discourse. *Studies in Second Language Acquisition.*, *7*, 184–99.

Faerch, C. and Kasper, G. (1987). *Introspection in Second Language Research*. Clevedon: Multilingual Matters.

Fang, Z. (1996a). A review of research on teacher beliefs and practices. *Educational Research*, *38*, 47–65.

—(1996b). What counts as good writing? A case study of relationships between teacher beliefs and pupil conceptions. *Reading Horizons*, *36*, 249–58.

Farrell, T. S. C. (1999). The reflective assignment: Unlocking pre-service teachers' beliefs on grammar teaching. *RELC Journal*, *30*, 1–17.

—(2001). English language teacher socialisation during the practicum. *Prospect*, *16*, 49–62.

—(2003). Learning to teach English language during the first year: personal influences and challenges. *Teaching and Teacher Education*, *19*, 95–111.

Farrell, T. S. C. and Lim, P. C. P. (2005). Conceptions of grammar teaching: A case study of teachers' beliefs and classroom practices. *TESL-EJ*, *9*, 1–13.

Feiman-Nemser, S. and Floden, R. E. (1986). The cultures of teaching. In M. C. Wittrock (ed.), *Handbook of Research on Teaching* (3rd edn, pp. 505–26). New York: Macmillan.

Fennema, E. and Franke, M. L. (1992). Teachers' knowledge and its impact. In D. A. Grouws (ed.), *Handbook of Research on Mathematics Teaching and Learning* (pp. 147–64). New York, NY: Macmillan.

Fenstermacher, G. D. (1986). Philosophy of research on teaching: Three aspects. In M. C. Wittrock (edn), *Handbook of Research on Teaching* (3rd edn, pp. 37–49). New York: Macmillan.

—(1994). The knower and the known: The nature of knowledge in research on teaching. *Review of Research in Education*, *20*, 1–54.

Fine, G. A. and Sandstrom, K. L. (1988). *Knowing Children: Participant Observation With Minors*. Beverly Hills, CA: Sage.

Flores, B. B. (2001). Bilingual education teachers' beliefs and their relation to self-reported practices. *Bilingual Research Journal*, *25*, 251–75.

Florio-Ruane, S. and Lensmire, T. J. (1990). Transforming future teachers' ideas about writing instruction. *Journal of Curriculum Studies*, 22, 277–89.

Fontana, A. and Frey, J. H. (1994). Interviewing: The art of science. In N. K. Denzin and Y. S. Lincoln (eds), *Handbook of Qualitative Research* (pp. 361–76). Thousand Oaks: Sage.

Ford, M. I. (1994). Teachers' beliefs about mathematical problem solving in the elementary school. *School Science and Mathematics*, 94, 314–22.

Foss, D. H. and Kleinsasser, R. C. (1996). Preservice elementary teachers' views of pedagogical and mathematical content knowledge. *Teaching and Teacher Education*, 12, 429–42.

Fowler, F. J. (2002). *Survey Research Methods* (3rd edn). Thous and Oaks: Sage.

Francis, D. (1995). The reflective journal: A window to preservice teachers' practical knowledge. *Teaching and Teacher Education*, 11, 229–41.

Fransella, F. and Bannister, D. (1977). *A Manual for Repertory Grid Technique*. New York: Academic Press.

Freeman, D. (1992). Emerging discourse and change in classroom practice. In J. Flowerdew, M. Brock and S. Hsia (eds), *Perspectives on Second Language Teacher Education*. Hong Kong: City Polytechnic of Hong Kong.

—(1993). Renaming experience/reconstructing practice: Developing new understandings of teaching. *Teaching and Teacher Education*, 9, 485–97.

—(2002). The hidden side of the work: Teacher knowledge and learning to teach. *Language Teaching*, 35, 1–13.

Gass, S. M. and Mackey, A. (2000). *Stimulated Recall Methodology in Second Language Research*. Mahwah, NJ: Lawrence Erlbaum Associates.

Gatbonton, E. (1999). Investigating experienced ESL teachers' pedagogical knowledge. *The Modern Language Journal*, 83, 35–50.

Gilhooly, K. and Green, C. (1996). Protocol analysis: Theoretical background. In J. T. E. Richardson (ed.), *Handbook of Qualitative Research Methods for Psychology and the Social Sciences* (pp. 43–54). Leicester: BPS Books.

Gillham, B. (2005). *Research Interviewing: The Range of Techniques*. Buckingham: Open University Press.

Glesne, C. and Peshkin, A. (1992). *Becoming Qualitative Researchers: An Introduction*. New York: Longman.

Gold, R. (1958). Roles in sociological field observation. *Social Forces*, 36, 217–23.

Golombek, P. R. (1998). A study of language teachers' personal practical knowledge. *TESOL Quarterly*, 32, 447–64.

Golombek, P. R. and Johnson, K. E. (2004). Narrative inquiry as a mediational space: Examining emotional and cognitive dissonance in second-language teachers' development. *Teachers and Teaching*, 10, 307–28.

Gomez, M. L. (1990). Learning to teach writing: Untangling the tensions between theory and practice (NCRTL Report 89–7). Retrieved 1 November, 2005, from http://ncrtl.msu.edu/http/rreports/html/pdf/rr897.pdf

Gove, M. K. (1983). Clarifying teachers' beliefs about reading. *Reading Teacher*, 37, 261–6.

Graber, K. C. (1995). The influence of teacher education programs on the beliefs of student teachers: General pedagogical knowledge, pedagogical content knowledge, and teacher education course work. *Journal of Teaching in Physical Education*, 14, 157–78.

Graham, P. (2005). Classroom-based assessment: Changing knowledge and practice through preservice teacher education. *Teaching and Teacher Education*, 21, 607–21.

Green, C. and Gilhooly, K. (1996). Protocol analysis: Practical implementation. In J. T. E. Richardson (ed.), *Handbook of Qualitative Research Methods for Psychology and the Social Sciences* (pp. 55–74). Leicester: BPS Books.

Green, T. F. (1971). *The Activities of Teaching*. New York: McGraw-Hill.

Grimmett, P. P. and Erickson, G. L. (eds). (1988). *Reflection in Teacher Education*. New York: Teachers College.

Grimmett, P. P. and Mackinnon, A. M. (1992). Craft knowledge and the education of teachers. *Review of Research in Education*, 18, 385–456.

Grisham, D. L. (2000). Connecting theoretical conceptions of reading to practice: A longitudinal study of elementary school teachers. *Reading Psychology*, 21, 145–70.

Grossman, P. L. (1989). A study in contrast: Sources of pedagogical content knowledge for secondary English. *Journal of Teacher Education*, 40, 24–31.

—(1990). *The Making of a Teacher: Teacher Knowledge and Teacher Education*. New York: Teachers College Press.

Grossman, P. L., Wilson, S. M., and Shulman, L. S. (1989). Teachers of substance: Subject matter knowledge for teaching. In M. C. Reynolds (ed.), *Knowledge Base for the Beginning Teacher* (pp. 23–36). Oxford: Pergamon.

Gutierrez Almarza, G. (1996). Student foreign language teachers' growth. In D. Freeman and J. C. Richards (eds), *Teacher Learning in Language Teaching* (pp. 50–78). Cambridge: Cambridge University Press.

Halkes, R. and Deijkers, R. (1984a). Introduction. In R. Halkes and K. J. Olson (eds), *Teacher Thinking*. (pp. 1–6). Lisse, Netherlands: Swets and Zeitlinger.

—(1984b). Teachers' teaching criteria. In R. Halkes and K. J. Olson (eds), *Teacher Thinking*. (pp. 149–62). Lisse: Swets and Zeitlinger.
Handal, G. and Lauvas, P. (1987). *Promoting Reflective Teaching: Supervision in Action*. Milton Keynes: Open University Press.
Harste, J. and Burke, C. (1977). A new hypothesis for reading teacher research: Both the teaching and learning of reading are theoretically based. In P. D. Pearson (ed.), *Reading: Theory, Research, and Practice*. (pp. 32–40). Clemson, S.C.: National Reading Conference.
Hashweh, M. Z. (2005). Teacher pedagogical constructions: A reconfiguration of pedagogical content knowledge. *Teachers and Teaching*, 11, 273–92.
Hayes, D. (2005). Exploring the lives of non-native speaking English educators in Sri Lanka. *Teachers and Teaching*, 11, 169–94.
Hewson, P. W., Kerby, H. W., and Cook, P. A. (1995). Determining the conceptions of teaching science held by experienced high school science teachers. *Journal of Research in Science Teaching*, 32, 503–20.
Hinkel, E. (ed.). (2005). *Handbook of Research in Second Language Teaching and Learning*. Mahwah, NJ: Erlbaum.
Hislam, J. and Cajkler, W. (2005). Teacher trainees' explicit knowledge of grammar and primary curriculum requirements in England. In N. Bartels (ed.), *Applied Linguistics and Language Teacher Education* (pp. 295–312). New York: Springer.
Holly, M. L. (1989a). Reflective writing and the spirit of inquiry. *Cambridge Journal of Education*, 19, 71–80.
—(1989b). *Writing to Grow: Keeping a Personal-Professional Journal*. Portsmouth, NH: Heinemann.
Holstein, J. A. and Gubrium, J. F. (1997). Active interviewing. In D. Silverman (ed.), *Qualitative Research: Theory, Method and Practice*. (pp. 113–29). London: Sage.
Holt Reynolds, D. (1992). Personal history-based beliefs as relevant prior knowledge in course work. *American Educational Research Journal*, 29, 325–49.
Horwitz, E. K. (1985). Using student beliefs about language learning and teaching in the foreign language methods course. *Foreign Language Annals*, 18, 333–40.
—(1988). The beliefs about language learning of beginning university foreign language students. *Modern Language Journal*, 72, 283–94.
—(1999). Cultural and situational influences on foreign language learners' beliefs about language learning: A review of BALLI studies. *System*, 27, 557–76.
Huang, J., Normandia, B., and Greer, S. (2005). Communicating mathematically: Comparison of knowledge structures in teacher and student discourse in a secondary math classroom. *Communication Education*, 54, 34–51.

Hulshof, H. and Verloop, N. (2002). The use of analogies in language teaching: Representing the content of teachers' practical knowledge. *Journal of Curriculum Studies*, 34, 77–90.

Jackson, P. W. (1968). *Life in Classrooms*. New York: Holt, Rinehart and Winston.

Janesick, V. J. (1999). A journal about journal writing as a qualitative research technique: History, issues, reflections. *Qualitative Inquiry*, 5, 505–24.

Jarvis, J. (1992). Using diaries for teacher reflection on in-service courses. *ELT Journal*, 46, 133–43.

John, P. D. (1996). Understanding the apprenticeship of observation in initial teacher education. In G. Claxton, T. Atkinson, M. Osborn and M. Wallace (eds), *Liberating the Learner* (pp. 90–107). London: Routledge.

Johnson, K. (2003). *Designing Language Teaching Tasks*. Basingstoke: Palgrave Macmillan.

Johnson, K. E. (1992a). Learning to teach: Instructional actions and decisions of preservice ESL teachers. *TESOL Quarterly*, 26, 507–35.

—(1992b). The relationship between teachers' beliefs and practices during literacy instruction for non-native speakers of English. *Journal of Reading Behavior*, 24, 83–108.

—(1994). The emerging beliefs and instructional practices of preservice English as a second language teachers. *Teaching and Teacher Education*, 10, 439–52.

—(1996). The vision versus the reality: The tensions of the TESOL practicum. In D. Freeman and J. C. Richards (eds), *Teacher Learning in Language Teaching* (pp. 30–49). Cambridge: Cambridge University Press.

—(1999). *Understanding Language Teaching: Reasoning in Action*. Boston, MA: Heinle and Heinle.

Johnson, K. E. and Golombek, P. R. (eds). (2002). *Teachers' Narrative Inquiry as Professional Development*. New York: Cambridge University Press.

Johnston, B. and Goettsch, K. (2000). In search of the knowledge base of language teaching: Explanations by experienced teachers. *The Canadian Modern Language Review*, 56, 437–68.

Johnston, F. R. (2001). Exploring classroom teachers' spelling practices and beliefs. *Reading Research and Instruction*, 40, 143–56.

Joram, E. and Gabriele, A. J. (1998). Preservice teachers' prior beliefs: Transforming obstacles into opportunities. *Teaching and Teacher Education*, 14, 175–92.

Kagan, D. M. (1988). Teaching as clinical problem solving: A critical examination of the analogy and its implications. *Review of Educational Research*, 58, 482–505.

Kagan, D. M. (1990). Ways of evaluating teacher cognition: Inferences concerning the Goldilocks principle. *Review of Educational Research, 60*, 419–69.
Kagan, D. M. (1992a). Professional growth among preservice and beginning teachers. *Review of Educational Research, 62*, 129–69.
Kagan, D. M. (1992b). Implications of research on teacher belief. *Educational Psychologist, 27*, 65–90.
Karavas-Doukas, E. (1996). Using attitude scales to investigate teachers' attitudes to the communicative approach. *ELT Journal, 50*, 187–98.
Kelly, G. A. (1955). *The Psychology of Personal Constructs*. New York: W.W. Norton.
Kennedy, M. M. (1991). An agenda for research on teacher learning. Retrieved 16 February, 2005, from http://ncrtl.msu.edu/http/sreports/sr391.pdf
Kern, R. G. (1995). Students' and teachers' beliefs about language learning. *Foreign Language Annals, 28*, 71–92.
Kettle, B. and Sellars, N. (1996). The development of student teachers' practical theory of teaching. *Teaching and Teacher Education, 12*, 1–24.
Kinzer, C. K. (1988). Instructional frameworks and instructional choices: Comparisons between preservice and inservice teachers. *Journal of Reading Behaviour, 20*, 357–77.
Kinzer, C. K. (1989). Mental models and beliefs about classrooms and reading instruction: A comparison between preservice teachers, inservice teachers and professors of education. In S. McCormick and J. Zutell (eds), *Cognitive and Social Perspectives for Literacy Research and Instruction (38th Yearbook of the National Reading Conference)* (pp. 489–99). Chicago, IL: The National Reading Conference.
Kinzer, C. K. and Carrick, D. (1985). Teacher beliefs as instructional influences. In J. Niles and R. Lalik (eds), *Solving Problems in Literacy: Learners, Teachers and Researchers* (pp. 272–9). New York: National Reading Conference.
Knowles, J. G. and Holt-Reynolds, D. (1994). Personal histories as medium, method, and milieu for gaining insights into teacher development: An Introduction. *Teacher Education Quarterly, 21*, 5–12.
Konopak, B. C. and Williams, N. L. (1994). Elementary teachers' beliefs and decisions about vocabulary learning and instruction. *Yearbook of the National Reading Conference, 43*, 485–95
Kounin, J. S. (1970). *Discipline and Group Management in Classrooms*. New York: Hot, Rinehart and Winston.
Kvale, S. (1996). *InterViews: An Introduction to Qualitative Research Interviewing*. Thousand Oaks: Sage.

REFERENCES

Lam, Y. (2000). Technophilia vs. technophobia: A preliminary look at why second-language teachers do or do not use technology in their classrooms. *Canadian Modern Language Review*, 56, 390–420.

Lapp, D. and Flood, J. (1985). The impact of writing instruction on teachers' attitudes and practices. In J. A. Niles (ed.), *Issues in Literacy: A Research Perspective. Thirty-Fourth Yearbook of the National Reading Conference* (pp. 375–80). Chicago: National Reading Conference.

Lawrence, G. P. (2001). Second language teacher belief systems towards computer-mediated language learning: Defining teacher belief systems. In K. Cameron (ed.), *C.A.L.L. – The Challenge of Change: Research and Practice* (pp. 41–52). Exeter: Elm Bank Publications.

Leinhardt, G. (1988). Situated knowledge and expertise in teaching. In J. Calderhead (ed.), *Teachers' Professional Learning.* (pp. 146–68). London: The Falmer Press.

Leu, D. J. J. and Kinzer, C. K. (1987). *Effective Reading Instruction in Elementary Grades.* Columbus, OH: Merrill.

Lightbown, P. M. and Spada, N. (1993). *How Languages are Learned.* Oxford: Oxford University Press.

Linek, W. M., Nelson, O. G., Sampson, M. B., Zeek, C. K., Mohr, K. A. J., and Hughes, L. (1999). Developing beliefs about literacy instruction: A cross-case analysis of preservice teachers in traditional and field based settings. *Reading Research and Instruction*, 38, 371–86.

Lortie, D. (1975). *Schoolteacher: A Sociological Study.* Chicago: University of Chicago Press.

Loughran, J. and Russell, T. (eds). (1997). *Teaching about Teaching: Purpose, Passion, and Pedagogy in Teacher Education.* London: Falmer Press.

Lumley, T. (2002). Assessment criteria in a large-scale writing test: What do they really mean to the raters? *Language Testing*, 19, 246–76.

Lyle, J. (2003). Stimulated recall: A report on its use in naturalistic research. *British Educational Research Journal*, 29, 861–78.

MacDonald, M., Badger, R., and White, G. (2001). Changing values: what use are theories of language learning and teaching? *Teaching and Teacher Education*, 17, 949–63.

Maloch, B., Flint, A. S., Eldridge, D., Harmon, J., Loven, R., Fine, J. C., Bryant-Shanklin, M., and Martinez, M. (2003). Understandings, beliefs, and reported decision making of first-year teachers from different reading teacher preparation programs. *Elementary School Journal*, 103, 431–58.

Mangubhai, F., Marland, P., Dashwood, A., and Son, J. B. (2004). Teaching a foreign language: One teacher's practical theory. *Teaching and Teacher Education*, 20, 291–311.

Markham, K. M., Mintzes, J. J., and Gail Jones, M. (1994). The concept map as a research and evaluation tool: Further evidence of validity. *Journal of Research in Science Teaching*, *31*, 91–101.
Maxwell, J. (1996). *Qualitative Research Design*. Thousand Oaks: Sage.
McCargar, D. F. (1993). Teacher and student role expectations: Cross-cultural differences and implications. *Modern Language Journal*, *77*, 192–207.
McCarthey, S. J. (1992). Teachers' changing conceptions of writing instruction (NCRTL Report 92–3). Retrieved 1 November, 2005, from http://ncrtl.msu.edu/http/rreports/html/pdf/rr923.pdf
McCutchen, D., Abbott, R. D., Green, L. B., Beretvas, S. N., Cox, S., Potter, N. S., Quiroga, T., and Gray, A. L. (2002). Beginning literacy: Links among teacher knowledge, teacher practice, and student learning. *Journal of Learning Disabilities*, *35*, 69–86.
McDiarmid, G. W. and Ball, D. L. (1989). The teacher education and learning to teach study: An occasion for developing a conception of teacher knowledge. Retrieved 5 December, 2005, from http://ncrtl.msu.edu/http/tseries/ts891.pdf.
McDonough, J. (1994). A teacher looks at teachers' diaries. *ELT Journal*, *48*, 57–65.
Measor, L. (1985). Interviewing: A strategy in qualitative research. In R. G. Burgess (ed.), *Strategies of Educational Research: Qualitative Methods*. (pp. 55–77). London: The Falmer Press.
Meijer, P. (1999). *Teachers' Practical Knowledge: Teaching Reading Comprehension in Secondary Education*. Leiden: University of Leiden.
Meijer, P. C., Verloop, N., and Beijaard, D. (1999). Exploring language teachers' practical knowledge about teaching reading comprehension. *Teaching and Teacher Education*, *15*, 59–84.
—(2001). Similarities and differences in teachers' practical knowledge about teaching reading comprehension. *Journal of Educational Research*, *94*, 171–84.
Meijer, P. C., Zanting, A., and Verloop, N. (2002). How can student teachers elicit experienced teachers' practical knowledge? Tools, suggestions, and significance. *Journal of Teacher Education*, *53*, 406–19.
Meloth, M. S., Book, C., Putnam, J., and Sivan, E. (1989). Teachers' concepts of reading, reading instruction, and students' concepts of reading. *Journal of Teacher Education*, *40*, 33–39.
Mergendoller, J. R. and Sachs, C. H. (1994). Concerning the relationship between teachers' theoretical orientations towards reading and their concept maps. *Teaching and Teacher Education*, *10*, 589–99.
Miller, J. and Glassner, B. (1997). The 'inside' and the 'outside': Finding realities in interviews. In D. Silverman (ed.), *Qualitative Research: Theory, Method and Practice*. (pp. 99–112). London: Sage.
Mitchell, J. and Marland, P. (1989). Research on teacher thinking: The next phase. *Teaching and Teacher Education*, *5*, 115–28.

Mitchell, R., Brumfit, C., and Hooper, J. (1994a). Knowledge about language: Policy, rationales and practices. *Research Papers in Education*, 9, 183–205.
Mitchell, R., Brumfit, C., and Hooper, J. (1994b). Perceptions of language and language learning in English and foreign language classrooms. In M. Hughes (ed.), *Perceptions of Teaching and Learning* (pp. 53–65). Clevedon: Multilingual Matters.
Mitchell, R. and Hooper, J. (1992). Teachers' views of language knowledge. In C. James and P. Garrett (eds), *Language Awareness in the Classroom* (pp. 40–50). London: Longman.
Moats, L. C. and Lyon, G. R. (1996). Wanted: teachers with knowledge of language. *Topics in Learning Disabilities*, 16, 73–86.
Mok, W. E. (1994). Reflecting on reflections: A case study of experienced and inexperienced ESL teachers. *System*, 22, 93–111.
Morine-Dershimer, G. (1993). Tracing conceptual change in preservice teachers. *Teaching and Teacher Education*, 9, 15–26.
Mosenthal, J. H. (1995). Change in two teachers' conceptions of math or writing instruction after in-service training. *Elementary School Journal*, 95, 263–77.
Muchmore, J. A. (1994). A statewide survey of the beliefs and practices of Chapter 1 reading teachers. *Remedial and Special Education*, 15, 252–59.
—(2001). The story of 'Anna': A life history of the literacy beliefs and teaching practices of an urban high school English teacher. *Teacher Education Quarterly*, 28, 89–110.
Mullock, B. (2003). What makes a good teacher? The perceptions of postgraduate TESOL students. *Prospect*, 18, 3–24.
Munby, H. (1982). The place of teachers' beliefs in research on teacher thinking and decision making, and an alternative methodology. *Instructional Science*, 11, 201–225.
Munby, H., Russell, T., and Martin, A. K. (2001). Teachers' knowledge and how it develops. In V. Richardson (ed.), *Handbook of Research on Teaching* (4th ed., pp. 877–904). Washington, D.C.: American Educational Research Association.
Murray, H. (2003). Tracing the Development of Language Awareness: An Exploratory Study of Language Teachers in Training (Working Papers in Linguistics 40). Bern, Switzerland: University of Bern.
National Institute of Education. (1975). *Teaching as Clinical Information Processing*. Washington. DC: National Institute of Education.
Nespor, J. (1987). The role of beliefs in the practice of teaching. *Journal of Curriculum Studies*, 19, 317–28.
Ng, J. and Farrell, T. S. C. (2003). Do teachers' beliefs of grammar teaching match their classroom practices? A Singapore case study. In D. Deterding, A. Brown and E. L. Low (eds), *English in Singapore: Research on Grammar* (pp. 128–37). Singapore: McGraw Hill.

Nisbett, R. E. and Ross, L. (1980). *Human Inference: Strategies and Shortcoming of Social Judgment.* Englewood Cliff, NJ: Prentice Hall.

Norman, K. A. and Spencer, B. H. (2005). Our lives as writers: Examining preservice teachers' experiences and beliefs about the nature of writing and writing instruction. *Teacher Education Quarterly, 32,* 25–40.

Numrich, C. (1996). On becoming a language teacher: Insights from diary studies. *TESOL Quarterly, 30,* 131–53.

Nunan, D. (1992). The teacher as decision-maker. In J. Flowerdew, M. Brock and S. Hsia (eds), *Perspectives on Second Language Teacher Education* (pp. 135–65). Hong Kong: City Polytechnic.

Olson, J. R. and Singer, M. (1994). Examining teacher beliefs, reflective change and the teaching of reading. *Reading Research and Instruction, 34,* 97–110.

Olson, M. R. and Craig, C. J. (2005). Uncovering cover stories: Tensions and entailments in the development of teacher knowledge. *Curriculum Inquiry, 35,* 161–82.

Oppenheim, A. N. (1992). *Questionnaire Design, Interviewing and Attitude Measurement* (New edn). London: Continuum.

Orton, R. E. (1996). How can teacher beliefs about student learning be justified? *Curriculum Inquiry, 26,* 133–46.

Pajares, F. (1993). Preservice teachers' beliefs: A focus for teacher education. *Action in Teacher Education, 15,* 45–54.

Pajares, M. F. (1992). Teachers' beliefs and educational research: Cleaning up a messy construct. *Review of Educational Research, 62,* 307–32.

Palfreyman, D. (1993). 'How I got it in my head': Conceptual models of language and learning in native and non-native trainee EFL teachers. *Language Awareness,* 209–23.

Patton, M. Q. (1990). *Qualitative Evaluation and Research Methods* (2nd edn). Newbury: Sage.

Peacock, M. (1998). Exploring the gap between teachers' and learners' beliefs about 'useful' activities for EFL. *International Journal of Applied Linguistics, 8,* 233–50.

Peacock, M. (2001). Pre-service ESL teachers' beliefs about second language learning: A longitudinal study. *System, 29,* 177–95.

Pennington, M. C. and Richards, J. C. (1997). Reorienting the teaching universe: the experience of five first-year English teachers in Hong Kong. *Language Teaching Research, 1,* 149–78.

Pennington, M. C. and Urmston, A. (1998). The teaching orientation of graduating students on a BA TESL course in Hong Kong: A comparison with first-year students. *Hong Kong Journal of Applied Linguistics, 3,* 17–46.

Pope, M. and Denicolo, P. (1993). The art and science of constructivist research in teacher thinking. *Teaching and Teacher Education, 9,* 529–44.

REFERENCES

Pope, M. and Keen, T. (1981). *Personal Construct Psychology and Education*. London: Academic Press.

Popko, J. (2005). How MA TESOL students use knowledge about language in teaching ESL classes. In N. Bartels (ed.), *Applied Linguistics and Language Teacher Education* (pp. 387–403). New York: Springer.

Porter, P. A., Goldstein, L. M., Leatherman, J., and Conrad, S. (1990). An ongoing dialogue: Learning logs for teacher preparation. In J. C. Richards and D. Nunan (eds), *Second Language Teacher Education* (pp. 227–40). Cambridge: Cambridge University Press.

Poulson, L., Avramidis, E., Fox, R., Medwell, J., and Wray, D. (2001). The theoretical beliefs of effective teachers of literacy in primary schools: An exploratory study of orientations to reading and writing. *Research Papers in Education*, 16, 271–92.

Powney, J. and Watts, M. (1987). *Interviewing in Educational Research*. London: Routledge and Kegan Paul.

Punch, M. (1986). *The Politics and Ethics of Fieldwork*. Beverly Hills, CA: Sage.

Reynolds, M. C. (ed.). (1989). *Knowledge Base for the Beginning Teacher*. Oxford: Pergamon.

Richards, J. C. (1996). Teachers' maxims in language teaching. *TESOL Quarterly*, 30, 281–96.

—(1998). What's the use of lesson plans? In J. C. Richards (ed.), *Beyond Training* (pp. 103–21). Cambridge: Cambridge University Press.

Richards, J. C., Ho, B., and Giblin, K. (1996). Learning how to teach in the RSA Cert. In D. Freeman and J. C. Richards (eds), *Teacher Learning in Language Teaching* (pp. 242–59). Cambridge: Cambridge University Press.

Richards, J. C., Li, B., and Tang, A. (1998). Exploring pedagogical reasoning skills. In J. C. Richards (ed.), *Beyond Training* (pp. 86–102). Cambridge: Cambridge University Press.

Richards, J. C. and Pennington, M. (1998). The first year of teaching. In J. C. Richards (ed.), *Beyond Training* (pp. 173–90). Cambridge: CUP.

Richards, J. C., Tung, P., and Ng, P. (1992). The culture of the English language teacher: A Hong Kong example. *RELC Journal*, 23, 81–102.

Richards, K. (2003). *Qualitative Inquiry in TESOL*. Basingstoke: Palgrave.

Richardson, V. (1996). The role of attitudes and beliefs in learning to teach. In J. Sikula, T. J. Buttery, and E, Guyton (eds), *Handbook of Research on Teacher Education* (2nd edn, pp. 102–119). New York: Macmillan.

Richardson, V. (ed.). (1997). *Constructivist Teacher Education: Building New Understandings*. London: Falmer.

Richardson, V., Anders, P., Tidwell, D., and Lloyd, C. (1991). The relationship between teachers' beliefs and practices in reading comprehension instruction. *American Educational Research Journal*, 28, 559–86.

Roberts, J. (1999). Personal construct psychology as a framework for research into teacher learning and thinking. *Language Teaching Research*, *3*, 117–44.
Robson, C. (2002). *Real World Research* (2nd ed.). Oxford: Blackwell.
Roehler, L. R., Duffy, G. G., Conley, M., Hermann, B. A., Johnson, J., and Michelson, S. (1990). *Teachers' knowledge structures: Documenting their development and their relation to instruction.* Unpublished manuscript, Michigan State University.
Roehler, L. R., Duffy, G. G., Hermann, B. A., Conley, M., and Johnson, J. (1988). Knowledge structures as evidence of the personal: Bridging the gap from thought to practice. *Journal of Curriculum Studies*, *20*, 159–65.
Roehler, L. R., Hermann, B. A., and Reinken, B. (1989). *Exploring knowledge through the ordered tree technique: A manual for use.* Unpublished manuscript, Michigan State University.
Rokeach, M. (1968). *Belifs, Attitudes, and Values: A Theory of Organization and Change.* San Francisco: Jossey-Bass.
Rubin, H. J. and Rubin, I. S. (2004). *Qualitative Interviewing: The Art of Hearing Data.* Thousand Oaks: Sage.
Russell, T. and Munby, H. (eds). (1992). *Teachers and Teaching: From Classroom to Reflection.* London: Falmer.
Sakui, K. and Gaies, S. J. (2002). Beliefs and professional identity. *Language Teacher*, *26*, 7–11.
—(2003). A case study: beliefs and metaphors of a Japanese teacher of English. In P. Kalaja and A. M. F. Barcelos (eds), *Beliefs about SLA: New Research Approaches* (pp. 153–70).Dordecht, Netherlands: Kluwer.
Samuda, V. (2005). Expertise in pedagogic task design. In K. Johnson (ed.), *Expertise in Second Language Learning and Teaching* (pp. 230–54). Basingstoke: Palgrave Macmillan.
Sanders, D. P. and McCutcheon, G. (1986). The development of practical theories of teaching. *Journal of Curriculum and Supervision.*, *2*, 50–67.
Sariscany, M. J. and Pettigrew, F. (1997). Effectiveness of interactive video instruction on teachers' classroom management declarative knowledge. *Journal of Teaching in Physical Education*, *16*, 229–40.
Sato, K. and Kleinsasser, R. C. (1999). Communicative language teaching (CLT): Practical understandings. *Modern Language Journal*, *83*, 494–517.
Scharer, P. L., Freeman, E. B., and Lehman, B. A. (1993). Literacy and literature in elementary classrooms: Teachers' beliefs and practices. *Yearbook of the National Reading Conference*, *42*, 359–66.
Scheffler, I. (1965). *Conditions of Knowledge: An Introduction to Epistemology and Education.* Glenview, IL: Scott, Foresman and Company.

Schommer, M. (1990). Effects of beliefs about the nature of knowledge on comprehension. *Journal of Educational Psychology*, *82*, 498–504.

Schön, D. A. (1983). *The Reflective Practitioner: How Professionals Think in Action*. London: Temple Smith.

—(1987). *Educating the Reflective Practitioner*. London: Jossey Bass.

Schulz, R. A. (1996). Focus on form in the foreign language classroom: Students' and teachers' views on error correction and the role of grammar. *Foreign Language Annals*, *29*, 343–64.

—(2001). Cultural differences in student and teacher perceptions concerning the role of grammar teaching and corrective feedback: USA-Colombia. *Modern Language Journal*, *85*, 244–58.

Scott, R. and Rodgers, B. (1995). Changing teachers' conceptions of teaching writing: A collaborative study. *Foreign Language Annals*, *28*, 234–46.

Seedhouse, P. (2004). *The Interactional Architecture of the Language Classroom: A Conversation Analysis Perspective*. Malden, MA: Blackwell.

Segall, A. (2004). Revisiting pedagogical content knowledge: The pedagogy of content/the content of pedagogy. *Teaching and Teacher Education*, *20*, 489–504.

Sendan, F. and Roberts, J. (1998). Orhan: A case study in the development of a student teachers' personal theories. *Teachers and Teaching: Theory and Practice*, *4*, 229–44.

Sengupta, S. and Xiao, M. K. (2002). The contextual reshaping of beliefs about L2 writing: three teachers' practical process of theory construction. TESL-EJ, 5. Retrieved 20 February 2006, from http://writing.berkeley.edu/tesl-ej/ej21/a1.html

Shaffer, C. (1989). A comparison of inductive and deductive approaches to teaching foreign languages. *The Modern Language Journal*, *73*, 395–403.

Shavelson, R. J. and Stern, P. (1981). Research on teachers' pedagogical thoughts, judgements and behaviours. *Review of Educational Research*, *51*, 455–98.

Shavelson, R. J., Webb, N. M., and Burstein, L. (1986). Measurement of teaching. In M. C. Wittrock (ed.), *Handbook of Research on Teaching* (3rd edn, pp. 50–91). New York: Macmillan.

Shi, L. and Cumming, A. (1995). Teachers' conceptions of second language writing instruction: Five case studies. *Journal of Second Language Writing*, *4*, 87–111.

Shulman, L. S. (1986a). Paradigms and research programmes in the study of teaching: A contemporary perspective. In M. C. Witrock (ed.), *Handbook of Research in Education* (pp. 3–36). New York: Macmillan.

—(1986b). Those who understand: knowledge growth in teaching. *Educational Researcher*, *15*, 4–14.

—(1987). Knowledge and teaching: Foundations of the new reform. *Harvard Educational Review*, 57, 1–22.
Shulman, L. S. and Elstein, A. S. (1975). Studies of problem solving, judgement, and decision making: Implications for educational research. *Review of Research in Education*, 3, 3–42.
Shulman, L. S. and Quinlan, K. M. (1996). The comparative psychology of school subjects. In D. C. Berliner and R. C. Calfee (eds), *Handbook of Educational Psychology* (pp. 399–422). New York: Macmillan.
Shulman, L. S. and Shulman, J. H. (2004). How and what teachers learn: A shifting perspective. *Journal of Curriculum Studies*, 36, 257–71.
Sikula, J., Buttery, T. J., and Guyton, E. (eds). (1996). *Handbook of Research on Teacher Education* (2nd edn). New York: Macmillan.
Silverman, D. (2001). *Interpreting Qualitative Data* (2nd ed.). London: Sage.
Smith, D. B. (1996). Teacher decision making in the adult ESL classroom. In D. Freeman and J. C. Richards (eds), *Teacher Learning in Language Teaching* (pp. 197–216). Cambridge: Cambridge University Press.
Smith, L. M. and Geoffrey, W. (1968). *The Complexities of an Urban Classroom*. New York: Holt, Rinehart and Winston.
Smith, M. U. and Siegel, H. (2004). Knowing, believing, and understanding: What goals for science education? *Science and Education*, 13, 553–82.
Sockett, H. (1987). Has Shulman got the strategy right? *Harvard Educational Review*, 57, 208–19.
Spada, N. and Massey, M. (1992). The role of prior pedagogical knowledge in determining the practice of novice ESL teachers. In J. Flowerdew, M. Brock and S. Hsia (eds), *Perspectives on Second Language Teacher Education* (pp. 23–37). Hong Kong: City Polytechnic.
Tabachnick, B. R. and Zeichner, K. M. (1986). Teacher beliefs and classroom behaviours: Some teacher responses to inconsistency. In M. Ben-Peretz, R. Bromme and R. Halkes (eds), *Advances of Research on Teacher Thinking* (pp. 84–96). Lisse, Netherlands: Swets and Zeitlinger.
Tercanlioglu, L. (2001). Pre-service teachers as readers and future teachers of EFL reading. TESL-EJ, 5. Retrieved 20 February 2006, from http://writing.berkeley.edu/tesl-ej/ej19/a2.html
Thomas, D. (1995a). Treasonable or trustworthy text. In D. Thomas (ed.), *Teachers' Stories* (pp. 1–23). Buckingham: Open University Press.
Thomas, D. (ed.). (1995b). *Teachers' Stories*. Buckingham: Open University Press.
Thompson, A. G. (1992). Teachers' beliefs and conceptions: A synthesis of the research. In D. A. Grouws (ed.), *Handbook of Research on Mathematics Teaching and Learning* (pp. 127–46). New York: Macmillan.
Tillema, H. H. (1994). Training and professional expertise: Bridging the gap between new information and pre-existing beliefs of teachers. *Teaching and Teacher Education*, 10, 601–615.

Tobin, K. and LaMaster, S. U. (1995). Relationships between metaphors, beliefs, and actions in a context of science curriculum change. *Journal of Research in Science Teaching*, *32*, 225–42.

Tsang, W. K. (2004). Teachers' personal practical knowledge and interactive decisions. *Language Teaching Research*, *8*, 163–98.

Tsui, A. B. M. (1996). Learning how to teach ESL writing. In D. Freeman and J. C. Richards (eds), *Teacher Learning in Language Teaching* (pp. 97–119). Cambridge: Cambridge University Press.

—(2003). *Understanding Expertise in Teaching: Case Studies of ESL Teachers*. Cambridge: Cambridge University Press.

—(2005). Expertise in teaching: Perspectives and issues. In K. Johnson (ed.), *Expertise in Second Language Learning and Teaching* (pp. 167–89). Basingstoke: Palgrave Macmillan.

Ulichny, P. (1996). What's in a methodology? In D. Freeman and J. C. Richards (eds), *Teacher Learning in Language Teaching* (pp. 178–96). Cambridge: Cambridge University Press.

Urmston, A. (2003). Learning to teach English in Hong Kong: The opinions of teachers in training. *Language and Education*, *17*, 112–37.

Verjovsky, J. and Waldegg, G. (2005). Analyzing beliefs and practices of a Mexican high school Biology teacher. *Journal of Research in Science Teaching*, *42*, 465–91.

Verloop, N., Van Driel, J., and Meijer, P. C. (2001). Teacher knowledge and the knowledge base of teaching. *International Journal of Educational Research*, *35*, 441–61.

Warford, M. K. and Reeves, J. (2003). Falling into it: Novice TESOL teacher thinking. *Teachers and Teaching*, *9*, 47–66.

Westwood, P., Knight, B. A., and Redden, E. (1997). Assessing teachers' beliefs about literacy acquisition: The development of the Teachers' Beliefs About Literacy Questionnaire (TBALQ). *Journal of Research in Reading*, *20*, 224–35.

Wham, M. A., Cook, G., and Lenski, S. D. (2001). A comparison of teachers whose literacy orientations reflect constructivist or traditional principles. *Journal of Reading Education*, *26*, 1–8.

White, C. S., Sturtevant, E. G., and Dunlap, K. L. (2003). Preservice and beginning teachers' perceptions of the influence of high stakes tests on their literacy-related instructional beliefs and decisions. *Reading Research and Instruction*, *42*, 39–62.

Wideen, M., Mayer-Smith, J., and Moon, B. (1998). A critical analysis of the research on learning to teach: Making the case for an ecological perspective on inquiry. *Review of Educational Research*, *68*, 130–78.

Williamson, J. and Hardman, F. (1995). Time for refilling the bath? A study of primary student-teachers' grammatical knowledge. *Language and Education*, *9*, 117–34.

Wilson, E. K., Konopak, B. C., and Readence, J. E. (1992). Examining content area and reading beliefs, decisions, and instruction: A case study of an English teacher. *Yearbook of the National Reading Conference*, 41, 475–82.

Wilson, S. M., Floden, R. E., and Ferrini-Mundy, J. (2002). Teacher preparation research: An insider's view from the outside. *Journal of Teacher Education*, 53, 190–204.

Wilson, S. M., Shulman, L. S., and Richert, A. E. (1987). '150 different ways' of knowing: Representations of knowledge in teaching. In J. Calderhead (ed.), *Exploring Teachers' Thinking* (pp. 104–24). London: Cassell.

Wing, L. (1989). The influence of preschool teachers' beliefs on young children's conceptions of reading and writing. *Early Childhood Research Quarterly*, 4, 61–74.

Witherell, C. and Noddings, N. (eds). (1991). *Stories Lives Tell: Narrative and Dialogue in Education*. New York: Teachers College Press.

Woods, D. (1991). Teachers' interpretations of second language teaching curricula. *RELC Journal*, 22, 1–19.

—(1996). *Teacher Cognition in Language Teaching*. Cambridge: Cambridge University Press.

Woods, P. (1986). *Inside Schools: Ethnography in Educational Research*. London: Routledge.

Wray, D. (1988). The impact of psycholinguistic theories on trainee-teachers' views of the teaching of reading. *Journal of Reading Education*, 14, 24–35.

—(1993). Student-teachers' knowledge and beliefs about language. In N. Bennett and C. Carré (eds), *Learning to Teach* (pp. 51–72). London: Routledge.

Xiao, Y. (2005). Raising orthographic awareness of teachers of Chinese. In N. Bartels (ed.), *Applied Linguistics and Language Teacher Education* (pp. 221–34). New York: Springer.

Yinger, R. J. (1986). Examining thought in action: A theoretical and methodological critique of research on interactive teaching. *Teaching and Teacher Education*, 2, 263–82.

Zacharias, N. T. (2005). Teachers' beliefs about internationally-published materials: A survey of tertiary English teachers in Indonesia. *RELC Journal*, 36, 23–38.

Zanting, A., Verloop, N., and Vermunt, J. D. (2003). How do student teachers elicit their mentor teachers' practical knowledge? *Teachers and Teaching*, 9, 197–212.

Zeichner, K. M., Tabachnick, B. R., and Densmore, K. (1987). Individual, institutional, and cultural influences on the development of teachers' craft knowledge. In J. Calderhead (ed.), *Exploring Teachers' Thinking* (pp. 21–59). London: Cassell.

Index

affective dimension of teaching
23, 30, 57, 153, 192, 298, 320
apprenticeship of observation
35, 60, 62, 64, 118, 180, 305
autobiographical accounts 303–9

beliefs 10, 12, 15, 19–20, 22, 25–6, 28–36, 38–41, 52–5, 58–9, 62, 63–4, 103
   about communicative language teaching 114–15, 152
   comparisons of teachers' and students' 97, 100, 136, 182–3, 191, 195
   impact of teacher education on 71–82, 94, 99, 129, 166–9
   of in-service language teachers 94–101
   of pre-service teachers 58–85
bilingual educators 95, 98–100, 205

CELTA 72–5, 84, 85
concept mapping 311–15
congruence between cognitions and classroom practice 12, 46, 114, 126, 141, 148–50, 156, 162–6, 170–1, 324–5,

contextual influences on teaching
17, 48, 69, 76, 77, 83, 89, 94, 100, 103, 143, 144, 150, 156, 163, 189, 324, 332, 334
collective teacher cognitions
102, 106, 110, 127, 152, 156, 175

ecological validity 162, 176, 216, 259
expertise in teaching 27, 47, 53, 119–25, 184, 187–8, 196, 207, 261, 263, 313, 327–8

grammar teaching 129–58
   grammatical terminology 132, 136, 145, 146, 152, 154, 213
   KAL 130, 132, 138, 141–2
   knowledge about grammar 130–3
   naturalistic studies of 144–53
   teachers' rationales for 147

improvisational teaching 109, 119, 120, 328
interactive decision-making
9–25, 35, 59, 120, 129, 245, 256, 323
interviews 221–63
   semi-structured interviews 236–44

scenario-based interviews 224–227
structured interviews 223–36
  see also repertory grid, think aloud protocols
ISATT 15–16

journal writing 294–303

literacy instruction 159–96

narrative inquiry 23, 102, 116, 126, 127, 308
novice language teachers 53, 87, 88–94, 119–25, 187–8

observation 265–91
  coding and analysing 285–8
  dimensions of 265–9
  disclosure of purpose 277–80
  observer role 273–5
  reactivity 277, 281
  recording 280–4
origins of teacher cognition research 5–48

pedagogical content knowledge 21, 26–7, 39, 88, 92, 94, 150, 151, 155
practical knowledge 14–15, 21–4, 26–8, 33–4, 36, 38, 44, 47, 57, 58, 67–71, 84, 101, 123, 149, 165, 170, 173–5, 223, 313–14

questionnaires see self-report instruments

reading instruction 159–76
  L1 reading instruction 159–69

L2/FL reading instruction 169–76
reflective writing 293–317
repertory grid 227–36
retrospective accounts 309–11

self-perception/confidence and teacher cognition 35, 68, 139, 146–7, 167, 172, 178
self-report instruments 197–220
  questionnaires 199–207
  scenario rating 207–11
  tests 211–16
SLA research 336–9
Standards for Foreign Language Learning in the 21st Century 97
stimulated recall 244–58

teacher education 1, 8, 11, 23, 26, 34–7, 39, 40, 46
  and grammar teaching in 142, 153–7
  and reading instruction 166–9
  and writing instruction 176–83
  in-service 110–13
  practicum 53, 59, 60–1, 64–7, 91, 122, 179, 294, 297, 301
  pre-service 58–85
  transfer to classroom of 88–9, 94, 153–7
teacher cognition and student learning 29–32, 39, 158, 334
teacher knowledge 20–5, 31–3, 37–9, 54, 88, 116, 143, 150, 157, 158, 176, 194, 338
teacher planning 9–25, 107, 173, 258–9, 312

teachers' theories   19–20, 22, 24, 102, 140, 192
teacher thinking   8–25, 28, 157, 163
terminology in teacher cognition research   20, 22, 53–7, 74, 76, 84, 136, 145, 146, 152, 154, 197, 213, 273, 294, 320, 321
theoretical orientations to reading   161–2, 165–6, 171, 176

think-aloud protocols   258–63
TORP   161–2, 165, 167, 193, 203, 204, 218, 330

writing instruction
   L1 writing instruction   176–83
   L2/FL writing instruction   183–90